THE MEANING OF SOCIAL POLICY

The Meaning of Social Policy

THE COMPARATIVE DIMENSION IN
SOCIAL WELFARE

BERNICE Q. MADISON

LONDON AND NEW YORK

First published 1980 by Westview Press

Published 2019 by Routledge
52 Vanderbilt Avenue, New York, NY 10017
2 Park Square, Milton Park, Abingdon, Oxon OX14 4RN

Routledge is an imprint of the Taylor & Francis Group, an informa business

Copyright © 1980 Bernice Q. Madison

All rights reserved. No part of this book may be reprinted or reproduced or utilised in any form or by any electronic, mechanical, or other means, now known or hereafter invented, including photocopying and recording, or in any information storage or retrieval system, without permission in writing from the publishers.

Notice:
Product or corporate names may be trademarks or registered trademarks, and are used only for identification and explanation without intent to infringe.

British Library Cataloguing in Publication Data

Madison, Bernice Q.
    The meaning of social policy.
    1. Social policy − Comparative method
    I. Title
    361   HN17.5
    ISBN 0-7099-0222-0

LC Card No: 79-3622

ISBN 13: 978-0-367-29380-2 (hbk)

CONTENTS

Acknowledgments

1. Introduction — 11

Part One: Framework for Cross-National Research

2. Values and Ideologies — 27
3. The Definition of Social Welfare and Social Policy — 46
4. Key Problems of Methodology — 69

Part Two: The Structure of Social Security

5. Themes in National Experience — 93
6. The Impact of Social Security on Society — 120
7. Social Security and the Individual — 155

Part Three: Personal Social Services

8. Comparative National Experience — 197
9. The Organization of Social Welfare — 222
10. Services for Special Groups — 235

Part Four: Planning

11. Social Welfare Planning — 275
12. Conclusion — 300

Select Bibliography — 313

Name Index — 324

Suject Index — 327

To Mike — patient, understanding and helpful

ACKNOWLEDGMENTS

I would like to thank Michael S. Lund for sending me his unpublished manuscript entitled 'Comparing the Social Policies of Nations: A Report on Issues, Methods, and Resources. Part I: A Review of the Literature', Draft No. 2, March 1972. This work added a few items to my bibliography and in several instances enriched my understanding of what was found in the literature.

I am especially grateful to the Woodrow Wilson International Center for Scholars in whose Kennan Institute for Advanced Russian Studies I spent the year 1977/8 as a fellow. This period of concentrated research, devoted to a comparison of social welfare in the Soviet Union and the United States, measurably strengthened my grasp of welfare policy issues in the two superpowers, and also renewed my interest in social welfare policy and planning in an international perspective.

1 INTRODUCTION

The importance of a cross-national approach to social welfare policy and planning is currently achieving growing recognition among social welfare scholars, administrators and practitioners and is being widely used by social scientists as they become more aware of the limitations of their own 'national' frames of reference.[1] The first international conference of ministers responsible for social welfare (1968) recommended that comparative studies should be among the first new directions to be explored (1:23). The International Labour Conference adopted a resolution on the need for developing internationally comparable statistics on social security in 1944 (at its 26th session). Behind this spreading and intensified interest in comparative studies and international perspectives in the social welfare field are both theoretical and practical considerations.

At the theoretical level, comparative studies are among the better instruments for establishing general laws about social life — for searching out the theoretically relevant similarities. Clear of irrelevant specifics, such laws transcend cultural and national settings and reveal whether what is found 'to be true in one society is a phenomenon that occurs under a given set of circumstances in all societies or whether it is relevant for that society only' (2:13). Alternatively, such laws indicate what is true to a particular situation, to specific circumstances of time and place. Discrepancies stimulate new hypotheses by pointing to new independent variables. Where circumstances cannot be experimentally varied, 'controlled observation of the same identifiable phenomenon in different places and at different times' (3:834) can help us understand causal relationships. When comparative studies shed light on the similarities and differences between the social institutions of two or more nations, they often reveal the causal links within each nation.

By comparing and contrasting public expenditures of many nations, Pryor was able to discover

> relationships which, for lack of perspective, can never be unearthed from study of such expenditures in a single country. If nations with different economic systems are used in such comparisons, additional generalizations with political and ideological significance can be derived which are unobtainable if we limit such comparison to nations with the same economic system (4:19—20).

By comparing and contrasting different cultures, Mead was able to discern the actual dimensions of a problem, complete a picture and thus restate the problem in new terms (5:214). By comparing youth in two worlds, Kandel and Lesser gained insights 'that would never have been forthcoming from a study in the United States alone or in Denmark alone' (6:xiv). By comparing work incentives and welfare reform in Britain and the United States, Rein showed that the real problem of disincentives among the able-bodied poor is the lack of jobs at non-poverty wages rather than the availability of high public assistance benefits — the latter, a widely held belief in the United States (7:151—95). In short, as Emile Durkheim noted in 1897 in his pioneering study, *Suicide*, 'only comparison affords explanation'; and if we refuse to compare ourselves with anyone else and deal 'solely with ourselves and our fantasies both on an individual and on a national level, we obliterate the possibility of a communal approach to experience', warn Gavin and Blakeley (8:74).

At a practical level, comparative studies make possible the detection of trends and the placing of a given system in clearer perspective, thereby contributing to a better understanding of the social policies of particular countries. Nations can draw upon the experience of others if methods of dealing with certain problems 'prove "exportable" ' (9:242), offering 'policy-makers a wider range of culturally adoptable possibilities and [helping them] to make better informed choices' (10:260). Some programs tried elsewhere may provide pilot experience worth studying further. By showing where specified conditions in one country stand in relation to those in other countries, cross-national research may stimulate questions about reasons behind the selection of a particular policy and this, in turn, may prompt creative thinking about alternatives — the varieties of policy options and the conditions required for their successful implementation. By permitting us to know where we stand in relation to others comparative studies often 'lead to new interpretations and fresh evaluations of social institutions with which [a particular country] has long been familiar' (11:13). Experts and policy-makers in different countries can make their experience more understandable and useful to each other, and prepare themselves better for intelligent international cooperation. The perspective gained through cross-national research helps to avoid the 'here and now' view which repeats previous mistakes and relies on a pseudo-inventiveness that ignores the experience of others. In short, it can help policy-makers decide what not to do, as well as what to do.

To what extent cross-national studies can be used for predictive

Introduction

purposes has been of concern for some time. Writing in 1966 as the editor of the influential book *Social Indicators*, Bauer explained that he deliberately used the word *anticipation* of the future instead of the more popular term prediction because he wanted

> to avoid certain prevailing errors in thinking about the future as a guide to action. For example, *prediction* ordinarily is thought of as identifying that future state of affairs which is considered to be the most probable of all the conceivable outcomes. However, a program of action must contemplate more possible states of affairs than solely that one which appears to be the most probable. It must take into consideration a whole range of events which are reasonably probable and reasonably important. For this reason, we prefer the broader concept of *anticipation* to that of prediction, which has come to imply concern with the single most probable future event among all those that are possible (12:17).

The predictive potential of comparative studies remains a moot point. While some social scientists think that social forecasting is feasible, they note that methodology for it is as yet in an underdeveloped state; in an international perspective the situation is complicated by the problem of transferability of social phenomena to different environments. Nevertheless, there is a growing conviction that the predictability of certain choices can be better assessed when evidence from more than one country is available. And Mouton points out that 'at a more modest level' comparative studies can 'try to discern some of the broad lines of future developments, bearing in mind present trends, the underlying factors which can also affect future prospects, and the possible solutions to problems [uncovered by them]' (13:159–60).

The helping professions in all societies — especially those concerned with health, education and welfare — attach great importance to experiential learning considered essential for acquiring therapeutic skills as well as for enhancing the professional's capacity to act as a change agent in societal evolution — to contribute effectively to policy and planning. If one agrees with Titmuss that

> It is only when one adopts a comparative approach and analysis that one can distinguish something of the nature of the real choices and priorities in social policy — which, in the ultimate, is all about the dilemmas of choice and change, individual liberty and collective responsibility (14:102–3),

14 Introduction

then it becomes obvious that helping professionals can gain a great deal, indeed, from comparative studies of social welfare policy and an international view of social welfare planning.

The purpose of this book is to survey the literature on social welfare policies and planning of different nations in order to explain some of the major problems that are encountered in comparative research and to highlight what has been learned so far. It is hoped that this preliminary effort will contribute toward a better understanding of a rapidly emerging field of scholarly endeavor, thereby stimulating creative thinking and more effective action by both scholars and practitioners concerned with social welfare.

The surveyed literature includes single-country and cross-national studies by scholars as well as those sponsored by organizations whose membership is composed largely of social welfare administrators and practitioners. Single-country studies are included because some are useful for comparative purposes — those that concern themselves with universal issues and those that explain the interconnections between a country's welfare evolution and its historical development, political and value systems, and cultural norms. They shed light on the reasons for similarities and differences in welfare subcultures, and reveal which societal forces are especially determining, in contrast to influences that are weak or transitory. Although the authors of such studies may not themselves explicate insights useful for comparisons, they may help some of their readers to do so and to apply these insights to their own work.

Cross-national studies produced under the auspices of administrators and practitioners, in addition to those written by scholars, are included because they furnish practically useful knowledge — about substantive provisions, administrative structures, bureaucratic processes, effects on recipients (actual and potential), and other aspects of what happens when legal and administrative blueprints are transformed into benefits and services. These studies also reveal the judgments of administrators and practitioners as to which problems are most in need of investigation, as these problems evolve out of the ever-changing social environment and demand a more effective response to new or only partially satisfied needs. From questions asked in the 'real world', researchers can derive guidelines for more effectively addressing the claims of both analytic and experiential knowledge. If comparative policy research is to fulfill both its theoretical and practical potentials, it must emerge at the point where theory and reality converge, where it can encompass both theoretical significance and policy applicability.

Only studies and reports available in English are included because it

Introduction

cannot be assumed that readers know many foreign languages. The surveyed literature does not pretend to provide an exhaustive bibliography. To attempt this would have questionable utility since almost all of the included studies incorporate thorough inventories of relevant research and extensive bibliographies which draw attention to other sources pertinent for deeper analysis into the subject being investigated. From these, readers can extract additional bibliography, specifically in areas of their special interest. My objective was to select works that seem to have considerable significance and/or usefulness within the limits imposed by definitions of social welfare policy and planning adopted for this book. A number of studies that fulfill this criterion only partially are included because they raise questions about seemingly well-established notions or juxtapose conflicting points of view, and thus illumine areas that need further investigation; others, because they focus on issues that are now emerging as important; still others, because they employ novel approaches to the analysis of both old and new problems; and a few, simply because so little information is available on the countries about which they are written. Certain welfare programs that are covered by my definitions are not discussed because I could not find a sufficient number of policy-oriented studies in regard to them to permit meaningful comparisons. Some studies that I would have liked to include were not available to me.

In regard to definitions I was guided by several considerations. Given the enormous expanse of 'social welfare', it was essential to reduce the scope of this preliminary undertaking to manageable proportions. To do so, compromises and arbitrary decisions had to be made which means, among other things, that my 'definitions' may not correspond to conceptualizations entertained by some of my readers. In the process, I became more and more aware of the subtleties of national welfare vocabularies which often defy precise translation, especially when they deal with relative concepts — relative in the thinking of the person who is writing about them, as well as in time and place. It is well known, for example, that many similarly labeled programs of different countries do not uniformly display the same characteristics. The category of income maintenance does not have a standard international meaning or dimension; the lack of standardization is even more pronounced in personal social services. In the international literature on welfare one quickly becomes aware of puzzling ambiguities in the meanings of many terms. Although the aim of welfare everywhere is the 'well-being' of people, well-being is seen differently in different societies and the designations used to refer to programs expected to improve or achieve it, range over a variety of formulations: social development programs, social programs, social measures, social action, social services, social welfare, social welfare services, etc. These inexactnesses are magnified by uncertainities about which programs are required by the 'normal population' in contrast to those deemed necessary for the 'vulnerable sections' of the society. Nor does the literature provide universally accepted guidelines for selecting and classifying programs. Efforts to achieve a usable differentiation are complicated by the requirement that services and benefits personify a constantly interacting balance between social and economic development as it affects well-being.

Yet, for the most part changes in social welfare concepts and policies seem to be induced by the need to deal with changes in existing programs — however these programs are structured and by whatever forces bring the changes about. This usually means that departures from major assumptions that underlie these programs are either rare or gradual, although periodic break-throughs that bring about sudden and far-reaching departures do take place. Consequently, to replace widely accepted perceptions and established terminology with new concepts and unfamiliar terminology would not be helpful either to policy-makers or to administrators. Nor is it likely that researchers who wish their findings to influence social policy would be successful if their concepts were not recognizably related to existing social welfare subcultures. Resort to conventional program categories, despite their shortcomings, was motivated by a desire to make my presentation more meaningful to all who are concerned with social welfare, whether policy makers and administrators, or scholars, researchers, students and the lay public.

As used here, *social welfare* encompasses social security and personal social services. Excluded as outside the scope of this book are comparative studies of poverty per se, although a major purpose of social welfare in a world-wide perspective continues to be the prevention, amelioration or elimination of poverty. Some material on poverty is used for illustrative purposes, however. The literature on this subject is enormous; a few studies that are relevant to an international view of poverty are included in the references for this chapter (15–21).

Social security, that is, transfer programs which provide cash income, include programs of social insurance (compulsory programs that are usually job related and financed at least in part by contributions), public assistance, and family allowances — all located in the public sector and all centered on income maintenance and income supports. The use of this definition is to provide a point of departure, not to

Introduction

impose an inappropriate uniformity and thus to project a value judgment as to the kinds of programs countries ought to have.

Personal social services refer to organized noncash programs concerned with prevention of social problems and with the developmental, rehabilitative, and access needs of people, such as day care, child welfare services, community-based and institutional services for the aged, and referral services designed to direct people to the community resources which they seek and/or need. To varying degrees personal social services involve professional staff, often with diverse skills obtained from dissimilar educational and training backgrounds.

Excluded are medical care, education, housing, and employment-training. These exclusions do not mean, however, that both social security and personal social services are not influenced, often decisively, by what these separate systems provide; or that social security and personal social services can reach a high degree of success when their activities are not harmonized with the provisions and procedures of these separate systems.

Studies of social welfare administration are included because the manner in which policy is implemented affects its very substance. As an action oriented plan, policy cannot ignore the continuing changes in the organizational, financial and staffing features of bureaucratic structures responsible for administering social welfare programs — to say nothing of having to take into account a dynamic variety of political and social changes. No policy, perforce put forward at a given point in time, can foresee all of these changes. Consequently, to remain operative, it must utilize the interdependence of the formulation and implementation processes on an ongoing basis. Furthermore, in an international perspective

> The increasing interdependence of nations and regions of the world makes comprehension of the conduct of administration of much more importance than in the past ... Various administrative devices developed abroad may prove worthy of consideration for adoption or adaptation at home. The influence of Western patterns of administration in the newly independent countries is well-known and easily understandable. Less obvious is the growing interest in larger countries concerning administrative machinery originated in smaller nations (22:4).

As noted, *social policy* is thought of as a plan of action. Through it social welfare can influence relevant subsequent actions and/or relationships within groups toward which it is directed. Expressing the 'general will' of the people through government activities, social policy can influence the quality of life of a society; ultimately the product of political decisions, it can distribute material resources, social rewards and sanctions. While social policy focuses more on ends than on means, with the reverse being true of planning, means and ends are inextricably related. Planning may focus on means not only for attaining the goals set by social policy but also for determining social policy itself.[2] Both involve a sequence of means–ends relationships and both are continuing processes in which ends and means shape each other.

It follows that *social planning* is thought of as an institutionalized process to achieve a more rational use of resources. It emphasizes ways of reaching goals for specific functional activities or sectors. To be effective, it must be intimately connected with the society's practical politics and its governmental machinery and, as the implementer of social policy, it must be purposive yet flexible.

In regard to the *comparative* dimension, the view taken here is that ' "making comparisons" implies that the underlying reasons for similarities and differences are sought' (26:3). It is not enough to explain what is provided, or how provisions are transformed into benefits and services by organizational structures and administrative practices. The question 'why' means that the researcher must possess some knowledge about the historical, cultural, political and socioeconomic features of the country or countries he is studying. It also means that to a reasonable degree, he must be able to use this knowledge to show the decisive interconnections between social welfare and the particular social milieu in which it is located.[3]

Following the introductory chapter, the book is divided into four parts. Part One is concerned with some of the major problems faced in cross-national research of social welfare policy and planning. The purpose here is to outline a framework within which the limitations (as well as the strengths) of comparative studies can be better understood, as well as to sketch in a broader view some of the elements that are likely to demand attention in cross-national research for those who wish to undertake it. The intent is not to furnish a complete and/or detailed listing of these elements, but rather to indicate the scope and diversity of the major factors that require consideration because, if ignored, they are liable to mar or constrict the potential usefulness of the findings.

Part One opens, in Chapter 2, with a discussion of values and ideologies — bodies of attitudes and doctrines basic to social welfare policy in all societies. Values and ideologies are among the major

Introduction 19

determining influences in relation to what policy undertakes to accomplish and how it intends to reach its goals, whether their impact is made manifest explicitly and directly or suggested implicitly and indirectly. Chapter 2 looks into the nature of values and the manner in which they evolve from the social matrix, and at the differences in the degree of consensus they represent at a high and general level of abstraction, on the one hand, and at lower levels of generalization, on the other. Examined as well are the controversies around the convergence theory and the meaning of freedom of choice as they are reflected in values. The influence that conflicts in values has on actual welfare provisions is illustrated by certain programs of social security and personal social services. Part One then moves, in Chapter 3, to a consideration of problems involved in defining social welfare and social policy — of concern to all researchers and scholars and especially acute in personal social services, although some do not devote as much effort to conceptualizing boundaries and content as others. The analysis of problems of methodology, in Chapter 4, leaves out those of a technical nature (such as, for example, when is regression analysis a good way to analyze data and when is it not). By no means does this signify that I do not appreciate the basic importance of technical know-how for social welfare. On the contrary, from observations in many countries it is clear to me that limitations of technical equipment, in people and machines, can severely circumscribe what even the best intentioned policy-makers and planners can do. Problems of a technical nature are left out simply as beyond the scope of this book. Chapter 4 looks at problems that are of a broader, more general character; namely, lack and ambiguity of data, and the need to establish criteria for selecting countries to be compared, to assess social reality and progress, and to assure a comparative dimension.

Social security and personal social services are presented separately in Parts Two and Three, respectively. This division is for clarity of analysis, and not because either in the literature or in 'real life' it invariably exists. In each of these two components of social welfare, examination of single-country studies precedes that of cross-national studies in order to help the reader see the relationship of the more detailed and specific issues raised by the former to the universal issues revealed by the latter; and in each the nature of the presentation is thematic to make clearer what the issues are. Part Two, in Chapter 5, centers on the principles and problems in social security as they emerge from single-country studies; then moves, in Chapter 6, to an examination of the impact of social security on the society and, in Chapter 7, to its

20 Introduction

impact on the individual — both chapters based on what was learned from cross-national studies. Part Three, in Chapter 8, focuses on the role of personal social services and on the individuals who comprise their clienteles, as this is demonstrated by single-country studies; the analysis then proceeds, in Chapter 9, to the organizational structure of services and, in Chapter 10, to what they provide for special groups in the population — both chapters likewise deriving their information from cross-national studies.

Part Four is devoted to social welfare planning in an international perspective. It opens with a brief overview of its significance and feasibility and of the types of planning that are or may be used by different societies. The discussion then addresses the conceptual and practical problems planning presents and the recommendations made to deal with them — in Chapter 11. Many writers note that social planners have a great deal of substance and consequence to offer about ways to improve the quality of life (28). Their efforts to do so, however, are often so sporadic, confused and impractical that they add up to only a minimal input into the planning process. This is generally attributed to several dilemmas in which social planners find themselves. There are the difficulties they seem to experience in seeing the objectives of economic and social planning as complementary rather than contradictory, at the same time insisting — and justly so — that the two must be integrated; there are the inconsistencies that arise when social welfare functions are defined so specifically that they tend to isolate personnel from being able to deal with underlying causes while insisting — and correctly so — that activities of personnel must be dynamically related to the societal matrix at all times; and there is the proneness to become immobilized in criticisms of the inadequacy of currently available statistics and resources, while making few determined efforts to improve them — at the same time insisting on being included in the planning process.

For Chapters 5–11, inclusive, the summary in each chapter is preceded by a section on what I saw as major policy issues, explicit and implicit, in the materials which I studied. Here as well my purpose was not to present a detailed, specific listing, but rather an overview of those issues which seemed to cut across national boundaries and to be of concern to all involved in social welfare, although in some countries they were faced more squarely than in others. Summaries attempt to highlight what has been learned so far, to suggest whether the available knowledge is adequate to deal with the issues at hand, and to indicate the areas in which it seems particularly thin. Some issues appear in

Introduction 21

several chapters, their persistence and importance underscored by the variety of contexts in which they play a role.

In the concluding chapter an attempt is made to indicate the most promising directions for future undertakings in cross-national research in social welfare policy and planning. This is done with the full realization that social welfare, like all human services, is a field of activity in constant evolution in response to many continually changing forces in the society. Its responses may be erratic, weak, steady, strong or in the shape of cataclysmic break-throughs followed by periods of relative rigidity, but they can never be final. Consequently, answers to policy issues in social welfare cannot be final. Yet some answers are better than others in the sense that they incorporate a more incisive grasp of the significance of change and of its possible consequences for the well-being of both the society and the individual.

Notes

1. There is a distinction between 'trans-national' and 'cross-national' research. The prefix 'trans' denotes that the vista of the scientific observer extends beyond the scope of one nation to another. The prefix 'cross' has a methodological connotation: it refers to a comparison of observations between at least two nations.
2. Thus, Frieden thinks that in the next 50 years, both the content and the management of urban planning will be changed in order to emphasize the distribution of resources to disadvantaged groups as a major policy goal (23). Perloff sees the social planning process as an instrument which coordinates social services with physical and economic activities in order to further a comprehensive, problem-oriented policy to community welfare (24). Social welfare administrators place emphasis on planning which helps governments formulate policies that fully express the role of social welfare in national development (1). And Popenoe prognosticates that in the near future city planning will promote social welfare policy through conscious social intervention (25:271).
3. Comparisons can be usefully made in regard to smaller or subordinate units within a nation such as localities or regions, provided the limiting conditions and what the researcher considers as uniform are explicitly stated and adhered to. In his case study of Venezuela, for example, Friedmann stresses that regional policy has a much more critical role in national development than economic planners have realized. Regional policy, he thinks, is a means of creating a spatial organization that can undergird and carry out national development goals (27).

References

1. United Nations (UN) Department of Economic and Social Affairs, *Proceedings of the International Conference of Ministers Responsible for Social Welfare, 3–12 September 1968* (New York, UN, 1969. Sales No. E. 69. IV. 4).

22 Introduction

2. Shanas, Ethel et al., *Old People in Three Industrial Societies* (New York, Atherton Press, 1968).
3. Yap, P. M., 'A Search for Order in Diversity', *International Journal of Psychiatry*, 8, no. 5 (November 1969), pp. 834–9.
4. Pryor, Frederic L., *Public Expenditures in Communist and Capitalist Nations* (Homewood, Illinois, Richard D. Irwin, Inc., 1968).
5. Mead, Margaret, *Blackberry Winter, My Earlier Years* (New York, William Morrow and Company, Inc., 1972).
6. Coleman, James, S., in foreword to *Youth in Two Worlds* by Kandel, Denise B. and Lesser, Gerald S. (San Francisco, Jossey-Bass, Inc., 1972).
7. Rein, Martin, 'Work Incentives and Welfare Reform in Britain and the United States', pp. 151–95 in Stein, Bruno and Miller, S. M. (eds.), *Incentives and Planning in Social Policy* (Chicago, Aldine Publishing Company, 1973).
8. Gavin, William J. and Blakeley, T. J., *Russia and America: A Philosophical Comparison, Development and Change of Outlook from the 19th to the 20th Century* (Boston, D. Reidel Publishing Company, 1976).
9. Rys, Vladimir, 'Comparative Studies of Social Security: Problems and Perspectives', *Bulletin of International Social Security Association*, 19, nos. 7/8 (July/August 1966), pp. 242–68.
10. Titmuss, Richard, 'Equity, Adequacy, and Innovation in Social Security', *International Social Security Review*, xxiii, no. 2 (1970), pp. 259–69.
11. Rodgers, Barbara N., *Comparative Social Administration* (New York, Atherton Press, 1968).
12. Bauer, Raymond A. (ed.), *Social Indicators* (Cambridge, Mass., MIT Press, 1966).
13. Mouton, Pierre, *Social Security in Africa. Trends, Problems and Prospects* (Geneva, International Labour Office (ILO), 1975).
14. Titmuss, Richard M., in Abel-Smith, Brian, and Titmuss, Kay (eds.), *Social Policy. An Introduction*, (New York, Pantheon Books, 1975).
15. Myrdal, Gunnar, *Asian Drama: An Inquiry into the Poverty of Nations* (New York, The Twentieth Century Fund, 1968), 3 vols.
16. Chandler, J. H., 'Perspectives on Poverty: an International Comparison', *Monthly Labor Review*, 92, no. 2 (1969), pp. 55–62.
17. Parsons, Kenneth H., 'Poverty as an Issue in Development Policy: A Comparison of United States and Underdeveloped Countries', *Land Economics*, xlv, no. 1 (February 1969).
18. Galenson, Walter (ed.), *Incomes Policy: What Can We Learn from Europe?* (Ithaca, New York State School of Industrial and Labor Relations, Cornell University, 1973).
19. Kravis, Irving B., 'A World of Unequal Incomes', *The Annals of the American Academy of Political and Social Science*, 409 (September 1973), pp. 61–81.
20. Drewnowski, Jan, 'Poverty: Its Meaning and Measurement', *Development and Change*, 8, no. 2 (April 1977), pp. 183–208.
21. Galbraith, John Kenneth, *The Nature of Mass Poverty* (Cambridge, Mass., Harvard University Press, 1979). See also the review of this book by P. T. Bauer, 'Breaking the Grip of Poverty', *Wall Street Journal* (April 18, 1979), p. 20.
22. Heady, Ferrel, *Public Administration: A Comparative Perspective* (New Jersey, Prentice-Hall, 1966).
23. Frieden, Bernard J., 'The Changing Prospects for Social Planning', *Journal of the American Institute of Planners*, xxxiii, no. 5 (September 1967), pp. 311–24.
24. Perloff, Harvey S., 'New Directions in Social Planning', *Journal of the American Institute of Planners*. xxxi, no. 4 (November 1965), pp. 297–303.

25. Popenoe, David, 'Review of Urban Development: Its Implications for Social Welfare, Proceedings of the XIIIth International Conference of Social Work', *Journal of the American Institute of Planners*, xxxiv, no. 4 (July 1969), p. 271.

26. Brislin, Richard W., Lonner, Walter J. and Thorndike, Robert M., *Cross-Cultural Research Methods* (New York, Wiley, 1973).

27. Friedmann, John, *Regional Development Policy: A Case Study of Venezuela* (Cambridge, Mass., MIT Press, 1966).

28. See for example, Sovani, N. V., 'Whither Social Planners and Social Planning?', pp. 46–69 in Gokhale, S. D. (ed.), *Social Welfare, Legend and Legacy* (Bombay, Popular Prakashan, 1975).

PART ONE:
FRAMEWORK FOR CROSS-NATIONAL RESEARCH

The problems discussed focus on values and ideologies, definitions and concepts, and certain methodological issues — three interrelated areas that must be considered in order to understand both the literature and the field of study. For example, it is often claimed that the available data are either too limited or too unreliable to provide the basis for comprehensive analyses that would yield viable and testable generalizations in regard to policy. But it is equally true that without good theoretical constructs it is not possible either to utilize the data that are available or to point out clearly where data are lacking and/or deficient. Nor is there any doubt that as methodological concerns increase, more reliable data are likely to be produced. Theoretical constructs, in turn, must come to grips with values and ideologies and definitions and concepts if they are to reflect reality and to explain how and why it came to be.

2 VALUES AND IDEOLOGIES

In any sizable work with comparative connotations, cognizance and/or discussion of values or ideologies is a *sine qua non*. Even those who believe that the importance of values in certain welfare areas has been exaggerated, recognize their overall influence and the complexities they introduce into cross-national research on policy and planning. Yet, according to Baier,

> One of the principal problems in studying values . . . is the lack of universal agreement about what values are or what morality is. There is, at present, no scientific working model of morality. We are forced to resort to pre-scientific terms like values and moral judgment which have many different connotations. The issue is further confused by the strong emotional concern which surrounds any effort to clarify questions about values . . . By values, what we usually mean is certain states of affairs toward which individuals or societies hold favorable attitudes and in whose beneficial effects they believe. But a favorable attitude alone does not turn something into a value. It becomes a value only if the individual devotes some of his resources to bringing about or maintaining the desired state of affairs . . . The concept of values has a rational element; in theory, at least, values represent attitudes based on relevant evidence and can be modified by the discovery of relevant facts (1:58).

Wishing to stress the subjective nature of the valuation process, Myrdal uses the word 'valuations' rather than 'values', in this way hoping to avoid the confusion between 'valuations in a subjective sense, the object of these valuations, and indeed often the whole social setting of valuations' (2:1). This setting is of fundamental importance since values (or valuations) become meaningful only when examined in the light of their psychological, social, and historical context. In a penetrating analysis, Marshall explains that welfare decisions

> are essentially altruistic, and they must draw on standards of value embodied in an autonomous ethical system which, though an intrinsic part of the contemporary civilization, is not the product either of the summation of individual preferences (as in the market) or of a

hypothetical majority vote. It is impossible to say exactly how these ethical standards arise in a society or are recognized by its members. Total consensus with regard to them is unthinkable, outside a devout religious community, but without a foundation of near-consensus, no general social welfare policy would be possible . . . (3:20).

And Donnison emphasizes that there is no escape from ideologies since governments 'need them to guide and coordinate their work, to secure the support of the governed, and to make the behavior of citizens orderly and predictable'. He defines 'ideologies' as 'patterns of attitudes and aspirations leading to programs of action and sustained by reasonably coherent (although possibly erroneous) sets of assumptions and prognoses about the working of society' (4:106).

Implicitly or explicitly, most social scientists tend to accept the notion that values appear when there is a good probability that they can be achieved, so that not only do people inherit values, they also create them. That values are instrumental in shaping social welfare policy and that, on a 'higher' and more general level, they are universal — minimally controversial, accepted and shared with relative unambivalence by persons from all major subgroups in the society — is not disputed. For example, Myrdal singles out the social and economic quest for equality as one such value and notes that it induced social change to create greater equality of opportunity (5:6–7). The United Nations Universal Declaration of Human Rights (1948) includes two articles delineating universal social welfare rights which personify universal values:

> Article 22: Everyone, as a member of society, has the right to social security and is entitled to realization, through national effort and international cooperation, and in accordance with the organization and resources of each State, of the economic, social and cultural rights indispensable for his dignity and the free development of his personality.

> Article 25: Everyone has the right to a standard of living adequate for the health and well-being of himself and of his family, including food, clothing, housing and medical care and necessary social services, and the right to security in the event of unemployment, sickness, disability, widowhood, old age, or other lack of livelihood in circumstances beyond his control.

Values and Ideologies

Support for high level universality also comes from Cantril's study of aspirations, fears and basic strivings of people in 13 countries in various stages of development — premobilization, mobilization, and relative maturity (6). Psychologically, mobilization means 'an extension of what people learn to want out of life as they perceive new potentialities for increasing both the range and the quality of satisfactions, as "quality" is defined by people in a culture' (6:220—1). Cantril found wide variations in the total volume, range and focus of concerns expressed by people in these countries, but concluded with a description 'of what seem to be the demands human beings everywhere impose on any society or political culture because of their very nature' (6:315). These eleven demands clearly represent the 'higher' and more general values such as 'human beings require freedom to exercise the choices they are capable of making', or 'people want to experience their own identity and integrity, more popularly referred to as the need for personal dignity'.

When however aspirations are studied at a lower level of generalization, differences emerge. Katona *et al.* examined the influence of aspirations on economic behavior in six Western countries, all of which participated in 'the trend toward improved well-being and increased opportunities for educational and occupational advancement' (7). He found that substantial differences existed in attitudes and expectations which, in turn, are traceable to differences in the cultural and social structure of the different countries.

Similarly, in regard to welfare values, consensus has been achieved only at a high and general level, primarily via the concept of the 'welfare state'. The essence of the ideal component at its core

is compensation to the individual for the negative consequences of a particular organization of life. Emphasis is placed on the common-needs principle, rather than on reward of individual productivity — an approach relied on to maximize equality, social justice, and freedom . . . But the common-needs principle is inextricably entwined with the imperatives of redistribution, planning, and intervention which inevitably encroach on individual freedom. Fulfilment of individual potential excludes certain kinds of potential; collectively provided services are designed to meet socially recognized needs. But social and individual needs are interdependent and change in relation to time, to need cycles of individuals and families, to prevailing notions of what constitutes a 'need' and in what circumstances, and to value judgments concerning the extent to which such needs should be met' (8:434).

Furniss and Tilton distinguish 'three kinds of interventionist regimes, the corporate-oriented *positive state*, the *social security state* with its assurance of a minimum standard of civilized life, and the radically democratic and egalitarian *social welfare state*'. They prefer the latter because they perceive the values on which it is based as 'human dignity, equality, liberty, democracy, security, solidarity, and economic efficiency' (9:x—xi).

But again, when discussion descends to a lower level of generalization, consensus is rare. At an intercultural seminar, participants were unable to agree on a definition of 'value' during three days of discussion and when they finally moved out of this impasse, they formulated only two dualities of values as cutting across the various cultures represented; namely, worth and dignity of man as related to the well-being and integrity of the group, and progress and development of the individual and society as related to their security (10:5—22). It was recognized that values may be normative (that is, thought of as ends) or instrumental (that is, thought of as means). While participants agreed that hard and fast distinctions between these two emphases should not be made, disagreement arose in regard to instrumental values — just as it had earlier in regard to the normative ones.

This seems to bear out Rein's view that the ideology of means is as formidable as the ideology of ends (11:299) — a view reflected in broader questions: does technology have a levelling effect on systems of values, given differences in history, culture, and tradition; do different political ideologies have a determining effect on the ability of societies to create, develop, and maintain a welfare state? The 'convergence' theory developed by some social scientists in the 1950s and early 1960s argued for a 'yes' answer to the first and a 'no' answer to the second of these questions. But such answers have come under review since then, leading to a continuing and widespread disagreement among social scientists that affects their thinking on policy and planning (12:445—7).

In his study of the role of altruism in modern society as exemplified in the giving of human blood in the United States, Japan, and Great Britain, Titmuss found very great differences in the proportion of blood donors of varying types in the three countries and concluded that explanations for these differences have to be sought in the history, the values and the political ideas of each society. His study, writes Titmuss,

Values and Ideologies

does not support the convergence theory — the notion that 'large-scale industrialized societies, increasingly ruled by technology and the demands of a mass consumption market, are tending to become more and more alike . . . in terms of their dominant value systems and political ideologies' (12:173). He thinks that social scientists who propound 'the end of ideology' err because they base their theories on indicators that can be measured and quantified and have excluded indicators that embody transactions and relationships in non-economic categories. Other scholars argue that it is the differences in national value systems which cause lags in social policy development in certain countries which are similar to socially more advanced countries in other respects. Still others note that basic values and traditions of a culture have a marked effect on the extent to which there is assimilation of new knowledge and techniques.

Heidenheimer, Heclo, and Adams found that in some policy areas American and European choices on social program content converge; on others, they continue to diverge; and on still others, developments are parallel, 'with countries moving in roughly the same direction but in their own distinctive ways'. The three explanations for policy differences they give are ideology, the structure of political institutions, and social conditions (13:257—9). The key role of political factors is emphasized by Alber who reports that preliminary analyses of social security in Western European democracies (15 countries) confirm the assumption that 'political factors, above all the political incorporation of the working class, and the stability of governments, are decisive in accounting for national variations of social insurance regulations' (14:16). And Leman found that in Canada and the United States old-age security policies 'have been profoundly influenced by the political contexts in which they have developed' (15:261).

On the other hand, for Cantril it became abundantly clear that

> except in certain critical situations such as war or revolution, the stage of social and political organization characterizing a nation appears more closely related to human concerns than it does to any ideology as such. While the conflicts of ideologies, with their different emphases concerning the use and organization of power, are obviously of the utmost importance for the psychologist as well as the political scientist, our current quest could be misleading if the emphasis were put on variations in ideologies rather than on variations in phases of development (6:301—2).

This theme is echoed by others. Pryor found that those who make decisions on public consumption expenditures face similar issues and make similar decisions in all nations, regardless of their political systems (16:285–6). Cutright became convinced that governmental social security activities are related to organizational requirements rather than to differences in ideological orientations (17).

In discussing deviance in Soviet society, Connor stresses the importance of recognizing that social problems characteristic of contemporary Soviet life owe their existence to both the character of the USSR's modernizing experience and to the ravages of World War II. Certain elements of this experience the USSR shares with other urban, industrial societies since socialism does not confer immunity (18:262). From her study of the Soviet welfare system, Madison concluded that Soviet advances and weaknesses are similar to advances and weaknesses in Western democracies, as are instruments used to achieve progress and cope with weaknesses (19:230–40). 'Looking at the medical scene in the United States and the Soviet Union', Field assumes

> that the United States will need to concentrate its efforts in the future on the distribution of health services. Such an effort will require more governmental intervention, a greater need for rationalization and planning, and decreased autonomy for the medical profession and hospitals. [He] would assume that in the Soviet Union the direction will be toward increasing the quality of health services and of medical research; this may lead to an increase in the overall status of the medical profession and to increased autonomy in professional matters. Whether one wants to call this convergence, coincidence, or resemblance, [he] would argue that the differences are decreasing and the similarities increasing (20:262).

Wolins interpreted his findings in regard to group care for children in Israel, Russia, Yugoslavia, and Poland as pointing to gradual convergence (21). On the basis of studies that deal with many facets of the status of women in Russia, Dallin concludes that the Soviet experience, 'despite the distinctiveness of Soviet ideology and the Soviet system . . . [presents] striking similarities in the general trends manifested in modern societies' (22:387).

But Osborn's study of Soviet social security, education, and urban communities led him to believe that even if there are some constants in man's response to the drastically new environment of the twentieth century, it would be a mistake to assume that 'the social policies of modern governments will somehow converge; or at least, this remains to be shown' (23:274). Osborn's view supports the position that it is essential to distinguish between the universal characteristics of modernization and the distinctive historical expressions in particular societies that provide them with a socio-political substance.

Mishra's study (1973), aimed at testing the convergence theory which postulates 'that the imperatives of industrial technology and economic development constrain societies towards a common institutional pattern' (24:535). He examined statutory programs of social security and education in 20 non-Communist Western industrial countries highest in per capita GNP in relation to four propositions derived from the convergence theory. His findings led him to conclude that these countries are indeed converging toward state responsibility for some measure of education, income security and medical care, but that the level of this social provision varies widely and is likely to continue to do so. To think that the 'logic' of industrialism will lead to a well-defined point of convergence seems unwarranted; while industrialism's structural constraints may limit the variation in social structures, 'these limits are wide and leave plenty of room for diversity. The forces that operate in this area of "freedom" may have little to do with industrialism *per se*' (24:556). Rather, these forces may emerge from a new institutional 'logic', developed in the process of industrialization, which influences the social structure in its own right.

Grant demonstrates that in the 1960s, successes and failures in dealing with concrete development problems occurred under a variety of ideological labels — capitalist, socialist and mixed — and that in changing the structure of their societies, developing countries need to, and can draw on experience from both sides of the ideological barrier (25:4). In fact, no social structure can deliver all the values which modern man believes he should have.

That differences will continue is clear from the outcome of a 1972 symposium on the social consequences of modernization in socialist countries: whether in relation to such consequences the modern industrial societies of the socialist and non-socialist worlds are converging toward patterns that have more in common than not is still a controversial question (26:5). This would have to include patterns of values. Some social scientists do not think that it is always possible or even desirable to strive for a 'harmonizing synthesis' of antagonistic values. Stating that 'it is only thanks to inconsistency that humanity has kept alive on this earth', Kolakowski explains that what he has in

34 Values and Ideologies

mind are 'the relations between thought and principle on the one hand and practical behavior on the other', and that in this relationship there may exist values that are mutually exclusive without ceasing to be values. In fact, he notes, 'contradictions will haunt us as long as we act within a world of values, or simply as long as we exist' (27:206, 202, 204). And Gartner and Riessman point out that 'value syndromes', even though they have been institutionalized, for the most part remain incomplete and sometimes become back-lashed (28:15).

In the meantime, efforts to explicate the values upon which social welfare ought to be based continue. In 1970, a New Zealand Royal Commission produced the following list of 'main values underlying income maintenance programmes': the values of life and health, of belonging and participating, of equality of economic well-being, of security and status. In relation to economic well-being, the values included dignity, independence, work, freedom, wealth, worthiness. It was noted that these values can influence coverage, conditions of eligibility, structure, or levels of provisions which increase or redistribute the levels of economic well-being within the community. All of them act as the basis for program construction and evaluation (29). Professionals in the social welfare field agree that uniqueness of values is not a necessary requisite of a profession. On the contrary, it is interrelatedness that is an inherent characteristic of all social phenomena, including professions. Hence, social welfare's values, as taught to those involved in the field, ought to be viewed as quite similar to those espoused by other professions (10:8).

What emerges from these efforts and the continuing clash in conceptual positions is a reaffirmation of the role of values in formulating and evaluating current policy and in advocating policy changes. There is no getting away from values because deliberate choices in decision-making are reflections of values. Thought of as beliefs that are non-scientific and not rooted in rational considerations, values appear to originate in the conviction that personal choice is real, that there is a moral element involved, and that ethical criteria are central in all human relationships. When facts do not coincide with beliefs, they are either rationalized with the beliefs or ignored. But it is arguable whether the source of values is genetic, or personal in the sense of being learned from one's immediate human and natural environment, or social in the sense of being inherent in the stage of the economy and polity. Those who argue that values are derived from a given type or level of economic structure seek to locate a convergence of values in similar economic stages while those who argue that values are personal

Values and Ideologies

seek to emphasize the cultural and subcultural differences which distinguish different ways of life and social organization.

The reality of the freedom of choice is an ancient concept. As a basic tenet in the Bhagavadgītā which dates back to the pre-Christian era, for example, it is explained to its millions of followers thus:

> There are certain factors in our lives which are determined for us by forces over which we have no control. We do not choose how or when or where or in what condition of life we are born. On the theory of rebirth, even these are chosen by us. It is our past karma that determines our ancestry, heredity and environment. But when we look from the standpoint of this life, we can say that we were not consulted about our nationality, race, parentage or social status. But subject to these limitations, we have freedom of choice. Life is like a game of bridge. We did not invent the game or design the cards. We did not frame the rules and we cannot control the dealing. The cards are dealt out to us, whether they be good or bad. To that extent, determinism rules. But we can play the game well or play it badly. A skilful player may have a poor hand and yet win the game. A bad player may have a good hand and yet make a mess of it. Our life is a mixture of necessity and freedom, chance and choice. By exercising our choice properly, we can control steadily all the elements and eliminate altogether the determinism of nature (30:48—9).

The Gītā's stress on unassisted individual responsibility for exercising freedom of choice wisely and rationally has been modified in the course of centuries by the view that freedom to choose is empty of meaning unless society carries out its obligation to ensure that people have access to the resources, services, and opportunities they need to exercise it — an obligation that is a basic welfare value. Because differences about what it takes to endow personal choice with genuine meaning bear directly on the relationship between the individual and the society, they can produce profoundly different policy decisions.

Just as welfare philosophy perceives society as a system with social values, so it is agreed that in order to guide policy, values must be defined through general consensus. How to arrive at consensus, however, turns out to be a task fraught with dangers and frustrations. There is the inescapable question: whose values, preferences or assumptions about what is desirable and good for the individual and the society are to be considered and given dominant weight? There is a conflict between the value system of the poor and the underprivileged, so prominent in welfare concerns, and the middle classes whose needs for and claims to what welfare has to offer are being more widely recognized everywhere. A meeting of minds on values between officials, elites and professionals, on the one hand, and the general public, on the other, is frequently absent, to say nothing of disagreements that divide officials, elites and professionals from each other. Although no one opposes the notion that welfare's purpose is to enhance well-being, the values that individuals and groups consider essential to move it toward this goal are often sharply different from the values of the so-called public interest, both in substance and in their relative importance in the attitudinal hierarchy.

This is especially visible in corrections, a services segment in which another basic welfare value — 'in providing societal resources, the dignity and individuality of the person served should be respected' — is put to a severe test. This value incorporates the democratic ideal; no person can be stripped of his dignity, no matter how grievous his actions against the general good. Gandhi reminds us that, since we cannot possibly know the absolute truth, we are 'therefore not competent to punish'; and Erikson's interpretation of the Golden Rule proclaims: 'The doer of the Golden Rule, and he who is done by, is the same man, *is* man' (31:243). Nevertheless, even those policy-makers and practitioners who are genuinely imbued with these ideals recognize that in real life there are limits to permitting individuals do their own thing if a livable situation is to be created for all. Nor is it possible to help people without at least some manipulation and some imposition of values, a reality which erodes the idea that you, the helper, are not better than I, the one being helped. Another problem erupts when within a given hierarchy of values, one value indicates one course of action, another a different course.

These various disaccords emerge throughout the policy-making process, that is, not only in relation to what is to be done, but why it should be done, how are the goals to be reached and how are the outcomes to be evaluated. Examples of this abound, only a few will be given here, drawn from social security and personal social services, all centered on the family — 'rediscovered' in the 1970s and universally valued as a basic social unit, its sustenance and nurture to be vigorously supported by welfare policy.

In the American system of social security, the wife's retirement allowance of 50 percent of her husband's benefit is based upon the need to protect the family unit whether the wife earns outside wages or not. The family is a basic social and economic feature of our way of life. The contribution of the wife in the home is not measurable by cash wages. Yet to deprive her of protection because her work is not directly measurable in dollars would leave millions of families with inadequate protection (32:137).

The 50 percent level is derived from the concept of adequacy which, in turn, is related to and supports the protective function. Brown explains that in recent years adequacy has been challenged by the concept of equity — a concept that jeopardizes social security's potential to protect the family. The challenge has come from working wives who argue 'that if non-working wives get "something for nothing" . . . working wives should get that 50 percent allowance plus an additional benefit related to their earnings' (32:137). The reason why this should not be done, argues Brown, is that to inject equity into a social provision would create a specially privileged class, wage-earning wives, at the expense of all other persons protected by the system, including single women. If the family is to be protected as the basic social unit, an adequate allowance for the dependent wife is socially justified.

The same philosophy has been used to justify the major cost of the widow's benefit and the desirability of providing it without delay after the husband's death. Liberalizations have raised an aged widow's benefit to 82.5 percent of her husband's primary benefit, but even this is found to be inadequate because of changes in women's life patterns and the increasing generation gap. Eligible as well are younger widows, with one or more dependent children of the deceased husband, and the children themselves (until age 18, 21 if attending school, no age limit applying to children who became permanently disabled before 18). The mother and each of the children now receive 75 percent of the deceased worker's benefit. But the adequacy principle is weakened by what Brown describes as 'an arbitrary and inconsistent basis for determination of the family maximum benefit' for survivors (32:140—50). It appears, therefore, that while the American system's philosophy of adequacy as it affects the family needs to be strengthened, its goal of protecting the family unit has been substantially implemented and remains basic to its concerns and purposes.

In contrast, in the Soviet Union the wife's noncash contribution in the home does not help her much in gaining entitlement to adequate protection: aged and unable-to-work women who are dependents of retired workers and employees receive only 10 percent of the breadwinner's basic pension; as dependents of collective farmers, they receive nothing. The contingent eligible to survivors' pensions is harshly limited: the wife is eligible only if she is caring for a child under eight years of age, attains the retirement age, or becomes disabled within five years after the death of the husband. His children are eligible until age 16 (18, if in school, indefinitely if they become disabled before 18). Clearly, a young or a middle-aged widow is not likely to qualify for a pension in her old age since she is not likely to turn 60 within five years after the youngest child under her care has reached the eighth year (retirement age for women in the Soviet Union is 55). In terms of adequacy, survivors' pensions are the puniest of all benefits in the social security system: for two survivors the minimum is below the poverty line for one person; a single survivor gets only about one-third of the old-age pension award. There is no doubt that destitution stalks the lives of survivors. All this makes clear that if the wife wants to assure for herself relatively adequate support in her old age, she should establish her own work record outside the home; and if she becomes a widow, she should get a job even if she has young children under her care. Nonwork participants are allowed only the meagerest of claims on social security's resources. Unmistakably, in social security the value placed on 'productive' work dominates, relegating the value of protecting the family as a basic social unit to a secondary role.

In Great Britain the protective function of cash benefits is achieved via a third scenario. Here married women who build up their own retirement pensions now have the option of paying contributions to qualify for benefits on their own insurance or not paying contributions and relying on their husband's insurance for a smaller range of benefits as dependents.

Whether its benefits foster incentives to strengthen and maintain the bonds of marriage and to carry out family responsibilities is a question that confronts social security policy in many other ways. Titmuss enumerates some of them. Should non-working men (unemployed and sick), with or without working wives, be placed in a better income position than men who do work, with working or non-working wives? Should single (or deserted) men or women living together with children in the home be better off than married couples with the same number of children? 'To what extent', he asks, 'can social security systems resolve such conflicting questions of equity and adequacy in these situations — which are often situations of poverty, hardship and low wages — when they have a duty to support the moral values that society

Values and Ideologies

places on work, marriage and the family?' (33:266). According to Stein and Miller, the fact is that

> In a world of scarce resources, a social policy uses some of these resources, reallocating them from their alternative uses. It is almost impossible to reallocate resources without redistributing income. Accordingly, a policy is likely to impose costs on some and benefits on others (34:5).

It seems that knowledge is not enough to assure both adequacy and equity, and that values and ideologies enter the stage at many points.

Conflicts between proclaimed values and those actually incorporated into programs likewise beset personal social services. Returning once again to the family, we find that in Great Britain families are still the primary providers of care for the frail elderly and for the mentally handicapped children. Yet, they receive fewer services than other groups, and their caring capacities are only minimally strengthened by welfare's ministrations. Despite policy pronouncements to the contrary, the welfare establishment is in fact continuing to emphasize its role as a substitute for the family, rather than its complementer and supporter, and policy directions are set in relation to the outcomes of substitution (35).

In the United States criticisms of foster care, a program that has been in operation in one form or another for over a century, have been multiplying. The National Commission on Children in Need of Parents condemns foster care as an 'unconscionable failure' that harms many of the children whom it is supposed to help. It maintains that a majority of the 500,000 children who live away from their parents could perfectly well be returned to their own families or placed in adoptive homes. But, claims the Commission, Federal assistance programs do nothing significant either to keep families together or to encourage adoption when children cannot be reared at home. An earlier report, by the Children's Defense Fund, arrives at similar conclusions stating that foster care is often 'psychologically devastating' and frequently unnecessary: many children have been removed from their families 'wrongly written off as too poor, too sick or too inadequate to bring up children'. Federal actions contravene announced policy: agreeing that 'families are vital to the healthy development of children', the Government spends less than $56 million a year for in-home care, and more than $300 million on out-of-home care. Moreover, Federal aid is cut off as soon as a foster child is adopted (36). A longitudinal study of more than 600 children in foster care in New York, published by two recognized scholars, also found that many of the foster children would have been better off if they had remained with their own, although less than ideally adequate, parents (37).

The task of achieving reasonable consensus on values is considered so conflict-ridden by some theorists that they have been inclined to dispute the whole idea of attaining a complete and soundly-based position on choices needed for policy development. Others imply that it is possible to attain such a position, but that this would require the entire international community to establish a generally agreed upon set of values that could guide the subsequent steps of goal-setting, priorities, planning and implementation of plans, both at the national and international levels. The fact remains, however, that all societies arrive at positions on preferences, whether as compromises worked out via the democratic process or as directives handed down by those who 'know best'. These positions and prescriptions may be either implicit in laws, regulations and provisions or explicitly enunciated, but they are almost certain to be imperfect in the sense of not reflecting the beliefs of everyone in the society equally. But people and societies cannot tolerate indecision which prevents action any more than they can tolerate for an indefinite time total exclusion from the decision-making process. Coleman points out that

> ... rational behavior in collective decisions requires rationality under uncertainty or risk, which opens up the possibility of expression of intensity of preference; ... in actual groups, the existence of a sequence of decisions gives actors the resources that allow the expression of such intensity, even if imperfectly and incompletely (38:1122).

Everywhere, the political process provides a milieu for reaching sufficient consensus to act, with the acting being modified and readjusted in the light of experience. In short, researchers and policy-makers must do the best they can.

Predictably, answers to how to go about doing the best they can are rather few and sometimes, vague. How do they find out what the prevailing system of values of a given society is — to say nothing of what its implications for social welfare policy are? For societies rooted in the Judeo-Christian ethics, there are, of course, the Ten Commandments and the Golden Rule, but they are interpreted differently even by those who want to obey them, and there are many

Values and Ideologies

who do not want to. The same can be said of all other great religious works and their teachings about individual conduct and human relationships — the Gītā, the Koran, the *Analects* of Confucius. Wide and unceasing reading of works on ethics and philosophy, of constitutions and legal codes, and of leading thinkers in the social sciences and in literature will help. Codes of ethics of the different professions (such as the well-known Hippocratic oath in medicine) are important although at least some of the principles they embody may not be shared by the populace, and some are likely to be instrumental rather than normative. Instrumental values focus on how the professional person is to conduct his activities in order to achieve the goals established by normative values (examples are socialized medicine; yoga which teaches that actions must be free of selfishness or expectation of rewards; respect for the person being helped, honesty in dealing with him, etc.). Normative values focus on the ultimate premises concerning the nature of man and on what kind of society is desirable for him.

Assuming that policy-makers overcome at least the major ambiguities and dilemmas sufficiently to produce a reasonably reliable constellation of primary values represented by the general consensus, what can they suggest about how to incorporate values into policy? It seems that the first thing for policy-makers to do is to recognize those issues in policy that involve value judgments, in contrast to those that require knowledge — the latter being thought of as information confirmed through scientific empirical investigation. This calls, among other things, for a separation of values from knowledge, not easy to achieve. Although knowledge and values differ in substance and in function and should not be used interchangeably, they are in fact so used in many instances because the moral issues they project are often interconnected, and because the technical problems that arise in the process of obtaining knowledge often present moral, social and legal dilemmas. For example, often enunciated as a value rather than as knowledge — admittedly, not always thoroughly confirmed knowledge — is the notion that the family is best for rearing children.

Difficulties in separating the two seem to become more pronounced as social welfare builds an ever more sophisticated body of scientific knowledge and seeks to develop greater skills in using it in order to assure scientific objectivity. Therein resides a hazard that social welfare researchers, planners and decision-makers must avoid: a one-sided and narrow preoccupation with scientific methodology may have the effect of pushing out of sight the very need to recognize those policy issues in which values are of primordial importance. Exciting technological vistas that promise an end to nagging human problems combined with the pragmatism that is inevitable in providing services — in any applied field — may then overemphasize questionable 'general characteristics' and turn individuals into proverbial statistics, in this way belittling their spiritual values and aspirations. Policies may then become callous, dehumanized and fragmented, harmful to those whose well-being they are supposed to enhance. All this is not to say that there is no crying need to foster and develop the scientific method in social welfare. On the contrary, appropriately used, this method will advance the cause of sorely needed precision and validity in social welfare's knowledge base, will organize and classify, and thus will help prevent the perpetuation of a morass of good impulses that are impotent in the face of destructive societal forces.

It is equally important for planners and decision-makers to be unceasingly aware of their own values as they evolve them in the life-long process of clarifying their philosophy of life, the basis for values. This will help them guard against injecting their own values into policy, rather than shape it in the image of the choices that make up the general consensus. Awareness, however, is not to be confused with neutrality on value-laden issues: to attain such neutrality is, strictly speaking, impossible and the very effort to do so is likely to atrophy value-judgment skill. Such skill can be nurtured and improved by careful and objective assessments and use of experience and knowledge — without sacrificing a genuine and abiding commitment to a humanistic philosophy.

Summary. While the workings of value systems confront the researcher, the policy-maker and the practitioner at every turn, the nature, evolution and meaning of values remain elusive and complex. Nevertheless, it is essential in comparative social welfare studies to make every effort to understand what the prevailing values of a given society are: failure to do so may lead policy-makers to assume that a particular society's values are like their own and consequently, they may judge what is done by their own standards. This skewed view may be aggravated by unfamiliar subtleties of the welfare vocabulary and, more importantly, by nonobservance of the difference between values that represent consensus and those that emanate from strivings to remain compatible with ideological positions of authoritarian elites. The researcher may be confused as well by the fact that recognition of the legitimacy of social welfare values in policy deliberations does not necessarily produce

Values and Ideologies

commitment to them, or that commitment will be operationalized in programs even if it exists.

Reaching a consensus on values that is sufficiently strong to be used for guiding social welfare policy is a difficult task. Involved is the requirement to balance individual needs against community needs and individual good against societal good; to reconcile the concepts of coercion and freedom of choice, of autonomy and paternalism, of benefits conferred as of right and benefits conferred by altruism. The resolution of these conflicts is often accompanied by insecurity and pain. And all this must be done without confusing a moralistic with a moral view of life. At the same time, consensus must not stand in the way of helping each individual to attain wholeness, to actualize his uniqueness as it projects a sense of value meaningful to others. Normally, within limits, each person finds scope in society for expressing his life, and social demands and standards are not felt as a bondage. But to submit completely to social authority would stunt growth and fragment individual integrity, diminishing an individual's chances of becoming aware of himself as an active and creative being who lives, in the vision of the teacher in the Gītā, 'not by the discipline of external authority but the inward rule of free devotion to truth'.

References

1. Baier, Kurt, 'Defining the Concept of Values', pp. 58–9 in *The Acquisition and Development of Values. Perspectives on Research*, Report of a Conference, May 15–17, 1968 (Washington, DC, US Department of Health, Education and Welfare (HEW), Public Health Service, National Institute of Child Health and Human Development. GPO: 1969, 0-351-894).
2. Myrdal, Gunnar, 'The Place of Values in Social Policy', *Journal of Social Policy*, 1, Part 1 (January 1972), pp. 1–15.
3. Marshall, T. H., 'Value Problems of Welfare-Capitalism', *ibid.*, pp. 15–33.
4. Donnison, D., 'Ideologies and Policy', *Journal of Social Policy*, 1, Part 2 (April 1972), pp. 97–117.
5. Myrdal, Gunnar, 'Social Values and Their Universality', *International Social Work*, xii, no. 1 (1969), pp. 3–12.
6. Cantril, Hadley, *The Pattern of Human Concerns* (New Jersey, Rutgers University Press, 1965).
7. Katona, George, et al., *Aspirations and Affluence, Comparative Studies in the United States and Western Europe* (New York, McGraw-Hill, 1971).
8. Madison, Bernice, 'The Welfare State: Some Unanswered Questions for the 1970s', *Social Service Review*, 44, no. 4 (December 1970), pp. 434–51. This material is based on Titmuss, Richard M., *Essays on 'The Welfare State'* (London, Unwin University Books, 1963), pp. 39–40.
9. Furniss, Norman and Tilton, Timothy, *The Case for the Welfare State. From Social Security to Social Equality* (Bloomington and London, Indiana University Press, 1977).

44 Values and Ideologies

10. Aptekar, Herbert H., 'The Values, Functions, and Methods of Social Work – An Interpretive Report of the Honolulu Seminar', in *An Intercultural Exploration: Universals and Differences in Social Work Values, Functions and Practice*, Report of an International seminar, The East–West Center, Hawaii, February 21–March 4 1966 (New York, Council on Social Work Education, 1967), pp. 3–63.
11. Rein, Martin, 'Social Policy Analysis as the Interpretation of Beliefs', *Journal of the American Institute of Planners*, xxxviii, no. 5 (September 1971), pp. 297–311.
12. Titmuss, Richard M., *The Gift Relationship. From Human Blood to Social Policy* (New York, Pantheon Books, 1971).
13. Heidenheimer, Arnold J., Heclo, Hugh, and Adams, Carolyn Teich, *Comparative Public Policy: The Politics of Social Choice in Europe and America* (New York, St Martins Press, 1975).
14. Alber, Jens, 'The Coverage of Social Insurance Schemes: Methodological Problems of International Comparisons', *International Social Work*, xix, no. 4 (1972), pp. 14–26.
15. Leman, Christopher, 'Patterns of Policy Development: Social Security in the United States and Canada', *Public Policy*, 25, no. 2 (Spring 1977), pp. 261–91.
16. Pryor, *Public Expenditures*.
17. Cutright, Phillips, 'Political Structure, Economic Development, and National Social Security Programs', *American Journal of Sociology*, lxx, no. 5 (March 1965), pp. 537–50.
18. Connor, Walter D., *Deviance in Soviet Society. Crime, Delinquency and Alcoholism* (New York, Columbia University Press, 1972).
19. Madison, Bernice, *Social Welfare in the Soviet Union* (Stanford, California, Stanford University Press, 1968).
20. Field, Mark G., 'Health as a "Public Utility" or the "Maintenance of Health Capacity" in Soviet Society', pp. 234–64 in Field, Mark G. (ed.), *Social Consequences of Modernization in Communist Societies* (Baltimore, The Johns Hopkins University Press, 1976).
21. Wolins, Martin, 'Some Theory and Practice in Child Care: A Cross-Cultural View', *Child Welfare*, 42, no. 8 (October 1963), pp. 369–77, 399.
22. Dallin, Alexander, 'Conclusions', pp. 385–98 in Atkinson, Dorothy, Dallin, Alexander, and Lapidus, Gail Warshofsky (eds.), *Women in Russia* (Stanford, California, Stanford University Press, 1977).
23. Osborn, Robert J., *Soviet Social Policies: Welfare, Equality, and Community* (Homewood, Illinois, The Dorsey Press, 1970).
24. Mishra, Ramesh, 'Welfare and Industrial Man: A Study of Welfare in Western Industrial Societies in Relation to a Hypothesis of Convergence', *The Sociological Review*, 21, no. 4 (November 1973), pp. 535–60.
25. Grant, James P., 'Accelerating Progress Through Social Justice', *International Development Review*, xiv, no. 3 (1972/3), pp. 2–9.
26. Field, Mark G., 'Introduction', pp. 1–19 in Field (ed.), *Social Consequences*.
27. Kolakowski, Leszek, 'In Praise of Inconsistency', *Dissent* (Spring 1964), pp. 201–9.
28. Gartner, Alan and Riessman, Frank, *The Service Society and the Consumer Vanguard. Introduction by Colin Greer* (New York, Harper & Row, 1974).
29. New Zealand, Royal Commission to Inquire Into and Report on Social Security, *Social Security Department, Paper 3*, 'Main values underlying income maintenance programmes' (Wellington, Social Security Department, March 1970); *Social Security Department, Paper 4*, 'Some Further Values Affecting Maintenance Programmes' (*ibid.*, April 1970).

Values and Ideologies

30. Radhakrishnan, S., *The Bhagavadgītā*, with an Introductory Essay, Sanskrit Text, English Translation and Notes (Bombay, Blacke & Son (India) Ltd, 1975).

31. Erikson, Erik H., 'Insight and Responsibility: Lectures on the Ethical Implications of Psychoanalytic Insight' (New York, W. W. Norton & Co., 1964).

32. Brown, J. Douglas, *An American Philosophy of Social Security. Evolution and Issues* (Princeton, New Jersey, Princeton University Press, 1972).

33. Titmuss, 'Equity, Adequacy and Innovation', pp. 259–69.

34. Stein, Bruno and Miller, S. M. (eds.), *Incentives and Planning in Social Policy* (Chicago, Aldine Publishing Co., 1973).

35. Moroney, Robert, *The Family and the State: Considerations for Social Policy* (New York, Longman, 1976).

36. *New York Times*, April 29, 1979.

37. Fanshel, David and Shinn, Eugene B., *Children in Foster Care. A Longitudinal Investigation* (New York, Columbia University Press, 1977).

38. Coleman, J. S., 'The Possibility of a Social Welfare Function', *American Economic Review*, LVI, no. 5 (December 1966), pp. 1105–23.

3 THE DEFINITION OF SOCIAL WELFARE AND SOCIAL POLICY

The phrases 'social welfare' and 'social policy' continue to be open to different interpretations which often determine both the content and the method of investigation. This chapter examines key reasons for these differences and illustrates their significance in policy formulation in an area of perennial and ancient social welfare concern.

Social Welfare. This term (as well as social services, social utilities, social programs, and social work) takes on different meanings in different countries. Writing in 1965, Wickenden explained that some of the reasons for this are that social welfare is dynamic and sensitive to political and economic changes; that 'its own functions are related to the total process of development and therefore undergo change as other aspects of the social structure produce new services, create new problems of adaptation, or stimulate new aspirations' (1:iv). Speaking at the International Conference on Social Welfare in 1972, she again emphasized that social welfare is a 'volatile term' and that 'its institutions reflect the society within which it operates. Because these take such varied and adaptable forms it can only be described functionally' (2:10).

The changes which social welfare has been and is undergoing were described by the European ministers responsible for social welfare in 1972. Social welfare is no longer directed solely towards the most under-privileged. Consequently, there is taking place a diversification of the motives for social welfare intervention and of the ways of intervening. While remedial action is still an essential task, there is increasing emphasis on preventive and rehabilitative functions. Changing conceptions of social welfare — from charity to solidarity, from spontaneous action to organized action, from the granting of favors to social rights — have combined into significant ideological shifts. Social welfare has moved away from a stress on individual morality to social causation as the dominant mode for explaining social problems; hence to a growing recognition of common needs and a belief in the necessity of collective/community responses to meet them. Such responses, in turn, require popular participation. The ministers emphasized that these changes subordinate economic growth to broader objectives of improving both individual well-being and the structures and operation of society as a whole. For them, this means that social welfare activities, marginal for a long time, should become the heart of the development process (3:5, 14–16).

Assuming that there exists a fair amount of consensus on this position among those concerned with social welfare, its practitioners are nevertheless finding it difficult to be indefatigable agents of development and at the same time help those whose lives are disrupted and who are made to suffer because of development. How to rehabilitate vulnerable individuals and groups and alleviate suffering among those left behind in the process of development and at the same time accord priority to welfare's developmental and preventive functions has remained an often insuperable problem. In many countries, efforts to cope with it require a major shift in social welfare policy and a marked reorientation of existing resources, programs and personnel.

The very breadth of the preventive–rehabilitative–developmental concept of social welfare has been among the main reasons for the continuing vagueness about the meaning to be given to social welfare both in individual countries and in an international context. This vagueness is especially pronounced in developing countries. In them, the failure to assign to 'social welfare' a distinctive and valid meaning as a specialized activity or a special professional discipline measurably diminishes its role in efforts to achieve the economic and social objectives of national planning. As a consequence, writes Livingstone, 'in national affairs and at the level of international organization, social welfare as a concept and a practice is widely misunderstood, sometimes rejected, and occasionally accorded no more than a peripheral role in the determination of planning objectives' (4:52). In international settings the problem of definition is compounded by the fact that as a concept, 'social welfare' has strong ideological overtones and is therefore likely to take on the characteristics of differing ideologies.

Efforts to produce more universally acceptable definitions have been made by a number of individual scholars, some program-oriented (5; 6; 7), others analytic (8; 9). International bodies have been active as well. At the UN, work on the problem of definition has been going on since 1950 (10:3–9). In 1963, for example, social welfare was described as a wide range of socially sponsored activities and programs directed towards community and individual well-being. Within this broad spectrum, 'social services' were delimited as a more specific functional area and 'social work', as the professional activity primarily concerned with social service functions. In 1967, social welfare as an organized function was seen as a body of activities designed to enable individuals, families, groups and communities to cope with the social problems generated by changing conditions. But at their 1968 meeting, the ministers responsible for social welfare could not arrive at a definition. They ended up by indicating their belief in certain principles: social welfare should insure that no person is left behind in the process of development, that no one is permitted to fall below the social standards that are every man's right, and that social welfare should be fully represented in national planning. The ministers supported giving priority to preventive and developmental programs that could affect a whole community, to programs affecting children and young people, and programs aimed at improving family life, particularly family planning. It was noted that

> The difficulties encountered in reaching an agreement on what is social welfare cannot be reduced to a problem of semantics. The uncertainties which do exist in social welfare terminology and the problem of finding equivalent terms for different languages would be easily overcome if the underlying concepts were commonly understood (11:34).

At their meeting in 1972, the European ministers seemed to return to the 1967 description, adding to it the notion (first enunciated in 1959) that social welfare is not a one-way operation since it aims at a *mutual* adjustment of individuals and their social environment; hence, it must influence the structures of society as well as the groups and individuals who compose it.

Continuing efforts at clarification are likewise evident in proceedings of the International Conference on Social Welfare (12; 13:9; 14:133; 15:98−100; 16:4; 17:37−8; 2:10). In this arena, some movement toward basic agreement is taking place, but a host of knotty problems, conceptual and semantic, remains. The notion that 'social welfare refers to the particular set of instrumentalities that a particular society develops to fulfill the goals of the "Welfare State" ' (18:13, reference 4) is not universally accepted − to say nothing of the fact that the very concept 'Welfare State' as an embodiment of the evolution from minimal to increased governmental responsibility for meeting basic human needs is neither understood nor accepted everywhere. Nor is there evident substantial consensus on social welfare as 'a broad term describing organized social methods of meeting basic needs for mutual support' (2:10).

The Definition of Social Welfare and Social Policy

The search for consensus is complicated by the inability of professionals, who provide a sizable segment of the personnel for social welfare programs, to define themselves, despite valiant efforts to do so. A recent attempt in the United States to clarify what social workers' purposes are and what they should be, what social workers are and should be doing, and whether there exists consensus among social workers that cuts across the profession's various specialties and interests, concluded that as yet social work remains unable to 'clearly and simply articulate to others what is common to the activities of all social workers' (19:444).[1] Similar problems, it appears, beset other social fields as well. In writing about public administration in a comparative perspective, Heady notes that 'despite several decades of development, consensus about the scope of public administration is still lacking, and the field has been described as featuring heterodoxy rather than orthodoxy. This may be a strength rather than a weakness, but such a feature does rule out a short, precise, and generally acceptable definition of the field' (21:2). Writing in 1969, Pusic urged social workers to recognize that in the context of the UN Developmental Decade (1961—70) which called for progress toward self-sustaining economic growth *and* development

> it seems particularly important to set up, perfect, make accepted and stabilize internationally valid standards defining the parameters of a profession: what training does it require, under what conditions is it practiced, with what codes of behavior and moral obligations. The 'cosmopolitanism' of the professions should receive its normative framework. It would then be easier for professional solidarity to extend beyond territorial limits and to give the moral and psychological support professionals working in other countries so badly need (22:9).

A decade later, in 1979, there is no reason to challenge either the soundness or the timeliness of Pusic's exhortation.

Some writers believe that efforts to arrive at a single definition of social welfare are premature and academic, in view of the fact that little empirical research has been done on welfare programs. They advise that scholars and researchers simply make explicit the particular concept of social welfare they employ in their particular undertakings. Others, more pragmatically inclined, argue that vagueness leads to failure to ascribe a distinctive quality to activities of social welfare personnel, to point up the uniqueness of what they do, thus hindering a meeting of

50 The Definition of Social Welfare and Social Policy

minds between them and the general public. It leads to difficulties in deciding where to locate social welfare within the broad range of social policies. Elkin points out that improved definitions are essential to long-range planning, priority-setting, cost analyses, statistical systems, studies of expenditures, definition of workload standards and measurement of effectiveness (23). They appear essential as well for organizing the service delivery system, for designing a more refined specification of service objectives, and a more rational manpower policy whose crucial importance is widely acknowledged. Writing in 1965, Donnison and Chapman pointed out that

> Discretion, vagueness and inexplicitness are only tolerable and useful if their limits are reasonably clear and their implications restricted in scope. Objectives which are too precisely defined tend to be restrictive, if cautious, or disruptive, if radical. But objectives which are too vague tend to destroy a sense of purpose, and provide no foundation upon which to establish proper standards of performance (24:241−2).

And it is added by other writers that in cross-national endeavors, clarifying definitions, however arbitrary and unsatisfactory, are essential for purposes of communication.

The need for a theoretical base for social welfare was emphasized by Pusic in 1971. He noted that basically different cultural and functional societies coexist, or adjoin each other, within nation-states (and, it may be added, within the world as a whole); and he argued that in order to understand what welfare is, we must achieve a better understanding of the nature of social development. Toward this end, it is necessary to construct theoretical models for analyzing the social welfare field (25:400−13). In his keynote address at the 16th International Conference on Social Welfare in 1972, Titmuss presented his 'institutional−redistributive' model fo social welfare/social policy.[2] This model

> sees social welfare as a basic integrated institution in society providing both universal and selective services outside the market on the principle of need. Universal services, available without distinction of class, colour, sex, or religion, can perform functions which foster and promote attitudes and behavior towards the values of social solidarity, altruism, toleration and accountability . . . Territorially then [social welfare/social policy], in its universalist

The Definition of Social Welfare and Social Policy

role recognizes no human boundaries or man-made laws of residence and race. The frontiers of social growth are open. As a model, it is in part based on theories about the multiplier diswelfare and disrupting effects of change, industrial, technological, social and economic, and in part on a conception of social justice which sees man not only as an individual but as a member of groups and associations. It follows, therefore, that this model not only incorporates and embodies the effects of past and present change but envisages a variety of roles for social welfare to play as a positive and dynamic agent of change: to promote integrative values, to prevent future diswelfares; to penetrate economic policies with social welfare objectives, and in all these ways to bring about a redistribution in command-over-resources-through-time. In doing so it challenges different societies at different stages of development and within different cultural contexts to determine a particular infrastructure of universalist services within and around which to develop selective or positively discriminating services provided, as social rights, on criteria of the needs of specific disadvantaged categories, groups and territorial areas . . . One of the assumptions underlying this model is that social welfare is not simply an adjunct of the economy or an ameliorative system providing services for poor people . . . while accepting a compensatory role . . . it also accepts a positive role through the development of social manpower policies, corrective regional and area economic policies, retraining and further education services and other instrumentalities designed to bring about an improvement in the standard and quality of life of the individuals concerned (26:40–41).

That this grandiose model is theoretically challenging and exciting — opening as it does enormous vistas into a world of high quality of life for everyone — cannot be denied. Given the problems of the 'real world' discussed earlier, however, it does not diminish but rather serves to accentuate the need for clarification and consensus in regard to 'social welfare'/social policy across the globe. For the social scientist working in a cross-national context, the breadth of the model offers a wide choice but also requires careful delimiting: he/she is to compare policies and plans in reference to what? Nor can administrators and practitioners, trying to help diverse individuals and groups in their particular countries cope with many-faceted social problems, avoid delimiting their functions — hopefully, in a manner that will facilitate coordination and strengthen social welfare's overall thrust toward objectives so trenchantly enunciated in Titmuss' vision.

52 The Definition of Social Welfare and Social Policy

Social Policy. Despite the fact that 'social scientists now have an overwhelming interest in "policy studies" ' (28:ix), and that there exists a large and burgeoning literature on social policy (among studies especially pertinent for social welfare policy, see 29, 30, 31, 9, 4, 32), this term remains ill-defined. Writing in 1976, Moroney stated that 'there is, by and large, no universal agreement as to what social policy is, its boundaries, nor appropriate methodologies for its analysis'. His own belief was that

> social policy is concerned with a search for and articulation of social objectives and the means to achieve these [and that the] 'non-ideological' activities involved include analysis of the issue, its dimensions and its implications, . . . a consensus of the body politic that the situation presents a current or future problem that should be addressed, [and] choosing among alternative strategies and developing structures to carry out specific interventions (18:2).

Noting in 1975 that the study of comparative public policy 'is rapidly becoming a busy cross-roads in the social sciences', Heidenheimer, Heclo and Adams asserted that 'there are as yet few signposts and still fewer agreed destinations'. They think that such study will continue 'to be subject to perpetual tension between the recognition of particularity and the quest for universality, between the claims of analytic and those of experiential knowledge' (33:Preface). Writing in 1976, Littrell explained that 'neither social scientists nor policy makers are quite sure how to bring the diverse methods of social research to bear upon the complex problems of social policy'. He considers the current issues in social policy research to be 'the nature of such research, strategy and perspective, and technical problems within highly specialized policy areas' (34:3). 'Social policy' continues to be an elusive term even within one culture and one language; it becomes more complex and more difficult to define across cultural, language and developmental barriers.

An insightful discussion by Boulding in 1967 suggests some of the difficulties in seeking agreement on what social policy is. He writes:

> If there is one common thread that unites all aspects of social policy and distinguishes them from merely economic policy, it is the thread of what has elsewhere been called the 'integrative system'. This includes those aspects of social life that are characterized not so much by exchange in which a quid is got for a quo as by unilateral transfers that are justified by some kind of appeal to a status of

legitimacy, identity, or community . . . By and large it is an objective of social policy to build the identity of a person around some community with which he is associated (35:3).

To achieve an 'integrative system', social policy must address numerous, often contradictory, aspects of the social environment.

Although some researchers do not seem to be too concerned with the role of values in final judgments on social policies — they emphasize, rather, that 'a policy may be bad in the sense that it would not necessarily have been adopted if the persons taking the decision had had greater knowledge or greater understanding' (36:1) — the majority agree that such judgments 'depend heavily on personal values and choice and, through them, on the values of a society at large' (33:212).

Thus, Rein identifies the terrain of social policy not by its subject matter but its procedures of analysis, and propounds the view that the most demanding task of those who undertake policy analysis is 'identification of their own values, along with an understanding of how these values blatantly and subtly bias analysis' (37:309). This, he realizes, leaves unsolved the ethical problem faced by analysts of how to act on their prejudices — something that may immobilize them as far as action and reform are concerned or whittle away their moral integrity. But action will take place in any case: Reubens argues that while in practice there are serious obstacles to implementing the goals (values) of policy ranked in some order of relative importance and priority, this does not negate the whole idea of attaining a complete and soundly based social schedule of preferences (as Arrow attempted to do: see 38). The fact is, he writes, that all societies do arrive at some such schedule because people will not long tolerate indecision which prevents action, 'and will rather find through the political process some rough-and-ready consensus which may then be modified and readjusted in the light of experience' (39:15). Unanimity, argues Rothenberg, is not a necessary condition (40). And Berliner reminds us that inaction is also a form of action (41:5). Explaining that 'the variety of definitions offered in the literature is almost as diverse as the number of writers who examine the subject', Weiner, Akabas, Kremen and Sommer decide that for the purposes of their study, social policy adds up to 'enunciated positions and courses of action reflecting an underlying set of beliefs about what ought to be done in relation to a given aspect of the human condition' (42:4). Donnison's value-oriented approach comes through when he argues that a choice between economic growth and distributive justice need not be made and provides the following blueprint:

54   The Definition of Social Welfare and Social Policy

1. When policies are to be decided, top priority should normally be given to the extension of liberty, particularly among those who have least of it — the people whose lives are most severely stunted by economic, social and political constraints.
2. To be freer, our society must be less deferential and therefore less constrained by social hierarchies. That is unlikely to happen unless its distributions of status, living standards and security become more equal.
3. In a peace-time democracy, the greater equality and the expansion of opportunities which we seek are unlikely to be achieved unless we maintain a higher rate of economic growth.
4. We should ensure, wherever possible, that our towns grow in ways that make it easier, not harder, for people to seize new opportunities, and to encounter and learn from others of different ages, races, classes and incomes.
5. Liberty will not have been effectively extended unless it provokes new demands, and unlocks new talents for meeting them. The 'virtuous circle' we seek would extend freedom, and thus encourage innovation, which hastens economic and social growth which furnish the resources for further progress towards equalization of attainment and living standards, which again extends freedom . . . (43:114–17).

Agreeing that social policy involves a blending of facts and preferences, scholars are also for the most part in accord that facts and preferences must be developed by means of a 'continuous dialogue between the policy analyst, the policy maker, and the policy implementer' (18:4) — if, as the actors who make the essential inputs, they are to understand and interpret the meaning of a given policy similarly and then be able to agree on the goals it is to achieve. The method chosen to implement a particular policy — including administrative details — contains the vital elements of the policy itself. Furthermore, argue Donnison and Chapman, 'the activities of "policy-makers" and "professional staff" are just as much a part of the administrative process as those of the staff who are called "administrators" ' (24:41). Consequently, 'it is crucial', writes Littrell, 'to understand how bureaucratic organizations gather, mold, and use data as well as how they implement and evaluate policy implementation'. Such an understanding may be hampered by the mistrust that often exists between social scientists and policy-makers. The sources of it, according to Littrell, other than individual 'idiosyncracies', are 'systematic' and 'structured': the former arise from differing conceptions of adequate knowledge'; the latter, 'from constraints inherent in the differential organizational bases of researchers and policy makers' (34:21 and 7).

In connection with administrative aspects, it must also be kept in mind that social policies are of several levels. On a national level they may be setting priorities, accompanied by massive rhetoric and propaganda, and determining their degree of effectiveness by shifting allocations of money and personnel. The lower the level of administration and hence, the more specific the priorities, the more difficult it becomes to maintain conceptual and programmatic purity. At the level of an individual within the social welfare subculture, policies may dissolve into personalities and other highly specific details. Comparisons of policies may trace particular social welfare programs from broad statements of national concern to very specific implementation within any one program or society; comparative studies may involve cross-national comparisons at one or more administrative levels, within a single society or among several.

Important as well, argue some writers, is the need to respond to ethnic diversity. In the United States, they suggest, this response should not ignore 'the common values that make up a specifically American consciousness'. Rather, they think, 'the ideal lies somewhere between assimilation and ethnic diversity', with the latter acknowledged in the formulation and implementation of specific public policies. If this does not take place, they warn, social policies will be ineffective (44:xii—xiii).

Other writers find that social policy is 'stalemated' because it fails to incorporate ' a developmental perspective': it does not take into account 'the emergence of a fluid life cycle' brought about by changes in the 'work-family system'. The decline in full-time, lifetime jobs or careers, combined with a more varied family composition requires policies, it is said, that would respond to needs generated by 'transitions between life states' (45:434—50).

Casting his view of social policy into a broad historical and social framework, Moynihan sees it in the United States as

> torn between two conflicting sets of assumptions about man: [on the one hand, there is the] 'utilitarian ethic', which assumes that man is a reasoning and responsible creature, and that social policy should entail incentives and deterrences to which the citizen might respond; [but this ethic] has increasingly given way to a new 'therapeutic ethic' that arose out of Freudianism and modern social science . . . [which] envisions man as a creature of circumstance . . .

56   The Definition of Social Welfare and Social Policy

> [for whom] 'therapeutic' social policy . . . requires a far greater degree of government intervention in order to 'restructure' [his] environment. [According to Moynihan], neither assumption . . . is empirically proved, and neither is a sufficient guide to policy-making. But much of the confusion, conflict and ineffectiveness which attend current social policies derive from the incompatability of the two assumptions in a polity in which both are widely and sometimes simultaneously held . . . (46:25).

It is reasonable to assume that such conflict, confusion and ineffectiveness may exist and to some extent, at least, for the same reasons in other Western democratic societies.

Another complicating factor is that social policy affects economic policy and 'economic policy is equally decisive for framing social policies . . .' (47:565). This interdependence is underscored by a recent UN study of 'the practical social policy aspects of the concept of a minimum level of living' which concludes that social security programs can have an important corrective impact on preventing poverty and on healing its effects, but only if policy makers do not overlook

> the fundamental fact that general economic policy, including policy of full employment, taxation and price policy constitutes a decisive framework for achieving a socially acceptable equitable income distribution and significantly improving the situation of social groups at the lower end of the income scale (48:39).

Rein emphasizes that interdependence ought not to be permitted to subordinate social policies to economic policies: rather, the latter ought to promote 'the social aims of redistribution and the reduction of inequalities' (47:585). To achieve this is extremely difficult, not only because of ideological constraints, but also because as yet analytical tools available to economists allow for more precision and for greater analytical skill than anything available to social policy makers and planners. Livingstone writes:

> Social concepts are still relatively ambiguous; the quantification of social achievement is rudimentary and imprecise. While it is true that the development process is indivisible — it is an artificial distinction to talk of an economic process and not of a social process — the aims and the consequences of development can be examined in either economic or social terms. What are these social and economic

elements in development? How are they related to each other? What is meant by the reference to 'socio-economic reality'? (4:103–4).

There is disagreement between the anti- and the pro-incrementalists. According to Titmuss, 'at best it is clear that the study of social policy cannot be isolated from the study of society as a whole in all its varied social, economic, and political aspects' (27:15). For Gil, social policy is the entire system of principles and measures which whole societies — not simply their governments — use to allocate and distribute economic resources, statuses and rights among individuals and groups, and thus to order social relationships. He rejects the position that incrementalism is an intrinsic aspect of democracy in a complex and pluralistic society (8). He proposes a comprehensive approach and emphasizes the need, in analyzing specific policies, to show their interdependence with other policies, their consistency or lack of consistency with these others, and the reasons for congruence or lack of it. But he does not provide a hierarchy of criteria to which the variables that finally determine a policy choice must connect. The need emphasized by Gil is recognized by Heclo who finds that policy 'harmonization' — the 'way any given policy can be shaped to take other policies into account and to reconcile an ever-widening range of factors' — is especially important in the income support area as distinctions between social insurance and public assistance become more and more blurred (49:213). For this area, he does suggest the 'other' policies that should be harmonized and also calls for harmonization to be a continuous process.

Other scholars, however, question the rejection of incrementalism, Moynihan points out that incremental reforms 'by never altering too much, being always subject to relatively easy corrective measures, produce better decisions and pose less of a threat to democratic consensus'; furthermore, he argues, it is not possible to say whether a change constitutes a 'fundamental change': this will be known only if it is adopted and 'is accompanied by fundamental effects' (50:551). Harris shows that not only do incremental shifts of policy involve the utilization of sizable human and financial resources, but that 'a series of changes in an existing program — incremental as each may be — can result in adoption of major new policy directions' (51:366). Kahn believes that 'nobody can offer one well-developed social policy paradigm, proven in its applicability to all decision-making in social services'. For him, it is not clear that a paradigm will or should evolve, since some of its dimensions have greater weight at one moment than at another. Hence, the hierarchy of choices depends upon both reality assessment and a balancing among values (7:129). According to Stein, 'in practice . . . [social policy] is born of conflicting goals and interests, . . . its various parts grow by accretion, . . . the process compounds existing goal conflicts within the system . . . and the resultant policy set can behave irrationally with respect to any or all goals' (52:2).

Still others are concerned with setting realistic limits to social policy. Thus, for Glazer, the 'elastic term social policy' is an effort to deal with traditional ways of handling distress. The traditional mechanisms, in his view, are located in the family, in ethnic groups, in churches and in neighborhoods. He compares the welfare system in the United States with the English and Swedish systems and concludes that the United States has gone further towards the destruction of tradition than England or Sweden. In this sense, he is convinced, the United States comes face to face with the limits of social policy more sharply than any other country (53).

A number of authors have indicated what must be taken into account in formulating social welfare policy. For developing countries, Livingstone's 'determinants' include economic, political and cultural factors, the family, celebrations (associated with many forms of personal spending), tradition and change, international aid, the interests of the donor (which have an influence on the purposes and provisions of this aid and on its effectiveness), the international consultant, and the interests of the recipient (4:66—86). For Titmuss, an essential background would include

> knowledge of population changes, past and present and predicted for the future; the family as an institution and the position of women; social stratification and the concepts of class, caste, status and mobility, social change and the effects of industrialization, urbanization and social conditions; the political structure; the work ethic and the sociology of industrial relations; minority groups and racial prejudice; social control, conformity, deviance and the uses of sociology to maintain the political status quo (27:15—16).

A seminar on cross-national research in social policy identified six groups of questions implied in social policy problems: cost—benefit; interest groups (who are the potential supporters and the likely opponents of the policy); policy-implementation; change (what are the likely directions in which circumstances relevant to the policy are going to change in the future); attitudes and values; and program evaluation and assessment of progress (who benefits; what are the benefits and the disbenefits) (54).

Given this wide-ranging spectrum of elements that must be considered, efforts to achieve the 'integrative system' that appears to be the essence of social policy inevitably run into complexities and difficulties. One such effort, faced with the need to integrate poverty policy into a much broader matrix of social welfare policy, will suffice to illustrate some of these complexities and difficulties in an international perspective.

There is widespread concern over the fact that despite the tremendous economic gains of the last 20 years, 'very little progress has been made by the poorest people and nations' (55:2) — to say nothing of the hardships that are still faced by many even in a country as rich as the United States. This concern translates into a desire to assure 'minimum levels of living', to meet 'basic needs' in both developing and developed nations. That the basic human needs concept should become a central purpose of development was endorsed by the Organization for Economic Cooperation and Development (OECD) in 1977. It was affirmed that 'while development cooperation concerned relations between governments, its objective was the well-being of individuals; development cooperation should therefore fulfill the dual purpose of growth of incomes and meeting basic needs of individuals in all developing countries'. It was noted that 'a basic needs approach is not primarily welfare or charity but productivity-oriented, aiming at increasing the productive income of the poor and strengthening the basis for long-term self-generating development' (55:2–3).[3] In 1972, the Conference of European Ministers Responsible for Social Welfare stated that 'one of the fundamental concerns of all European countries today is to achieve a more equitable distribution of income and resources among individuals, social groups and various parts of the country' and, among other things, recommended that 'criteria must be established that will allow for selectivity of benefits and social services in favour of population groups with particular needs, and for the gradual modification of the advantages they are afforded, while always maintaining the principle of the universality of social welfare' (3:4, 6). To establish such criteria, it was important to determine 'a socially acceptable minimum level of living and [to use] it as a practical guideline for specific policy measures, in order to orient existing resources more directly to the needs of the poor, to improve the situation of the deprived members of society and, at the same time, to provide for a more equitable income distribution' (48:1).

To define acceptable minimum levels of living (which presumably would fulfill basic needs) demands the resolution of complex and many-faceted issues. 'There is no universally relevant definition of poverty. It depends on the standards adopted by a community at a given time' (58:141). 'Minimum level' (the 'poverty line' which divides those in and out of poverty) may refer only to minimum material resources; or it may in addition include other elements considered essential for ensuring optimum participation of each individual in community life. In Sweden, for example, the items adopted as a basis for ascertaining the minimum level of living in 1970 included not only economic resources, but work, health, education, childhood and family conditions, housing, diet, leisure time, recreation and political resources (58:142). That such items are not likely to be considered for inclusion in Latin America is strongly suggested by the estimate of Portes and Ferguson which places more than half of the urban population of that part of the world in poverty (59:78); that such items perhaps ought not to be included in most African nations is indicated by Eames and Goodé who found that European models of welfare programs borrowed by them fail to take into account differences in social and demographic situations and tribal heterogeneity and are, consequently, less than effective (60:113–14); and Gilbert proposes 'alternative' measures of social protection for the rural sector of developing nations, measures that are neither traditional (individual efforts and reciprocal obligations of extended family and village) nor classical (government-sponsored social security) (61).

Furthermore, whichever standards are adopted, they are constantly subject to change, although social change is much slower in some countries than in others. How the poverty line is drawn – whether the absolute or the relative method is used – has important implications. In the United States, the absolute method (which determines a minimum subsistence level for basic maintenance for a family of a given size and fixes the market price of the included necessities – a price that is periodically adjusted to reflect changes in the value of money) has prevailed. Appelbaum found that, given this method,

> the actual level of living deemed necessary for poverty-level families has risen . . . that they have been considered to need less than working-class families by a relatively constant ratio. Thus, while the level of living provided by a poverty-line budget has improved, the status of these families relative to the rest of society has remained static (62:514).

In contrast to the absolute American poverty line, explains Zimbalist, Britain's line is relative; that is, its minimum subsistence level has been adjusted over time

The Definition of Social Welfare and Social Policy

to reflect not only the changing prices but also changing *standards of living* in the broader society. Thus, it perceives poverty not in terms of fixed needs but, rather, in terms of relative deprivation, at a given time ... [The] British assistance recipient has bettered his position vis-a-vis national norms while his American counterpart has lost ground in this same relationship (63:421, 431).

He demonstrates that unless the difference between the absolute and relative concepts is taken into account when differences in poverty trends in the two countries are compared, conclusions are likely to be spurious. But in a carefully reasoned presentation, Wilson warns that the relative concept 'can be pushed so far that the measurement of poverty becomes closely identified with the measurement of inequality'. He recognizes that relative social deprivation must be addressed since it is part of the problem, but he believes that it would 'be wrong to claim that poverty should be simply identified with inequality and measured only by some index of inequality' (64:8, 9). Marshall expressed the same view when he wrote that there has taken place

a reaction against the idea of the 'poverty line' in favor of the view that the concept 'poverty' has no meaning except in a relative sense, whereas the 'poverty line' implies that it can be conceived in absolute terms. This has been accompanied by the contention that the real problem is not poverty, but inequality. If this means that poverty is relative to the standard of civilization of the country concerned, it is beyond dispute. If it means that I may not say that A is poor, but only that he is poorer than B, I cannot accept it. If it means that inequality is a major social issue of which poverty is a part, that is beyond dispute. But if it means that the problems of poverty and inequality are identical and inseparable, so that one could not eradicate poverty without solving the problem of inequality, then I cannot accept that either ... in a democratic—welfare—capitalist society ... poverty is a disease, but inequality is an essential structural feature (65:27-8).

In an effort to provide comparable data in a cross-national context, a study by the OECD created a 'standardized relative poverty line' which is the rounded (unweighted) average of the official or quasi-official poverty lines provided by the included countries.[4] It was found that for one person this average was 66.6 percent; that is, 'a person would be poor if his income was below two-thirds of the average disposable income in his country'. Adopting this averaging procedure, percentages of average per capita disposable income that would be necessary to provide a minimum level of living were obtained for families of various sizes (two persons, 100 percent; three persons, 125 percent; four persons, 145 percent; five persons, 160 percent). The creators of this distribution are aware of the many limitations contained in their method, but they believe that their standardized poverty line is a convenient way 'of making broad comparisons between different countries and of obtaining a general impression of the extent of poverty and does not of course provide a precise measure' (66:66).

This example of the difficulties that continue to surround policy formulation is concerned, it must be remembered, with poverty — not a new subject but rather, in the words of Stein and Miller, 'the relief of poverty must be the oldest task for social policy' (67:9).

Movement toward resolving at least some of these difficulties will perhaps be stimulated by work that is being done on the integration of social theory and social policy — work that seeks 'to establish more clearly the constraints under which policy-makers operate and to clarify the consequences that are likely to follow when certain kinds of policies are adopted' (68:1) by delineating general variables 'which transcend space and time and present a scheme that permits the analysis of numerous policy sectors across time and across societies' (69:vii).

In the meantime, from an international point of view, most useful is a UN publication (1969), *Social Policy and the Distribution of Income in the Nation* (70). This document discusses the most expedient socio-economic policy goals for different types of societies, analyzes the methodological problems involved in measuring redistribution and provides an excellent bibliography on both subjects.

Summary. 'Social welfare' describes a field of human activity whose goals, forms and content change as the society changes. Although the transformations that take place are not identical in all societies, major differences seem to grow out of the pace of change and the emphases placed on specific programs rather than out of differences in the overall direction of social welfare's movement. In an international perspective, movement is from the residual to the institutional concept, that is, from benefits and services provided only to those who qualify and are in crisis to incorporating benefits and services into the normal functioning of the social system; from granting assistance out of altruistic motives to social rights; from provision for special groups to universal provision; from efforts to reform the individual to joining these efforts with

The Definition of Social Welfare and Social Policy

reforms of the society itself; from primary dependence on voluntary and spontaneous action to public, organized action; and from providing a minimum of help — sometimes only enough for survival — to making available enough help — both in quantity and diversity — for a genuine improvement of the quality of life which, in turn, makes it possible for individuals to fully develop their potentials and to contribute constructively to their communities.

The far-reaching scope of its activities and the fact that its functions require close working relationships with many professions make it difficult for social welfare to define itself and its boundaries — either to the satisfaction of its own practitioners or to that of other professionals or of the general public. As yet unachieved are generalizations that would be acceptable in most societies as well as concepts that would be widely acceptable within particular societies. The continuation of this state of affairs reflects a dearth of well-conceived empirical studies and a lack of consensus among social welfare practitioners about what the social welfare field ought to encompass and ought to do — as well as the underdeveloped state of social welfare's theoretical base. Vagueness and disaccord make for difficulties in locating responsibility for carrying out the policy-planning process and in implementing the decisions that flow out of it. All this often has a chilling effect on the allocation of resources for welfare undertakings.

'Social policy', despite the fact that it is increasingly claiming the attention of a growing number of social scientists, likewise remains an elusive term, with no universal agreement evident on its content, its goals, or the most promising methods for its analysis. A number of reasons are contributing to this situation, some more weightily than others. Recognition of the interdependence of social and economic factors in social policy has yet to reduce measurably either the technical or the ideological problems in achieving it. Genuine interdependence, it is argued, exposes the need for greater redistribution of income and a more decisive reduction of social inequality than have been achieved so far; this, in turn, demands far-reaching (often, structural) changes in both the economic and social domains. Not surprisingly, many do not accept this view, consequently, the debate continues. A complementary controversy is precluding a meeting of minds between advocates of a holistic concept of social policy which insists on a comprehensive approach to what whole societies do to order social relationships — and those who are inclined not to rule out the incremental approach, both because it takes into account reality assessment and a balancing of values and because it offers more possibility for relatively easy corrective measures.

64 The Definition of Social Welfare and Social Policy

Nevertheless, progress has been made in several directions. A better grasp of the major factors that present problems for social policy research and of the major questions implied in policy-oriented problems is apparent. Evident as well is the recognition of the fundamental importance of identifying values, both those held by the researcher and by the society he is investigating, if policy analysis is to be effective and purposive. There is greater appreciation of the manner in which the interplay of forces in the political arena, especially the activities of interest groups and bureaucracies, shapes social policy. Studies of bureaucracies have also revealed the need for a continuous and frank dialogue between the policy analyst, policy-maker and policy implementer because the administration of what social policy provides and of its outcomes can make or unmake the policy itself.

Notes

1. The deleterious effects of these uncertainties in an educational context (undergraduate social work curriculum in America) can be deduced from the observations made by an educator in March 1979. She said: 'Any curriculum... is a statement about the profession and what we deem its purpose to be... fuzziness, lack of definition, and disagreement about the essential professional purpose of social work just won't do for baccalaureate curriculum developers and managers... when faculties sit down across this country to develop curricula which will produce practitioners who have... mastered the fundamentals... for beginning-level practice, there must be some common understanding of what those fundamentals are. This, in turn, should flow from agreement about our professional purposes' (20).

2. For Titmuss, this is the best of three possible models. The other two are (1) the residual welfare model of social policy which is based on the premise that there are two 'natural' (or socially given) channels through which an individual's needs are properly met: the private market and the family. Only when these break down should welfare institutions come into play and then only temporarily; and (2) the industrial achievement–performance model of social policy which incorporates a significant role for social welfare institutions as adjuncts of the economy. It holds that social needs should be met on the basis of merit, work performance and productivity (27:30–31).

3. As a new employment-oriented approach to development, the basic human needs concept originated in employment conferences and research undertakings sponsored by the International Labour Organisation (ILO) beginning in 1969. A Declaration of Principles and Programme of Action for a Basic Needs Strategy of Development was adopted at the World Employment Conference in June 1976 (56). Those who challenge the 'human needs' strategy in development argue that it departs from viewing development as growth; distorts the term investment, since services to meet human needs may be an investment in the survival of the least educated, least healthy and least capable, but (in the absence of any specific or predictable future return other than survival) are not development investments (57:29).

4. The OECD member countries are: Australia, Austria, Belgium, Canada, Denmark, Finland, France, Germany, Greece, Iceland, Ireland, Italy, Japan,

The Definition of Social Welfare and Social Policy

Luxembourg, Netherlands, New Zealand, Norway, Portugal, Spain, Sweden, Switzerland, Turkey, United Kingdom, United States, and 'special status', Yugoslavia.

References

1. Wickenden, Elizabeth, *Social Welfare in a Changing World. The Place of Social Welfare in the Process of Development* (Washington, DC, HEW, Welfare Administration, 1965).
2. Wickenden, Elizabeth, 'Advanced Working Paper', pp. 9–21 in *Developing Social Policy in Conditions of Rapid Change. Role of Social Welfare*, Proceedings of the XVIth International Conference on Social Welfare, The Hague, Netherlands, August 13–19, 1972 (New York and London, Columbia University Press, 1973).
3. UN Economic and Social Council, *Conference of European Ministers Responsible for Social Welfare*, The Hague, Netherlands, August 22–26, 1972 (E/CONF. 64/1. February 8, 1972).
4. Livingstone, Arthur, *Social Policy in Developing Countries* (London, Routledge and Kegan Paul, 1969).
5. Rodgers, *Comparative Social Administration*.
6. George, Victor, *Social Security: Beveridge and After* (London, Routledge and Kegan Paul, 1968).
7. Kahn, Alfred J., *Social Policy and Social Services* (New York, Random House, 1973).
8. Gil, David G., *Unravelling Social Policy. Theory, Analysis, and Political Action Towards Social Equality* (Cambridge, Mass., Schenkman Publishing Co., 1973).
9. Rein, Martin, *Social Policy: Issues of Choice and Change* (New York, Random House, 1970).
10. Lally, Dorothy, *National Social Service Systems. A Comparative Study and Analysis of Selected Countries* (Washington, DC, HEW, Social and Rehabilitation Service, September 1970).
11. UN Department of Economic and Social Affairs, *Proceedings of the International Conference of Ministers Responsible for Social Welfare, 3–12 September 1968* (New York, UN, 1969. Sales No., E.69.IV.4).
12. *Tenth International Conference of Social Work*, Rome, Italy, January 8–14, 1961, 'Statements on the Use of the Term "Social Work" (taken from the National Reports)'. Mimeographed.
13. Leaper, R. A. B., 'Report of the Pre-Conference Working Party', in *Social Progress Through Social Planning*, Proceedings of the XIIth International Conference of Social Work, Athens, Greece, September 13–18, 1964 (International Conference of Social Work, 1965), pp. 3–35.
14. Winston, Ellen, 'Social Policy and Human Rights in Development Toward a Welfare Society', in *Social Welfare and Human Rights*, Proceedings of the XIVth International Conference on Social Welfare, Helsinki, Finland, August 18–24, 1968 (New York, Columbia University Press, 1969), pp. 133–42.
15. Feliciano, Gregorio M., 'New Strategies for Social Development: Role of Social Welfare and Perspectives for the Future', in *New Strategies for Social Development, Role of Social Welfare*, Proceedings of the XVth International Conference on Social Welfare, Manila, Philippines, September 6–12, 1970 (New York, Columbia University Press, 1971), pp. 96–103.
16. Fox, Morris G., 'Report of the Pre-Conference Working Party', in *ibid.*, pp. 3–37.

17. Schottland, Charles I., 'Welfare's Historic and Continuing Commitments', in *ibid.*, pp. 34–47.
18. Moroney, *The Family and the State*.
19. Briar, Scott, 'In Summary', *Social Work*, Special Issue on Conceptual Frameworks, 22, no. 5 (September 1977), pp. 415–16, 444.
20. Baer, Betty, in NASW, *NASW News*, vol. 24, no. 4 (April 1979), pp. 1, 4.
21. Heady, *Public Administration*.
22. Pusic, Eugen, 'The Role of Social Welfare in International Development', *International Social Work*, xii, no. 2 (1969), pp. 3–11.
23. Elkin, Robert, *A Conceptual Base for Defining Health and Welfare Services* (New York, Family Service Association of America, 1967).
24. Donnison, David V. and Chapman, Valerie, *Social Policy and Administration. Studies in the Development of Social Services at the Local Level*, National Institute for Social Work Training Series, no. 3 (London, George Allen & Unwin, 1965).
25. Pusic, Eugen, 'Levels of Social and Economic Development as Limits to Welfare Policy', *Social Service Review*, 45, no. 4 (December 1971), pp. 400–13.
26. Titmuss, Richard M., Keynote Address, pp. 33–43 in *Developing Social Policy in Conditions of Rapid Change. Role of Social Welfare*, Proceedings of the XVIth International Conference on Social Welfare, The Hague, Netherlands, August 13–19, 1972 (New York and London, Columbia University Press, 1973).
27. Titmuss, *Social Policy*.
28. Furniss and Tilton, *The Case for the Welfare State*.
29. Marshall, T. H., *Social Policy*, 3rd edn (London, Hutchinson University Library, 1970).
30. Titmuss, Richard M., *Commitment to Welfare* (New York, Pantheon Books, 1968).
31. Schorr, Alvin, *Explorations in Social Policy* (New York, Basic Books, 1968).
32. Gilbert, Neil and Specht, Harry, *Dimensions of Social Welfare Policy* (Englewood Cliffs, New Jersey, Prentice-Hall, 1974).
33. Heidenheimer, Heclo, and Adams, *Comparative Public Policy*.
34. Littrell, W. Boyd, 'Editor's Introduction: The Translation of Social Science Data into Policy Knowledge', pp. 3–28 in Littrell, W. Boyd and Sjoberg, Gideon (eds.), *Current Issues in Social Policy* (Beverly Hills and London, Sage Publications, 1976).
35. Boulding, Kenneth, 'The Boundaries of Social Policy', *Social Work*, 12, no. 1 (January 1967), pp. 3–11.
36. Kaim-Caudle, P. R., *Comparative Social Policy and Social Security. A Ten-Country Study* (New York, Dunellen Publishing Co., 1974).
37. Rein, Martin, 'Social Policy Analysis as the Interpretation of Beliefs', *Journal of the American Institute of Planners*, xxxviii, no. 5 (September 1971), pp. 297–311.
38. Arrow, Kenneth Joseph, *Social Choice and Individual Values* (New York, Wiley, 1951).
39. Reubens, Edwin P., *Planning for Children and Youth Within National Development Planning* (Geneva, UN Research Institute for Social Development and UN Children's Fund, 1967).
40. Rothenberg, Jerome, *The Measurement of Social Welfare* (Englewood Cliffs, New Jersey, Prentice-Hall, 1961).
41. Berliner, Joseph S., *Economy, Society and Welfare: A Study in Social Economics* (New York, Praeger Publishers, 1972).
42. Weiner, Hyman J., Akabas, Sheila H., Kremen, Eleanor, and Sommer, John J., *The World of Work and Social Welfare Policy* (New York, The Industrial Social Welfare Center, Columbia University School of Social Work, March 1971).

43. Donnison, D., 'Ideologies and Policy', *Journal of Social Policy*, vol. 1, part 2 (April 1972), pp. 97–117.
44. Cafferty, Pastora San Juan and Chestang, Leon (eds.), *The Diverse Society: Implications for Social Policy* (Washington, DC, National Association of Social Workers, 1976).
45. Hirschhorn, Larry, 'Social Policy and the Life Cycle: A Developmental Perspective', *Social Service Review*, 51, no. 3 (September 1977), pp. 434–50.
46. Moynihan, Daniel P., 'Social Policy: From the Utilitarian Ethic to the Therapeutic Ethic', pp. 25–51 in Kristol, Irving and Weaver, Paul H., *Critical Choices for Americans. The Americans: 1976* (Lexington, Mass., Lexington Books, 1976).
47. Rein, Martin, 'Equality and Social Policy', *Social Service Review*, 51, no. 4 (December 1977), pp. 565–88.
48. UN, Division of Social Affairs, *Minimum Levels of Living and Their Role in Social Policy. Comparative Study*, Working Paper no. 1, prepared for the Expert Group on Minimum Levels of Living which met in Czechoslovakia in October 4–8, 1976 (UN, Geneva. SOA/SEM/64/WP. 1.GE. 76-6169). Mimeographed.
49. Heclo, 'Income Maintenance: Patterns and Priorities', pp. 187–226 in Heidenheimer, Heclo and Adams.
50. Moynihan, Daniel P., *The Politics of A Guaranteed Income. The Nixon Administration and the Family Assistance Plan* (New York, Random House, 1973).
51. Harris, Robert, 'Policy Analysis and Policy Development', *Social Service Review*, 47, no. 3 (September 1973), pp. 360–72.
52. Stein, Bruno, *Work and Welfare in Britain and the USA* (London, The Macmillan Press, 1976).
53. Glazer, Nathan, 'The Limits of Social Policy', *The Commentary*, 52, no. 3 (September 1971), pp. 51–8.
54. Vogel, Lynn Harold and Lund, Michael S., *Cross-National Research in Social Policy, Report of a Seminar, April 14–16, 1972*, Sponsored by The Center for the Study of Welfare Policy, School of Social Service Administration, University of Chicago.
55. Williams, Maurice J., 'Development Cooperation: Efforts and Policies of the Members of the Development Assistance Committee, 1977 Review' (Paris, November 1977). Summary of this report, entitled 'Sheer Scale of Extreme Poverty Together with Mounting Unemployment in Third World Challenges Social and Political Order — Thus Growing Urgency to Make Basic Human Needs Centerpiece of Development Cooperation', is in *Survey of International Development*, xv, no. 1 (January/February 1978), pp. 1–7.
56. For a comprehensive summary of the Declaration and Programme, see *Survey of International Development* (July/August 1976).
57. Darling, Roger, 'A Return to Valid Development Principles', *International Development Review*, xix, no. 4 (1977/4), pp. 27–31.
58. UN, *1974 Report on the World Social Situation* (UN, Sales No., E.75.IV.6).
59. Portes, Alejandro and Ferguson, D. Frances, 'Comparative Ideologies of Poverty and Equity: Latin America and the United States', pp. 70–105 in Horowitz, Irvin Louis (ed.), *Equity, Income, and Policy. Comparative Studies in Three Worlds of Development* (New York and London, Praeger Publishers, 1977).
60. Eames, Edwin and Goode, Judith Granich, *Urban Poverty in a Cross-Cultural Context* (New York, The Free Press, 1973).
61. Gilbert, Neil, 'Alternative Forms of Social Protection for Developing Countries', *Social Service Review*, 50, no. 3 (September 1976), pp. 363–88.
62. Appelbaum, Diana Karter, 'The Level of the Poverty Line: A Historical Survey', *Social Service Review*, 51, no. 3 (September 1977), pp. 514–24.

63. Zimbalist, Sidney E., 'Recent British and American Poverty Trends: Conceptual and Policy Contrasts', *Social Service Review*, 51, no. 3 (September 1977), pp. 419–34.

64. Wilson, Thomas (ed.), *Pensions, Inflation and Growth: A Comparative Study of the Elderly in the Welfare State* (London, Heinemann Educational Books, 1974).

65. Marshall, T. H., 'Value Problems of Welfare-Capitalism', *Journal of Social Policy*, 1, Part I (January 1972), pp. 15–33.

66. The OECD, *Public Expenditure on Income Maintenance Programmes*, Studies in Resource Allocation, no. 3 (Paris, July 1976).

67. Stein, Bruno, and Miller, S. M. (eds.), *Incentives and Planning in Social Policy* (Chicago, Aldine Publishing Co., 1973).

68. Hage, Jerald, and Hollingsworth, J. Rogers, 'The First Steps Towards the Integration of Social Theory and Social Policy', *The Annals of the American Academy of Political and Social Science*, Issue on Social Theory and Public Policy, 434 (November 1977), pp. 1–24.

69. Hollingsworth, J. Rogers, 'Preface', *ibid.*, pp. vii–viii.

70. UN, *Social Policy and the Distribution of Income in the Nation* (New York, UN, 1969).

4 KEY PROBLEMS OF METHODOLOGY

No less formidable than value questions and definitional difficulties are the methodological problems involved in cross-national studies. That they must 'be confronted more solidly before current speculation and anecdotal impressions can be converted into scientific findings' (1:831) is widely recognized — as is the fact that such confrontation demands new and ingenious methodologies, let alone impressive knowledge and skills. Thus, Littrell explains that the laboratory experiment, 'often believed to be the ideal embodiment of the principle of methodological adequacy', if closely approximated in social policy research, would cause policy-makers to nullify social science data. The reason for this is that such an experiment is bound to 'exclude contingencies, narrow [the] focus of attention, and eliminate uncontrollable sources of variation'. As a result, moral, legal and political questions would be discarded, relevant interests of policy-makers' constituents would be omitted; and, as policy issues became more complex, additional, specific studies (to deal with variables) would be required, perhaps to be undertaken by 'different disciplines employing various perspectives and methods of research'. Then policy-makers would have to read, coordinate, and interpret diverse findings (an impossible task), and 'if the findings do not converge or are contradictory, to ignore them altogether'. Littrell suggests two ways to overcome the frequent rendering null and void of social science data: multidisciplinary teams and interpretive adequacy to go hand-in-hand with methodological adequacy (2:10, 11, 13).

This discussion will be confined to four problem areas, recurring and interrelated.

1. *Lack and Ambiguity of Empirical Data.* The literature on social welfare policy and planning is full of references to the lack of detailed, objective and/or comparable data; to the need for new and more relevant data; and to hardships in gaining access to available data. The situation is complicated by semantic and cultural problems, and by ethical dilemmas. The researcher is often confronted by differences in reporting procedures, variances in definition and terminology, diversity of sources and of their range. Survey schedules often ask questions that are meaningful in one country but not in another. Non-comparability is

70   Key Problems of Methodology

accentuated by secondary data gathered in different ways and for different purposes — the only kind available in many situations.

In regard to social security, for example, detailed information on the extent of coverage or the level of benefits is available for only a few nations (3:539). Historical series for less developed nations do not exist (4:5). Validity of international comparisons is impaired by important differences in the national concepts and institutional arrangements for social insurance (complicated by the diffusion of social insurance provisions over several separate schemes), and by the lack of uniformity in the definitions and methods underlying national statistics (5:16 and 20). Because of such gaps, Rys believes that 'to find ways and means of obtaining' data is one of the tasks of social scientists engaged in crossnational studies (6:244).

In child welfare, sufficient worldwide statistical data on children's needs, either for complete current analysis or for bench-marks against which to measure progress in the future, are not at hand. UNICEF's experience indicates that the best prospects for improvement 'lie in more country and regional studies and in sample collections of statistics' (7:14). In child mental health there is a scarcity of data in both developing and developed countries — despite the latter's specialized knowledge (8:7).

In psychiatry, hospital records in many countries supply only limited information about the epidemiology of mental illness and often exclude such variables as education which makes comparison impossible (9:840).

At international social welfare conferences, reports emphasize that pertinent, accurate and systematized data required for planning are generally lacking or scant (10:23; 11); that 'in most if not all countries we actually have all too few facts to provide solid bases for realistic, forward-looking social policy' and for evaluating results (12:139).

Even in an advanced country such as the United States, appraisal of social services 'becomes hazardous speculation without specific datacollection procedures established for the purpose of evaluation' (13:221) — and such procedures are yet to be established.[1]

The literature likewise often refers to the ambiguity of data in the social welfare field — a feature that is generated by the ambiguity of the social world. Littrell discusses two types of ambiguity in social science data: relational, 'when the meaning of key concepts . . . depends in part upon meanings of other key concepts . . .'; and 'ambiguity of doubtful signification, . . . when key concepts cannot be shown to be clearly standardized' or '. . . to have multiple meanings'. He suggests that these ambiguities may be handled by interpretive social science grounded in

Key Problems of Methodology

'theories of social organizations, and particularly theories of . . . bureaucracies' (2:15, 20, 21).

2. *Criteria for Selecting Countries to be Compared.* The question how to select the countries to be compared confronts all researchers in the cross-national field.

For her study of child welfare administration, Kammerer selected the United States and Great Britain because, despite some sharp points of contrast, there were sufficient similarities in philosophy and in problems of management to produce a comparison that would make apparent the common problems involved in directing this field (16:4). In selecting the United States and Great Britain for his study of 'work and welfare', Stein hoped that a comparison of countries similar in values and in certain historical developments would generate insights drawn from dissimilarities in policy and programs (17). For Shanas, the marked basic similarities in the composition of the older population in Denmark, Great Britain and the United States seemed to offer special advantages for comparative research because analysis 'would help to reveal what changes in the life-situation of old people are the result of age, and what are the result of differences in cultural milieu and expectations' (18:13). To Shlakman the advantage of concentrating on 'countries with comparable economic capacities and situations lies in the useful fact that history does not put the same problems on various national agendas at precisely the same time' (19:194). Rodgers believed that by confining her study of social administration to modern Western societies, she would be able to address the many likenesses among them, likenesses sufficiently significant and relevant to warrant straightforward descriptive comparisons of certain problems and services (20). Kilby and Taira believe that the selected countries must 'form a meaningful statistical universe'. In line with this criterion they limited themselves to 19 developed countries of the West or of Western origin which constituted a distinct 'culture realm' and were at similar levels of economic development (21:140).

A somewhat different reason motivated Inkeles' selection of six developing nations for his study of modernization. They represented the overwhelming majority of such nations on three continents where they are found, ranging

> from the newest nations which have only recently won their independence to those with a long history of self-government; from those only now emerging from tribal life to those with ancient high

cultures, and from those furthest removed from, to those most intimately linked to, the European cultural and industrial social order (22:209).

By so doing, Inkeles and Smith were able to establish 'that there is a set of personal qualities which cohere as a syndrome empirically designating a type of man we may properly call modern' (23:52).

Pryor included nations with different economic systems in his study of public expenditures because 'generalizations with political and ideological significance can be derived which are unobtainable if we limit such comparison to nations with the same economic system' (24:20). The reason why the study of the group care of infants by Meers and Marans addressed both communist countries and Western democracies was that the enormity of the undertaking in the former 'merits attention in and of itself . . . The consequences of caring for millions of babies under such a radical change in child-rearing methods are of greatest importance for science and society' (25:239).

In discussing this issue in her study of the hard-to-employ, Reubens takes the position that

> When one explores the programs of another country for relevance to American problems, it is helpful but not essential if conditions in the foreign nation are closely comparable to ours in nature and scope. We can learn about programs for the integration of minority groups, for example, from countries where minorities are a much smaller part of the population than they are in the United States. And we should not offer our larger and more complicated problems as an excuse for a troublesome backlog of unresolved issues. All the more reason to have initiated earlier and greater preventive and remedial action! A confrontation with alternative sets of values and priorities or with different national styles provides the opportunity to reassess features of one's country which are generally regarded as fixed and immutable (26:383).

It is not altogether clear what reasons 'based . . . in theory' led Kahn and Kamerman to select the particular eight countries for their crossnational study of personal social services. Apparently, the two authors wished to include federated republics as well as relatively centralized countries; those with 'varying degrees of social service development and with known differences in basic approaches to social service organization'; 'rich and poor lands'; and 'socialist and free-enterprise

Key Problems of Methodology

systems'. Reasons 'based . . . in practicality' were also important: 'funding and collaborative arrangements made it possible to include these countries and not others . . .' (27:ix, x).

3. *Assessing Social Reality and Progress: 'Where Are We and Where Are We Going?'* Essentially, these questions call for measuring social change — an undertaking tied into social reporting and social indicators.

In their analysis of the 'social indicators movement' (from its origin in the United States in 1933 to the present), Parke and Seidman explain that renewed impetus for this movement in the 1960s was generated by 'doubts about the easy equation of economic growth and social progress and a widening sense that economic indicators alone no longer sufficed to measure that progress' (28:2). At that time, there was consensus that social indicators should develop and use statistics for measuring social (in contrast to economic) dimensions of well-being, and that the resulting information was bound to improve social policy formulation. Hence, both social scientists and public administrators advocated the development of an inclusive set of indicators to show social progress or retrogression and the preparation of an annual report that would attempt to assess the social health of the nation.

Toward a Social Report, published in the United States in 1969, explored the feasibility of such an undertaking. It was found that there was no government procedure for periodic stocktaking of the social health of the nation (29:XI), but that there was considerable agreement on what would be desirable indicators of progress or retrogression in health, education, and income status (30:38). The *Report* defined social indicators as 'direct measure(s) of welfare', and made a distinction between them and the more readily available measures of government expenditures (29:97). As noted by Parke and Seidman, however, this distinction is neither exhaustive nor unambiguous, and ' "direct measures of welfare" do not include many of the variables central to an understanding of the social process' (28:4). Writing in 1970, Sheldon and Freeman insisted that it is not possible to use indicators to set goals and priorities, to evaluate programs, or to develop a balance sheet. In their view, 'the social indicator movement [could] contribute (1) to improved descriptive reporting; (2) to the analyses of social change; and (3) to the prediction of future social events and social life' (31:103). But they thought at that time that 'any reasonably definitive effort to develop a social report to the nation' was prevented by the 'elusive boundaries of the social indicator movement' (31:109). Writing in 1972, Henriot defined social indicators, in general terms, as 'quantitative data that serve as measures of socially important conditions of society' (32:3). For purposes of social policy analysis and application, such measures may be represented by specified sets of indicators — biological, cultural, demographic, economic, social. In discerning policy effects on the quality of life, indicators may measure both objective conditions (for example, health, education, crime, mobility) and subjective perceptions of life experiences (for example, satisfactions, aspirations, alienation). Members of a commission concerned with 'The Evaluation of Social Policy' at the XVIth International Conference on Social Welfare in 1972 agreed that

> Social indicators can be defined as quantitative data that serve as indexes to the level of social development of a society. They are indispensable in formulating social policy on the basis of accurate knowledge about the dimensions of social problems and about differential location of high problem areas among age groups, sex groups, socio-economic groups, etc. By giving clearer visibility to social conditions and by helping to develop public interest, they permit the establishment of base line from which the impact of social policy can be more properly evaluated . . . such indicators are most helpful in evaluating the impact of social programs . . . [But] social indicators are useful only to the extent that objectives of social policy and social programs are properly defined . . . (33:240).

Work on social indicators by experts from diverse intellectual backgrounds has continued since the need for it is ever more widely recognized. In addition to focusing on the structural and social-psychological aspects of social change, attention is being directed to relating social measurement to antecedent and consequent political considerations. This is because all measures of the quality of life have implications for public policy and thereby may well have political impact.

Problems and critical appraisals have also continued. In 1971, Rivlin found that while considerable progress has been made in identifying and measuring social problems and in improving 'our knowledge of the distribution of the initial costs and benefits of social action programs . . . little progress has been made in comparing the benefits of different social action programs [and] little is known about how to produce more effective health, education and other social services' (30:7). In a 1972 review, Plessas and Fein reported that, at that time, the social indicator movement had produced few measures of social welfare and of social

Key Problems of Methodology

progress, and that a unified body of theory was still lacking (34). They stated that among many disagreements a basic dispute concerned the necessity for immediate action versus the equal importance of scientific validity. Another difference divided those who believed that social indicators can replace political decision-making from those who saw indicators as representing subjective feelings that can supplement or replace the quantitative data presently largely relied on in decision-making. In 1972 Fisher did not think that the expectations of some that social indicators 'may bypass the need to coordinate competing social programs and make simpler the inclusion of sectoral "social" programs in an enlarged national socio-economic plan' were realistic (35:19). Nor did he think that an integrated and uniform picture can be presented by efforts to supplement the national social accounts, based on product and income, by social indicators. While he saw social indicators as providing some insight into the development of each sector of a society's concern for the welfare of its members, he also saw them as remaining outside a unified system. Recent commentaries as well voice reservations. Furniss and Tilton, who see the social indicator movement (and social experimentation) as exemplifying 'the drive to evaluate and measure the impact of specific public policies', find that 'these promising fields of study are too often locked into narrow behavioral, historical, normative, or descriptive styles of analysis which fail to confront the current issues of social policy' (36:ix). Discussing the data on income and consumption in *Social Indicators, 1976* (37), Danziger and Lampman conclude that these data tell them 'what has happened, but not how or why' (38:31).

A controversial question is whether social indicators need to have a normative direction. Land and Spilerman seem to circumvent the normative issue by recognizing two types of indicators: descriptive and analytic — the latter being a rigorous analysis (model) of the interrelationships among several indicators. They stress that 'both for reporting changes in social conditions and for the guidance of social policy, there are great benefits to be derived from the analysis model . . .' (39:2). According to Parke and Seidman, *Social Indicators, 1976* (37) 'removes the constraint of direct normative relevance and defines indicators simply as "statistics or statistical measures . . . which indicate the general status of the population with respect to certain aspects" of "certain topics of broad social interest . . ."' — in this way legitimating the inclusion 'of a broader range of statistical material concerning social conditions and trends' (28:13).

Work on social indicators is going on in a number of countries. By

1976, at least 29 nations issued or prepared statistical compilations which can be used for purposes similar to those fulfilled by social indicators; a modeling approach has been developed under UN auspices[2]; work on measuring perceptions and assessments of the quality of life is going on 'in comparative studies of well-being based on surveys taken in various countries' (28:11, 8). Many feel, however, that this work has not progressed to the point where it can be used for meaningful and valid international comparisons. At a 1969 UN meeting on social policy and planning, participants felt that it is more important for each country to have useful indicators for its own planning purposes than to have standardized indicators to permit international comparisons. Concern was expressed that indicators may become translated into targets, displacing true social goals, even though, when detached from such goals, they are meaningless (40:4). Writing from an international perspective in 1972, McGranahan took the position that 'in social development field most main goals like "health", "education", "security", "equity" and other objects of social policy are not directly measurable in their totalities or even clearly defined, and indicators commonly serve as proxy or partial measures of these entities' (41:92–3). He also explained that

> Indicators are useful for developmental analysis, for general diagnosis of developmental conditions and needs, and for general evaluation of progress. But while they can measure progress, they should not be confused with targets for planning . . . They may be used in evaluation but they should not be assumed ordinarily to reveal the impact of different factors upon each other . . . They do not automatically or ordinarily reveal programme impact over time, because of the many influences at work in the interdependent process of development. Special studies are required for programme and project evaluations . . . In other words, indicators are not a substitute for research but a tool of research (41:100).[3]

This does not invalidate the views held by many social scientists that certain ideas regarding social information proposals of developed nations may be extremely useful for specific problems of developing nations — even though differences in social problems in these nations are so great as to require entirely different kinds of social information in each (42:1).

A carefully planned development program on social indicators, currently in progress, was launched by the OECD in 1971. This

Key Problems of Methodology

initiative was spurred by the realization that despite substantial improvement in the material situation of most of the population in member countries, increasing concern was being expressed by many about the quality of life in them: questions were being raised about the qualitative aspects of economic growth and its unfavorable side effects on society and on individuals. The first objective of the program was to draw up a list of social concerns of sufficient common interest to serve as a basis for developing common indicators. A 'social concern' was defined as an identifiable and definable aspiration or concern of fundamental and direct importance to well-being (in contrast to instrumental or indirect importance). This phase of the work was completed in 1973 with the identification of 24 concerns in eight primary goal areas: health; individual development through learning; employment and quality of working life; time and leisure; command over goods and services; physical environment; personal safety and the administration of justice; and social opportunity and participation (43).

The next objective was to specify these concerns towards indicators. In this process, concerns were modified and refined. Among refinements and extensions of particular significance in a social welfare context were those in regard to the family as part of the social environment, command over goods and services, social opportunity and participation, and accessibility. Concern with the family had been left out of the 1973 list. Subsequently, because it was felt that to conceptualize the family only in its legal and anthropological meaning was too restrictive (as a fundamental element of well-being, it is the quality of interpersonal relationships rather than formal structure that matters), a new goal area was added. It focused on the qualitative aspects of the primary as well as the wider social environment.

Kinship, and hence the Family, was to have an additional importance, but on a mediating level, with respect to many of the other fundamental social concerns. Thus, kinship affects personal development, health, the transfer of wealth between generations, attitudes to work, etc. This mediating role will have to be taken into account when relating levels of well-being in various social concerns to influencing factors (44:17).

'Command over goods and services' was replaced with 'personal economic situation'. This was done in order to deemphasize consumption as the main element that counts; rather, it is the results of consumption as it affects well-being that matter. By using the new title, increased emphasis was placed on economic resources to acquire goods and services, 'on security of these resources under adverse circumstances, on availability of at least minimum resources, and on the mechanisms which enable the consumer to make effective choices' (44:18).

Additional work on 'social opportunity and participation' was generated by the recognition that the concerns listed in 1973 under this goal cut across other concerns in the list and also embody important values that influence relationships between concerns and over time (for example, equality, mobility, participation in decision-making). It was thought that clarity of identification might be enhanced by including such concepts as freedom, justice and self-fulfillment (44:18).

As to 'accessibility', it was implicit in several of the concerns included in the 1973 list. It was felt desirable, however, to adopt a more general approach to this concept and to apply it more broadly.

> First of all, through the notion of accessibility, choice is introduced as an element of well-being in itself. Secondly, accessibility to various services, . . . would seem to be as important as actual use. Thirdly, accessibility would provide a direct link between elements of well-being and policy variables, since access to services is relevant and amenable to policy action. Lastly, the distributional aspects of access assume particular importance from the points of view of equity and justice (44:19).

Accessibility was defined as the absence of barriers in the way of an individual wishing to use a service, one of such barriers being the cost of using services — in money, time, discomfort, etc. As to types of accessibility, included were physical, economic and perceived accessibility, as well as time constraints and eligibility conditions (44:144–9).

A survey of research on 'perception and satisfaction' in relation to working life, undertaken because it was believed that these concepts could contribute to indicator construction for 'subjective' elements, failed to yield clear guidelines for social indicator development (45:17).

As the work on social indicators progressed, a clearer notion of their main purposes emerged; namely, description, analysis, program evaluation, policy development and normative considerations. It was found that achievement of these different purposes imposed different requirements, in terms of the kinds of measures that are appropriate and the levels of disaggregation (or aggregation) that are called for. For program evaluation and policy development,

Key Problems of Methodology

disaggregations identify influencing factors amenable to policy intervention. Programs are often aimed at groups of individuals defined as disadvantaged in terms of their *well-being characteristics*, e.g., the unemployed, slum dwellers, single parents, ex-prisoners and the physically and mentally handicapped. Such disadvantages are often crystallized among categories of people with particular *ascribed characteristics* — ethnic groups, the elderly, immigrants and youth. Thus, for program evaluation and policy development purposes, the desired disaggregations tend to fall into categories similar to those used for analytical purposes, though the emphasis is somewhat different. In general terms, analytical frameworks will be more abstract or theoretical while program evaluation and policy development will be more specific and concrete (46:15–16).

Those involved in the continuing OECD program on social indicators believe that its 'social concerns', while perhaps more germane to the economically developed nations, as a whole apply to both developed and developing nations alike, as well as to the relations between them (44:10). Furthermore, they think that 'while strict international comparability of social indicators may be impossible to achieve, indicators permitting broad and reasonable comparisons are feasible'. To achieve international comparability, it is necessary to develop a common conceptual framework; standard definitions and formulae; and equivalent statistical methods and comparable coverage of the primary data (45:40).

4. *Assuring a Comparative Dimension.* Useful descriptive facts about welfare programs, often in the form of synoptical tables, summaries or sketches, are found in official government publications. In the field of social security, a report issued biennially by HEW since 1937, *Social Security Programs Throughout the World* (47), contains a highly summarized description of the evolution and current content of all existing programs.

Of additional substantive relevance for social policy and planning in social security are publications of the International Social Security Association (ISSA). Founded in Europe in 1927, ISSA's membership is composed largely of national social security institutions and funds, represented at its meetings and conferences by social insurance administrators and technicians. Quite often, however, 'the problems considered by ISSA and the treatment given them "go beyond administrative and technical concerns", with the result that many

80 *Key Problems of Methodology*

committee reports contain information . . . on program content and policy questions' (48). This is especially true of its research reports and studies which, in addition to descriptions of program content in various countries, contain summaries of the major issues that emerge from their findings as well as from discussions that usually follow their presentation. ISSA publishes the *International Social Security Review* (formerly the *International Social Security Bulletin*) which is a source for current developments in a world-wide perspective, particularly useful for those regions from which scholarly writings on social security that analyze its various aspects within a policy context are rarely available.[4]

The social security branch of the ILO, which publishes the *International Labour Review*, performs a similar function.[5] In addition, the ILO periodically makes available compilations useful for researchers and administrators alike. For example, a recent manual (1976) provides a concise but exhaustive description of the origins, principles and main types of social security, and the benefits granted under social security schemes (49).

Biennial reports on Scandinavian social security (*Social Security in Nordic Countries*, Statistical Reports of the Northern Countries, Stockholm) have been available since 1952. Other sources of data may not be as well known. For example, the Historical Indicators of the Western European Democracies project at the University of Mannheim in West Germany is engaged in data collection on participants of social insurance systems in Western Europe. Besides compiling a statistical handbook with time-series data on the societal development of Western European Democracies and a bibliography of statistical sources, the project is attempting to analyze the development of the 'welfare state' concept in the 15 participating countries (50).

Information of this kind from official publications is not as readily available for social services. A report concerning national social service systems in selected countries, providing some background and brief but adequate descriptions, was published by HEW in 1970 (51), but it has not been updated. Special reports, dealing with specific problems in an international perspective, do appear from time to time (52). Current developments in various countries are described in journals supported by voluntary professional organizations. Among them are, for example, *International Social Work* and *International Child Welfare Review*; and articles that enhance the understanding of poverty-related problems in developing countries frequently appear in the *International Development Review*.

Some undertakings, of a non-continuing nature, are important as well. Among these, of special interest is the International Symposium on Social Welfare Research, sponsored by HEW and the Brookings Institution (May 23–June 9, 1971). In addition to a report from the UN, papers were presented by participants from the United States, Israel, Africa, Europe, Latin America, and Asia. Stein focused on the difficulty of defining 'social welfare' in an international context; on the need for international data in the social welfare field, for adequate pretesting of social welfare programs, and for social indicators to define social goals, gauge changes in social trends, evaluate the effectiveness of social policies, indicate areas for research, and provide a picture of the quality of life in a given society. Schottland discussed six important questions: what kind of society do we want? can we achieve social goals through rational planning? what barriers exist to rational planning, particularly as related to social welfare? can social welfare programs be quantified in order to receive equal consideration in the distribution of a society's resources? does political power need to be redistributed to meet social needs? what is the role of international organizations, especially the UN? Issues important for social welfare research, listed by Rosenfeld, included the identification and development of social indicators, of evaluative criteria, of programs applicable to similar population groups, and of studies concerned with systems of social service delivery. Group discussion ranged over ways of building a data base, the role of the social scientist in policy making, and the need for thorough knowledge about the workings of the administrative process and of individual policy-makers' positions (53).

All of the sources mentioned above, although their major purpose is not to produce cross-national studies, do provide information that is useful as an essential first step in comparative social policy analysis. It must be kept in mind, stresses Rys, that cross-national surveys are expensive, and also require a network of competent and willing persons for the fact-collecting work — the latter normally available free of charge to international organizations, but not so easily accessible to individual scholars. At the same time, Rys believes that international organizations often lack the skill to carry out cross-national surveys in a scientific manner (54). Works that provide samplings of factual programmatic material concerning various segments of the welfare field abroad usually lack a conceptual framework which would allow for comparability. Because they do not provide socio-cultural perspectives on the program discussed, such works make possible only a somewhat superficial understanding of their content and leave the reader unclear as to its relevance for our own situation. In addition to information essential for a first step, much more is needed to provide a basis for systematic and scientific comparisons since 'no interesting and valid comparisons are to be found in the mere juxtaposition of parallel descriptions' (55:11). Many social scientists feel that 'there is no point in saying anything about several countries in a comparative fashion until one has thoroughly studied the history and politico-economic sociology of each country' (21:139–40).[6]

A somewhat different purpose, but again not a comparative one, is served by the worldwide views contained in periodic UN publications that deal with the 'world social situation' (56), or with special groups on our planet (57)[7]. In them the reader finds sweeping panoramas of social developments describing major trends, continuing and evolving problems and needs, and of actions taken, as well as a pointing up of areas particularly important for future investigation.

Most researchers would probably agree with Rys that the ideal comparison is holistic because the workings of social institutions cannot be understood nor compared outside the social whole (54:261). Hence, the institution or system being studied must be understood as an entity in constant interaction with its total environment – social, physical, geographic, cultural, economic and political – as well as an entity which is constantly evolving, that is, in historical perspective. Discussion of the literature that follows will show, however, that most studies do not attain such a holistic level.

Summary. The four methodological problem areas discussed above confront all researchers, although their relative importance may differ between studies. Lack of valid, reliable and unambiguous data, for example, ranges from total absence in relation to many welfare programs in many countries; to partial, fragmented, and speculative data about many programs in many other countries; to adequate data, quantitatively and qualitatively, in relation to some programs in some countries. There are no countries, it seems, that can boast adequate, continuously updated data for all social welfare programs they offer.

Guidelines for selecting countries to be included in cross-national comparisons useful for all investigators are not in evidence. Rather, criteria for selection are determined by each investigator in line with the purposes he has in mind: to shed light on common administrative problems, on dissimilarities in policy and programs, on how cultural and demographic factors affect programs – all in countries with similar philosophies and value systems and at similar levels of economic maturity; or to illumine developments in nations with comparable economic capacities but different from the point of view of political, cultural and geographic characteristics; or to find out whether generalizations in regard to content, financing and administration of programs can be derived from comparing nations with different economic and political systems, etc. Whatever the purpose, overall there are more studies that compare countries at similar stages of economic and technological development than countries that are dissimilar in these respects. Furthermore, it appears that because some countries already have adequate data for the investigator's purposes (usually those that are in the 'developed' group), they are compared over and over again. On the other hand, countries in which such data are lacking — requiring the investigator to obtain them firsthand — are frequently left out of the comparative sphere.

Consequently, we are by no means presented with a global view. The non-entrants include most Catholic nations (in South America, for example) and a majority of those in the Middle East, Asia, Africa and the Pacific region. India includes social welfare in her five-year plans and produces a sizable amount of material on social welfare (58, 59, 60, 61) but this material has not been used for comparative purposes, either with similar or dissimilar nations. Reasons for these gaps are unclear. It is suggested by some that indigenous social scientists in certain parts of the world do not engage in social welfare research. Researchers in developed nations tend to concentrate on countries which, they believe, can usefully inform their policy deliberations because of similar levels of development and similarities in historical, cultural or psychological backgrounds.

The art of assessing social reality and progress, so vital for social policy, has yet to achieve a full fledged scientific status. Although movement in this direction seems to be gaining momentum, deterrents persist. The continuing dearth and ambiguity of data, the difficulties around presenting a comprehensive view, the subtleties of evaluating the extent to which values are incorporated in programs all enter in, to say nothing of the realization that social indicators can be 'useful only to the extent that objectives of social policy and social programs are properly defined'. Nevertheless, work that is now going on has clarified their main purposes and has developed better techniques for fulfilling the research requirements of these purposes. The controversial question, do social indicators need to have a normative direction?, is still to be answered. But what seems to be emerging is that one of the main purposes of social indicators is to make known the nature of normative considerations that enter into the process of specifying them. Overall, social indicators can now explain the 'what' of social policy, but their capacity to explain the 'why' is still limited, and the propriety of using them to show what 'should' be done is in question.

Individual countries and international organizations provide a substantial amount of information that is useful as an essential first step in comparative social policy analysis, for both cross-sectional and time-sequential comparisons. The former seek to find degrees of similarity or difference at any given moment of time among societies (or particular aspects of societies) along any given continuum (for example, developed—developing; with planned economics—with market economies). Time-sequence comparisons seek to compare processes of change and development of any particular society as they shape aspects of policy over a span of time. Such studies tend to emphasize the specific geographic, social and historical context within which the process of development occurs.

In regard to both types of studies researchers have learned to be cautious about simplistic solutions to the problems they encounter. It is not reasonable to infer, for example, that any particular process or stage of historical development is necessary or inevitable, simply because cross-sectional differences between societies can be observed at one point in time. 'Immersion' in an alien language and culture is likely to be a relative experience at best. Regardless of how intimately and empathetically one learns to perceive another society, this perception has little to do per se with the problems of comparing societies — parts or wholes — with which one is intimately familiar, or with comparing any society at a particular moment in time with that same society earlier or later than the period of time one happened to know well.

As to what constitutes comparability, it is generally agreed that in addition to *what*, comparative studies should show *why*, that is, explain the influence of the social—economic—cultural environment, within which the subject being investigated (problem, provision, relationship) had its genesis, developed, and is now operating. But there is no agreement on whether it is the gathering and presentation of data (or *what*) or the construction of theoretical frameworks (that speak to both *what* and *why*) that should come first. At the same time, none dispute that whichever side the investigator is on, at whatever point in time the world of reality and the world of theory meet to make their contribution to his undertaking, unless the final outcome achieves integration of the two, the question 'why' is not likely to be answered and the study is not likely to be 'comparative'.

Notes

1. Inadequate data hamper the work of social scientists in general. Heady notes 'the absence or inadequacy of reliable information on bureaucratic structures and behavior in a large majority of the nation-states of the modern world' (14:105). Myrdal reports that in South Asia information about health conditions and all aspects of education is either deficient or totally lacking (15:3).

2. A considerable amount of work toward developing this approach has been done by the UN Research Institute for Social Development. See, for example, Drewnowski, Jan, *Studies in the Measurement of Levels of Living and Welfare* (Geneva, UN Research Institute for Social Development, Report no. 70.3, 1970) and McGranahan, D. V., Richard-Proust, C., Sovani, N. V., and Subraminian, M., *Contents and Measurement of Socio-Economic Development. An Empirical Enquiry* (Geneva, UN Research Institute for Social Development, Report no. 70.10, 1970). The first is concerned with a level of living index that can be applied to cross-country comparisons, showing the differences between the levels of living in various countries in the same period of time. Levels of living are measured 'by indicators of the flows of goods and services to the individuals of a society' that affect their welfare over a period of time. The level of living index is designed 'as a unitary index combining the several indicators of the flow' and is used as a means of measuring the flow of welfare. The second study is 'an exploratory study of ways of analyzing and measuring development in its combined economic and social aspects'. Three main tasks are attempted: 'to select the best available indicators of social and economic development; to establish the relationships among these indicators at different levels of development; and to combine them into a synthetic indicator of development'. It was found that among factors of development there exists a certain coherence and that factors appear to adjust themselves to each other as parts of an evolving system; that the response to a factor input will depend not simply on the nature and amount of the input, but also on the nature of the existing system; and that an important role is played by the effectiveness of a given factor and the nature of the connecting links between factors.

3. The need to use different criteria for different programs and to assign relative weights to conflicting criteria in special evaluative studies is recognized. See, for example, Marmor, Theodore, 'On Comparing Income Maintenance Alternatives', *American Political Science Review*, lxv, no. 1 (March 1971), pp. 86–90; and Gilbert, Charles E., 'Policy-Making in Welfare: the 1962 Amendments', *Political Science Quarterly*, lxxxi, no. 2 (June 1966), p. 221. Considerable literature on social program evaluation exists, for example, Carter, Genevieve W., 'The Challenge of Accountability — How We Measure the Outcome of Our Efforts', *Public Welfare*, 29, no. 3 (Summer 1971), pp. 267–77; and Tripodi, Tony, Fellin, Phillip, and Epstein, Irwin, *Social Program Evaluation: Guidelines for Health, Education, and Welfare Administration* (Itasca, Illinois, F. E. Peacock Publishers, Inc., 1971). For survey and other research methods for evaluating social development projects in a variety of countries, see Turner, Herbert, D., 'Principles and Methods of Program Evaluation', *International Development Review*, xviii, no. 3 (1976/3), pp. 26–30. A thought-provoking method for analyzing the impacts of public policy is described by Cook, Thomas J., and Scioli Jr, Frank P., 'A Research Strategy for Analyzing the Impacts for Public Policy', *Administrative Science Quarterly*, 17, no. 3 (September 1972), pp. 327–40. For social security, see ILO, *Methods of Evaluating the Effectiveness of Social Security Programmes* (ILO, Geneva, 1975), a report of a research conference held in Vienna, from September 10–12, 1975. Prefaced by papers on the objectives of social security research and evaluation

and on the general framework for the evaluation of social security programs, a range of specific methods currently used in evaluation are described and commented on.
  4. See, for example, (1) Weise, Robert W., 'Early Retirement under Public Pension Systems in Latin America', xxv, no. 3 (1972), pp. 255–61; (2) Wadhawan, S. K., 'Development of Social Security in Asia and Oceania', xxv, no. 4 (1972), pp. 395–424; (3) Gobin, Maurice, 'The Role of Social Security in the Development of the Caribbean Territories', xxx, no. 1 (1977), pp. 7–20.
  5. See, for example, (1) Mallet, Alfredo, 'Diversification of Standardisation: Two Trends in Latin American Social Security', 101, no. 1 (January 1970), pp. 49–83; (2) Seng, You Poh, Bhanoji, Rao, and Shantakumer, G., 'Social Policy and Population Growth in South-East Asia', 109, nos. 5 and 6 (May and June 1974), pp. 459–70, in which the ways in which demographic changes affect social security are discussed.
  6. Efforts to develop more genuinely comparative analyses are not lacking. See, for example, Berton, Peter, 'A New Phase in the Development of Comparative Communist Studies', *Studies in Comparative Communism. An Interdisciplinary Journal*, vi, nos. 1 and 2 (Spring/Summer 1973), pp. 3–7. This Journal's new editorial policy wishes 'to encourage horizontal studies comparing different societies, vertical studies treating a given topic within a society in historical perspective, and diagonal studies examining different societies in different historical periods (so long as their stages of development make such comparisons fruitful)'.
  7. Recent compilations appear to be in the tradition of earlier efforts. See, for example, (1) League of Nations, Secretariat, *The Placing of Children in Families*, I.C.260.M.155 (1938); (2) League of Nations, *Study of the Legal Position of the Illegitimate Child*, C.70.M.24 (1939); (3) UN, Department of Economic and Social Affairs, *The Prevention of Juvenile Delinquency in Selected European Countries* (UN, April 1955. ST/SOA/SD/6. Sales No., iv, 12, 1955); (4) UN, Department of Economic and Social Affairs, *Comparative Analysis of Adoption Laws* (New York, UN, June 27, 1956. ST/SOA/30); (5) UN Commission on the Status of Women, *Parental Rights and Duties, Including Guardianship* (New York, UN, 1968) – as well as Freund, Ernest, *Illegitimacy Laws of the United States and Certain Foreign Countries* (Washington, DC, US Department of Labor, Children's Bureau, Legal Series No. 2, Bureau Publication No. 42. GPO, 1919).

References

  1. Wynne, Lyman C., 'Methodologic Prerequisites for Crosscultural Conclusions', *International Journal of Psychiatry*, 8, no. 5 (November 1969), pp. 831–3.
  2. Littrell, 'Editor's Introduction'.
  3. Cutright, 'Political Structure'.
  4. Kassalow, Everett, M., 'Introduction', pp. 1–20 in Kassalow, Everett M., (ed.), *The Role of Social Security in Economic Development* (Washington, DC, HEW, Social Security Administration, Office of Research and Statistics, Research Report no. 27, 1968).
  5. Alber, 'The Coverage of Social Insurance Schemes'.
  6. Rys, Vladimir, 'Comparative Studies of Social Security'.
  7. UN Children's Fund, *Strategy for Children*, A Study of UNICEF Assistance Policies, Report of the Executive Director to the UNICEF Executive Board (New York, Publication 67.iv.29; E/Icef/559/rev. 1, 1967).

8. Houwer, Dan Q. R. Mulock, 'Children's Needs in Today's World', pp. 3–9 in David.
9. Wittkower, E. D., 'Reply to Discussants', *International Journal of Psychiatry*, 8, no. 5 (1969), p. 840.
10. Leaper, 'Report of the Pre-Conference Working Party'.
11. UN, Department of Economic and Social Affairs, *Proceedings of the International Conference of Ministers Responsible for Social Welfare, 3 to 12 September 1968* (New York, UN, 1969. Sales No., E.69.IV.4).
12. Winston, 'Social Policy and Human Rights'.
13. Carter, Genevieve E., 'Public Welfare', pp. 193–232 in Maas, Henry S. (ed.), *Research in The Social Services: A Five-Year Review* (New York, National Association of Social Workers, 1971).
14. Heady, *Public Administration*.
15. Myrdal, Gunnar, 'Investment in Man', *International Social Work*, xii, no. 4 (1969), pp. 2–16.
16. Kammerer, Gladys M., *British and American Child Welfare Services. A Comparative Study in Administration* (Detroit, Wayne State University Press 1962).
17. Stein, *Work and Welfare*.
18. Shanas, et al., *Old People*.
19. Shlakman, Vera, 'The Safety-Net Function in Public Assistance', *Social Service Review*, 46, no. 2 (June 1972), pp. 193–212.
20. Rodgers, *Comparative Social Administration*.
21. Kilby, Peter and Taira, Koji, 'Differences in Social Security Development in Selected Countries', *International Social Security Review*, 22, no. 2 (1969), pp. 139–54.
22. Inkeles, Alex and Smith, David H., *Becoming Modern. Individual Change in Six Developing Countries* (Cambridge, Mass., Harvard University Press, 1974).
23. Inkeles, Alex, 'The Modernization of Man in Socialist and Nonsocialist Countries', pp. 50–9, in Field, Mark G. (ed.), *Social Consequences of Modernization in Communist Societies* (Baltimore, The Johns Hopkins University Press, 1976).
24. Pryor, *Public Expenditures*.
25. Meers, Dale R. and Marans, Allen E., 'Group Care of Infants in Other Countries', pp. 237–82, in Dittman, Laura (ed.), *Early Child Care: The New Perspectives* (New York, Atherton Press, 1968).
26. Reubens, Beatrice G., *The Hard-to-Employ: European Programs* (New York, Columbia University Press, 1970).
27. Kahn, Alfred J. and Kamerman, Sheila B., *Social Services in International Perspective, The Emergence of the Sixth System* (Washington, DC, HEW, Social and Rehabilitation Service, Office of Planning, Research and Evaluation (SRS) 76-050704. 1976). Country reports were prepared by and/or under the supervision of H. Philip Hepworth, of Canada; Dieter Schaefer of West Germany; Jacqueline Ancelin of France; Abraham Doron of Israel; Jan Rosner of Poland; Barbara Rodgers of the United Kingdom; Vitomir Stojakovic (principal investigator) and Marko Mladenovic (country director) of Yugoslavia; and Alfred Kahn and Sheila Kamerman of the United States. The Canadian reports are published in a ten-part monograph series by the Canadian Council on Social Development, Ottawa. The US report is published as *Social Services in the United States* (Philadelphia, Temple University Press, 1976). All other country reports appear in a ten-volume imprint series from Xerox University Microfilms, Ann Arbor, Michigan, in its 'publication on demand' program (1976).
28. Parke, Robert and Seidman, David, 'Social Indicators and Social Reporting', *The Annals of the American Academy of Political and Social Science*, 435 (January 1978), pp. 1–23.

29. US, HEW, *Toward a Social Report* (Washington, DC, GPO, 1969).
30. Rivlin, Alice M., *Systematic Thinking for Social Action* (Washington, DC, Brookings Institution, 1971).
31. Sheldon, Eleanor Bernert and Freeman, Howard E., 'Notes on Social Indicators: Promises and Potentials', *Policy Sciences*, 1 (Spring 1970), pp. 97–111.
32. Henriot, Peter J., *Political Aspects of Social Indicators: Implications for Research* (New York, Russell Sage Foundation, 1972).
33. Lory, Louis, 'The Use of Social Indicators', pp. 239–42 in International Council on Social Welfare, *Developing Social Policy in Conditions of Rapid Change. Role of Social Welfare*, Proceedings of the XVIth International Conference on Social Welfare, The Hague, Netherlands, August 13–19, 1972 (New York, Columbia University Press, 1973).
34. Plessas, Demetrius J. and Fein, Ricca, 'Review Article: An Evaluation of Social Indicators', *Journal of the American Institute of Planners*, xxxviii, no. 1 (January 1972), pp. 43–51.
35. Fisher, Paul, 'Social Reports of the German Federal Republic, 1970–71', *Social Security Bulletin*, 35, no. 7 (July 1972), pp. 16–29.
36. Furniss and Tilton, *The Case for the Welfare State*.
37. US Department of Commerce, Office of Federal Statistical Policy and Standards and Bureau of the Census, *Social Indicators, 1976* (for sale by the Superintendent of Documents, Washington, DC, 20402. Stock #041-001-00156-5).
38. Danziger, Sheldon H. and Lampman, Robert J., 'Getting and Spending', *The Annals of the American Academy of Political and Social Science*, 435 (January 1978), pp. 23–40.
39. Land, Kenneth C. and Spilerman, Seymour (eds.), *Social Indicator Models* (New York, Russell Sage Foundation, 1975).
40. UN Economic and Social Council, *Social Policy and Planning in National Development*, Report of the Meeting of Experts on Social Policy and Planning held at Stockholm, 1 to 10 September 1969 (New York, UN, March 1970. E/CN/5/445).
41. McGranahan, Donald, 'Development Indicators and Development Models', *The Journal of Development Studies*, A Quarterly Journal Devoted to Economic, Political and Social Development, no. 3 (April 1972), pp. 91–103.
42. Galnoor, Itzhak, special editor, 'Social Information for Developing Countries', *The Annals of the American Academy of Political and Social Science*, 393 (January 1971).
43. OECD, The OECD Social Development Programme, 1, *List of Social Concerns Common to Most OECD Countries* (Paris, 1973).
44. OECD, The OECD Social Indicator Development Programme, 3, *Measuring Social Well-Being. A Progress Report on the Development of Social Indicators* (Paris, 1976).
45. OECD, The OECD Social Indicator Development Program, *1976 Progress Report on Phase II. Plan for Future Activities* (Paris, 1977).
46. OECD, The OECD Social Indicator Development Programme: Special Studies, no. 4, *Basic Disaggregations of Main Social Indicators* (Paris, 1977).
47. US, HEW, Social Security Administration, Office of Research and Statistics, Research Report No. 50, HEW Publication No. (SSA) 78-11805, *Social Security Programs Throughout the World, 1977* (the most recent report at this writing).
48. Rohrlich, George F., 'Social Security in World-Wide Perspective', *Social Service Review*, 38, no. 4 (December 1964), pp. 443–54.
49. ILO, *Introduction to Social Security: A Workers Education Manual* (Geneva: ILO, 1976).
50. *HIWED Report No. 1* (Mannheim, West Germany, 1975). Mimeographed.
51. Lally, *National Social Service Systems*.

52. David, Henry P. (ed.), *Child Mental Health in International Perspective*, Report of the Joint Commission on the Mental Health of Children (New York, Harper & Row, 1972).

53. Bubeck, A. E., *International Perspectives on Social Welfare Research: Report of an International Symposium* (Washington, DC, The Brookings Institution, 1971).

54. Rys, 'Comparative Studies'.

55. Rodgers, *Comparative Social Administration*.

56. UN Department of Economic and Social Affairs, *1974 Report on the World Social Situation* (New York, UN, Sales No. E.75.iv.6).

57. For example, UN Department of Economic and Social Affairs, *Report on Children* (New York, UN, 1971).

58. *Encyclopedia of Social Work in India*, issued on behalf of the Planning Commission, Government of India (Delhi, Government of India Press, 1968).

59. *Social Development and Voluntary Action*, Report of Workshop on Social Development, Madras, January 1973 (Bombay: Indian Council of Social Welfare, 1974).

60. *Education, Training and Rehabilitation of the Handicapped* (New Delhi, Government of India, Department of Social Welfare, 1974).

61. *Towards Equality*, Report Of The Committee On the Status of Women In India (Government of India, Department of Social Welfare, Ministry of Education and Social Welfare, December 1974).

PART TWO:
THE STRUCTURE OF SOCIAL SECURITY

The selected studies — single-country and cross-national — address a variety of questions, at various levels of theoretical and practical importance. Some are relevant for several questions and levels. They differ as to the degree of clarity and directness with which they provide insights into causal relationships useful for policy analysis: some require only an intelligent reading; others demand a considerable amount of analytic perception in order to draw out policy implications. Grouped into studies concerned primarily with social security, that is, transfer programs which provide cash income, they progress from a micro- to a macroscopic view: from studies dealing with single countries to those dealing with two or more countries. When single-country studies precede comparative analyses, it is possible to assess with more certainty what is useful and desirable for policy when several countries are compared. It is hoped, therefore, that this progression will provide a more logical channel for cumulating discrete policy-oriented theories and practical ideas into concepts of a more general nature.

5 THEMES IN NATIONAL EXPERIENCE

The studies discussed in this chapter differ in scope and emphasis. For the most part, they range over the entire spectrum of social security programs and over many issues that have required resolution in the course of these programs' development in the particular countries. Political and value concerns provide the points of departure for some analyses; others focus on the role of social security in meeting income maintenance objectives; still others devote major attention to important aspects of policy implementation, that is, to organizational structure and administrative processes. The latter involve relationships between different levels of government, and between government agencies and groups and organizations outside government; qualifications required of personnel and the training they receive before and after employment; relationships between agencies concerned with welfare and those responsible for other areas of human services. In their various ways, these studies augment our understanding of the influence of social forces on policy issues and policy decisions in social security.

Program Development and the Social Environment. Morgan (1969) presents a masterful account of the evolution of the Canadian program, relating its characteristics to major features of the country's population and economy, and showing how it has been shaped by particular social forces. The more potent among the latter have been a growing desire for a more equitable distribution of opportunities, rising income and wealth and concern about poverty in the midst of plenty, the latter sharpened by a multitude of old and new social problems that accompany rapid urbanization. Morgan explains that Canada's income maintenance programs progressed from a series of fragmented provisions, 'each inaugurated to meet particular social, economic, and political pressures' (1:105), to a coherent pattern based on a universalist infrastructure. In this process, the role of the federal government was modified from that of a hesitant and partial participant to one of an active senior partner. As a result, the federal government has taken the lead in financing and operating large-scale income maintenance programs, principally the demogrant, the social insurances, and the means-tested benefits. Constitutional questions, especially those concerned with the division of responsibilities for welfare between the federal and provincial governments, are yet to be resolved.

Friis links the development of the Danish social security program (1969), characterized by increases in benefits and extensions in coverage in recent decades, to 'attitudes toward major social security issues in Denmark' (2:129). A striking attitude, in evidence from 1933 on, has been the high degree of political consent to the program's expansion: 'there has generally been agreement among all major political parties about the social content and aim of this expansion, and no decisive step in this expansion has been undertaken without support from all these parties' (2:130). At the same time, much more attention has been devoted to policies for old-age pensions than to those for children's allowances. Problems presented by the former have dominated social security discussions and have generated many government committees and much legislation, all seeking 'to augment pensions beyond the increase secured through automatic cost-of-living adjustments' (2:136).

In contrast, no influential political party has presented concrete proposals for major cash transfers to families with children, even though existing provisions are by no means adequate or free of problems. Consequently, expansion has been slow and at the time of writing, Friis found no increase in the general interest in family policy. Friis thinks that this contrast is the result of a 'widespread view that pensions have been too low [a view which] has influenced politicians of all parties' (2:143) and has given rise to feelings of relative deprivation among the beneficiaries. On the other hand, 'among families with children there is not any strong feeling of relative deprivation, from which pressure and a pressure group might develop' (2:148). Furthermore, most people expect to support children during part of their lives; hence, estimates of the cost of children to parents, sporadically made, have exerted little influence on general opinion.

For the purpose of his book (1961), Kuusi defines social policy as the 'support and assistance given by the community to its inactive members' (3:65). Consequently, he leaves out as beyond the scope of his book such topics as income redistribution, wage and taxation policies. In a democratic society — based on political equality but economic inequality — the function of social policy is to equalize income so as to ensure the possibilities of consumption for people outside the productive process and for those whose consumption is the most limited. To carry out this function, the society uses social income transfers. After these transfers have assured a minimum level of consumption, there is movement toward higher goals, a movement that

Themes in National Experience

is in constant evolution as aspirations rise. Kuusi thinks that there are five stages in the planning of social policy: '(a) estimation of the future development of population; (b) estimation of the future development of national income; (c) estimation of the future cost of the social policy schemes now in operation; (d) decisions with regard to the size of the share of social income transfers in national income; (e) allocation of the share of national income available for new social security schemes among different purposes' (3:104).

There are three ways, according to Kuusi, for solving the question of size of old-age and disability pensions: to use a means test; to pay flat-rate pensions which guarantee a certain specified minimum income; and to base the pension on former earnings. All three have advantages and disadvantages. The means test smacks of poor relief; the flat rate is inequitable in relation to standards prior to retirement; income-related pensions are costly and even though financed by contributions from workers, employers or both, are in the last analysis paid for by the productive life and economy of the country. Whatever method is used, the decent minimum it provides must be reasonably comparable to the consumption standards of the general population. He warns that within the situation of the aged in general, there are differences from case to case so that there are many who still live in poverty.

For Kuusi the task of social assistance goes beyond providing the needy with economic help: it must also make available services that are individualized, given according to need, are temporary and preventive. Its ultimate objective is to help each person improve his situation through his own efforts; hence, if successful, social assistance becomes superfluous. He believes that because the phenomena social assistance 'fights' — need, distress, infirmity, helplessness, apathy, maladjustment — are too complex for accurate measurement, planning for dealing with them is more difficult.

> Our plans for social assistance must be necessarily less ambitious in respect to comprehensiveness and rationality than for the other sectors of social policy: we cannot design a plan where we could say with serious conviction that its implementation will result in a reduction in the frequency of the occurrence of the phenomena we are fighting against (3:247).

In his study of social welfare in France (1962), Friedlander shows how social security developed from medieval charities to its modern form, and points up its unique features, particularly in the area of family allowances and, to some extent in the social insurances. These features, he found, are shaped by two sometimes conflicting conceptions about how best to enhance human well-being. On the one hand, there is 'the deep devotion to individualism, the desire for personal freedom, for intellectual, economic and social independence, the strong concern for privacy in family life, affection for children, and the preservation of health'; on the other, there is 'the recognition that the striving for social security . . . cannot be fulfilled without a national program of aid to the needy and collective measures for health protection and the education of children . . .' (4:vii). The French system strives to integrate these two mental attitudes.

Laroque's analysis (1969) of the evolution of the French social security system shows that when it was set up in 1945, it attempted to respond to three factors peculiar to France at that time: the decline in birth rate, existence of numerous older laws, and influence of democratic traditions. As a result, the programs that emerged were dominated by a preoccupation with family problems, by the need to unify former arrangements into one overall agency and to cover the whole population against every threat to economic and social life, and by a desire to have a democratic administration. Although development along these lines has taken place, Laroque finds that in the process the system's features have been profoundly altered. 'Its extension has been realized at the expense of unity': it is characterized by 'a juxtaposition of systems, overlapping, unequal, sometimes competitive, always distrustful and jealous of one another, in which the concern for national solidarity is increasingly alien' (5:175). This has come about, in Laroque's view, because of the power and the rugged individualism of social and economic groups in France which exert strong influence on political decision-makers. As a counterbalance to the decline in 'a healthy conception of national solidarity' which is likely to project a negative future influence, there is the fact that social security has become an essential part of daily life for all Frenchmen to which all are deeply attached.

Stevens focuses her carefully researched study on French public assistance (1973). She shows how its development and its program patterns have been influenced by the ideas that shaped the country's socio-political structure, and locates public assistance within the total income support network. This is followed by an evaluation of the program's relative importance as a form of discretionary aid, administered by decentralized, elected councils — and of the effect of the French version of the means test, both inside and outside the public assistance system, on benefit levels. Her assessment concludes that

> Despite post-war hopes to the contrary, social aid still has an important role to play in the total scheme of social services in France. [But] its function is chiefly to support provision in social security, and it has little that is peculiarly its own. Post-war developments, even in means-testing, have taken place for the most part in social security . . . It is in the areas in which social security has remained weak that social aid is strongest . . . It seems probable that the differences between the schemes will continue to narrow . . . Social aid seems likely to continue in its three functions of provider of benefits, provider of services and co-ordinator of welfare activities, although the importance of each of these may vary from time to time and may not be the same in all areas (6:83—5).

George centers his discussion of the British social security system (1973) on the relationship between social security development and the role of the country's ruling class in determining the resources allocated to it. This relationship is illustrated by an analysis of the system's impact on various groups in the population: the poor, the low-paid, the unemployed, and the aged. George argues that in order to obtain sufficient financing to provide adequate and equitable protection, the disadvantaged have had to mount a power struggle against the ruling class. For the poor, he maintains, the ruling class has attempted to cut certain subsistence payments in order to minimize dissatisfaction among the middle and the working classes. Low-paid workers, he explains, have been benefited by supplementary family income, family allowances and the national minimum wage. But these provisions for raising family income have been accompanied by criticisms that they encourage dependency. For the unemployed — their number increasing due to structural factors and not because of personal inadequacies — work has been made more appealing by providing low-quality and low-paid jobs, not a proper solution. Social security's effects have been most positive for the aged: they are taking advantage of their benefits because of increasing longevity and because they are seeing retirement as a time for a more leisurely life-style, and not only because they are being displaced from the market and/or relegated to a low social status (7).[1]

According to Fisher (1972), pensions, health insurance and family allowances in Japan combine into a complex mosaic. He was able, however, to discern two determining characteristics in program development: 'the relatively low level of certain cash benefits, measured against the basic needs of the beneficiaries and, in particular, against the considerably improved income of the labor force; and the way in which the social insurance system mirrors Japanese labor-management relations' (8:3). The latter is exemplified by the 'retirement allowance', a uniquely Japanese social invention. It pays large lump sums based on final wage and length of service to 'permanent' employees when they reach the traditional retirement age of 55. Despite its many shortcomings, the 'allowance' is so firmly rooted in the social fabric that Fisher does not think it can give way to a modern pension system in the near future. Growing concern about the slow rise in benefit levels and the insufficient resources devoted to social security has been voiced in the Japanese press. A much lower proportion of GNP is being allocated to social security in Japan as compared to other industrial nations, while labor productivity is higher than in these other nations. To what extent and when Japanese social policy will change to make it possible for social progress to catch up with economic growth remains to be seen.

Analyses by two Japanese writers elaborate on Fisher's evaluation. In 1970, 70 percent of Japanese men and 40 percent of the women in their late 60s were working. This is extremely high compared with other industrialized countries, and even higher than in developing countries. The pensionable age in the Employees' Pension program and in the National Pension program is 60 and 65 years, respectively. But almost all Japanese enterprises set the mandatory retirement age at 55; consequently, there is a gap between the retirement age and the eligible age for receiving retirement benefits. The system of lump sum benefits at retirement — which distributes these rewards in accordance with age, educational level and the length of service — is justified as a device to stimulate the employees' full commitment to the company. On the average, in 1974 these lump-sum retirement benefits amounted to $10–15,000, amounts that can cover the average expenditure for a household for about two years where the head is 55–60. In connection with this, it should be kept in mind that in 1971, the average life expectancy at 55 was more than 20 years for men and more than 24 years for women.

All these factors combined signify that in Japan retirement means retirement from one firm and transfer to another, since continued work is essential for financial reasons. Because of this the government has been paying increased attention to facilitating the labor force participation among the elderly. This has met with considerable success (in 1970, 75 percent of those who reached the mandatory retirement

Themes in National Experience 99

age in the previous five years were reemployed), but the problem is that
the elderly are reemployed at a lower status than when they were
younger than 55. Also, their working conditions are generally very bad
compared with those of younger workers in large-sized firms. Reasons
for this unsatisfactory situation are demographic and cultural: the
number of persons 65 and older doubled between 1920 and 1965 and it
is projected that by 1985 it will reach 10 percent of the population
while the younger population is estimated not to increase. As for
cultural factors, the most important are the long-established norms
concerning family self-sufficiency. It is feared that liberalization of the
social security system will weaken the sense of family responsibility as
well as social cohesion (9, 10).

In a study of statutory health insurance in West Germany, Safran
(1967) focuses on the extended controversy about how to reform
it (11). He traces the course of a set of legislative proposals from their
conception to their ultimate veto by a miscellany of political actors,
among whom interest groups were prominent. These proposals resulted
from a rethinking of social policy issues, stimulated by the rising costs
of social security which outstripped the growth of national income. The
major issues involved were 'welfare state or individual initiative;
compulsion or freedom of choice; coddling or responsibility' (11:17).
Safran found that government can use legal restraints effectively even in
democratic (non-socialist) societies; that key interest groups not only
wield influence on government, but are themselves influenced by what
government does.

Hasan's conviction that India ought to measurably improve her social
security system without further delay (1969) stems from his knowledge
of the huge and growing need for this type of protection as it is
aggravated by demographic, social and economic factors. His description
of existing programs – centered on coverage, structure and character of
administration, the nature and standard of benefits, conditions of
eligibility, and financing – reveals the profound inadequacy of
resources that have been allocated to them so far. Appearing in a book
which deals with social security and health services in the United States
and in four developed Western democracies, the Indian programs are
included because they are 'of interest by contrast'. And, indeed, the
shortcomings and inadequacies of Indian provision are startling and
discouraging because social security has existed in India since the 1920s.
Hasan concludes by noting that although 'the time seems to be ripe for
the development of a comprehensive social security scheme for India',
such a scheme will not be introduced because of the underdeveloped

state of its economy. He argues, however, that efforts in this direction cannot 'be postponed indefinitely as the country awaits the attainment of a particular state of economic development' (12:208).

The development of social security in Israel, according to Nizan (1973), is unlike that in most other countries because in them 'the state preceded its institutions, a parliament was active before there were trade unions, cooperatives, medical associations and services or social security systems' (13:1), while in Israel the process was reversed: people preceded the state. Consequently, during the 30 years of the 'nascent' period (when the country was a British Mandate) it was the Jewish Labour Movement, founded in 1920, which introduced and developed social insurance, continuing the work done by the Union of Agricultural Workers in the Galilee which founded the first sickness fund in 1912. Labor's involvement was spurred on by the fact that 'under the Mandate there was no social insurance legislation as such, nor were any ILO recommendations on minimum standards ever carried out' (13:2).

Soon after the establishment of the State of Israel in 1948, the debate on the pros and cons of a national insurance scheme was in full swing, between those who demanded a comprehensive state social security system, covering all risks and the entire population, and those who did not see how an infant and an underdeveloped state, already burdened with the costs of the War of Independence, could take on the additional heavy financial burden that a comprehensive system would impose. The National Insurance Bill, embodying compromise solutions that commanded substantial consensus finally went into effect in 1954. Subsequent amendments have liberalized coverage and benefit levels. The main fields of social security (national insurance, sickness funds and pension funds) account for the major available provisions; 'a complementary role in striving to better the welfare of the public as a whole' is played by other programs administered by governmental, public and voluntary agencies. Future goals focus on 'the liquidation of existing centres of poverty' and preventing new poverty by means of expanding current provisions and by reforming payments for low-income families (13:27). It is also projected to introduce state health insurance even though the voluntary scheme covers up to 90 percent of the population.

As was to be expected, the Revolution in Russia brought about profound changes in the country's welfare system. At its beginning the Soviet regime took a firm stand in favor of the 'institutional' approach which regarded welfare as an ongoing, comprehensive social institution

Themes in National Experience

whose major function was to prevent social breakdown, but which also made help available as a right to those who were qualified if a breakdown occurred. Soviet theoreticians rejected the 'residual' concept, dominant before the Revolution, invariably associated with the detested means test and the humiliation of charity. They claimed that such an approach was appropriate only for a capitalist society, which cares nothing about eliminating social risks that have disastrous consequences for the working class, and that institutionalization of social welfare can come to full fruition only in a socialist society (14). But, beset by a myriad of economic and administrative difficulties, the Soviets have never been able to adhere consistently to the policies and principles that these positions personified. In fact, the dismantling of the familiar 'from each according to his abilities, to each according to his needs' as a practicable policy began early after the new regime came to power and continued as the process of industrialization, urbanization, and the creation of a powerful military complex gained momentum. Currently, many of the major features that characterize Soviet social security and many of the problems that beset it are similar to those that mark 'capitalist' social security systems.

Programs and Values. Although philosophy and values are ever present components of social environment as it affects social security policy, some studies explicate them more clearly than others.

Completed within the short period of five months and based on Canadian reports and studies that often suffer from a dearth of adequate data, Brown's report on retirement policies in Canada (1975) is nevertheless a cogent analysis. Imbued with a philosophy which stresses the importance of harmonization, the report presents the totality of retirement policies and the interaction between them and thus offers 'a wider perspective within which detailed special studies can be placed'. Discussion of current policies – those that govern the age at which people retire, the reality of choice they have in retiring or continuing to work, the income they will receive and the opportunities and services which will be available to them in retirement – is made incisive by attention to some of their unanticipated consequences. Suggestions about alternatives that can be utilized to create 'better' policies are made, inevitably leading to a consideration of the value question, the need 'to establish some explicit principles by which policies and programs can be judged'. Among these principles, the author speaks of those she considers particularly important: for example, 'independence and control over one's own life pattern' in retirement — 'the right to have one's human dignity fully respected even when dying, which will perhaps be the last wish of all of us' (15:237).

In Denmark, according to Friis (2), the major principles that shaped social security expansion fall into four categories: (1) extension of coverage to all occupational groups, while confining unemployment insurance and compensation for industrial injuries to wage and salary workers; (2) exclusion of persons with higher incomes, except for almost free hospitalization; (3) tax financing which in 1964 absorbed two-thirds of the cost; and (4) administrative decentralization. But the first three of these principles were violated to some extent during the 1950s and 1960s. The principle of inclusion of all occupational groups was broken 'because wage earners represented by the labor unions pressed for increased benefits' (2:133); a universalistic trend overcame the principle of excluding persons with higher incomes; tax financing of social security, while still dominant, has become somewhat less important because contributions from employers and employees have been increased to meet the additional costs resulting from the introduction of sickness benefit and supplementary pension schemes. Criticisms that surfaced because of these departures ranged from accusations that the social security system brought about income equalization which is harmful to business and individual initiative, made by those on the right, to claims that it was responsible for crippling the soul of modern man and for exacerbating his immaturity, dependence and anxieties, made by intellectuals — to allegations that by overconcentrating on the payment of cash benefits, the system neglected to pay attention to preventing need, made by social security experts (2:131).

Schorr (1965) found that the major components of the ideology of French social security are 'solidarity, social justice, family policy, a categorical approach to risks or needs, benefits as a right, mutuality, decentralization and flexibility' (16:2). Solidarity implies the rejection of benevolence on the part of employers and the state based on a contract that returns benefits for payments. Instead, benefits are related to presumed need so that a record of contributions only determines the form that benefits take. Social justice is an outcome of solidarity since the latter redistributes national income in favor of those who have special need. Family policy in the French setting conceptualizes the family as a unit, with attention centered on families with children while childless families are overlooked. A categorical approach means that each insurance program is buttressed by its own

Themes in National Experience

supplemental assistance program for those judged to be in need.

Schorr shows that social aid (public assistance) in France is likewise organized in a categorical pattern. This diminishes the differences between insurance and assistance, that is, benefits as of right as distinct from discretionary benefits — a situation seen by the French not as ambiguous but as one that humanizes and makes flexible the various parts of the system. The concept of mutuality, which marks the program as nongovernmental, is implemented by the requirement that social security be governed by elected administrative councils, local, regional and national, a structure that results in decentralization of decision-making. Schorr notes that this unique national system contains a number of contradictions and reveals a 'hodgepodge of private and public responsibilities'. Nevertheless, it 'functions perhaps with waste, but in a coordinated fashion, carrying conviction about the ideas that are important to Frenchmen' (16:40).

In his book on French pensions Lynes (1967) presents a detailed description of the governing regulations and of the income and services pensions provide, and takes a close look at the relationship between the individual beneficiary and the pension administration as it reflects the presence of democratic control. All this is discussed in the context of social solidarity, a concept which he, like Schorr, discovers to be the kingpin among the basic tenets of French social security. Explaining its significance, he writes:

> There are many possible ways of judging the merits of a system of social security. The most obvious criterion is the extent to which it succeeds in providing adequate protection against poverty. But social security is much more than a source of income geared to particular events or circumstances in the life of the individual or the family. It is a social institution which both reflects and modifies the ideologies and aspirations of society; which can perceptibly change the patterns of distribution of income and wealth; and which, above all, can symbolise the cohesion of a society or of classes within a society. This quality of social cohesion is expressed in French by the word which recurs frequently in reports and debates on social security — solidarité (17:46).

The impact of values on program development is vividly demonstrated by policy dilemmas generated by experience with universal and selective services which continue to receive attention (18, 19,20). In Great Britain, although universal programs have become dominant, selectivity persists in the form of the large Supplementary Benefits program and a network of means-tested local services. At the same time, greater concern is being voiced about the need to consider not only those in poverty, but the working poor and the unemployed as well. As explained by Titmuss (1969),

> We are beginning to see that we are more concerned with inequality and with issues of equity than with a pre-determined population of poor people. The more that standards are raised in noncontributory income maintenance programs, the greater the challenge will be to the social security programs and the problem of low wages and low earnings among both women and men. There is, of course, a danger in this development in Britain, a threat to social security as of right . . . But the risk will be minimized if the commission and the government continue to be convinced of the necessity to develop policies aimed at identifying categories, groups, and classes of income maintenance needs within the Supplementary Benefits programs and transferring them, stage by stage, to expanding social security programs (21:168–9).

Titmuss returns to the problems of equity in 1970 — problems that are being enlarged and complicated by forces of social and economic change, accompanied by changes in expectations. Among them are the desire of people everywhere for higher benefits; the expectation that treatment of individuals, groups, classes and categories will become more equitable, that is, 'that people (and classes of people) in like circumstances of need and fulfilling like conditions of eligibility [will] be treated alike in social security systems' (22:261); movement toward equal status between the sexes; more frequent job changing and greater occupational and territorial mobility; increasing numbers of illegitimate children, divorces, and, with longer life expectancy, longer periods of widowhood. Difficulties in reconciling equity and adequacy are especially pronounced in the case of the disabled, widows and divorced wives. The 'right to maintenance' concept is being incorporated into discretionary systems such as public assistance, resulting in less clear-cut distinctions between benefits as of right and benefits based on need. Titmuss' analysis underscores the untenable nature of 'the notion that there could be some kind of final solution to the problems of social security and income maintenance in modern industrialized societies', for 'not all good things are compatible, still less all the ideals of mankind, in the realm of social security as in other areas of human life' (22:259).

Themes in National Experience

The continuing British dilemmas in income inequality and income maintenance are highlighted by Abel-Smith in 1973(23). He discusses the change from flat rate to earnings-related contributions and the failure to eliminate poverty. In his view the problem of poverty cannot be resolved without much wider changes in the distribution of income. Like Titmuss before him, he is convinced that inequality is the key problem and the attempt to isolate poverty as a separate issue is a diversion from the central social dilemma of modern society.

The proposition that 'not all good things are compatible' emerges as boldly in the Soviet Union as it does in democratic societies. Osborn (1970) shows that it is incorrect to assume that because they were derived from a single ideology, political and social purposes had been made explicit and pervasive in the Soviet Union, that the gap between values and legislation had been closed. On the contrary, there are 'gaps in the array of values derived from Soviet Marxist ideology' (24:1) which are apparent in many areas of social provision including the responsibility of society for all its members in the social security realm — an important ideological tenet of the Soviet state. Nor, as shown by Madison, is there any guarantee that the responses of beneficiaries to what social security provides and to the administrative style it exhibits will support, rather than conflict with, program intent (25). This is demonstrated, she finds, by many beneficiaries who have grievances, but are not encouraged to insist on a fair resolution: the restricted nature of the administrative appeals machinery rules out judicial review and raises doubts about its objectivity and accessibility. In many instances, for example, the review is by persons who handed down the original decision. Furthermore, Soviet literature is devoid of statistical information on appeals, of the reasons for grievances, and of the outcomes of decisions in appealed cases. Thus, the question *whose* values and intent do governing policies represent is a vital one.

In contrast, Rosenthal's (1967) description of the evolution of Sweden's social security (as well as health, welfare and related programs) notes that in Sweden special attention has been paid to built-in devices in the law designed to maintain individual freedom. This helps to explain the type of programs that have been developed and the lack of alarm over expanded government activity in the country's social undertakings. As a consequence, a comparison of Swedish and American programs finds that the major distinction lies in the greater willingness of Swedish citizens to rely on public rather than private agencies to meet social needs (26).

Social Security and Income Redistribution. The problem of income inequality is dealt with more specifically in studies that center on the income redistribution effect and potentials of social security transfers.

In his study of the French 'welfare state' Petersen (1960) wished to show 'the extent to which the nation's social security system has become an instrument for the redistribution of income . . . ; and . . . [to] analyze the manner in which the pattern of income distribution is altered as a result of welfare expenditures by the government' (27:2). In addition, he analyzed the impact of certain structural characteristics of the French economy on the functioning of her 'welfare state'. From a comparison of income redistribution via transfer expenditures in the French economy on an aggregate basis with similar practices in Great Britain and the United States, Petersen finds that inequality in income between social classes is 'mitigated to some extent by the transfer mechanism' which serves chiefly 'to bolster the income position of persons in the nonactive population', and that social security benefits are 'on the whole progressive in their effects'. The same situation obtains in regard to distribution of income between income classes: 'a considerable inequality in the *initial* distribution of income is modified by the system of transfer payments, the bulk of which are directed to households in the lower income ranges' (27:99). But

> the efficiency of the welfare state as a means to cope with the problem of the distribution of income is limited. In other words, the welfare state idea may achieve desirable results with respect to the distribution of income in a society up to a point, but thereafter the principle of diminishing returns sets in (27:107).

George (1968) arrives at the conclusion that very little vertical redistribution of income has taken place in Great Britain since the last war, and that therefore the country has to know in a detailed manner the ways in which the economic system opens or closes doors of opportunity to people of different social classes. These findings are derived from an examination of the recommendations of the Beveridge Report which came out in 1942, and of social security developments since then – an examination which entails a detailed look at social security legislation, at the extent to which benefits had been used by the public, and at the role of the state in the social security domain. How the economic system affects opportunity cannot be answered by rising standards of life for 'improved standards do not satisfy expectations for ever; they merely prod them on to demand even better standards' (28:235).

Habib's effort to ascertain the current redistributive effects of national insurance (1975) — if 'only to determine what is left for the other income support programs to do' since the primary goal of national insurance is not the reduction of income inequality — is most informative. He precedes it by a lucid and cogent exposition of the problems involved in the resolution of the redistribution issue; of the opposing views of economists and other scholars concerning it; of the ways in which national insurance may redistribute income; and what each of these ways requires for its assessment of the final outcome. Habib's own investigation first addresses the distribution of direct taxes and transfers by income groups; then it examines the effect of national insurance on the distribution of income, by family size and by age; and finally, estimates the role of national insurance in the total redistribution of income due to all taxes and transfers.

The major findings indicate that (a) the total reduction in inequality due to insurance benefits in 1960 was 5.7 percent, with various programs differing considerably in the degree of progressivity; (b) contributions are regressive, with regressivity being greatest if the employers' share is shifted to consumers in the form of price rises; (c) nevertheless, insurance benefits do reduce inequality by 4 percent; and (d) reduction in inequality is greatest within age and family-size groups, in contrast to redistribution between demographic groups where it is very small. This means that claims that insurance merely redistributes over the life cycle or between generations are incorrect (29:11). It is also noted that in regard to the important changes introduced into the insurance system in Israel since 1969, 'it can . . . be said with assurance that national insurance now plays a much greater role in the total redistribution of income' (29:36). Habib stresses that in order to predict changes in redistributive effects on an ongoing basis, better and more accessible data are needed.

In Sweden, according to Uhr (1966), 'the combined effect of the increases in social services and cash benefits and of the development of the supporting system of financing seems to be a redistribution in the range of 8—10 percent of the national income from those in the top four deciles of the income distribution to families and individuals in the three bottom deciles' (30:129). Among the included social provisions are those for employed mothers and for housewives and children of low-income families. Considered as well are unemployment assistance and measures to stimulate employment. Development of the social security system is seen as a response to changes in the country's post-war social, economic and demographic trends. Uhr doubts that an assumed additional economic expansion — which might have been achieved 'if social security had not expanded, if taxes had been correspondingly lower, and if the amounts thus added to disposable income had been utilized for increased investment' — could come about without a higher rate of inflation (30:157).

The Organization and Administration of Social Security. Oram's study of New Zealand's social welfare system (1969) is divided into a three-part analysis. The first centers on a review of the country's system of income maintenance (as well as of health, education, welfare and housing), describes each income support program and evaluates income maintenance 'in context of economic and social welfare in New Zealand'. The second part examines the administrative structure of the different programs and the third, their level of expenditures and their patterns of financing. Analysis in each part encompasses both the public and voluntary sectors. Oram devotes his entire final part to emphasizing New Zealand's need for coordination — between levels of government and between public and voluntary sectors. This need, he notes, is recognized world-wide by a diverse group of countries: Great Britain, United States, Canada, Nordic Countries, Thailand, Russia and Czechoslovakia (31).

Despite the fact that the data limitations in respect to the People's Republic of China — even concerning such basic features as total work force, covered employment, actual benefits paid, the number of retiring workers — are, in Kallgren's words, 'particularly acute', she succeeds in sketching in the major distinguishing characteristics of the country's labor insurance system as it has developed since 1949, the assumptions and policy decisions they personify, and the problem their implementation presents, to the government and to the intended beneficiaries. This material is contained in three papers, published or prepared in 1968, 1971 and 1977 (32,33,34). In the 1977 paper she compares the existing situation with what she found earlier and attempts to answer such questions as: how are the benefits funded and how are the financial deposits handled? how are benefits determined and distributed? and how is an increasing population of aged and near aged workers (in major enterprises under direct control of central government) faring in terms of the relevant welfare programs?

Kallgren finds that there has been little change in basic benefits for the country's industrial workers in centrally directed enterprises and to a lesser degree, in other work settings. These benefits continue to differ in scope and degree of protection. They may depend on a

Themes in National Experience

person's individual status as worker: in industry covered by national labor insurance; in a local cooperative where the provision of limited benefits (medical care and modest child care facilities, but no old-age or disability pensions) is determined by the cooperative; and in a commune, where benefits are fixed by the particular commune. Nor have there been any substantial changes in funding procedures. She notes that enterprise workers can neither expect a higher standard in benefits nor can they predict the level of support that will be available to them when they qualify. Some welfare supplements are available in some enterprises, but commonly it is children who help parents to supplement insurance payments. Kallgren concludes that

> the full scale enforcement of the low wage policy, combined with the fact that not all workers can expect to reach the top grade, means that the floor guaranteed to retired workers appears to be lowering ... At the same time, the wages of younger workers providing some assistance to their parents also remain low ... [At best], the competing needs for supporting their own families inevitably will bring pressures upon a diminishing source of funds ... [These problems will influence future funding arrangements.] As established in the 1950s, the Chinese government, though guaranteeing the rights of social welfare, has not been involved in the funding of the program ... It would seem, however, that the central government will, of necessity, become more involved, specifically in terms of financing (34:18—19).

Knowledge and understanding about the Soviet social security system are available from official reports and scholarly works. A 1960 HEW report provides a straightforward description of Soviet programs of cash benefits and welfare services (35), including their financing and administrative structure. The two aspects commented on are the non-universality of general social security provisions which did not cover collective farmers (who at that time constituted 40 percent of the population) and the extremely slow pace of benefit level adjustments which meant that pensioners lived in hardship over many years. A second HEW report, published in 1972, describes major developments since 1960 among which extension of social security to collective farmers in 1964, on a limited scale in terms of coverage and level of protection, was the most important (36). Pointed up is the unwillingness of Soviet authorities to recognize the need for a decent public assistance program for those unable to work, those who do not qualify for social insurance, or whose insurance benefits are too low for survival. Subsequent Western estimates show that such need was and is quite extensive (14) and that much suffering results from the continuing failure to meet it (37).[2] The 1972 report also noted the existence of a conflict between welfare considerations and work incentives built into the social security system, designed to get people productively employed early and to keep them in the labor force as long as possible.

In her first study of Soviet social security and welfare services systems (1960), Madison reviews their components against a brief historical backdrop of pre- and post-Revolutionary developments. Analysis encompasses administration, coverage, financing and adequacy of benefits, as well as the manner in which changes in principles governing social security were used to implement the regime's social goals. She saw the transformations that took place during the post-Revolutionary period as largely Soviet counterparts of changes in welfare throughout the world. But, she noted, 'the benefits of modernization have not been and are not now available to those opposing the regime, however indirectly . . .' (39:536). Especially disturbing was the pervasive silence about the situation of needy people excluded from the system.

In a major work (1968) Madison expands, deepens and updates her examination of the Soviet social security system (as well as personal social services for families, children, the aged, and the disabled) — this time within the framework of social policy formation during 1917—66 as it had been influenced by the nation's pre-revolutionary heritage and by Soviet psycho-social and economic theories (14). Current practice — as shaped by administrative patterns, organizational structure, qualifications of personnel and the nature of the helping methods — is critically reviewed. Illumined are the government's unrelenting demands that the individual participate fully and uninterruptedly in productive work — 'he who does not work, neither shall he eat'[3]— and the continuing emphasis on differentiation as opposed to egalitarianism in regard to what the beneficiary can receive from social security — 'from each according to his ability, to each according to his *work*'. These demands produce inequalities and inequities since their impact is greatest on the weakest members of the society, those disadvantaged by physical, emotional and social disabilities. Light is also shed on conditions in which the state replaces all other agencies in providing all forms of welfare and on the dilemma of a feedback system representing interests that do not represent themselves.

Themes in National Experience 111

Problems generated by the Soviet system's efforts to simultaneously achieve two objectives, to raise productivity and to meet minimum welfare needs, are elaborated by Madison in 1973 (40). That progress toward a minimum level of protection is not lacking is demonstrated by liberalizations introduced since 1967 and by those projected for the future. Nevertheless, the gap between social security for collective farmers and the system for workers and employees continues wide, at least one half of all pensioners exist at a level below the official 'minimum of material well-being', and poverty among families with children is widespread. Plans for a program of 'allowances' for children in poor families mark a departure from previous policy: the introduction of a public assistance system for more than a third of all children under age eight in whose families the aggregate per capita income from all sources is below the official poverty line.[4]

In a 1977 publication Madison looks at income maintenance provisions (and social services) for women in Russia (41). To achieve a clearer analysis, she discusses these provisions in relation to the different roles women play — as wives, mothers, parents, workers — recognizing that in practice, some programs and the problems they address are interrelated and overlap. Examined are maternity leave provisions, family allowances, the new public assistance program for poor children, social security and social insurance benefits, public assistance and institutional care for the aged and the totally disabled. Inadequate benefits, both for women who receive them on the basis of their own work records and those who qualify as dependents, underscore the larger gaps that continue to divide the policy blueprint from what is actually made available — as well as to raise questions about the reality of values so loudly proclaimed in official pronouncements.

A more detailed and updated analysis of Soviet administration of social security and how it operates in 'real life' is given by Madison in a 1979 publication (25). She analyzes the relative powers and responsibilities of the organs involved in administration (the USSR Council of Ministers, its Union—Republic State Committee on Labor and Social Questions, the 15 Republic Ministries of Social Security, and the trade unions), and then concentrates on the specifics of the trade union role in this power structure. Problems experienced by unions are examined in relation to the organizational structure's effectiveness, both from the point of view of the needs of potential and actual beneficiaries and of the continuing drive to implement the government's social goals via social security. On the basis of this assessment she concludes that 'the administration of welfare benefits by trade union committees is not a resounding success, although it is by no means a dismal failure' (25). In regard to future developments, what to Madison appears 'least amenable to change is the lack of human rights in welfare, the freedom to challenge the government when beneficiaries consider decisions to be unjust' (25).

Policy Issues. Policy issues that emerge from the mass of detailed material contained in single-country studies lend themselves to being presented in relation to groups of countries divided into developed democracies, developing socialist and nonsocialist societies, and developed socialist nations.

In Canada, the 'real questions' are located in administrative and value areas. In the former, what needs to be achieved are balance and effectiveness: balance between income maintenance and other social programs, between contributory and tax-supported programs, between central, provincial and municipal responsibilities, and between national and sectional interests; effectiveness calls for meeting the needs of people in a fast-changing industrialized society by provisions that are socially acceptable, free of stigma, and do not deprive recipients of their dignity and of control over their own lives.

In Denmark major policy issues emanate from a lack of clarity about the changing goals of social security and hence, from disagreements about the most efficient organizational structure to attain these goals. What needs to be clarified is how to develop effective preventive, therapeutic and rehabilitative services that would provide real security for each individual in every situation of need. Then it will be possible to decide whether existing provisions and structures should be replaced by new forms or whether they can be sufficiently improved to remain in place.

A somewhat different scenario emerges from the French situation. Because of a rising proportion of aged people in the population and a more prolonged period of education for the young, and above all, more costly medical care, there has taken place a constant increase in expenses, greater than the increase in resources. Costs have been augmented as well by a categorical approach in social security and public assistance with its series of diversified supportive provisions which have tended to narrow the differences between social insurance and public assistance. The basic questions are how to develop a workable plan of acceptable priorities in relation to needs, a plan that would not further erode, but would rather enhance social cohesion (solidarité) without, however, stifling individualism; and how to restructure the system — eliminating anarchy, unnecessary proliferation and unjustified inequalities — so that it apportions available resources on a rational basis and makes possible the implementation of agreed upon priorities.

Inequity and inequality are the twin issues that continue to dominate the social security debates in Great Britain, the elimination of the former apparently desired by all, while the demise of the latter is somewhat less universally advocated. In this connection, it is pertinent to note that proposals by some to make social security a means for achieving social equality seem to depart from the principles of the Beveridge Report — a milestone in the evolution of the philosophy of social security world-wide — since the latter's objective was not so much to do away with inequality, as to provide a floor below which no-one would be allowed to fall. Views in regard to inequity and inequality underlie controversies as to whether in democratic societies it is social conflict between the ruling and the working classes that plays a dominant role in the development of social security or whether many different interest groups wield important influence on final decisions; whether inequality and poverty can or cannot be seen as separate problems; whether a universal or selective approach is more likely to bring about social justice; whether diminution of poverty can be achieved faster by accentuating its absolute rather than its relative aspect; and whether those who receive cash benefits on the basis of need ought to be gradually transferred to join those who receive them as of right, or whether the two ought to be separate and distinct. While studies in France, Great Britain and Israel show that social security does redistribute income and that it can do so to a greater extent, there is not a consensus on whether this is an appropriate goal, or on how to structure benefits, if indeed it is appropriate.

In Japan the major policy issue illustrates the hold of culturally induced values on current provisions: how to overcome or modify cultural ways of life so that they will not act as deterrents to the creation of a modern system of social security to replace old arrangements which are recognized as no longer serving the needs of a modern and wealthy society.

New Zealand's pressing issues revolve around the need to better define the aims and content of policy. This would help clarify the responsibilities of central and local governments in the welfare field and to make more precise the roles of research, planning and action in formulating and implementing policy. A better definition would also assist in establishing criteria for selecting among options open to the public welfare sector in making use of voluntary agencies for some aspects of this sector's work. Combined, these improvements would lead social welfare to become more effective in managing public relations to advance its cause, a crucial requirement for progress in a democratic society.

The most important problem in the Swedish system — a network of provisions considered by some as the fullest fruition of the welfare state attained so far — is how to contain mounting costs without deterring steady movement toward more adequate protection and greater individual freedom than are now bestowed by the legally prescribed provisions.

In developing countries policy issues raise a different set of questions. Among them the most important is: at what level of economic development can and should a country consider itself ready to initiate or measurably improve a publicly supported social security program? This presents the underlying value questions in especially sharp relief. It demands a decision about the relative importance of human well-being, both in itself and as an element in accelerating economic progress, as contrasted to greater capital investment which then becomes unavailable for social programs in general, and for social security in particular. That decisions differ is illustrated by Israel and India, even though the two countries are similar in that both fought to obtain their independence from Great Britain and both are democracies. Apparently, it is the differences in the degree of dominance exerted by a variety of factors that coalesce into value positions — historical, religious, social and cultural — that mold the final policy decisions.

In the People's Republic of China, a socialist developing country, the major issues appear to stem from the failure of the central government to become involved in financing benefits — although in principle it has 'guaranteed' the right to social welfare for all since 1950. This has resulted in differences in the scope and degree of protection that existing benefits provide, elicited, as they are, by uneven responses from a variety of local organs and from adult children. It is possible, if one is to judge by the Israeli experience, that when publicly provided protection is not comprehensive and does not cover every qualified or needy person, people learn to help each other and to rely on their own collective efforts to ameliorate problems of want in daily life. Perhaps this is especially so in an ancient culture whose people have lived under foreign domination for long periods of time. At the same time, there is no doubt that even if this happens to some appreciable extent, the results are meager and uneven and become less and less acceptable in the process of industrialization and urbanization.

The Soviet Union, its transformation from an underdeveloped to a developed nation initiated by a profound social revolution, presents an especially interesting case as a mature socialist society and one of the world's two super-powers. The policy issues of its social security system have their roots in the government's view that social security must serve broader goals of social policy as well as the welfare needs of the non-productive, the latter to be subordinated to the former if necessary. Consequently, a persistent issue is how to make provision for the weakest and most disadvantaged without plunging them too far below a meager subsistence level and without placing them in a seriously disadvantaged position vis-à-vis the active population. This, in turn, is a manifestation of the equity—equality problems which the government in principle wishes to overcome but so far without success. Difficult as well is the problem of insufficient dynamism throughout the social security system: a poverty line, unchanged since 1967 and meager even by its outdated standards, still exerts its baleful influence on the level of all benefits. Perhaps more sharply than other issues, the constricted nature of the fair hearings process raises questions about the relationship between the individual and the state. Whose values and goals are dominant: those of officials bent on adhering strictly to the ideological line, of administrators caught between demands of the Party and the needs of people who come within their purview, or of the eligible and the needy who want help and more adequate protection granted in a dignified and humane manner?

Summary. The detailed information contained in single-country studies sheds light on the more significant forces at work in social security developments. Some arise from values firmly embedded in the social fabric and often resistant to change, even in the face of rapid industrialization. Others spring from changes of a social and demographic nature; still others are the consequences of changes in the labor market, occupational distribution, and the overall economic position of a given country, especially as it influences the level of living. Both in countries with market and planned economies, these forces are likely to develop further and to shape social security even more decisively than they do now — comparatively rapidly in modern, industrialized societies, slowly and haltingly in tradition-bound, developing nations. These forces of change affect all central policy issues: decisions about what constitutes adequacy at a given point in time; patterns of eligibility, entitlement and qualifying conditions; allocation of resources sufficient to meet the adequacy standard; positions on narrowing or retaining differences between benefits as of right and benefits based on need; views on universality as opposed to selectivity. Underlying all this are the diverse views in regard to the meaning of social justice as it is reflected in equity and equality.

Illumined as well, in some instances with exceptional clarity, is the interplay of theory, policy and effective implementation in social security. It becomes clear that often the policy blueprint and its implementation in 'real life' are two different things, sometimes far apart. At times, policy designed to enhance human well-being produces unforeseen consequences. These may assume sizable diswelfare proportions, leading to only an inadequate fulfillment of needs for which the proclaimed policy promised so much. Involved are the values prevalent in a given society, especially attitudes about the non-productive or the minimally productive. These attitudes are shaped by historical, religious, social and cultural factors which interact in a complicated fashion that pushes certain values to the forefront while others are relegated to the shadows during the decision-making process which, in the final analysis, is political in nature. As a result, even when social security problems in different countries are similar in substance, they are dealt with differently. In this connection, much depends on the workings of delivery systems charged with transforming legal provisions into benefits — especially the philosophy of personnel and the extent to which balance, coordination and harmonization are attained on an ongoing basis.

In the midst of all the problems, injustices and inadequacies two things are unmistakable: the desire of people everywhere for more comprehensive, adequate, and equitable social security protection, and the realization that there are no final solutions for social security because it is a living organism undergoing unceasing evolutionary change.

Notes

1. Historical accounts from Great Britain are copious. Described are the beginnings and histories of particular welfare programs, major social reforms, welfare traditions, trends, effects of deprivation, etc. A few of the many works that are useful for understanding the development of British social policy are:

(1) de Schweinitz, Karl, *England's Road to Social Security, from the Statute of Laborers in 1349 to the Beveridge Report of 1942* (Philadelphia, University of Pennsylvania Press, 1943). (2) Owen, David E., *English Philanthropy: 1660–1960* (Cambridge, Mass., Belknap Press of Harvard University, 1964). (3) Farndale, James (ed.) *Trends in Social Welfare* (Oxford, Pergamon Press, 1965). (4) Bruce, Maurice, *The Coming of the Welfare State,* revised edn (New York, Schocken, 1966). (5) Gilbert, Bentley B., *The Evolution of National Insurance in Great Britain: Origins of the Welfare State* (London, Michael Joseph, 1966). (6) Hanes, David G., *The First British Workmen's Compensation Act, 1897* (College Series, no. 8. New Haven, Yale University Press, 1968). (7) Gilbert, Bentley B., *British Social Policy: 1914–1939* (Ithaca, New York, Cornell University Press, 1970).

2. The only persons eligible for public assistance are the totally disabled (in all 15 Republics) and the aged (in nine Republics). The tough eligibility conditions require 'absence of any means for existence', as well as absence of relatives legally responsible for support. Such relatives include parents, children, stepchildren and grandchildren. Support payments can be exacted by civil suit and are set at levels proportional to the supporter's income. The level of assistance is extremely low: ten rubles a month in urban communities and nine rubles in rural villages. This can be compared to a minimum wage of 70 rubles a month. The number of needy persons certainly runs into the millions (38:53–4).

3. Faced with a progressively more severe labor shortage, the government decided on a policy of accentuating the potential of social security as an incentive to keep people working. Efforts to do so began in 1961; regulations which came into force on April 1, 1964 granted a flat 50 percent of full pension in addition to wages to workers and employees in many industries and occupations, if they continued to work full time. In the Urals, Siberia and the Far East, they became entitled to 75 percent of pension. In 1970, full pensions were made payable in a wide variety of occupations throughout the country, and the wage-plus-pension ceiling was raised to 300 rubles per month (38:30–7).

4. The poverty line, established in 1967 for the period 1965–70, was based on a minimum budget (free services and privileges having been excluded from both income and expenditures) for a family of four. The method for developing this budget was to apply predetermined consumption norms to the least expensive goods and services among those selected for inclusion. The resulting gaunt absolute poverty line has been used without adjustment since 1967 throughout the income-maintenance system, despite Soviet writers' stress on the necessity of adjusting minimum budgets to each higher stage of the country's economic development and the fact that prices have been subject to inflation (38:47–9).

References

1. Morgan, John S., 'An Emerging System of Income Maintenance: Canada in Transition', pp. 105–28 in Jenkins, Shirley (ed.) *Social Security in International Perspective* (New York, Columbia University Press, 1969).

2. Friis, Hennino, 'Issues in Social Security Policies in Denmark', pp. 129–50, *ibid.*

3. Kuusi, Pekka, *Social Policies for the Sixties. A Plan for Finland* (Helsinki, Finnish Policy Association, published in Finnish in 1961; translated into English in 1964).

4. Friedlander, Walter, *Individualism and Social Welfare: An Analysis of the System of Social Security and Social Welfare in France* (New York, Crowell-Collier Publishing Co., 1962).

118 Themes in National Experience

5. Laroque, Pierre, 'Social Security in France', pp. 171–89, in Jenkins, *Social Security*.
6. Stevens, Cindy, *Public Assistance in France*. Occasional paper in Social Administration, no. 50 (London, G. Bell and Sons, 1973).
7. George, Victor, *Social Security and Society* (London, Routledge and Kegan Paul, 1973).
8. Fisher, Paul, 'Major Social Security Issues: Japan', *Social Security Bulletin*, 36, no. 3 (March 1973), pp. 25–39. For a detailed description of this 'complex mosaic', comprising nine independent programs, see Japanese Government Social Insurance Agency, *Outline of Social Insurance In Japan* (1975).
9. An unpublished, mimeographed paper given to me in Japan. Sodei, Takako (Tokyo Metropolitan Institute of Gerontology), 'The Career Pattern after the "Retirement Age" in Japan', undated but probably written in 1972.
10. Murayama, Saeko, 'The Potential for US–Japanese Cross-National Research in the Area of Work, Retirement, and Income', paper prepared for presentation at Conference on the potential for Japanese–US cross-national research on aging in September 1974. Also an unpublished, mimeographed paper given to me in Japan.
11. Safran, William, *Veto-Group Politics: The Case of Health Insurance Reform in West Germany* (San Francisco, California, Chandler Publishing Co., 1967).
12. Hasan, Saiyid Zafar, 'Social Security in India: Limited Resources, Unlimited Needs', pp. 190–208 in Jenkins, *Social Security*.
13. Nizan, Dr A., *Social Security in Israel*, Submitted to the ISSA (Jerusalem, National Insurance Institute, July 1973).
14. Madison, Bernice, *Social Welfare in the Soviet Union* (Stanford, California, Stanford University Press, 1968).
15. Brown, Joan C., *How Much Choice. Retirement Policies in Canada* (Ottawa, The Canadian Council of Social Development, November 1975).
16. Schorr, Alvin L., *Social Security and Social Services in France* (Washington, DC, HEW, Social Security Administration, Division of Research and Statistics, Research Report no. 7, 1965).
17. Lynes, Tony, *French Pensions*, Occasional Paper in Social Administration, no. 21 (London, G. Bell and Sons, 1967).
18. Eimicke, William B., 'Debate over Welfare in Britain', *Social Work*, 18, no. 5 (September 1973), pp. 84–91.
19. Hoshino, George, 'Britain's Debate on Universal or Selective Social Security: Lessons for America', *Social Service Review*, 43, no. 3 (September 1969), pp. 245–59.
20. Madison, 'The Welfare State'.
21. Titmuss, Richard M., 'New Guardians of the Poor in Britain', pp. 151–70 in Jenkins, *Social Security*.
22. Titmuss, Richard M., 'Equity, Adequacy, and Innovation in Social Security', *International Social Security Review*, xxiii, no. 2 (1970), pp. 259–69.
23. Abel-Smith, Brian, 'Perspectives of Income Inequality and Income Maintenance: Some Dilemmas from British Experience', pp. 202–23 in Booth, Philip (ed.) *Social Security: Policy for the Seventies*, Proceedings of the Seventh Social Security Conference (Ann Arbor, Michigan, The University of Michigan–Wayne State University, Institute of Labor and Industrial Relations, 1973).
24. Osborn, *Soviet Social Policies*.
25. Madison, Bernice, 'Trade Unions and Social Welfare', in Kahan, Arcadius and Ruble, Blair A. (eds.) *Industrial Labor in the USSR* (Elmsford, New York, Pergamon Press, 1979).

Themes in National Experience

26. Rosenthal, Albert H., *The Social Programs of Sweden: A Search for Security in a Free Society* (Minneapolis, University of Minnesota Press, 1967).
27. Petersen, Wallace C., *The Welfare State in France* (Lincoln, Nebraska, University of Nebraska Press, 1960).
28. George, *Social Security: Beveridge and After*.
29. Habib, Jack, *Redistribution Through National Insurance in Israel by Income and Demographic Groups* (Jerusalem, The National Insurance Institute, November 1975).
30. Uhr, Carl C., *Sweden's Social Security System* (Washington, DC, HEW, Social Security Administration, Research Report no. 14, 1966).
31. Oram, C. A., *Social Policy and Administration in New Zealand* (Wellington, New Zealand University Press, 1969).
32. Kallgren, Joyce K., 'Social Welfare and China's Industrial Workers', pp. 540–74 in Barnett, A. Doak (ed.) *Chinese Communist Politics in Action* (Seattle, Washington, University of Washington Press, 1968).
33. Kallgren, Joyce K., 'Chinese Welfare Programs', Paper prepared for the 1971 Annual Meeting of the American Political Science Association, September 1971, Chicago, Illinois. Mimeographed. Incorporated into an amended statement made at Hearings before the Joint Economic Committee, Congress of the United States, 92nd Session, June 13, 14, 15, 1972, pp. 69–87.
34. Kallgren, Joyce K., 'Welfare Options in Post-Mao China', Paper prepared for the 1977 Annual Meeting of the American Political Science Association, September 1977, Washington, DC. Mimeographed.
35. US, HEW, Social Security Administration, *A Report on Social Security Programs in the Soviet Union*, prepared by the US team that visited the USSR under the East-West Exchange Program in August–September 1958 (Washington, DC, US Government Printing Office, 1960).
36. US, HEW, Social Security Administration, *The US Social Security Mission to the Union of Soviet Socialist Republics* . . . report on the 1971 cultural exchange visit by the American delegation (Washington, DC, DHEW Publication no. (SSA) 73-11901, February 1972).
37. Madison, Bernice, 'Russia's Social Security Mess', *Wall Street Journal*, (May 19, 1978).
38. Madison, Bernice, *Soviet Income Maintenance Programs in the Struggle Against Poverty* (Colloquium, Kennan Institute for Advanced Russian Studies, Woodrow Wilson International Center for Scholars, Washington, DC, June 20, 1978).
39. Madison, Bernice, 'The Organization of Welfare Services', pp. 515–41 in Black, Cyril E. (ed.) *The Transformation of Russian Society* (Cambridge, Mass., Harvard University Press, 1960).
40. Madison, Bernice, 'Soviet Income Maintenance Policy for the 1970s', *Journal of Social Policy*, 2, part 2 (April 1973), pp. 97–116.
41. Madison, Bernice, 'Social Services for Women: Problems and Priorities', pp. 307–33 in Atkinson, Dorothy, Dallin, Alexander, and Lapidus, Gail Warshofsky (eds.) *Women in Russia* (Stanford, California, Stanford University Press, 1977).

6 THE IMPACT OF SOCIAL SECURITY ON SOCIETY

The cross-national studies included in this section range from worldwide panoramas that sketch in highlights of a half century of change and/or forecast future trends to in-depth analyses of social security in two countries, related to the unique features of their historic, political, economic and social development. Some address only one program or issue; others deal with a whole network of programs and many issues, both substantive and administrative. As explained earlier, these studies are arranged according to the major areas or aspects of social security to which they speak, and within this context, chronologically. It is hoped that this pattern will assist in bringing out differences that may have emerged in policy-oriented concerns over time, and will shed light on the kind of policy issues that are common to many countries in contrast to those that are specific to particular nations — as well as explain or at least suggest the reasons for these similarities and differences.

Trends and Forecasts. Several studies provide a worldwide panorama for the purpose of shedding light on trends in the evolution of social security at the international level. As explained by Rys, 'in view of the importance of external sociological factors for the formation and the development of national social security schemes, the study of international trends is of direct interest to national social policy planning' (1:264).

In his 1964 review, Rohrlich gave an account of developments and trends during the years 1961—3 as they emerged in discussions at the ISSA conference of that year. At that time, the only truly comprehensive programs protecting against all categories of social risks outside of Euro-American societies were found in Japan and Israel. Programs for the unemployed, involving income maintenance, training and rehabilitation, were not at all widespread. Africa and areas of Asia and Latin America lagged behind the West in unemployment compensation; but Mexico and Uruguay had adopted advanced unemployment programs in the preceding decade (2).

Fisher covers developments and trends for the three-year period 1967—9. He finds that there is a growing recognition in developing countries 'that social security protection, which replaces older patterns of family support [is] essential for a smooth transition to an industrial society' (3:10); and in advanced countries, that it is beyond political realities to provide a social security benefit which by itself, without regard to any other income, would assure the pensioned a livelihood, however it may be defined. This fact once again raises the question as to

> whether social insurance or social assistance should be expected to carry the main burden in the fight against poverty and to what extent the burden on both programs could be reduced by a general attack on poverty wherever it ocurred in the nation through the whole gamut of social policy and taxation measures (3:39—40).

In a paper prepared for a Senate hearing in 1969, entitled 'Social Security for the Aged: International Perspectives', Rohrlich stated that the trend everywhere was to raise expectations for protection against want in certain common contingencies of life. These rising expectations emphasized that this protection be made available for all persons exposed to such contingencies; that it embody socially acceptable standards; and that it be given as of right. The three institutions that offered such protection, he said, were social security, social assistance and universal pensions. He defined the latter as an unconditional minimum income guarantee upon attainment of age; and social assistance, as a method that recognized a right to benefit, but conditional on proof of need.

Social security, the most important institution world-wide in this context, relies heavily on the social insurance — the 'earned right' — approach. Its shortcomings, pointed out Rohrlich, are several: less than universal coverage; inadequate benefits; 'a loss in the real value of benefits . . . [and] a relative decline in the socioeconomic position of social insurance beneficiaries vis-à-vis the bulk of the economically active population' (4:2). There are, however, a number of ways that countries around the world have developed for coping with or at least minimizing these shortcomings and these Rohrlich analyzes, indicating the strengths and weaknesses of each one.

Perrin describes the tremendous expansion of social security programs during the 50 post-World War I years and the role played by the ILO (1969). This expansion is an attempt to respond to a need that has become fundamental in the concerns of modern societies — an expression of 'collective responsibility with regard to the right to health and to a guaranteed social income' (5:262), based on two principles: universality and 'unity of social security's role considered in relation to social and economic policy as a whole' (5:257). Despite diversity of national methods, certain common trends are discernible: to extend coverage; to provide more effective protection; to administer programs in a unified and coordinated manner which, however, allows for diversification; and to emphasize the role of social security in income redistribution.

The most serious current problems that require policy and planning decisions, Perrin finds, arise out of the need to reexamine social security's relationship to the economy, to society and to the level of development. Among several suggestions, he explores the possibilities of using social security to further social adaptation through its welfare activities. The latter, he believes, are 'destined to become more important as the circle of protected persons grows wider and more effective income security is provided' (5:279) and as emphasis on the 'qualitative aspect, connected with the diversification and individualisation of collective assistance' (5:280), becomes imperative. Doubting that social security's role in income redistribution can be appreciably strengthened within the traditional national framework, he calls for international solidarity and planning which would address 'new forms of international assistance as an incentive to the social investments that are indispensable if social security is to be effective ... ,' and he argues that the recognition of social security as an essential social right 'imposes responsibilities on the international community that cannot be evaded on the grounds of underdevelopment' (5:281).

In another important article, also published in 1969, Perrin attempts to forecast future developments, not merely in relation to what went on before, but 'in the light of the general evolution of the societies in question'. He finds that the protection offered by social security is characterized by 'active trends' and 'latent conflicts'. In regard to trends, two are especially powerful: the trend toward universality as to persons covered, and growing concern about the capacity of social security to fully meet the needs of protected persons. As to universality (apparent in both developed and developing countries, but for different reasons), the trend is from coverage for lower-paid workers in industry, to all wage earners, to entire working populations, or even to all citizens or residents. As to level of benefits, the trend is away from viewing benefits as a defence against excessive poverty to seeing them as a means of assuring income security. This involves moving toward a guaranteed wage in both short-term and long-term contingencies since it is acknowledged that the needs of the aged are equivalent to those of the young — apart from family dependents.

In regard to tensions (also apparent in both developed and developing countries, but differing in relation to inequalities in levels of development), Perrin argues that they arise because of contradictions in the active trends — 'divergencies between the hopes aroused by these trends and the means available, and . . . incompatibilities of the social environment' (6:7). In developed countries, universality brings on financial crises; in developing countries, there is a clash between development of the environment and the normal functions of social security. For example, income security has no relevance in a subsistence economy. He prognosticates that progress of social security in poorer countries will be very slow if it continues to depend on their economic growth.

Having designed this conceptual model, Perrin proceeds to discuss an 'outline of a prospective strategy', projecting separately for developed countries and for 'neo-industrial societies' since he believes that unequal development will limit the international application of an ideal system. He concludes by discussing 'new dimensions in social security' from the perspective of functions, structures and internationalization. Functions, he thinks, will change from satisfying needs to satisfying aspirations; structures will change because of the change in functions, and will be influenced as well by the nature of technical means placed at the disposal of social security. The problems of unification vs diversification, centralization vs decentralization, and bureaucratic vs an individual approach will still have to be dealt with. As for internationalization, Perrin thinks that dealing with inequalities of social development requires 'harmonization' between social security and regional economic integration. Overall, he is convinced that social security 'will not disappear but will not remain the same' (6:26).

In 1975 Mouton published a masterful study of social security in 42 countries in Africa. He presents a unified analysis, rather than a detailed description, of the changes that have taken place since 1960.[1] Its purpose is a double one: on the practical side, to clarify the goals of social security and help adapt available means and methods to these goals; on the theoretical side, to provoke thinking about a reappraisal of social security policies for the future.

The first part of the study traces the stages and the main trends of the development of social security in Africa, and reveals the problems that have emerged as they are generated by and relate to the specific economic and social environment of the African countries. The second part examines these problems — the place of social security in development, the relationship between social security and the demographic situation, medical care, 'and the implantation of social security in African societies' (7:vi) — in considerable depth. In concluding, Mouton outlines the future prospects for social security in Africa.

As to stages and trends, Mouton found that there are wide differences between the 42 countries in dates at which social security systems were introduced, in their nature, in the rate of their growth, and in the tendencies exhibited by their development. At the same time, certain general similarities and a slow convergence can be discerned which, Mouton thinks, will become more pronounced in the future — a direction encouraged by the common elements of the economic and social situations of the studied countries, as well as by the promotion of international standards first formulated by the ILO. When discussing coverage, administrative and financial arrangements, and protection afforded national and immigrant workers (recent progress in protecting immigrants is important because Africa is one of the principal centers of international migrations and because foreign workers have endured oppressive discrimination), Mouton points up reasons for similarities and differences.

As to problems, Mouton thinks that many spring up because allocations to social security invariably represent but a small part of the national income, but that even more important is the social context in which social security has developed. He writes:

Social security legislation, which always includes a substantial family component, may have a substantial, but fairly contradictory, influence on the development of the African family. Being designed along the lines that fit the Western type of family, it is conducive to change by virtue of the content of its provisions and by the very fact of its existence; however, it must often be adapted to the most persistent characteristics of the indigenous families and may consequently also tend to slow down this process of change (7:147).

It is these persistent characteristics that have led many social security funds to provide family benefits in kind and certain types of welfare services.

As to the future, Mouton believes that in order to achieve optimum development, social security should adapt itself 'to the real requirements, particular circumstances and possibilities of the African countries' (7:160). He thinks, however, that the integration of social security into development planning will continue to be hampered by inappropriate methods and by lack of comprehensive and reliable statistics. And in some of the African countries, the growing volume of social transfers may cause social security to lose some of its autonomy. He is convinced that

> the emphasis should be placed on prevention and welfare services, just as much as on the protective role of social security. In Africa even more than in the industrialized countries, social security should be a dynamic concept so that the institution can 'contribute more directly to psychological security' (7:166).

Mouton sees African social security relying primarily on domestic means for its future development, but hopes that a system of international financial cooperation will be organized, to assist the African people and to further the cause of a world community.

The most recent overview was published by Tracy in 1976. It is

> a survey of developments in the social security systems of more than 125 countries from 1971 to 1975 [which] found that most programs are undergoing significant growth. This pattern is reflected primarily by the adoption of additional programs and new provisions designed to raise benefit levels, provide flexibility in retirement practices, expand coverage, and cope with demographic changes, inflationary trends, and growing costs. The new measures tend to ... [provide] a greater proportion of the population with more comprehensive protection and [to set] higher benefit rates to replace income lost because of old age, disability, sickness, work injury, unemployment, or death (8:14).

Within this broad framework, Tracy gives details on ways of coping with inflation (via general and minimum wages, and by price indexing, a device used in 33 countries); on retirement age (lowering it, permitting early retirement from hazardous or arduous employment because of ill-health and partial disability or because of involuntary unemployment; and by providing the worker with a number of choices); on efforts to unify the programs that provide sickness-disability benefits (those that apply to short-term illness and long-term invalidity, not job-connected as well as job-related); on 'constant attendance' supplement (a cash allowance paid on behalf of disabled beneficiaries who require an attendant's care for a specified number of hours a day); on means-tested benefits (now available in 26 countries for those whose social insurance benefits are insufficient to cover minimum needs and those who are not eligible for insurance benefits); and on extensions of coverage in both less developed and developed countries.

The Pace and Impact of Social Security. Gordon (1963) examined social security expenditures as a percentage of national income in 30 countries for the years 1950–7. She included both the total amounts spent and the variations in expenditures for the different programs – social insurance, family allowances, public employee benefit schemes, public health services, public assistance, and veterans' benefits – and she discusses the reasons for these variations. She found not only a 'tendency for the countries with the oldest social security programs of a relatively modern type . . . to maintain comparatively high benefit levels . . .' (9:16), but also that these same countries are likely to support reasonably adequate public assistance payments. She suggests that

> where both types of systems exist side by side, there are both political and economic forces at work which tend to preserve a certain relationship between benefit levels under the two types of programs (9:20).

As for the relationship between expenditures on statutory programs and those in the private sector, Gordon found that in industrialized countries, it has an 'inverse' character, leading to a sort of substitutive association between the two. Her analysis reveals a recognition that while economic and political factors influence social policy, the reverse is also true: policy decisions on public spending can reduce or expand spending in the private sector and this, in turn, can strengthen or diminish political pressure on public spending.

Cutright's study (1965) analyzes the relationship between 'social insurance program experience' (measured by the total number of years of program operation of five major types of social security) and economic and political variables in 76 nations, rich and poor. He finds that this experience correlates most powerfully with levels of economic development (measured in terms of energy consumption), and that differences in these levels are somewhat more determining among poor than among rich nations. He also finds that 'social security growth is less likely to follow a negative political-representativeness index change than a positive change . . .' (10:547); that is, movement toward democracy. But when levels of economic development are controlled, there are no significant differences in experience between more and less democratic nations within the same economic group, except among the richest nations. In them, social insurance experience seems to be related to political variables more significantly than to levels of economic development. In nations at low levels, a rise in level must precede the introduction of social insurance — even if there is pressure from the people to do so without waiting for a rise. On the other hand, governments may introduce social insurance when there is no popular pressure to do so, provided resources are available. Welfare provisions are seen as 'intimately related to the problem of maintaining motivation and order . . .', and as being generated by 'deeper strains affecting the organization of society', rather than as unequivocal responses to economic and political forces.[2]

Aaron (1967) compares expenditures in 22 advanced countries — those that devoted 5 percent or more of national income to social security in 1949—57 (11).[3] Like Gordon he found that the single most influential variable is the age of the programs: countries that introduced major programs early spend relatively more than the latecomers. Nor is the importance of age diminished by differences in the political and value atmosphere at the time programs are started or by changes in this atmosphere in years following the programs' initiation. Aaron discovered further that high per capita social security outlays accompany high per capita income, although the response of the latter is less than proportionate. Financing out of general revenues rather than earmarked taxes provides less adequate income maintenance. This is because general revenue financing, resulting in greater income redistribution, generates opposition to increasing the levels of benefits. According to Aaron, leftist regimes generate more initiatives in social security than the more conservative ones. He writes:

> The political complexion of the governments in power when social security programs are first introduced is usually rather similar. Moderately leftist governments, which come to power on promises of social reform, take the first steps (11:17).

In his pioneering study (1968), Pryor examined welfare expenditures in seven communist and seven capitalist nations, differentiating them as countries with planned and market economies. For the purposes of study, he defined welfare expenditures as all assistance payments, public pensions, public income-support programs and social insurance payments, excluding those for medical care. The most important factor explaining variations in expenditures is again the number of years the social insurance systems have been in operation — not the type of economic system. He also argues that among the most developed countries, the level of economic development is an underlying but not an immediate determining influence on welfare expenditures. He writes:

> two factors seem to work in the establishment of social insurance systems — the level of economic development, which is the deeper and more basic cause and the relative importance of unionization, which is related to more immediate and political influences. The importance of the political factor seems to be increasing — witness the establishment of social insurance programs in economically underdeveloped nations after World War II where political mobilization of the masses was strong (12:173).

Program age, according to Pryor, can refer either 'on the demand side to the basic climate of opinion in nations for governmental intervention in the welfare field' or 'on the supply side [to] the institutional momentum which appears to build up in certain public programs . . .' (12:133).

As for the relationships between expenditures on statutory and nonstatutory programs (in the United States), Pryor finds that

> the ratio of public consumption expenditures for welfare to the GNP is quite low, but that this ratio is increasing at a very fast rate over time. Since the ratio of total welfare expenditures to the GNP is rising and the share of privately financed welfare expenditures in the total is very slowly declining, this suggests that a large part of the growth of public expenditures can be traced to the filling of unmet welfare needs, rather than encroachment on the private sector (12:142).

His examination of expenditures on governmental old age pensions and on private life insurance in 16 countries reveals that the share of the latter in the GNP rises with per capita GNP, and that the amount spent on it is inversely related to the amount spent on governmental old age pensions. 'In other words, there appears to be a substitution effect of private for public welfare expenditures' (12:143). Overall, Pryor

The Impact of Social Security on Society

concludes that

> First, in a great many cases, the degree of variation among nations with the same economic system is much greater than the variation between the two economic systems, even after the influence of other determinants has been removed. This phenomenon overrides in importance any of the statistical difficulties in comparing public consumption expenditures between systems . . . Second, a number of general economic features . . . underlie the differences in public consumption expenditures between nations which are related neither to the system of property ownership nor to the method of resource allocation . . . These results suggest . . . that the policy dilemmas facing decision makers in public consumption expenditures are quite similar in all nations, regardless of system . . . If the basic economic circumstances . . . are similar and the policy dilemmas are similar, it should not be surprising that the decisions taken are also roughly similar (12:285).

The available evidence, he finds, transcends positive economics and points to the decisive importance of normative analysis since value judgments enter at all points.

Kilby and Taira (1969) confined their comparison to 19 developed countries of the West or of Western origin, a group that they saw as constituting a distinct 'culture realm' in which levels of economic development were similar. Their analysis centered on ten variables related to expenditures on social security as a percent of GNP in 1953, 1958, and 1968, as well as on two geographical variables related to membership in the Common Market. They found that two institutional factors explain most of the differences in social security development: program age and geographical location — that is, 'distance from the center of Western Europe measured broadly by two or three stages of country groups' (13:152). The highest expenditures were found in countries closest to the European continent, a finding that suggests that ideas in the social security domain seem to spread, facilitated by proximity. Combining age and geographical variables, the authors were able to explain up to 80 percent of the variations in their culture realm. Economic factors were, therefore, much less significant. At the same time, they found that high-income countries in this realm tended to spend less on social security than the low-income countries. In their view, this situation may not be as anomalous as it appears because 'frugality and prudence that make a person save may also make him willingly participate in social security schemes' (13:147); it reflects 'differences in socio-political climate . . . rather than a rational or normal relationship between income and social security' (13:146). This leads them to conclude that in high-income countries, differences in social security developments are not likely to be incisively explained unless economic and socio-political analyses are combined. They write:

> In recent years, economists have been paying increasing attention to noneconomic aspects of economic activities. Nowhere does this recognition of noneconomic factors seem more important than in the analysis of social security. Clearly, well-conceived research by political scientists and sociologists has promise of adding greatly to our understanding of this subject . . . It is clear that within the Western 'culture realm' neither resource availability nor the logic of economic choice in the strict sense can be said to determine a nation's social security policy. History and geography still dominate the pattern of international social security development (13:152–3).

In an impressive study (1975), Wilensky explores post-industrial societies; first, from the point of view of 'the interplay of affluence, economic system, political system, and ideology'; and second, in terms of the effect of social organization on decision-makers who allocate scarce resources to government programs of health, education, welfare and housing. His analysis is based on cross-sectional data on welfare categories and military spending in 64 rich and poor countries. He also carried out a detailed time-series analysis of these data for 22 most affluent countries, complemented by intensive historical case studies of some among them which he divided into welfare-state 'leaders, laggards, and middle-rank spenders'. Wilensky finds that welfare and military spending is 'mutually subversive'. Sharp divergences in levels of spending arise out of differences in economic development, but the economic factor is influenced by the age structure of the population (the higher the proportion of aged, the more is spent). As for the divergences among affluent countries, Wilensky indicates that they can be explained by specific differences in political, social, and economic organization, rather than by differences in ideology — by 'the degree of centralization of government, the shape of the stratification order and related mobility rates, the organization of the working class, and the position of the military' (14:xiv).

Miller (1976) questions Wilensky's claim that his path-analysis model provides 'the best explanation of welfare effort for many countries with a wide spread of economic levels' (15:47). Using ingenious statistical calculations, while basing his work almost entirely on Wilensky's data, Miller develops another, 'improved', model. Improvements consist in making clear and more direct the relationships that in Wilensky's model appear vague and hidden — such as those between increased resources and the welfare effort and between the military and welfare efforts. Miller's 'improved' model not only establishes that political systems 'matter', but also 'precisely by how much', and likewise furnishes a quantitative estimate of the rate of change of the welfare effort caused by the increase of aged in the population. It does not contradict Wilensky's finding that the age of the system does influence the welfare effort, but shows that this influence is relatively small — considerably smaller than in Wilensky's model (15:75—8).

Caputo compares all government expenditures and separately, those for defense, health and education, for the years 1950—70 in four Western democracies — Australia, Sweden, the United Kingdom, and the United States. He uses national income as a measure of economic growth in these countries. His research focuses on the yearly fluctuations of expenditures and on the statistical relationships existing among the variables under changing conditions.

Caputo's findings suggest that the assumption of an explicit trade-off between defense and welfare expenditures is questionable. He writes:

> Specifically, increased defense spending does not lead to a decrease in health expenditures, and may be responsible for their increase. Earlier findings concerning the trade-off between education and national defense expenditures are confirmed, but the findings are not statistically significant. Based on the general findings, it appears that the assumption of an explicit trade-off between defense and welfare expenditures should be re-examined and broadened to include both a comparative and a longer time perspective. [The results of the investigation of] trade-offs between defense and welfare policies under varying national defense and income situations [again] . . . indicated that prior research deserves reconsideration as the relationships often said to exist either did not do so or were found to lack statistical reliability' (16:445—6).

Convinced that his findings cannot be ignored, Caputo urges that the basic methodological and policy questions that are involved be further researched by more sophisticated methods; to wit, by 'comparative and longitudinal research, combined with intensive specific policy and country analysis' (16:446). If this is not done, he warns, 'vast misunderstanding of the resource allocation process in the world community with precious few resources to waste' might result.

The recent OECD study of public expenditures on income maintenance (July 1976) was undertaken because of concern with their rapid rise in the past ten to 15 years. Its aim was to make clear the broad trends and the major forces that stimulate expenditures, concentrating on main policy issues rather than on detailed descriptions of each country's social security system (in all, 17 countries were included). Income maintenance programs were defined as transfer payments on account of old-age pensions, child allowances, sickness cash benefits, unemployment benefits, and social assistance. Throughout, the study is characterized by painstaking explanations of method, meaning and limitations, and by a consistent avoidance of comparisons that cannot be made with a reasonable degree of validity (17).

A summary of 'the very aggregate findings' concerning the four social insurance programs (leaving out social assistance for the moment) notes that they absorb nearly 6 percent of Gross Domestic Product (GDP): 10 percent of the population receives a pension equal to about one-third of GDP per capita; 25 percent of the population benefits from very low child allowances; 1.75 percent of the population is paid relatively high unemployment and sickness benefits. As to trends (from 1962 to 1972), the study found that coverage has expanded greatly, but that a similar increase in the scale of benefits has not occurred (in terms of GDP per capita, child allowances fell). The study attempts to project expenditures for the coming decade. Because data are inadequate and in many countries programs and policies are in constant evolution, the researchers resort to a set of 'hypothetical scenarios for 1985 [variants A, B and C], based on a number of alternative assumptions'. It is prognosticated that purely demographic factors are not likely to induce large future expenditure increases, and that extensions in coverage will probably play a larger role. Overall, given the assumptions made, expenditures will continue to rise as a share of GDP in the next decade.

Since achievement of a minimum standard of living, that is, the relief of poverty, seems to be one of the objectives for the programs included in their study, the OECD addresses the question: to what extent has this objective been reached? Absolute and relative concepts of poverty are discussed and it is noted that 'industrialized societies tend to view poverty more as a relative than an absolute concept' (17:63). Comparisons are then made between 'standardized' (see discussion in Chapter 1, 'Social Policy') and national (set by individual countries themselves) poverty lines. This leads to the conclusion that when national poverty lines are used, relative poverty in OECD countries affects between 15 and 20 percent of the population; but when the 'standardized' poverty line is applied and West Germany and Sweden are excluded, only 5 to 10 percent are affected. As for changes in the extent of relative poverty in the preceding decade, the OECD researchers believe that no reliable conclusions can be reached.

The OECD study attempts to suggest 'the more immediate reasons' for the paradox of widespread relative poverty in countries that allocate substantial (and growing) proportions of their GDP to income maintenance. In this effort, it examines the relationship between expenditures on income maintenance and the 'income deficit' experienced by the poor, describes the composition of the groups who benefit, and considers the 'feedbacks' that may offset the positive effects of income maintenance programs. These feedbacks may shed light on 'the original distribution of income which may work counter to transfers intended to relieve relative poverty, and . . . on the size of the "target group" which may, for instance, increase the size of the population covered by a program by more than had been anticipated' (17:77). One reason for the paradox described above is that income maintenance programs have not been designed 'solely or even primarily' to relieve poverty, and that benefit and assistance levels in many countries are below the 'standardized' and sometimes, below the national, poverty lines.

The OECD study concludes with a discussion of policy implications for two issues which are considered especially important in view of the study's major findings; namely, how to proceed if the objective is to reduce poverty rather than to increase benefits for all, regardless of income; and how to proceed to minimize the burden of heavier expenditures, if the objective is to improve benefits in most or all programs.

The Role of Social Security in Economic and Social Development.
Laroque (1966) sees the spreading acceptance of the concept of social security as itself a stage in social development: the first stage is social assistance, the second and more advanced, is social insurance, and the third, the most advanced at this point in time, is social security. For

him, the major characteristic of social security is that

> [It] represents a guarantee by the whole community to all its members of maintenance of their standard of living or at least of tolerable living conditions, by means of a redistribution of incomes based on national solidarity (18:84).

He urges developing countries to assign an important place to social security in such redistribution because its benefits are often an essential factor in the growth of the economy.

The papers of a seminar sponsored by HEW in 1968, edited by Kassalow, interrelate the processes of economic development and social security system building, 'with experience from developed countries being drawn upon primarily as a means of shedding light on possible alternative choices for the new nations' (19:2). More and more, economists as well as experts from other disciplines, recognize that social provisions such as old age pensions and health insurance can generate incentives and/or supports that affect economic behavior — in work, saving, and spending — and can, therefore, have at least an indirect effect on productivity.

In this context, Singer questions both the capital investment and the human investment models of development: the former neglects social factors; the latter mixes cause and effect and therefore fails to resolve the question of whether higher levels of spending on health and education are the results rather than causes of development (20). He favors a third model: translating economic growth into human betterment — into better health, education, nutrition, and the like — and making this betterment the measurable objective. He notes, however, that there is a critical minimum level of social investment that must be reached before social improvement can feed back effectively into the economic development process. This level is a crucial factor. But other factors, such as a society's organizational capacities, its values, its political leadership, are also important. Singer considers social security both as an objective for human betterment and a tool for more effective development planning.

Galenson (21) and Tinbergen and Bouwmeesters (22) attempt to fill the quantitative information gap regarding social security and development. The latter two analyzed social insurance expenditures in seven developed nations at five points in time between 1907 and 1960. Their findings, showing a significant but *relatively* low correlation between social insurance and economic growth, suggest that there are other 'explanatory variables' in these relationships.

Galenson examined data from 40 countries — 20 developed, ten semideveloped and ten underdeveloped — comparing their social security expenditures with rates of economic growth in the industrial sector over a decade. His findings support Singer's views that there is a critical minimum level of social investment that must be reached before social improvement can feed back effectively into the economic development process. In Galenson's view, social security's potential for increasing productivity is greatest at 'intermediate' stages of development: at such stages, characterized by a substantial investment of capital and a sizable growth in the labor force, the marginal value of increases in production is high. When, however, almost the entire population becomes white-collar and quite affluent (in developed countries), the value of benefits furnished by social security declines in relation to personal income and privately provided benefits. As a result, the effect of social security on productivity may decline.

Paukert employs the level of social security expenditures as an explanatory variable for international differences in redistribution of income (23). He concludes that in developed countries, the flow of benefits to the lower income groups outweighs any regressive taxation. Hence, in these countries, the movement is 'from top to bottom'. But in less developed countries, the movement is 'from the top and the bottom to the center'. How to counter the movement of income from the bottom is an important policy issue.

Both Rimlinger — concentrating on Western nations undergoing rapid industrialization (24) — and Rohrlich — dealing with underdeveloped countries (25) — conclude that the emergence of some form of social security is inevitable as countries move from agrarian to industrial societies; that experience elsewhere can illumine some of the relevant questions; but that there is no single set of guidelines for selecting a social security system at a given stage of development.

In closing remarks, Fisher recognizes that the competing needs of consumption and savings — current income maintenance and investment — are severe in developing nations (26). He believes, however, that 'the tasks of simultaneously providing more adequate social protection in the present and a more productive economy in the future can be mastered'. Overall, the thinking of participants at this seminar points in the direction of the position so eloquently argued by Titmuss in 1971 (27); namely, that going beyond sheer survival unquestionably requires a surplus of resources. But, equally important, a society's decision as to when survival has been assured and to what ends surplus resources can be allocated is shaped by ideological and political factors. This has been true in the past and will continue to be true in the future.

Writing in 1971, Higgins expressed doubts that 'development economists (or any economists, for that matter) have much to offer by way of a scientific approach to programming social security as part of the over-all development program' (28:55). These doubts originate from his study of social security functions in which he used traditional tools of economic analysis in an effort to quantify security objectives and fit them into existing economic planning patterns. He found, however, that there is no clear relationship between 'the degree of social security' and either individual or national income. In his view, existing econometric studies are broadly inconclusive as to the exact nature of the relationship between social security and economic growth. The fact that all over the world people want social security proves the existence of a 'social demand' for it; but, he argues, the evaluation of this demand is outside the scope of current economic analysis.

Rys believes that Higgins' findings support his own position that social security ought to be designed to help attain social, rather than economic, objectives of planning. At the same time, he recognizes that the economic side-effects of social security programs are important, more so in developing than in industrialized countries (29:337,342).

Socio-political Factors and Social Security. Some social scientists have argued that 'politics of welfare' deserve to be studied in a comparative context, especially because only in this way is it possible to overcome cultural relativism inherent in specific political manifestations in different countries (30:207). A political perspective on policy, more so than other approaches, is likely to integrate aspects of the social environment that must be considered when formulating or implementing policy. In turn, it is the social environment that influences the minds and actions of decision-makers (1). Nevertheless, this area of analysis has been neglected until fairly recently so that most studies of the political process as a determinant in social security policy have appeared in the last decade.

Mencher's study (1967) of economic security policies in Great Britain and the United States since the sixteenth century is included here because it explores not only the two countries' social and economic order but also their dominant political and cultural patterns.

The Impact of Social Security on Society 137

He divides the 400-year period under consideration into four segments: the mercantilist era; from mercantilism to laissez-faire; the era of laissez-faire; and the era of movement toward the welfare state. His analysis of income security policies in each of these periods, in addition to providing a historical perspective, uncovers the ideological roots of human behavior and motivation in the social security domain. Mencher found that the theme that has dominated the two societies since mercantilism has been the 'shifting balance between the concepts of status and contract' (31:405) seen as inherently in conflict. It was not until the emergence of the welfare state that

> The earlier dichotomy between a society in which the individual's interests were subordinated to his membership in the whole and a society in which the whole gave way to the interests of the individual was no longer necessarily tenable. The former abstract notions of natural law and human nature, the stumbling blocks to imaginative social reform, had lost much of their magical appeal, and in their place there was a gradual proliferation of the rights of man and the goals of social justice (31:406−7).

Mencher shows that often, apparent similarities between the two countries are superficial. Up to the Civil War, the United States did not have provisions that could be considered as 'public welfare', whereas Great Britain already had a firmly established poor law system. It was not until the latter part of the nineteenth century that the United States began to build a foundation for its public welfare institution, and it was not until the end of that century, 'as the social and economic developments of the two nations converged' (31:405), that the earlier traditional values came to the fore and brought about a greater similarity in policies governing economic security. For both countries, the movement toward the welfare state has created many and complex problems — social and economic — which demand new policies, new strategies, and new techniques (31:407).[4]

Rimlinger's study of social security in West Germany, England, France, the United States, and the Soviet Union was published in 1971 (32). His purpose was 'to put the issues of economic insecurity and the means of dealing with it into . . . the context of economic and social development' (32:vii). He paid special attention to the relationship between these countries' political institutions and the development of their social security programs. In regard to the countries chosen for study, he writes:

The countries compared are selected to reflect different economic, social, and political tendencies. They represent the traditions of liberalism and patriarchalism in the West and the tradition of Marxist socialism in the East. The time path of the study ranges from the preindustrial era to that of modern industrialism (32:7).

Thus, the three 'routes' leading to modern social security systems which he explored were the liberal tradition, paternalism and collectivism.

The main 'themes' that run through the study are: the changing nature of the problem as societies move from their preindustrial periods to mature industrialism; class relations as an influential factor in the development of protection from want; the political system as a determinant of this type of protection; the ways used to adapt social security to economic systems; and the changing positions in regard to the reciprocal rights and duties of the individual and the state. Although each of the three routes produces a different relationship between government provided benefits and changes in the social environment resulting from industrialization, certain inevitable outcomes are reached by all three. His analysis demonstrates, Rimlinger claims, 'that social security programs can be integrated with either pure market economies or centralized communist economies' (32:333), that they are essential under socialism as under capitalism, and that everywhere they are one of the major ways of securing a new status for the masses.

In an article published in 1973 (33), Heidenheimer attempts to identify the more significant contrasts between the priorities and allocation patterns in social security (as well as in health and education) evolved in the United States and West European countries — Great Britain, Sweden, and West Germany. Although the United States was about a generation behind Europe in introducing public social insurance and some other kinds of income maintenance programs, once introduced, these programs grew at rates that narrowed the distance between them. Explaining the differences in 'take off' and subsequent growth, Heidenheimer writes that

> The timing of the introduction of public pensions seems to have been determined by complex relationships between the growth of labor unions, the prevailing ideologies, and the strategies of social demand anticipation on the part of governments (33:317).

In regard to unions, for example, in Europe, governments resorted to a pre-emptive strategy of granting benefits to workers in hopes of containing their support for socialist parties. Prior to 1914, sizable segments of European upper classes found programs of social protection for working classes ideologically acceptable. This did not hold true for American upper classes. Furthermore, in the United States, the growth of workers' organizations was too slow and irregular to stimulate pre-emptive action. Additionally, in the United States reformers of the Progressive period, unlike their European counterparts,

> did not view existing governmental agencies, even at the national but especially at the local levels, as capable of assuming new administrative responsibilities. Later, state and local governments varied greatly with regard to even the formal provision for merit systems, and it was only the Social Security Act which forced merit systems on the states, as a condition for administering grant-aided public assistance programs. This and subsequent steps have only marginally improved the reputation of state and local bureaucracies, many of which are still frequently associated with corruption and scandal (33:326—7).

Heidenheimer hypothesizes, therefore, that political variables, such as political institutions and interest groups, have powerfully influenced the divergent allocation patterns. This notion needs to be tested further, he proposes, since it is not supported by some other 'respected' researchers.[5]

Heclo's excellent study (1974) addresses the development of unemployment insurance, old-age pensions, and national superannuation in Great Britain and Sweden during the last century (34). His aim was 'to assess the effect of democratic politics' on these programs and thus to gain an understanding of the political process 'and its relationship to the collective social choices embedded in public policy'. He defines social policy as 'state interventions designed to affect the free play of market forces in the interest of citizens' welfare' — interventions shaped by economic growth and social change, political developments, and policy inheritance. In political developments he includes such variables as percentage of population entitled to vote, party strengths, popular vote by party, and the civil service. The similarities and differences between the two countries are lucidly delineated and the complicated manner in which 'agents of policy development' — socio-economic changes, elections, parties, interest groups, administrators — enter into the decision-making process is masterfully unraveled.

In Heclo's view, each of these agents contributes to the unending process of policy development, but it is the bureaucracy that exerts the most telling influence, while ' "democratic" factors — elections and parties — are . . . much less significant in the development of the "Welfare State" than has often been suggested.' Bureaucracies (including ministers, members of commissions and task forces, Cabinet officials, and top policy-makers) exert themselves to remove what they believe to be deficiencies in policy, to propel new proposals forward for consideration, to support these proposals and to influence important others to do so. Among these 'others' are interest groups and key individuals, usually outside the government, concerned with particular welfare issues. Although 'officials have rarely been able to fire up, by themselves, sufficient political steam to create new policies *ex nihilo*', this does not diminish their influence because 'much of social policy development has been and remains an elaboration rather than redirection of the original liberal framework' (34:304). He calls this activity 'political learning' and contrasts the formulation of policy in the process of such learning with what takes place when policy is seen as the result of a shifting power struggle.

Heclo's study indicates that neither Great Britain nor Sweden has solved the ancient dilemmas surrounding the provision of income support to the able-bodied; that in relation to old-age pensions government actions were not expressions of the ideology of the party in power but rather 'correctives for the perceived difficulties of past policies', and that no one has yet succeeded in proposing social policy capable of winning 'general and permanent assent'.

In a work concerned with comparative public policy in Europe and America, authored by three scholars (1975), Heclo wrote the chapter on income maintenance — usually the largest item in government spending in rich nations. He concentrates on social insurance and public assistance (these 'more overt' programs being prominent in welfare state political controversies), but emphasizes the need for harmonization because 'what is done in any one area of policy greatly affects what can be done in other areas' (35:213) and because distinctions between social insurance and public assistance are becoming more and more 'blurred'. Particularly decisive for income maintenance are tax systems which preserve the disposable income of some and diminish it for others; the often 'heavy element of income subsidy for social or political purposes' in public and publicly subsidized private employment; and changes in earnings levels brought about by government intervention in the labor market.

The Impact of Social Security on Society

Heclo's analysis of the two 'more overt' programs ranges over a network of determining factors: dates of first statutory programs, political and economic variables, experience with administering them, relationship between the bureaucracy and these programs as they evolve. In regard to all of them, he draws out a number of general conclusions, some that confirm the findings of other scholars, others that to an important degree are original with him. He writes, for example, that

> It is significant that one can discuss the growth of programs, coverage, and standards without necessarily referring to the differences between political systems. The same basic income support programs can be found in democratic and nondemocratic countries, in countries with one, two, or many political parties, in federal as well as unitary states. Nor does spending on these programs appear to differ significantly because of differing political arrangements (35:190).

But he argues that major exceptions can be found to each of the 'aggregate' factors laid down by Wilensky as associated with higher expenditures on social security by rich nations (more politically centralized government, stronger working-class organizations, less influential military interests, and less prominent or unified middle classes). Heclo's most provocative contribution resides in illumining the role of bureaucracy in social insurance evolution. Bureaucrats, he again maintains, have been important in introducing social insurance and 'even more important in the continuing evolution of [social insurance] policies'. To support this position, he examined recent policy developments in West Germany, Great Britain, Sweden, and the United States. He stresses that

> The pivotal position of government administrators stems from their remaining at the center of policy making despite political vicissitudes, from their having the specific knowledge to deal with detailed policies and new alternatives, and from their being involved in day-to-day operations so as to discover prevalent weaknesses that are in need of correction (35:205)

but that this does not relegate parties, interest groups, and elections to a secondary role.

In order to show the reader how the 'kaleidoscopic interaction' of the many income support programs available in developed nations affects clients, Heclo analyzes the income and status of the one-parent family in the four countries. By concentrating on this one client group, he demonstrates the value of a disaggregated analysis which does not obscure or lose vital information necessary for a more meaningful understanding of policy. In 'practicable politics and human lives', he writes, 'these program details matter greatly' (35:210).

Leman's thoughtful article (1977) explores differences in the political contexts of Canada and the United States and their implications for the social security policy-making process. He maintains that in Canada this process has been a continuous one, with major steps (in 1927, 1951, and 1965) occurring in times of relative prosperity; in contrast, in the United States the 1935 Social Security Act was passed in the crisis of the Depression with later amendments confirming to the Act — hence, continuous versus episodic development. He argues that the major reason for the episodic scenario in the United States is the country's division of power at both national and regional levels.

> This arrangement often prevents elections, bureaucracies, or others from achieving important changes in policy. No single agent has the initiative when stalemate prevails . . . Not only does a program become institutionalized, it becomes subject to empire-building . . . [particularly] a program with as broad appeal as Social Security . . . (36:264).

Canada can innovate, replace existing programs or curtail their growth so that later new programs can be added on top of them, without crises. Yet, Canada lacks the centralized political structure associated with these features. Leman thinks that the explanation for this parodox lies in a certain kind of regionalism:

> a unique two-party system that gives a Parliamentary foothold to regionally based third parties, and hence provides a platform for their proposals, [and] . . . a federal-provincial system of shared jurisdiction whose tendency toward deadlock injects special urgency into policy-making (36:280–1).

Leman contrasts Heclo's model of continuous policy development in Great Britain and Sweden with 'political learning' that occurs through crises in the United States and Canada: in the United States, because crises are not seen as endangering the survival of the political order; in Canada, because they are seen in this light and must, therefore, remain latent.

The book published by Furniss and Tilton (1977) 'attempts to develop a perspective which will elucidate the structural characteristics and political possibilities of advanced western societies' (37:x) in social welfare policy choices. The first half of the book is devoted to a vigorous defense of the authors' preference for a 'radically democratic and egalitarian *social welfare state*', rather than for the 'corporate-oriented *positive state*' or the '*social security state*' — the nature of these three states exemplified by Sweden, United States, and Great Britain, respectively. This defense argues for the values on which the authors believe the welfare state is based, and attempts to show how this state can 'improve the functioning of a capitalist economy', how it can 'redress the distributional inequity' resulting from unregulated markets, and how it can enhance participatory democracy and 'give public guidance to community life'. The defense also attempts to answer criticisms of the welfare state, from both conservative and radical quarters.

Furniss and Tilton then proceed to a comparison of the 'origins, structure, and performance' of welfare policies in Britain, Sweden, and the United States, in the process clarifying their strengths, weaknesses, limitations, and potentials. This analysis draws on social, economic, political and 'attitudinal' features of each country as they evolved from the Elizabethan Poor Law in Britain, from the early 1900s in Sweden, and from the end of the nineteenth century in the United States. In their final chapter, the two authors propose a nine-point program that in their opinion 'tackles the system as a whole rather than simply tending to particular details'. Proposals that deal most directly with social security include 'maximalist full employment', 'a national health service' (a public insurance program covering health costs is considered second-best but acceptable), 'housing allowances', 'a public pension system', and 'a guaranteed annual income'. The authors' discussion of problems that would arise in implementation and of objections they anticipate is brief, simply a blueprint.

One thought-provoking aspect of this book is the authors' rejection as useless the classifications of political regimes as 'totalitarian', 'democratic', 'capitalist', 'communist', 'industrial', and 'post-industrial'; and as limiting and obscurantist, the political categories of 'radical', 'liberal', and 'conservative'. The book is distinguished by its emphasis throughout on the primordial importance of a distinct set of values in shaping welfare policy as well as in creating instruments to implement it. For Furniss and Tilton, deliberately desirous of presenting a value-oriented analysis, the values that constitute the major goals of policy and therefore, the context within which political choices must be made, are 'equality, liberty, democracy, security, solidarity, and economic efficiency. . .' (37:203). It is in relation to these normative standards, they claim, that the 'moral inadequacy' of the *positive* (American) *state* is revealed.

Social Security and National Social Policy. In his study of social security schemes in ten Western democracies (1973), Kaim-Caudle examined five programs: employment injury, temporary disability, old age and invalidity, unemployment, and family endowment. His choice of countries was influenced by their having several significant characteristics in common; namely, 'a relatively high average standard of living, their governments require the support of the electorate at regular intervals, most of their people are of European stock, and they speak one of the Germanic languages' (38:14). His choice of programs was influenced by his desire to follow the definition and scope of the term 'social security' adopted by the ILO.[6] His three objectives were (1) 'to heighten the reader's understanding of the nature and implications of the social security provisions of his own society', (2) 'to enable him to learn from the experiences from the different provisions of other societies', and (3) 'to make him familiar with an important part of the social organization of other countries' (38:vii). Kaim-Caudle focused on social policy via four approaches: 'a brief history of the provisions in force in 1969, the economic and social implications of these provisions and the general direction in which benefit levels have moved' (38:290). For this task he amassed a large amount of information presenting it in such minute descriptive detail that it obscures the kind of analytic view the author enunciated in his objectives. Overall, Kaim-Caudle found that major influences on the level and nature of social security provisions emanate from 'policy considerations', demographic trends and economic levels. As he himself notes, however, he left unanswered three questions often posed by those concerned with social policy: why the differences between the countries' social security provisions? why the differences in their benefit levels? to what extent do existing programs meet existing social needs? Reasons that make it difficult to answer these questions are given in the concluding chapter.

The two monographs published simultaneously by Lawson and Reed

The Impact of Social Security on Society 145

(1975) are centered on comparing policy in social security (and medical care) in Britain and the Continent, and in social security (and medical care) in countries of the European Community. The major conclusion that emerges from their careful examination is that it is the differences, rather then similarities, in approaches to social security (and medical care) that must be emphasized. They write:

> Indeed, when one considers some of the practical issues involved in European integration, the most important point to be stressed is the great variety of provisions, procedures, and structures, not only between the different countries but also within them . . . [If] the Community attempts to make serious moves [to integrate, rather than merely co-ordinate, social policies], it will have to face squarely the fact that many of the differences are not purely technical in character. They also reflect the numerous ways in which social problems can be viewed and tackled, or not tackled; and this, in turn, reflects the long-standing and still quite profound differences between countries in attitudes to social relationships and to the responsibilities of the state and the individual (39:34).

The reasons for these differences are discussed from a historical perspective. In West Germany, for example, the influence of institutions and practices associated with Bismarck's reforms is still felt in the country's strong work orientation, the most distinctive aspect of its social policy. In France, on the other hand, the most distinctive feature has been the emphasis on provisions for the family, also going back to the late nineteenth century. Influenced 'by the Catholic emphasis on a "social wage" proportional to the needs of the family', many employers 'set up occupational family allowance schemes' (39:35). While France and Belgium still have the most generous family allowances and the most favorable tax treatment of families in the EEC, they lag behind other countries in pensions. Differences in financing health insurance likewise can be traced to historical developments. But, in addition, the reimbursement principle, brought into being by the political strength of the medical professions, is dominant in France and Belgium. Patients in these two countries 'are expected to pay for most medical services, and are then reimbursed up to 80 percent of a tariff of fees which is fixed by the social insurance agencies in negotiation with the medical profession' (39:36).

Lawson and Reed demonstrate that to develop common social policies in the EEC countries is an extremely complicated undertaking.

Nevertheless, they point to convergence at many points that has taken place in the past 20 years and conclude that a more common approach to social policy in the future should not be ruled out.

An article by Minkoff and Turgeon (1977) compares the Soviet income maintenance program with those of countries of the Soviet bloc (Bulgaria, Czechoslovakia, the German Democratic Republic (GDR), Hungary, Poland and Rumania). Some comparisons with programs in capitalist states are also made. They define income maintenance as 'embracing only those measures that are designed to substitute for the interrupted or discontinued customary earnings of employees' (40:178); consequently, their analysis is confined almost entirely to the industrial labor force.

The two authors begin by presenting what they consider to be the five principles of Soviet income maintenance: nonuniversality, especially as it discriminates against the agricultural population; variations in the level of benefits in the industrial sector by occupation; tying of benefits to earnings; guaranteeing employment and hence, the absence of unemployment compensation (this type of social insurance was discontinued in 1930); exclusive state responsibility for income maintenance and its funding for the nonagricultural labor force. These principles are briefly discussed and comparisons are made with Soviet bloc countries; a caustic attack on capitalist countries for their failure to prevent unemployment and subemployment is made.

The comparison itself takes in the sick benefit, old-age, disability and survivor pensions, and special provisions for women. Similarities and differences, strengths and weaknesses are clearly brought out. The aim is to show the degree of income protection offered to the populations of the studied countries, to ascertain the extent to which the bloc countries imitate the Soviet model, and to point out which ones provide the most equitable benefits. The two authors use descriptions of program to 'illustrate how the Soviet program is designed to further the government's socio-economic goals' (40:177) — quite often, it seems, to the detriment of welfare objectives in which the recipients are no doubt deeply interested. The weaker the recipient (from a health and/or social point of view), the worse his/her lot: disabled pensioners are described as 'impoverished'; and 'destitution stalks the lives of survivorship pensioners'. It is not indicated how impoverishment and destitution are measured. The single measure of the level of support provided is the percentage of current average wage it represents. Using this measure, Minkoff and Turgeon find that with the exception of GDR, the socialist countries 'furnish a very respectable level of support for *newly retiring* persons' (40:193, emphasis added) but they also note that none make 'provision for regular periodic increases in benefits . . . Thus, in these countries, the income of pensioners tends over extended periods to lag behind the constantly rising standard of living' (40:182). The most generous are the sick and maternity benefits. Minkoff and Turgeon (like Kallgren and Madison) discern an extensive use of incentives in social security policies, both to retain individuals in the labor force and presumably, to increase their productivity.

In their final, summarizing table the two authors rank the seven socialist countries in relation to eight variables of income-maintenance programs (1 = best). The Soviet Union is not best on any of them; it earns a '2' on only one variable (sick benefit); a '3' on two (employment required and the payment rate for a dependent and two children in disability pensions); for the remaining five variables, it is ranked '6' and '7'.

In his comparison of social security programs in Sweden, Yugoslavia, and Japan (1977), Woodsworth examines the manner in which the social security programs of each country relate to each other and how they reflect the political and cultural traditions of their national environments. This he does 'in order to get behind the surface resemblances of national programs'. He selected Sweden 'because of its socialist politics, capitalist economy, and industrial success; Yugoslavia because of its decentralized communist politics and style of industrial self-management; Japan because of the paternalistic, technologically efficient and integrated management of both government and industry' (41:6). In addition to describing each system's coverage, eligibility, contributions, and benefits, he gives some attention to questions of management and as a background, sketches in a brief portrait of each country's political, demographic and economic features. In concluding statements for each country, he attempts to highlight the major characteristics of these elements, to clarify the intent of social policy, and to prognosticate possible future developments. In the final chapter, he compares goals, benefits, participation and power in the three countries, and draws out some of their implications for the Canadian system of social security.

In terms of goals, Woodsworth found that 'all three countries tend to look for collective solutions, even though there are wide differences in the structures expressing their collective goals, and corresponding variations in the public acceptance of differences in levels of income or social class' (41:133). Work is the basic condition of eligibility in all three; when eligibility is based on membership in society rather than on work, benefits are much lower. While Sweden and Yugoslavia strive for equalization, this is not the case in Japan. Yet the value system represented by wide coverage, less disparity in benefits, and wider distribution of statuses and roles (as in Sweden and Yugoslavia) does not necessarily produce a better distribution of goods and a greater feeling of security than programs with wide disparities and central management (as in Japan) — at least not in the short run. In regard to material aspects of benefits, similarities outnumber differences: all have cash sickness benefits, including allowances for pregnancy and maternity designed to approximate the worker's standard of living; all provide retirement, disability and survivors' pensions but Woodsworth found it difficult to compare the actual benefits because of the complexity of formulae in each country; principles governing manpower policy and unemployment insurance are the same, less effective in Yugoslavia because of its decentralized pattern of management.

As for participation and power, in Yugoslavia contributions for all types of social security benefits are assessed against the enterprise as the collective economic base of the community, and since each individual is a member, he has to participate in decision-making. In Sweden, contributions made by individuals confer the right to take part in decision-making in social policy. In Japan, concentration of power at the top — as well as a wide range of inequities in benefits — seem to be acceptable because 'roles are at least clearly defined and assured' (41:139). For Woodsworth the major question of social policy is 'how political and economic power relate to each other, and how the worker relates to both, as contributor and as policy-maker. The form of relationships of structures carrying these powers and their legitimacy in the historical understanding of the people' (41:145) will determine what is provided by social security and how the provisions are implemented.

Policy Issues. World-wide, developments in social security and the impact they make on the society at large reflect, more or less emphatically, the detailed and constantly evolving issues brought to light by single-country studies (Chapter 5). But there are some issues among those that cross national boundaries that are especially pervasive and important.

Everywhere a fundamental issue that begets a large brood of subsumed questions revolves around what should be the major goals of

The Impact of Social Security on Society

social security — to prevent poverty by providing a floor below which no one would be allowed to fall, to replace income, to provide income security? Can or should social security be expected to serve as the main force in preventing poverty and as the main protector of those who experience it after all, or should at least the function of prevention be allocated throughout the economy, that is, to measures that implement employment, fiscal, health, educational, housing and many other social policies?

Closely related to these questions is the issue around the role of social security in income redistribution, assuming that this is a desirable goal from a social welfare perspective. Just as social security now prevents some poverty and certainly shields many from its most harmful effects, so it does redistribute income in some measure. The problem is one of degree. Can its redistributive potential be strengthened within traditional national frameworks? In developing countries, can the flow of benefits be directed to redistribute income from the top and middle groups to the ones at the bottom instead of from the top and the bottom to the middle, as is now the case? In developed countries, can the movement from top to bottom be strengthened by reducing the weight of regressive taxation?

In industrialized countries the tendency is to view poverty as a relative rather than an absolute concept. Despite substantial and growing allocations of financial resources to income maintenance — both in absolute terms and as proportions of their GNP — these countries have been unable to do away with relative poverty. How can they deal with this paradoxical situation? Can they reduce poverty and increase benefits for all in order to cope with inflation while, at the same time, keeping down costs to a level that will not become unbearably burdensome? Or should these functions as well be allocated to broader economic measures such as the fixing of general and minimum wages, putting in place anti-inflationary legislation, providing employment for the unemployed, etc.?

There is some evidence that social security provisions generate incentives and/or supports that affect economic behavior. At least indirectly, therefore, they affect productivity. This seems to hold at certain stages in the movement of developing countries toward higher economic levels — not so much in developed countries where, in fact, the reverse may be true. Does this mean that social security should have, by design, built-in incentives to higher productivity in developing countries but not in the rich nations? Or are incentives inappropriate because tying benefits to wages (which reflect productivity) relegates to a disadvantaged position the weakest segments of the population and thus endangers welfare objectives — to say nothing of deterring the achievement of social justice? In regard to the able-bodied who are victimized by contingencies that often accompany industrialization (unemployment, unequal opportunities, etc.), how is social security to provide decent protection without destroying their incentive to work?

In some countries, social security and welfare services are integrated. This is in order to endow cash benefits with the ability to improve social adaptation thereby helping beneficiaries to use income supports to greatest advantage. Social adaptation, unlike mass collective provision personified by benefits as of right, calls for diversification, individualization, decentralization — all combining to produce or enhance a qualitative (in contrast to a largely quantitative) dimension in social security. Is this compatible with its goals?

Summary. Like single-country studies, cross-national research has produced a large amount of information. Nor surprisingly, some questions have been researched more thoroughly than others. Thus, the economic and institutional factors that explain variations in social security expenditures, the role of social security in development, and its effect on income redistribution have been more extensively analyzed than its relationship to social and economic policy as a whole, reasons why the need for income conditioned transfers (public assistance) has not decreased, why the rise in benefit levels does not necessarily keep pace with economic growth, and why the 'quality of life' that social security makes possible still smacks of charity for many.

What has been learned, however, is impressive. There is by now universal recognition that social security is essential for a smooth transition to an industrial society and that it is just as essential under socialism as under capitalism. This is demonstrated by the tremendous expansion of programs since World War I, most of them striving to respond, more or less successfully, to rising expectations for protection against want by expanding coverage, raising benefit levels, and emphasizing the receipt of benefits as of right — the latter personifying the movement away from abstract notions of natural law and human nature to rights of man and social justice. At the same time, there are apparent great variations in provisions, procedures and structures between countries, as well as differences in dates at which social security is introduced, its value base, its rate of growth, and its direction. Some similarities and a slow convergence at some points are, however, observable.

There is also visible a growing recognition that external societal factors importantly affect the formation and development of social security policy and planning, that this policy is, in fact, part and parcel of a given society's overall socio-economic aspirations, and itself influences the direction and nature of these aspirations. Among factors that strengthen the impact of social security on a given society by providing the more comprehensive and generous protection, the most potent are its age, its geographic location, and the level of its society's economic development — not the type of economic system. As to age, there is some evidence that at least in some parts of the world the timing of the introduction of social security is influenced by relationships between the growth of labor unions, the prevailing ideology and the strategies a government uses to anticipate social demand. In regard to geography, it appears that proximity facilitates the spread of ideas. In developed nations, the level of economic development is an underlying but not an immediate determining influence on social security; in developing nations, a critical minimum level must be reached before resources can be allocated to social security.

In both, however, values, organizational capacities and politics are equally important. As to the political arena, there is some disagreement about who the really important players are. Some hold that it is the ruling and the working classes, in combat; others find that it is the bureaucracy that exerts the most telling influence while democratic factors such as elections and parties are much less significant. Still others plump for a group of interacting players — the changing character of social problems, social class relations, the political system, and changes in the reciprocal rights and duties of the individual and the state.

All this suggests that social security provisions are not automatic responses to any single force, but rather to several deeper strains affecting the organization and the distinctive features of the society. Consequently, knowledge and understanding of what is involved in social security policy would be greatly improved if economic and socio-political analyses in relation to it were combined, instead of continuing to pursue their separate paths.

Notes

1. Mouton does not include North Africa because he wishes to make his work comparable to a 1961 analysis and because there are wide differences between North Africa and the rest of the continent. The 1961 study is 'Social Security in Africa South of the Sahara', *International Labour Review*, lxxxiv, no. 3 (September 1961), pp. 144–74.

2. Cutright's cross-national linkage of macro-quantitative aggregate analysis to policy analysis was criticized by Rys as not particularly relevant. Writes Rys:

> In view of the underdeveloped state of research in this field, the first relationships to be examined should be those which are known to be relevant to the phenomenon under investigation, and only subsequently should the examination be extended to relationships which may be interesting but cannot in advance be considered relevant. It would be advisable to give priority to factors which in the socio-economic environment of the institution observed, are in close relationship to it and have a direct bearing on its formation and development rather than to the factors of general economic or cultural environment which are connected with the institution observed only inasmuch as all phenomena are inter-connected in a social whole (Rys, 'Comparative Studies of Social Security', p. 266).

3. Aaron uses the definition of social security developed by the ILO in *The Cost of Social Security 1949–57* (ILO, Geneva, 1961). It includes not only core programs such as old age insurance, family allowances, health insurance, and other pensions and direct payments, but also assistance, public relief, public health expenditures, pension programs for civil servants, former members of the armed services and war victims, and workmen's compensation. He excludes programs not administered by public, semi-public, or autonomous agencies, although workmen's compensation is included even if the carrier is a private insurance company.

4. Many of the studies concerned with historical development of social security policy in Great Britain listed under single-country studies (see footnote 1 in *Social Security – Single-Country Studies*) do discuss the influence of British policies on what took place in the United States and in some instances, make limited comparisons. A book that concentrates on the comparative aspects in a somewhat more focused manner is Martin, E. W. (ed.) *Comparative Social Welfare* (London, George Allen and Unwin, 1972).

5. Marshall stressed the major importance of the relationships between bureaucracies, their clients and professional groups when it came to initiating and supporting social welfare legislation (*Social Policy*). The same point was made by Rys. He listed as especially influential, interest groups, trade unions, employers' confederations, mutual benefit societies, the private insurance industry, pensioners' organizations, and service personnel associations ('Comparative Studies of Social Security').

6. The ILO refers to rights of individuals to provisions which have the object of (a) granting curative or preventive medical care; (b) maintaining income in case of involuntary loss of earnings or of an important part of earnings, or (c) granting supplementary incomes to persons having family responsibilities.

References

1. Rys, 'Comparative Studies of Social Security'.
2. Rohrlich, 'Social Security in World-Wide Perspective'.
3. Fisher, Paul, 'Developments and Trends in Social Security Throughout the World, 1967–69', Address delivered at the XVIIth General Assembly of the ISSA, Cologne, West Germany, September 1970. Mimeographed.
4. Rohrlich, George F., *Social Security for the Aged: International Perspectives*, A Working Paper Prepared for a Hearing on 'International Perspectives on the Economics of Aging', August 25, 1969. Special Committee on Aging, US Senate (US Government Printing Office, 1969).
5. Perrin, Guy, 'Reflections on Fifty Years of Social Security', *International Labour Review*, 99, no. 3 (March 1969), pp. 249–92.
6. Perrin, Guy, 'The Future of Social Security', *International Social Security Review*, xxii, no. 1 (1969), pp. 3–28.
7. Mouton, *Social Security in Africa*.
8. Tracy, Martin B., 'World Developments and Trends in Social Security', *Social Security Bulletin*, 39, no. 4 (April 1976), pp. 14–22.
9. Gordon, Margaret S., *The Economics of Welfare Policies* (New York, Columbia University Press, 1963).
10. Cutright, Phillips, 'Political Structure'.
11. Aaron, Henry, 'Social Security: International Comparisons', pp. 13–48 in Eckstein, Otto (ed.) *Studies in the Economics of Income Maintenance* (Washington, DC, The Brookings Institution, National Committee on Government Finance, 1967).
12. Pryor, *Public Expenditures*.
13. Kilby and Taira, 'Differences in Social Security Development'.
14. Wilensky, Harold L., *The Welfare State and Equality. Structural and Ideological Roots of Public Expenditures* (Berkeley, University of California Press, 1975).
15. Miller, Leonard S., 'The Structural Determinants of the Welfare Effort: A Critique and a Contribution', *Social Service Review*, 50, no. 1 (March 1976), pp. 57–79.
16. Caputo, David A., 'New Perspectives on the Public Policy Implications of Defense and Welfare Expenditures in Four Modern Democracies: 1950–70', *Policy Sciences*, iv (1975), pp. 423–46.
17. OECD, *Public Expenditure on Income Maintenance Programmes* (Paris, France, July 1976), Studies in Resource Allocation. no. 3.
18. Laroque, Pierre, 'Social Security and Social Development', *Bulletin of the International Social Security Association*, xix, nos. 3–4 (March–April 1966), pp. 83–90.
19. Kassalow, Everett M., 'Introduction', pp. 1–20 in Kassalow, Everett M. (ed.) *The Role of Social Security in Economic Development* (Washington, DC, HEW, Social Security Administration. Office of Research and Statistics, Research Report no. 27, 1968).
20. Singer, Hans W., 'Social Factors in Development: an Overview with Special Emphasis on Social Security', pp. 21–38 in *ibid*.
21. Galenson, Walter, 'A Quantitative Approach to Social Security and Economic Development', pp. 51–66 in *ibid*.
22. Tinbergen, Jan and Bouwmeesters, Jan, 'The Role of Social Security as Seen by the Development Planner', pp. 39–50 in *ibid*.
23. Paukert, Felix, 'Social Security and Income Redistribution: Comparative Experience', pp. 101–28 in *ibid*.
24. Rimlinger, Gaston, 'Social Security and Industrialization: the Western

154   The Impact of Social Security on Society

Experience, with Possible Lessons for the Less Developed Nations', pp. 129–54 in *ibid*.
    25. Rohrlich, George F., 'Social Security and Economic Development: the Evaluation of Program Needs at Successive Stages of Development', pp. 187–210 in *ibid*.
    26. Fisher, Paul, 'Social Security and Development Planning', pp. 239–59 in *ibid*.
    27. Titmuss, *The Gift Relationship*.
    28. Higgins, Benjamin, 'Planning Allocations for Social Development', *International Social Development Review*, no. 3 (1971), pp. 47–56.
    29. Rys, Vladimir, 'Problems of Social Security Planning in Industrialized and Developing Countries', *International Social Security Review*, nos. 2–3 (1974), pp. 314–46.
    30. Aiyar, Sadashin Prahakar, 'Introduction', pp. xv–xxiii in Aiyar, S. P. (ed.) *Perspectives on the Welfare State* (Bombay, Manaktala and Sons, 1966).
    31. Mencher, Samuel, *Poor Law to Poverty Program. Economic Security Policy in Britain and the United States* (University of Pittsburgh Press, 1967).
    32. 'Rimlinger, Gaston V., *Welfare Policy and Industrialization in Europe, America and Russia* (New York, John Wiley and Sons, 1971).
    33. Heidenheimer, Arnold J., 'The Politics of Public Education, Health and Welfare in the USA and Western Europe: How Growth and Reform Potentials Have Differed', *British Journal of Political Science*, 3, Part 3 (July 1973), pp. 315–40.
    34. Heclo, Hugh, *Modern Social Politics in Britain and Sweden. From Relief to Income Maintenance* (New Haven and London, Yale University Press, 1974).
    35. Heidenheimer, Heclo, Adams, *Comparative Public Policy*.
    36. Leman, Christopher, 'Patterns of Policy Development'.
    37. Furniss and Tilton, *The Case for the Welfare State*.
    38. Kaim-Caudle, *Comparative Social Policy and Social Security*.
    39. Lawson, Roger and Reed, Bruce, *Social Security in the European Community*. Lawson: *Social Security and Medical Care in Britain and the Continent*; Reed: *Social Security and Medical Care in the Context of the European Community* (London, Chatham House: PEP, 1975).
    40. Minkoff, Jack and Turgeon, Lynn, 'Income Maintenance in the Soviet Union in Eastern and Western Perspective', pp. 176–211 in Horowitz, Irving Louis (ed.) *Equity, Income and Policy. Comparative Studies in Three Worlds of Development* (New York, Praeger Publishers, 1977). A shorter version, entitled 'Income Maintenance in Eastern Europe', may be found in *Social Policy*, 6, no. 5 (March–April 1976), pp. 33–45.
    41. Woodsworth, David E., *Social Security and National Policy, Sweden, Yugoslavia, Japan* (Montreal and London, McGill–Queen's University Press, 1977).

7 SOCIAL SECURITY AND THE INDIVIDUAL

In recent years, concern about social protection for different population categories has become more pronounced, sparked by demographic trends, changes in family patterns, diversification of women's roles in the home and in the society at large, and pressures from a variety of interest groups. Attention centered on the aged has been gaining momentum as their number in the populations of many countries has increased, absolutely and relatively, and as the 'frail elderly' among them have become more numerous. Involved in the situation of the aged are changes in family patterns that reflect attempts to adjust to urbanization and industrialization, and the more insistent desire to fulfill rising social and economic expectations that, taken together, spell higher levels of well-being.

Concern about the social security position of women — catapulted into sharp focus by the movement to attain full legal, social and economic rights for women and to grant them equal status with men and by changes in women's occupational roles — became especially prominent in the 1970s resulting in numerous and wide-ranging studies. This burgeoning discussion has widened to include not only provisions for aged women who are no longer in the labor force or who have not worked outside the home, but also the rights under social security schemes of widows (young and old), divorced women, one-parent families (usually headed by women), and women whose employment is interrupted by pregnancy and maternity. In the course of this discussion the interdependence, substantive and philosophical, of provisions for women and men has been clarified, sometimes illumining more fundamental questions about the position of the sexes in modern societies.

As for children, a perennial area of concern, studies of what is done for them by social security are, predictably, tied into what is done for their families — whether the families are intact or broken, or headed by survivors of intact families or by parents who have not been legally married. That this concern should intensify is suggested by the fact that many countries are turning into aging societies, with relatively few children and rising numbers of elderly. Consequently, as the current demographic trends continue, children are increasingly becoming a scarce resource. This may lead to a more genuine view of children as perhaps the most valuable national asset in all societies which requires priority attention.

A crucial feature underlying the entire gamut of social security concerns is adequacy of benefits. Inevitably, the issues raised by adequacy lead to a consideration of the substantive features of public assistance and of the role this needs-related program plays in the total income support network. The limitations of cash provisions in meeting the diversified, individual social needs of those who come within the purview of social security lead, in turn, to an examination of the relationship between programs of cash benefits and programs of noncash services.

Aged. A 1977 OECD study of old-age pension schemes in member countries is a wide-ranging exposition which presents the emerging issues in this most important segment of social security within a context of interacting demographic, social and economic factors. Surveyed is the growth of the aged population, both in absolute terms and as a proportion of the active population, with projections into the 1980s. Traced is the historical development of principles underlying the various systems, giving rise to the three current categories of protection:

> collective retirement pensions for former workers, administered by the Social Security or by private institutions; individual assistance for the elderly; and basic pensions intended for all residents over a certain age (1:21).

Data for the three categories are presented in absolute numbers and as indices per thousand aged in the population. They demonstrate that while the number retired as former workers has increased steadily in both dimensions, the group receiving means-tested benefits has decreased. Similar data are given for survivors, revealing an upward curve. Figures on the amounts paid reveal a steady increase for the first category, but a decrease for the second: that is, for former workers in contrast to assistance recipients.

The entire galaxy of problems connected with old-age pensions (level of benefits, ancillary benefits, survivors' pensions and death grants, differences based on sex, pensions and taxation, adjustments required by inflation) is then discussed in sufficient detail to furnish a solid understanding of each problem's dimensions, the reasons for its persistence, and changes that may lead to acceptable solutions. There is evident a trend to relax the rules governing pensions in order to increase freedom of choice in regard to retirement age and the manner in which an individual stops working. That part-time work should be available for those who wish to continue to work is a position gaining in popularity. Although important improvements have been achieved in OECD countries, much still remains to be done before every old person in every member country receives a pension that provides a decent standard of living and before such payments are no longer, as is still too often the case, regarded as charity (1:177).

Women. In his article (1972), Laroque challenges the traditional principles underlying widows' pension schemes in the light of the evolution of ideas and realities in the modern world, particularly the demand for equality of treatment between the sexes. He begins his argument by noting that the rules governing widows' pensions have traditionally depended on three factors: assigning to a woman the status of her husband's dependent both in the family and in society; the material difficulties faced by a dependent widow and children; and 'the wider question of old age', that is, the fact that many women survive their husbands (women's average life-span is longer than men's in most countries and women are usually younger than their husbands). If a woman devoted herself entirely to her home during marriage, 'or if she worked for too short a time or was too poorly paid to gain entitlement to an adequate retirement pension', widowhood may reduce her standard of living to the level of indigence. It is the first factor, dependency upon the husband, that Laroque considers the most influential and at this stage of societal changes, the least defensible.

He then briefly analyzes 'the law as it stands', and concludes that

> All these rules, despite their differences, show how much the situation of the widow depends on that of her husband. Not only the conditions of entitlement but also the methods of calculating and paying the pension are governed by the constant concern to maintain the woman in a situation broadly corresponding to that which she would have had if she had continued to depend on her husband (2:3).

Laroque's criticisms of reasons behind the law as it stands are convincing and do open its basic philosophy to question. The author proposes a financial statute for widows based on the 'needs resulting from widowhood' – not on the loss of marital status. This statute outlines provisions suitable for the variety of circumstances that may be faced by widows, old and young, with or without children. Several of its features are likely to be especially controversial. He believes, for example, that (subject to relief of the burden arising out of the presence of dependent children) a woman of working age, after she has been helped to resume an occupation or to find a new one, 'must earn her living from it and so ensure her personal independence'. He thinks that in calculating old-age pensions, contributions into the social security fund should not be required of a woman during the years she devoted to bringing up young children, but that 'fictitious remuneration' equal to half of her husband's earnings should be counted as her earnings (if there are no young children but the woman stays home, the husband would contribute for her on half his salary). The effect of such changes, which Laroque views as logically flowing out of women's rights in the modern context, is to abolish widows' pensions – as well as to confer equal social security rights on widowers. He believes that the concept of widowhood can retain a social sense only if there is respect for the equality of husband and wife, of widower and widow.

In 1973 Haskins and Bixby published a study concerning entitlement of women to social security in five countries – Belgium, France, West Germany, Great Britain and the United States (3). Within the overall provisions governing each country's scheme, the authors present the main issues which elicit special concern. This is done clearly and cogently. The proposals for change that are being considered are then discussed, including an analysis of the reasons that generate them, and their probable effects on social security for women are examined. A careful reading yields a deeper understanding of the policy process in regard to the subject of study and how and why it differs between the studied countries.

The main issues in Belgium concern the family allowance program, the inequitable treatment of contributions and benefits of insured women as compared with men, and the need to protect more effectively the social security rights of women who temporarily leave the labor force to care for their children. In France concern centers on the 1972 amendments, designed to reflect France's continuing preoccupation with a pronatalist family policy and a greater commitment toward giving mothers a freer choice between remaining at home and working. The reform proposals in West Germany are chiefly concerned with the disadvantaged position of women in the old-age and survivors' insurance program. Great Britain has devised a new system for dealing with the rights of married women who build up their own retirement pensions: they now have the option of paying contributions to qualify for benefits on their own insurance or not paying contributions and relying on their husbands' insurance for a smaller range of benefits as dependents. In the United States social insurance has an uneven effect on women and men, partly because of economic and demographic factors outside the social security system and partly because of the diversity of women's roles.

Likewise in 1973, ISSA published a report of its conference on women and social security which took place the previous year (4). The conference's focus was on research then in progress in which ISSA members were involved. The two introductory papers surveyed the changing role of women in various societies, the second described current employment patterns of women in West Germany. Presentations of research studies which followed were grouped under five headings: long-term benefits for women; short-term benefits for women; benefits for women in the event of widowhood, divorce, or separation; family, maternity and child-care benefits; and social security for women in developing countries. These presentations, by participants from ten countries (Austria, USA, Canada, Belgium, Great Britain, France, Israel, Czechoslovakia, Hungary and Mexico), for the most part confined themselves to their own countries with only occasional references to Spain and Italy; the Mexican participant, however, discussed Latin America as a whole.

The tremendous scope of the issues that emerged precludes a detailed summation. Only some of the highlights will be mentioned in order to give the reader a notion of major policy implications suggested by the presented materials.

A paper on social security benefits for older women in the United States, based on two recent surveys conducted by the Social Security Administration, showed that the main characteristic of the American system is that it provides benefits to women both as dependents and as retired workers. In relation to questions posed by the assumption that wives should not be dependent on husbands, it was shown that although the increased labor force participation of women since World War II has substantially altered the basis upon which women receive social benefits, almost two-thirds of all wives and widows who are now 65 and over have been primarily dependent on their husbands' earnings throughout their lifetimes. It is not known how long it would take for this situation to change significantly. But it seems clear that for the near future both bases of entitlement, as dependents and as retired workers, must continue.

A paper on recent trends in benefits for widows, a particularly sensitive and unstable area, brought out priorities among problems that ought to be addressed by decision-makers, mindful of the legal situation and the continuing uncertainty that is likely to characterize legal developments due to the rapid social changes that shape advanced industrial societies. The most urgent current issues are related to the evolution of the occupational role of women and the demand for equality between the sexes. Addressing them is no easy matter because, in addition to the values involved, the conditions for eligibility to benefits are highly complicated. The presenter's findings indicated that there is a trend toward relaxing these conditions, by reducing the minimum age required to qualify, by increasing the income level beyond which entitlement is denied, and by modifying or eliminating conditions around the duration or date of marriage. But this does not mean that countries are moving to clear and precise solutions that would be generally acceptable: none of the modern pension systems recognize the unconditional right of a widow to receive a pension, although in some she is able to receive it because of invalidity or old age, without jeopardizing the granting of family benefit or orphan's allowances that favor widowed mothers. The presenter suggested a future policy in the following words:

> [It] should have due regard to the objectives of income maintenance inherent in the concept of social security, of equality of rights between men and women, of freedom of choice between occupational activity and household duties for persons with family responsibilities, of the social adjustment of widows during the initial period of widowhood and where appropriate of their subsequent re-entry into employment, and finally of the need to ensure adequate protection for children, which cannot in practice be distinguished from the protection of the surviving spouse. [All this should be] set within the broader perspective of assistance to incomplete families, where the surviving spouse with children is only one particular case (4:152–3).

A paper on the effect of maternity allowances on the employment of women in Czechoslovakia was based on a sample survey undertaken six months after the Maternity Allowance Act came into effect on July 1, 1970. The Act introduced maternity allowances for women employees giving birth to their second or subsequent child; this allowance was payable after completion of maternity leave until the child was one year of age. In 1971, an amendment extended the duration of the allowance until the child was two years old and also provided that the allowance was to be granted to all women regardless of whether or not they were employed before the birth of their second or subsequent child. The sample survey included ten branches of the national economy which were then employing 54.5 percent of all economically active women and 47.2 percent of the total labor force (men and women) in the branches concerned.

From its findings it was concluded that the rate of absenteeism on grounds of maternity is influenced by availability of maternity leaves and extended leaves of absence: the maternity allowance is a contributory factor in the almost one-third increase in the number of women deciding to take leave following the birth of their second and subsequent child. There are significant differences between different branches of the economy: favorable birth rates were found in textile and food industries and agriculture, but 'extremely unsatisfactory' ones in education. The replies of enterprise managers showed that the high absenteeism rate of female employees for reasons of maternity results in operational difficulties, and that many fear any further measures which might increase absenteeism.

The paper on 'the institutional protection of women in Latin America with special reference to social security systems' painted a sombre picture. In social security, 'a great disparity exists between the protection provided in law and the actual application of these norms'. Women participate in the labor force 'commonly in conditions that violate all the established principles'. There is a crying need for restructuring provisions in relation to maternity, job security, and general health and welfare of women, especially for family and self-employed workers. Economic conditions are such that women are obliged to take any kind of job and thus become a source of cheap labor. 'This at the same time means discrimination in wages without more benefits being granted than those specified in legal regulations, and sometimes not even these are obtained'. Their wages are often inferior to those of men. Cultural and socio-economic characteristics of Latin American societies relegate women to household duties and deny them access to education, and this, in turn, results in their educational levels being lower than those of men and hinders the application of equal rights for women for employment according to capacity. The high birth rate and excessive dependence on their families also restrict their training and employment opportunities. Provision of nurseries for working mothers, although required by law in a few countries, are not implemented.

In summing up the conference, Merriam noted that current attitudes and objectives relating to the treatment of women in social security systems exhibit serious ambiguities which will make more difficult the task of these systems to adapt to changing conditions. Questions of equity, for example, will be faced by them for some time to come. But there are also problems specific to social security that offer opportunities to 'shape the programs in advance of changes that we can see coming in the position and role of women — and men — in society'. Research can assist policy-makers in essential ways. She outlined three types of research which would be especially helpful: more factual information; research into the consequences of alternative forms of social welfare protection; and technical research.

Weise's article deals with pensions for housewives (non-working women) in ten countries: Belgium, Canada, Denmark, France, Great Britain, West Germany, Italy, Norway, Sweden, Switzerland (1976). He provides a straightforward description of what is available now and what is being discussed. He finds that approaches to this type of social provision 'vary according to the type of social security coverage already existing in the country and the objectives being pursued to make women more self-sufficient' (5:37). He discerns six main approaches

(1) the traditional system, under which wives become eligible for a dependency benefit based on the earnings-related pension of their husbands;
(2) the universal system, under which uniform benefits are awarded to all men and women who have reached the retirement age;
(3) options for voluntary contributions by working women under compulsory wage-related systems;
(4) voluntary contributions for the coverage of housewives;
(5) combining the retirement credits of husbands and wives or the splitting of such credits between them; and
(6) special retirement credits awarded to mothers on the basis of the number of children raised (5:37—8).

The 1977 OECD study on old-age pension schemes referred to earlier (1) contains a substantial amount of material that deals specifically with women. It makes clear that men and women are not always treated on a strictly equal basis. Differences relate to the statutory age at which the pension becomes payable, to the level of contributions, and to the level of benefits including supplements for a dependent spouse and benefits for the surviving spouse. Thus, in regard to level of benefits in earnings-related pensions, because of lower earnings and shorter contribution periods, women's pensions are usually smaller than men's. On the other hand, women live longer, so that on average, they receive pensions longer than men. Many schemes provide supplementary pensions to dependent wives but seldom to dependent husbands; even less frequent are survivors' pensions to widowers. Pension rights for married women in employment are handled in two ways: they either contribute to their own pensions but cannot cumulate them with benefits from their husbands' pensions and end up with the higher of the two; or, in line with what is considered a better solution (in Great Britain), they have two choices: to contribute and receive pensions in their own right at age 60, or not to contribute and draw only their husbands' supplementary pensions at age 65. In many countries a divorced wife who supports herself on alimony does not enjoy the same rights as a dependent wife. Her situation can become especially deprived when the husband remarries, retires or dies. In cases of remarriages, sharing of benefits between wives or paying a full survivor's pension to each wife are not satisfactory solutions: in the first instance, because none would get enough to live on; in the second, because it would be too costly. It is suggested that the best solution may be a flat-rate pension scheme for the whole population under which a divorced wife who has not remarried becomes entitled to benefits as any other single person upon reaching pensionable age.

Divorced persons. The 1972 ISSA conference on women referred to earlier (4) generated a widespread interest in the effect of divorce on the rights to social security benefits which resulted in the publication of a study on this subject by Cockburn and Haskins in 1976 (6). ISSA's members were especially concerned with this subject because in almost all countries of Europe and North America, there was taking place greater resort to divorce, on the one hand, and liberalization of divorce laws, on the other. The study presents an overview of provisions in 26 countries as they existed in 1974. As a background, the two authors give the available statistics on divorce rates in the studied countries and note the trend toward shorter marriages at the point of divorce.

Among many findings, several appear especially important. In regard to survivors' pensions for divorced wives the studied countries fell into four categories: those that grant such a pension only if the divorced woman meets certain qualifying conditions and *only* if she was also receiving alimony from her ex-husband at the time of his death (nine countries); those that grant it if she meets certain qualifying conditions (four countries); those which administer universal or assistance-based schemes which permit the divorced spouse, along with the widowed spouse (if there is one) and other women alone, to receive benefits which are in some cases subject to a means test (four countries); and those that do not grant such a pension (nine countries). This latter is a heterogeneous group which includes Belgium, Canada, Finland, France, Israel, Japan, Mexico, Romania and the USSR. For the 15 countries which sent in information as to whether provisions also apply to the divorced widower, only seven answered that they do. Incomplete data (from 17 countries) indicate that survivors' pensions under employment injury and occupational diseases schemes, if available, require that the divorced person be the recipient of alimony or maintenance from the ex-spouse.

In countries with universal-type family allowances (that is, programs not related to employment), divorce does not affect the right of children to continue to receive allowances. What has to be decided is to which parent are the allowances payable. In the great majority of cases it is the mother since it is with her that the child usually lives and who has the day-to-day care of the child. In two countries, Norway and Denmark, divorced as well as single mothers benefit from general allowances that are paid over and above the regular allowances. In countries that have earnings-related types of allowance programs, divorce may pose problems if the parent with whom the child lives is not working. In Western European countries, if the mother who is actually caring for the child is not working, the allowance is paid anyway. In Eastern European countries, in the relatively few cases when the mother is not working, the allowance continues on the insurance of the ex-husband if there is such insurance (presumably, when there is not, the allowance ceases).

Sickness cash benefits are restricted to those who are gainfully occupied. Consequently, unless the divorced spouse is working, she is normally not entitled to benefits. The same is true of unemployment insurance.

In 1977, Kirkpatrick published a short description of alimony and public income support provisions in 13 countries — Australia, Austria, Denmark, Finland, France, Great Britain, Israel, Netherlands, New Zealand, Norway, Poland, Sweden, and the United States (7). It is explained that when the divorced parent who is supposed to pay alimony fails to do so, 'the social welfare institution [which may have to provide assistance, particularly when dependent children are involved] often steps in to help locate the delinquent parent, tracing him through work records and, in some cases, instituting legal action to ensure payment' (7:1). How the tracing process is carried out and the problems and difficulties it encounters, are discussed. Examined as well are the two methods used to provide income support to divorced women whose alimony payments are in default; namely, assistance and advance maintenance grants. The latter, defined as 'a guaranteed public payment that is made available when private support obligations are not, or cannot be, met', originated in the Scandinavian countries and appears to be a more generous and less deterrent type of provision than the traditional assistance payment. Increasing interest has been shown in this innovative approach and by now, France, Israel, and Poland have established modified programs of advance maintenance grants.

One-parent Families. In 1975 ISSA published the report of a research project on income maintenance for one-parent families, undertaken at the request of the British Committee on One-Parent Families (8).[1] ISSA's study of five countries — Denmark, Norway, Sweden, West Germany and Netherlands — focused on the cash and cash-equivalent provisions, an almost bewildering array of diversified programs of allowances, grants, benefits, pensions and social assistance. Considered as well were maintenance advances and payments, education and training grants, housing allowances, day-care arrangements, and taxation regulations.

'Despite the complexities, and often contradictions, found within any nation's policies' (8:8), the researchers were able to discern several broad policy patterns. To begin with, in none of the five countries are one-parent families treated as absolutely distinct from or as completely identified with two-parent families, Within this range, 'some coherent variation' exists. Thus, Netherlands goes farthest on treating all families alike, with few 'concessions' to one-parent families. West Germany, its policy strongly work-oriented, goes farthest in meeting the needs of one-parent families through tax allowances and subsidized kindergartens and housing administered by employment authorities. The Scandinavian nations provide 'the most distinctive attention to single-parent families, and generally do so in ways which offer a higher proportion of family income support through non-means-tested aid'

(8:8). In this connection, the advance maintenance grants program (see earlier discussion) as a child-oriented method, obviates difficulties that usually arise when parents' income or cohabitation are checked; but this orientation does not necessarily provide sums 'sufficient nor intended to support fully the adult parent as such' (8:9). One feature is common to all the countries surveyed: the superior position afforded to widows.

The researchers conclude that 'no nation provides simple answers concerning how distinctively, "equally", or effectively one-parent families are treated by social policy' (8:158). They suggest that much can be learned from unsolved problems which exhibit 'strong cross-national similarities' despite differences in policy. Among such problems they include the finding that most single mothers receive *assistance* benefits subject to means tests: only widowed mothers' benefits are granted as 'of right', being part of the social insurance scheme. The child-oriented character of Scandinavian programs still leaves unsolved 'the problem of parental vulnerability once the child leaves the family unit, particularly where single mothers are not closely attached to the labor force' (8:59). Everywhere, the problems one-parent families face are interrelated which means that policies, if they are to be effective, must support each other – not always the case. The several services to which single-parent families must usually turn almost always lack internal consistency in their structure and eligibility conditions. Furthermore, policies are neither automatically operative nor are the services they govern easily accessible. These features bring about hardships more often for one-parent families than for other people. Means-tested programs which are based on common standards and which take account of the benefits each provides – so that they would be attuned to 'interlocking tests' – are rare. It became clear to the researchers that 'there is no single answer to the question of positive discrimination' (8:60) in income support provisions for single-parent families.

What they see as shown by their comparative analysis is 'that the choice facing society is not whether to have a family policy but what kind of family policy to have' (8:60).

Children. In a paper on guaranteed minimum income programs in foreign countries which he presented to a Congressional committee in 1968, Schnitzer analyzed family allowances – regular cash payments to families with children – in Canada, Denmark, France, Great Britain and Sweden (9). In these five countries, the family allowance comes closest to what can be considered a guaranteed income. In France, it is an important measure which, as a transfer payment, represents about 5 percent of national income, and can constitute a sizable proportion of personal income for lower income families. The allowance is less important in Great Britain. Since its introduction there in 1945, the rates had been changed only three times and in terms of real income, the allowance was less important in 1968 than in 1945. In Sweden, the allowance likewise represents a small proportion of total income to the typical Swedish family, but for lower income families with several children, this proportion is sizable. It has not kept up with the cost of living, however, and as a percentage of personal income has declined since its introduction in 1948. In Denmark the allowance discriminates between families on the basis of income: families below a prescribed income level receive a general allowance over and above the regular allowance. The general allowance decreases as family income rises to a prescribed minimum. In Canada, allowance payments, introduced in 1945, are low, but are of importance to low-income families with several children. The main differences between the studied countries are three: source of revenue, eligibility requirements, and rate of allowance (9:84–86).[2]

The report of an important conference concerned with the relationship of children's allowances to the economic welfare of children was published in 1968. A substantial part of the proceedings was given over to papers read by participants from four countries: Canada, France, Great Britain and Sweden. Since allowances in these countries were introduced and developed for a variety of reasons and aimed to achieve differing objectives, the specific provisions of their programs also differed. Yet, noted Burns in her concluding remarks, all four were strongly in favor of allowances,

> despite the fact that each indicated there were some shortcomings or inconsistencies in the programs. Thus, in Canada and Great Britain, it was noted, the levels of allowances have not kept pace with either the increases in other social security benefits or the rise of prices. Even in France and Sweden, where sizable adjustments have to some degree reflected price changes, the increases in children's allowances have not kept pace with the rising levels of national incomes and earnings. Except for Sweden, policies regarding exemptions on deductions for children under the income tax system have not been nationally coordinated with the payment of children's allowances. All four authors recognized that an effective

children's allowance program is costly, but regarded such a measure as an essential element in a comprehensive family welfare policy (10:185—6).

In 1972 Haanes-Olsen published a study of children's allowances in five Western type democracies (11). He selected the particular countries because they responded to different reasons for introducing allowances and because they represent different approaches to benefit patterns, actual and relative size of benefits and financing. Within a historical framework, he compares the size and composition of benefits, their relationship to earnings, to total social security expenditures, and to the Gross National Product, as well as financing and tax policies. He finds that perhaps the most striking development is the recent reliance upon general revenue financing, a fact which suggests that these countries are accepting the idea that the responsibility for bringing up children must be shared by all (11:28).

The Kafka and Underhill comparative study of certain aspects of family law in 16 European and Mediterranean countries (1974) is part of a larger investigation concerned with children of migrants, initiated by the International Union on Child Welfare (IUCW). 'Migrant' is defined in its widest sense as anyone working in a foreign country; in 1974, laws on migrants affected 12 million people. Part I of the study analyzes family allowances and compulsory maintenance provisions (12).

Migrant workers who bring their families with them are usually entitled to the same family benefits as the nationals of the country in which they are employed, although in some countries there are residence requirements. But for families of migrant workers who have been left behind the situation is complex because entitlement to family benefits as nationals of the country in which the worker is employed depends on the existence of a bilateral or multilateral agreement between the sending and the receiving country. Such agreements do exist in the countries studied and for the most part they support worker's right to family allowances according to the legislation of the country in which he is employed, even if his children are living abroad. Other requirements limit the receipt of allowances to one country only (rather than to both the sending and the receiving country); permit cumulating periods of employment in sending and receiving countries (if certain length of employment is essential); and specify the entitled children as legitimate, legitimated, recognized natural, adopted, or orphaned. Age limits and the number of children the family must have are also indicated. Kafka and Underhill present a table of 37 bilateral agreements in effect in 1974 which shows the dates of basic laws and types of programs, coverage, qualifying conditions, and size and manner of calculating the family allowance.

As for maintenance, migration creates a complex problem: that of recovery of maintenance obligations abroad. Once he emigrates, the migrant worker often abandons his dependent family which then usually applies for assistance. If a reconciliation cannot be effected, two types of legal action are possible: to bring action in the sending country and to enforce the decision in the receiving country, or to bring action in the receiving country. The first alternative comes up against the fact that in most countries the foreign judgment carries little weight; the second involves costs which may be 'overwhelming' (travel to the receiving country by the wife may be required). Even more complicated is the situation that involves an illegitimate child 'because most countries make a distinction as far as maintenance obligations are concerned between children born in and out of wedlock' (12:34). Some progress has been made, however, by resort to conventions: the Hague Convention of March 1, 1954 on civil procedure; the New York Convention of June 20, 1956 on recovery abroad of maintenance obligations; the Hague Convention of October 24, 1956 on the law applicable to maintenance obligations; and the Hague Convention of April 15, 1956 on the recognition and enforcement of decisions relating to maintenance obligation toward children — all of which Kafka and Underhill discuss briefly and in tabular form present the member states for each, the date of ratification by each country, and the date the convention came into force. While all countries adhere to the obligation to provide maintenance, they differ as to who is responsible for it, both parents or only the father. In all countries the obligation is enforceable by law and in some, failure to do so may lead to severe penalties.

Social Security for Young Adults. Horlick's study (1971) brings together the available information on 'the income security needs of young adults who are not yet full-time workers, or are just entering the labor force' (13:29), in the industrialized countries of the West. The programs involved in responding to these needs include family allowances, health insurance, survivor benefits, workmen's compensation, disability provisions, old-age pensions, and unemployment insurance. Although the survey is, by design, descriptive, important policy issues become visible. For example:

should workmen's compensation cover only young on-the-job trainees, or should it be extended to students in vocational schools, technical institutes, and general education in line with the argument that students are in training for a career, no matter what the form of preparation? In cases of work connected disability, is it equitable to calculate benefits on the basis of loss of current earnings when the injured worker is a young apprentice or trainee? Should the periods spent in education and training be credited toward the years of coverage required for an eventual old-age pension, given the delay in entering employment brought about by the demand for greater skills in a technological society? What, if any, special provisions should be created for young workers, or potential workers, who are not able to qualify for unemployment compensation because they have not contributed for the required period of time?

Unemployed. A study by Blaustein and Craig (1977) is concerned with unemployment insurance programs in 36 countries throughout the world, centering particularly on industrialized nations (14). The researchers encountered many difficulties in getting the information they needed. Countries vary in the amount of data they have that are useful for explaining their programs and in ways their data are treated; the data in some are factually inconsistent. Other difficulties revolve around translation problems, lack of standard usage of terminology and of a common understanding of concepts. The study uses the system in the United States as the basis for comparisons and also gives relatively greater prominence to the Canadian system (which shares experience relevant to unemployment with the United States) than it does to that of other countries.

Despite the difficulties, the study succeeds admirably in achieving its limited goal: to describe the provisions of unemployment schemes in the selected countries. This description ranges over all substantive features, as well as financing arrangements, administrative structures and procedures, and activities to promote the employment of the unemployed. As stated by the two authors, the study does not analyze the experience of countries in implementing their programs, nor does it deal with the reasons for differences between nations or with the implications of these differences for policy. Nevertheless, the clarity with which the material is presented (including ten tables) and its carefully organized details make it possible to make comparisons which, in turn, suggest policy issues and approaches.

Adequacy of Social Security Benefits. In 1970 Fisher examined the adequacy of minimum old-age pensions in 17 countries — so far, the most sophisticated study of its kind in the literature (15). For the first part of his analysis, criteria of adequacy included consumer expenditures, public assistance benefits and poverty standards; for the second, average earnings, minimum wages and national income. He found that although the minimum benefit is larger than it would be if strict wage-related or contribution-related formulae were used, it is in general insufficient and may fall below the level of public assistance payments and of poverty lines. Minimum pensions are relatively higher in developing than in developed countries in relation to average earnings, minimum wages, and national per capita income at current prices. In the developing countries

> paucity of individual savings, inadequate supplementary private insurance arrangements, a different view as to the role of the State as guarantor for the income needs of the retired, lead . . . to a different emphasis upon the income guarantee as distinct from the income replacement function of the social insurance system (15:229).

While the level of benefits is influenced by the level of economic development, this alone does not provide an adequate explanation of the differences that exist. The fact is that each program is unique within the context of its historical antecedents, social policy, and economic and political constraints (15:298).

A number of other studies by members of the Office of Research and Statistics of the Social Security Administration in HEW, all important but, by design, limited in scope, examined various aspects of foreign pension systems that have a bearing on adequacy of benefits: replacement rates of old age benefits; adjustments of old age pensions; role of the contribution ceiling in social security programs; the functions of private pension plans; and the roles of the retirement test (16,17,18,19,20).[3]

Kreps' meticulously executed study of 'lifetime allocation of work and income' (1971), while it does not address the question of adequacy of benefits directly, is suggestive in this connection because it takes into account, among other factors, the growing role of income transfers in influencing 'the economics of aging' — in West Germany, Great Britain, Sweden, Switzerland and the United States. Labor force activity and leisure-time patterns are related to variables such as regional rates of activity for men and women, rates by stage of industrialization, trends, and age. Workyear and worklife comparisons illumine the influence of socio-economic development on work and leisure. Consideration of the growing role of income transfers in retirement is preceded by elucidating the reasons for recent changes in patterns of work and earnings through the lifespan, recent and projected growth of nonworking time, levels of income by age and occupational groups, and the effect of economic growth on retirement benefits. This provides a much broader, a 'lifetime' vista, of what leads to the economic position of the aged in the studied countries, including an insight into the importance of adequacy in benefit levels (21).

In 1974 Schulz *et al.* published a study of old-age pensions provided by social security in the United States, Sweden, West Germany, Belgium and Canada which, by focusing on a common set of questions within an analytical framework, achieved a genuinely comparative and conceptually an unusually consistent examination. Focusing on the proper objectives of social security for the aged, Schulz and his colleagues emphasize that these objectives can be clarified and reached *if* the widely varying economic position of the aged is duly appreciated, that is, when they are not submerged into generalizations that are meaningless. Then, rather than concerning themselves with ways to improve the poverty or near-poverty incomes of the aged, the researchers advocate more flexible gauges of adequacy for the United States to the end of creating a pension system that will 'provide the elderly with pensions that permit them to maintain or more closely approach their pre-retirement living standard in retirement and, perhaps, even improve it' (22:22). Toward this objective, the other countries studied by Schulz and his associates have moved much further than the United States — at least in terms of income-loss replacement ratios for the average worker.

The major technical problems and policy issues that must be considered in efforts to achieve 'dynamic pension systems' — at what level should benefits be pegged at initial determination in relation to lifetime and pre-retirement earnings and prevailing economic conditions; how is this level of adequacy to be maintained after retirement — are competently explored and cogently presented. The researchers' overall conclusions note that dynamic systems must be national in scope and must deal effectively with the need in retirement for '(1) universal and equitable protection; (2) protection against the problems of economic instability — inflation and recession; and (3) growing pension benefits as the nation's productivity, hence total per capita output, increases' (22:270).

A book edited by Wilson and published in 1974 is concerned with the situation of the aged 'in societies that are both affluent and inflationary' in a wide-ranging perspective. As described by the editor, the book addresses such questions as:

> How has concern [for the elderly] found practical expression in the various pension schemes and other forms of assistance adopted in different countries? What meanings may be given to 'the poverty level'? In what ways are the elderly protected against poverty and with what degree of success? How much stress should be placed on the replacement of previous incomes? How may pensions be financed? How can the elderly be protected against inflation and given a share in economic growth? (23:v).

Since private occupational pensions contribute importantly to the incomes of the elderly in many countries, some attention is devoted to them, as well as to other types of provision such as assistance with housing and medical care.

This is the framework within which studies of policies for the elderly in six European countries — West Germany, the Netherlands, Sweden, France, Italy and Belgium — are presented. This material is expanded by a review of current policy issues in regard to the aged in Great Britain and the United States.

In the opening chapter, Wilson provides a clarification of the methodological and conceptual problems in dealing with poverty, noting that in many countries, minimum standards have been changed much more frequently than anticipated as they were reconstructed after World War II. His discussion of social insurance, after referring back to concepts of the Beveridge Report, incisively analyzes graduated (in contrast to flat) benefits and supplementary programs, public and private. In the concluding chapter, Wilson summarizes the main features of policies adopted by the studied countries, compares them to policies followed in Great Britain and the United States, and attempts to assess 'the merits of the different approaches to common problems'. He finds that these approaches differ greatly from country to country. For example: differences are considerable in regard to financing, expenditure as a fraction of GNP, benefit levels (including maximum cutoff), and income-replacement rates. He explicates the difficulties that must be confronted if the EEC countries wish to attain harmonization in fiscal policies. In connection with this, Wilson pays special attention to the comparative position of women (both dependent spouses and those who try to earn pensions in their own right), reviews the impact of the various existing pension systems on poverty, the pros and cons of recent tax and funding proposals, and the alternative future roles of private schemes.

In his 'final comments', Wilson summarizes his findings as follows:

there has been a large and general improvement in the provision made for the aged since the early post-war period when the welfare state was reconstructed in many countries . . . Over the trend pensioners have been more than protected against rising prices and have shared in growth. [He notes that much genuine improvement may be obscured by using a measurement of selectivity as an unequivocal measurement of poverty] . . . It is still necessary to consider whether the various minimum benefits are set at levels generally felt to be appropriate . . . The effects of inflation have been offset over the trend but rising prices can still bear hardly on the elderly in the short run. Even apart from inflation, we must continue to express concern about those groups of elderly people in a number of countries who, by any reasonable standard, must be deemed to be in distress (23:395—6).

In a recent HEW publication (September 1976), Kirkpatrick analyzes the experience of six foreign industrial countries — Belgium, Canada, France, West Germany, Norway and Sweden — in efforts to protect social security beneficiary earnings against inflation. These include not only automatic adjustments of benefits already in payment but also revaluation of past earnings. France and Germany base their revaluation on a wage index; Canada, Sweden and Belgium, on a price index; and Norway, on a mixed earnings-price index. In contrast, the adjustment legislated in the United States in 1972, and added to the social security system in 1975, 'involves automatic cost-of-living benefit increases equivalent to the increases in the consumer price index, if there is at least a 3 percent movement in the index and the Congress has taken no action to adjust pension levels. The index is applied to both newly awarded benefits and benefits in force' (24:1).

Kirkpatrick follows her description of the adjustment formulas in the six countries and how they work by applying 'each of the formulas to the earnings record of an "average" United States worker to show what would happen if the United States system were indexed by each of the foreign systems selected' (24:2). She explains the problems that she had to overcome in the process of this exercise (how to record and maintain a worker's earnings, and how to apply the index which adjusts the worker's earnings to a given year) and how she dealt with them. The care and skill that characterize this undertaking throughout make for confidence in the soundness of the findings. In all except the Belgian and Canadian *price-indexed* models, the revalued earnings average stands well above the final earnings level, ranging from 115 percent for the Canadian *earnings-indexed* model to 138 percent for the Norwegian price-wage indexed model. The picture is about the same, except for the German model, when revalued earnings are compared to average yearly (rather than to final) earnings.

Public Assistance. By way of introducing this program of social protection, it may be useful to present certain findings from a 1968 report by Schnitzer referred to earlier (9). He examined the welfare schemes that existed at that time in Canada, Denmark, France, Great Britain and Sweden, paying special attention to methods of financing and redistribution effects. He found that

> well-defined programs to eliminate poverty do not exist for the reason that there has been little or no preoccupation with the subject. Defined levels of poverty in these countries do not exist. On an a priori basis it is easy to select the lowest one-fifth or one-tenth of persons in an income distribution and designate them as 'poor'. This would mean that unless everyone made the same incomes, the bottom one-fifth or one-tenth of any income distribution would always be poor by definition. This is an arbitrary criterion. Even though income tax data is available for each country, the income distribution break-down ignores the effects of transfer payments. It is however, possible to identify low-income groups in these countries by using some percentage of average income as a mechanical divider between low and middle incomes (9:84).

In 1970, Marmor, Rein and Van Til published their analysis of the lessons of European experience in relation to the whole issue of preventing poverty in prosperous industrial countries through governmental income transfers (25). In this experience were included pensions, child allowances and public assistance. Their findings point up the fact that although European nations wished to provide protection for clearly defined risks through nonincome-conditioned transfers, the need for income-conditioned transfers has not decreased.

The problem of providing economic security to *all* in need in a dignified, equitable and efficient manner that preserves incentives to work has not been solved. In 1973, Rein enlarged on and brought up to date developments in income maintenance policy in Sweden, Britain and France, but in a somewhat narrower context than was done in 1970 (26).

Shlakman's examination of public assistance (1972), confined largely to the United States and Great Britain, reviews the reasons which cause people to 'slip through the meshes of first-line programs' and to land in the residual, safety-net schemes, invariably available as a last resort in the social security systems of industrial societies to those who fail to qualify for preferred benefits. These reasons are generated by these individuals' exceptional needs; by the way in which program boundaries have been drawn; by levels of benefits in first-line programs; 'and by the private-market insurance theories that have dominated the benefit and financing patterns of social insurance' (27:203).

The administration of safety-net benefits is attended by the exercise of discretionary judgment, even though attempts to reduce such judgment have been made. As a result, the residual function is not located at a fixed point in a given program, but is rather found somewhere 'between the extremes of complete discretion and precise statutory benefits programmed for impersonal delivery', and is 'moved, enlarged, or expanded, shaped and reshaped by the differentiating processes of social security systems' (27:207).

Schlakman thinks it important to gain more accurate knowledge about the structure of public assistance and the impact it has on people who come within its purview because its provisions shed light on all the other components of income-maintenance in a given country. She believes that to attain this more inclusive view, comparisons with other countries are useful. She writes:

> Making allowance for tradition, policies, and cultural differences, cross-national comparisons open to analysis an array of social welfare techniques that can be studied at the different stages of development which they present. The advantage of learning from the policies and programs of other countries with comparable economic capacities and situations lies in the useful fact that history does not put the same problems on various national agendas at precisely the same time (27:194).

The difficulties surrounding efforts to provide adequate support for public assistance recipients without destroying the incentive to work are incisively analyzed and lucidly explained by Rein in a comparative study of experience in the United States and Great Britain (1973). In the United States, the incentive strategy was based on the belief that if by working, people would gain economically, they would want to work. But this approach ran into tough problems, namely, how to provide 'strong incentives for the poor to work without discouraging those already on the job'; how to secure 'a decent basic allowance to those on welfare, along with a low rate of taxation on earned income, without prohibitively raising the cost of the program'; and 'how to coordinate the work-incentive features of the negative income tax with other means-tested programs' (28:159,160,163). Experience showed that to encourage work, to reduce poverty, and to keep down costs are conflicting aims, especially in periods of rising unemployment. Conflict was intensified by the desire of political decision-makers to achieve a number of additional aims by resort to incentive strategy, such as to reduce family break-up, decrease regional migration, etc.

Among the many motives that generated the British interest in the negative income tax, a desire to alter work behavior was not of primary importance. 'Rather, . . . a new principle for distributing public funds [which would concentrate scarce resources on those in greatest need] was sought' (28:169). The Family Income Supplement scheme (FIS) is a form of negative income taxation which is designed for families with children where the head of the family is in full-time work and which sets an income limit above which no benefit is payable. Two problems developed in implementing it: take-up, which refers to failure to reach the poor whose income it was designed to augment; and tax inequities, that is, the subjecting of those judged in need of benefits to income tax. FIS

> also made visible the potential work disincentives which arise when the poor and near-poor pay income and social security taxes as well as high implicit marginal taxes which lead to 'the poverty trap'
> — over 100 percent marginal tax rate (28:179).

Rein argues that while both the United States and Britain accepted a work test as a condition for eligibility (in the United States, work registration; in Great Britain, full-time employment), the purposes of policy in the two countries having been different, the outcomes were also different. In the United States, where the purpose was both to relieve poverty *and* to alter work behavior, 'costs of constraints encourage[d] the expanded use of restrictive policies'; in Great Britain, where the purpose was to expand consumption of the working poor, efforts to deal with the problems of take-up and incentives 'altered the rank-ordering of families in the income distribution' and made visible the inequities arising from the poverty surtax' (28:194). And this, in turn, may lead to tax reform with greater potential for redistribution. Overall, Rein concludes that each system has its limitations, that changes create new problems, and that 'there are no final solutions'.

A 1973 article by Rein and Heclo produces an eloquent and carefully researched debunking of the several arguments used by those who lament that welfare in the United States is in a state of crisis. They do this by exposing the fallacies of these arguments when they are related to the key pertinent characteristics of public assistance — the components of spending, recent trends in expenditures, the federal share in these expenditures, recipient rates, the increase in single-parent households, and the nature of American welfare statistics which, among other things, makes it difficult to understand what is happening to families who receive public assistance and exaggerates the prominence of one-parent families.

The two authors then make some comparisons with Great Britain and Sweden, and by so doing show 'that the so-called welfare crisis is *not* distinctively American with respect to these characteristics. What is distinctive is our response to them' (29:62). They also shed some light on reasons for the high Swedish work rates among welfare families despite the absence of a work incentive formula, in contrast to our failure to persuade the welfare recipients to work despite the ever lower *de facto* rates of marginal taxation on their earnings in the American system.

Warning that there are no easy solutions, Rein and Heclo urge 'a more realistic reorientation of the welfare debate'.

> Rather than hiding, or extending, or rehabilitating, or computerizing its categories of paupers, American welfare should strive to become a general residual facility available to any distressed citizen, and it should be interrelated with other forms of social support such as social security, retraining grants, housing assistance, health insurance, and effective enforcement of maintenance obligations toward the child (29:82).

In an important study (1973), Horlick presents his findings concerning 'income-tested benefits' (cash monthly payments made to the needy elderly) in five countries — Austria, Belgium, Finland, France and Switzerland. Their inclusion was influenced by such considerations as the availability of data, the opportunity to confer with officials, and the variety of approaches their programs utilize — as well as by the fact that four of these countries 'have pension plans that yield some of the highest earnings-replacement rates in the world. Yet their elderly frequently require financial help' (30:2). In his introductory chapter Horlick considers demographic trends, outlines the problems that have made it impossible for the social security systems of the selected countries to provide adequate benefit for all of their elderly without resort to means-tested benefits, and summarizes the main characteristics of their means-tested systems. He then discusses the basic provisions of the social security and means-tested system of each country (the former seen as a prelude to the latter), identifies who the recipients are, describes the size and cost of each national program, and compares benefit levels.

Horlick learned that two basic approaches are used to determine the size of means-tested benefits: either the fixing of a specific monthly amount on the basis of a means test, but varied in line with the family situation, geographic location, or other factors; or the bringing up of the applicant's income to a national or regional subsistence level via the means-tested benefit. Not only is the means test usually unpopular with the elderly and their families from a social point of view, but it is also difficult to administer. Especially cumbersome is the introduction of disconnected programs to fill specific gaps, and of separate means tests for many beneficiary categories called forth by efforts to tailor payments to needs. In all five countries the number of pensioners is growing faster than the labor force or the population as a whole, and among them the largest increases have come from those who needed assistance in the past, that is, single beneficiaries, particularly survivors. This has happened despite the fact that most of the included countries have highly developed economies, have social security systems among the oldest (except Switzerland), and have very high replacement rates. The most important reasons for this seemingly anomalous situation are that a country's oldest citizens may have been victimized by changes introduced into its social security system; 'incomplete or "mixed" career involving persons who may have worked all of their lives, but had only sporadic coverage' (30:45); low wages, declines in employment (especially in agriculture, mining, and self-employment), inflation; failure to ever contribute to social security or to be connected with it.

180 *Social Security and the Individual*

As to the proportion of pensioners who receive means-tested benefits, it ranged from 24—38 percent in four countries to 76 percent in Finland. The reason for this striking difference is that the former are providing supplements to earnings-related pensions, 'while Finland is providing a general supplement to a low-level universal pension' (30:54). The relative number of recipients of means-tested benefits declined in the 1960s, in all countries but Finland where it has held steady. This decline is due largely to a shrinking in the number of those recipients who were already retired or approaching retirement age when the means-tested program was introduced.

A larger percentage of pensioners in rural than in urban areas, among the self-employed, and among blue-collar than among white-collar workers needs means-tested benefits. In 1969, their cost, as a percent of the total spent on old-age pensions varied widely: for four countries it ranged from 4.98 percent (Belgium) to 16 percent (France), while in Finland it came to 59.6 percent. Horlick closes with a brief description of 'solutions' undertaken or studied by Belgium, Switzerland, and France to cope with the problem recognized by all selected countries as still intractable, namely, that the level of their means-tested benefits is too low.

In her paper (1975), Fishbein provides a brief overview of social insurance and social assistance programs in the industrialized democracies (31). Because of difficulties in securing comparable data, she warns that certain figures 'may be more misleading than elucidating' (31:15). Nevertheless, her tables on program costs as related to GNP and on family allowances provide a useful summary. Her major contribution is twofold: she makes the point that it is impossible to compare public assistance programs meaningfully without comparing all other means-tested programs as well; and she relates her data to the historical development of attitudes toward welfare in the countries she includes and to their socio-political structures as they changed over time.

In a 1976 book Stein explores the interdependence of income maintenance policies and manpower policies in Great Britain and the United States, an interdependence that can either support or weaken the achievement of their goals. Succinctly and skillfully he describes the two countries' income-maintenance and manpower programs and highlights their historical antecedents, bringing out the major similarities and differences in values and in a variety of social and economic features that illumine constraints in policy development. He argues that in both countries, the incentive framework and contradictions in the effects of assistance and training programs have stymied the attainment of desired goals, and have contributed to criticisms of their huge bureaucracies. There is an administrative separation of welfare-oriented and employment-oriented programs, with the latter not genuinely interested in services that would enhance employability. Income maintenance programs often create disincentives to work while training programs often are but feebly linked to actual market conditions.

Stein suggests that in order to enhance the incentive to work for those judged to be employable and simultaneously provide adequate support for those judged to be unemployable, work incentives must be built into the level and structure of assistance benefits. In other words, manpower training for recipients of such benefits (most of them, persons caught in the poverty-unemployability cycle) must be integrated into welfare-oriented programs. He cautions that international comparisons, because of differences in cultural backgrounds and value judgments in the countries being compared, are likely to distort 'an analytic signal'; hence, Stein has 'sought to play the role of the value-free analyst, in the scientific traditions of economics', but he does visualize a utopia — 'a place in which every person is at minimum entitled to as good as job as he is capable of learning to do' (32:6).

In a short but informative article (1977), Husby and Wetzel contrast public assistance in Sweden and the United States as to eligibility conditions, payment levels and employment incentives. Differences in eligibility conditions result in a startlingly different composition of the public assistance population: in Sweden (in Malmo) only 11 percent are single women with children; in the United States, they account for 73 percent of recipients. Swedish social aid is far more generous than public assistance in the United States. In Sweden, benefit levels approach wage levels (average earnings in manufacturing) and median incomes; in the United States, Aid to Families with Dependent Children (AFDC) payments in the median state are 40 percent of the after-tax manufacturing wage, and AFDC and food stamps combined amount to only 39.2 percent of median income. No financial incentive not to work is incorporated into public assistance in Sweden; in the United States, a 1967 amendment to the Social Security Act lowered the implicit marginal tax to 66.7 percent of earnings. Yet, in Sweden, the population is not flooding the welfare rolls. Aware of Sweden's 'advantages' — a relatively homogeneous population which augments social cohesion and may contribute to a strong work ethic — and of the difference in the role of women in the two countries, the authors do not advocate a wholesale transplantation of the Swedish approach. They suggest only that

> Higher benefit levels should be tried and greater bureaucratic coordination among training centers, employment and public aid offices, and other welfare facilities should be implemented (33:31).

That social insurance programs can have an important 'corrective' bearing on preventing poverty and on 'healing' its effects (hence, on the situation of potential and actual public assistance recipients) is widely recognized. 'In this sense', it is noted, 'the adoption of the minimum level of living concept as a major guideline for effective action in the field of income support could play a major role' (34:39). It is likely, therefore, that in the future social policy will increasingly concern itself with how much reliance should be placed on earnings-related social insurance and how much on needs-related public assistance, and how best to integrate the two approaches into a unified system.

Social Security and Social Services. The realization that cash benefits alone may not be the most effective way of helping people in need has been spreading among experts, administrators and the general public. Wrote Rys in 1974:

> A strong trend has appeared in social security development throughout the world over the past 15 years towards complementing income maintenance measures by social services. While, in some cases, cash benefits may be sufficient to deal with critical situations of short duration, they may clearly be insufficient in other cases, particularly when a social accident results, for the victim and his family, in a more or less prolonged, if not permanent, social declassification. While cash benefits constitute a mechanical device released on the occurrence of a contingency, social services are able to deal with individual situations of stress; their obvious objective is not only to provide the people in need with a certain amount of material help but also, as far as possible, to bring them back to normal life in society (35:327).

This is echoed by the expert group concerned with minimum levels of living. In concluding their deliberations in 1976 they note:

At the same time, it is generally recognized that even ensuring a socially acceptable minimum income to everybody as a citizen's right would not suffice by itself to eradicate poverty and that other measures are called for, measures that involve an efficient and purposeful combination of education, training, rehabilitation and professional re-education, health services, social and legal counselling, housing opportunities, cultural services, etc. (36:39).

Rys pointed out further that in developing countries (in contrast to industrialized nations), the social service approach will 'certainly gain more importance . . . in view of the particular need for adaptation of people to a new social environment'. Referring specifically to Africa, he explained that an expanded structural (rather than functional) concept of social security, in addition to protecting people, would teach them how to live better — especially those who leave the extended family to become income earners in urbanized communities. At the same time, such a concept can be most beneficial to people who continue their traditional style of living in rural communities since 'measures in favor of people living on the margin of the money economy [can] only take the form of social services. . .' (35:336). A new approach to the problem of social services is called for.

That such an approach is being used in Africa is reported by Mouton. On this continent, many social security funds provide family benefits in kind (milk, flour, soap, etc.); many employ family workers who offer advice, help with housework, make referrals (especially to agencies that provide medical care or distribute medicine free to needy persons); many establish and manage kindergartens and nurseries, organize holiday camps, help families to obtain housing, award scholarships, organize ambulance services, set up centers for the prevention of work-connected accidents, etc. Policies governing these activities so far have been centered on family assistance and health care. This is called for both because the traditional, extended, African family 'is still very much alive and continues to play a vital role in African society', and because there is beginning to take place a breakdown, at least in urban areas, of the indigenous pattern (37:35–6,147).

The difficulties of integrating social services into social security are revealed in an article by Borelli (1971) which is concerned primarily with the extent to which social security systems in five Central American States (Guatemala, Nicaragua, Honduras, El Salvador, and Costa Rica) are effective in efforts to establish a basic minimum level of social services, or to serve as a nucleus for developing a basic social services program (38). These five countries exhibit certain common socio-economic traits (population growth and urban growth, stage of economic development), but also certain differentiating characteristics (ethnic groupings, political structures). Borelli found that both the social security systems and the social service programs within them are limited in terms of coverage and the scope of protection and services they offer. He thinks that individually these countries are unable to bear the costs of more extensive systems, and recommends a regional approach.

The question of what should be the relationship between social security and social services has been extensively studied by ISSA since 1959. Between that year and 1967, a number of reports were made to ISSA's XIVth, XVth, and XVIth General Assemblies (1961, 1964, and 1967, respectively), the latter followed by a round-table discussion at which the whole subject was reviewed and the interaction of social security and social services was again explored, with particular attention directed to the situation of developing countries. All of the six reports to the Assemblies and two articles analyzing the discussions at the 1967 round table have been published. These materials provide not only a factual picture of practices in social security administrations in relation to social services, but reflect over the years the thinking about the relationship between these two forms of social provision. They reveal that this relationship is determined by a complex of factors — 'the historical development of a social security system, the intrinsic link between cash benefits and benefits in kind in certain branches of social security, [as well as] the social and political organization of a country' (39:151) — which vary from country to country. These materials support very few generalizations about advantages and disadvantages of the different methods of providing and of administering social services. Consequently, the need for further research is repeatedly stressed, especially because changes have been taking place both in administrative practice and in thinking about the role of social services in social security. The task of the round table convened under ISSA auspices in 1973 was

> to seek to identify current trends in different parts of the world and in varying economic and political situations, to explore the role presently being ascribed to social services in the totality of social protection and to analyze more closely the implications from the point of view of the social security institution as well as from that of the citizen as beneficiary and as contributor and taxpayer, of

Social Security and the Individual 185

making available the social services that are everywhere regarded as necessary components of full social security (39:152).

The more than 40 participants, representing 22 countries, produced five overview papers: on the Socialist countries, Western Europe and North America, Latin America, Africa, and on Asia and Oceania. These were detailed and expanded by auxiliary reports on individual countries in the part of the world with which each overview paper dealt — a total of 22 reports.

The major issues that emerged in the discussions encompassed a wide spectrum of concerns. Where there is integration of cash benefits and services, both being provided directly by the same authority (as in socialist countries), greater efficiency is likely to result — but at a price: many who are not social insurance beneficiaries may be excluded from social services which they sorely need; also, this restriction may segregate groups from each other in the general population. Where cash benefits and social services are administered by separate agencies, needed coordination may be difficult to achieve. In this connection it was noted that social workers, a professional group involved in the delivery of social services, might play a major role in assisting citizens to gain access to all available forms of help.

The increasing attention to social security planning may lead to a greater awareness of the complementarity of cash benefits and social services and thereby lessen the competition for scarce resources. Such competition can be observed in Western Europe and North America where the two parts of 'full social protection' are separated — but not without an advantage: greater ease in analyzing particular social services as to their scope and function in broad areas of social policy. Family services, for example, become visible as part of general family policy and beyond that, as part of population policy. It was suggested that at the planning stage, services and cash benefits might be treated as associated measures, but that administration might be decentralized and vested in separate agencies.

While the tie-in between benefits and services in certain social security provisions (unemployment compensation which in many cases must be accompanied by employment and training services; work injury benefits, often requiring rehabilitation services) is appreciated, this is not enough to deal with constantly emerging new needs. For example, the increase of married women in labor force participation means the need to provide child care facilities; growth in the number of old-age pensioners often calls for counselling services to prepare for retirement. Legal stipulations that services must be provided do not offer solutions to the thorny problems of quality, discretion, and differentiation. A large proportion of the participants agreed that

> what was important in a comparative study of the role of social services in social security was not *how* different countries administered these measures of social protection but *why* different methods were preferred and what the implications were in terms of efficiency and effectiveness (39:7).

Policy Issues. The broader policy issues in social security discussed in Chapter 6 are reflected in more detailed and specific forms when the impact of cash benefits is examined in relation to individuals. In regard to the aged, the main questions again center on whether benefits should replace or guarantee income, that is, on whether they ought to strive to provide a preretirement level of living in retirement or to improve it, if this is necessary to attain what is considered a decent minimum. Involved are questions about how to deal with inflation and recession in order to protect benefits from erosion by economic instability, and how to adjust benefits, on a continuing basis, to increases in productivity and in per capita income in order to assure adequacy of the retirees' living standard as compared with the standard enjoyed by the active population. Underlying all these questions are the issues of equity, universality and freedom of choice regarding retirement age — the latter bearing on whether part-time work should be made available to retired persons as a matter of policy. How to create and apply a dynamic concept of adequacy continues as an issue of paramount importance throughout the entire system of cash benefits, whether for the aged, for adults or for children.

It is becoming clear that social insurance and public assistance ought not to be viewed as two unrelated systems, the former granting benefits as of right, the latter on the basis of need. What social insurance does or does not do in regard to eligibility conditions, coverage, adequacy and equity profoundly influences what public assistance does in regard to these crucially important elements — to say nothing of the fact that the very concepts of 'rights', equity and adequacy are in constant evolution that affects both. Consequently, an emerging issue that will demand more and more attention is how to integrate social insurance and public assistance into a unified system.

The large number of specific issues raised by the reexamination of the position of women and children in the social security realm may be subsumed under more general questions. How to create a family policy (one that responds to the needs of traditional and new family forms) which would take into account its interconnections with population and economic policies, and make visible the role of social security and social services in achieving its goals? How to combine adequate protection with equality of rights of men and women? How to combine freedom of choice, by persons with family responsibilities, between work outside the home and household duties, with adequate protection if they choose the latter? How to assist a widow to carry out her functions as a mother by providing adequate protection for the children and at the same time help her adjust socially to widowhood, this adjustment to include preparation for subsequent entry into the labor force? How should the social security rights of women who temporarily leave the labor force to care for their children be protected?

The general agreement that even adequate cash benefits are not enough and must be buttressed by services, coupled with the realization that auspices under which services are provided are important determinants of their nature and goals, raise the question: should social security be fused with social services? The many difficult issues that have to be dealt with in answering this question include not only specific considerations but those of wider significance as well. Among the latter, for example, is the argument of proponents that unification may initiate a trend toward universality of services, an outcome they consider desirable. The universality versus selectivity debate clearly goes beyond the fusion question as such, producing disagreements about many features of both cash and noncash programs. Among specific considerations, an important one is quantification, widely applied in social security, but still in its infancy in social services and regarded by many as inappropriate for services because they aim at qualitative changes, social and cultural, that do not lend themselves to quantitative measurement. This militates against accountability, so pronounced in social security. Social security is by now quite firmly embedded in the social fabric of many countries and quite widely understood and accepted, while services are still fighting an uphill battle in many nations. They are still, to an important extent, responses to crises and urgent needs, rather than to long-range plans that govern social security. Financing sources and patterns are dissimilar. Nor is there a meeting of minds about administration — degree of centralization, nature of staffing patterns and the extent to which professionalization rather than on-the-job training is relied upon, the importance of responding to traditional ways of life and to individual needs. Views prevalent about the composite image of the 'client' being served often diverge, even when divergence is not called for by reality. All this tends to keep the debate on fusion wide open.

Summary. The information now available on how social security affects various categories in the population, although not equally thorough for all (the unemployed and young adults, for example), is nevertheless quite detailed and inclusive for most, in the sense of yielding insights into the kinds of problems their members experience as beneficiaries. Especially gratifying is the expansion of the data base in regard to women, hitherto an underdeveloped area of investigation. But much more is known about the situation of women beneficiaries in developed countries than elsewhere in the world. This expansion has shed light on the complexities around the fundamental issues of equity and adequacy as they affect women specifically. Furthermore, more and better knowledge has brought out of obscurity the intricacies generated by the intimate connection between income protection for women, on the one hand, and for their children, on the other, as well as between cash benefits for women and the wider areas of population and family policy — even when this connection is not explicitly recognized in social security provisions. It is likewise encouraging that a beginning has been made in studying the legal position of migrant children (and their families), a growing contingent in the international social security arena. Here too the problems are knotty, involving as they do differences in substantive provisions as well as in the rights which countries accord to legitimate, legitimated, illegitimate, recognized natural, adopted, and orphaned children — to say nothing of differences in what nations will accept as legally binding across national boundaries.

Better information has made it possible to assess with more certainty the reasons why beneficiaries experience problems. Factors that affect adequacy in old age pensions, for example — such as the level at which benefits are pegged at initial determination, effects of inflation, contribution ceilings, retirement tests and lifetime allocation of work and income, and the relationship between compulsory and private plans — are now much better understood. In regard to women, the reasons that bring about inequitable treatment of contributions and benefits of insured women as compared with men — resulting in an uneven effect of social insurance on the sexes — have been more precisely explored and their dimensions more clearly outlined. Progress has been made toward gaining more knowledge about the specific

Social Security and the Individual 189

circumstances that affect the income position of widows, divorced women (both those who do and who do not receive alimony), housewives, and unmarried mothers — all areas that are especially sensitive and unstable.

Reasons for the continuing need for public assistance, even in countries with mature and generous social insurance schemes, are being more incisively clarified, as are the reasons why so far little progress has been made in building work incentives into the level and structure of assistance benefits. This, in turn, brings into focus the nature of the interrelationship between benefits as of right and benefits based on need, both being essential forms of income support.

Overall, certain proposals for change are based on more solid grounds than has been true in some places and at some times in the past. But because policy decisions are not made solely on the basis of knowledge, many proposals gain only partial acceptance and others are either indefinitely postponed or rejected. This seems to be the case in regard to the especially intractable problem of providing adequate support for the needy able-bodied without destroying their incentive to work, considered by some as incapable of solution. Some questions cannot be answered without more and more reliable empirical data. This is the case in regard to fusion of social services and social security. What is required are data that would shed light on advantages and disadvantages of alternative arrangements and on the kinds of administrative and organizational forms and capacities that would be required by fusion, including its impact on professional status of personnel and on the attitudes and values which give form to staff performance.

Notes

1. This Committee completed a British Study, *Report of the Committee on One-Parent Families* (London, HMSO, Cmnd 5629 and Cmnd 5629-1, two vols., published in July 1974), but was interested in obtaining a broader, comparative, policy-oriented view.

2. As a method of assuring a guaranteed income, Schnitzer also discussed the negative income tax, defined as the payment of a cash grant to families or individuals whose incomes are below a specified minimum income level — the amount of payment depending on the negative taxable income and the negative tax rate. In reference to the United States, he reviewed the plans proposed by Friedman, the Ripon Society, Lampman and Tobin. The cost, Schnitzer noted, would depend on (1) definition of poverty; (2) rate of negative income taxation used; (3) whether present transfer payments will be maintained or eliminated; and (4) proportion of those eligible who would take advantage of the plan. None of the five countries he studied used negative income taxation and he discerned no interest among them in this approach (9:3–8, 84). An interesting source on the

guaranteed income politics in the United States is Moynihan, Daniel P., *The Politics of A Guaranteed Income. The Nixon Administration and The Family Assistance Plan* (New York, Random House, 1973).

3. What promises to be an important source for information in regard to adequacy of benefits is ISSA, *Problems of Social Security under Economic Recession and Inflation*, Studies and Research no. 10 (Geneva, ISSA, 1978). Unfortunately, this report − a series of technical papers by social security experts from various nations − was not available to me at the time of writing.

References

1. OECD, *Old Age Pension Schemes* (Paris, France, 1977).
2. Laroque, Pierre, 'Women's Rights and Widows' Pensions', *International Labour Review*, 106, no. 1 (July 1972), pp. 1−10.
3. Haskins, Dalmer and Bixby, Lenore E., *Women and Social Security: Law and Policy in Five Countries* (Washington, DC, Research Report No. 42, HEW, Social Security Administration, Office of Research and Statistics, 1973. HEW Publication No. (SSA) 73-11800). A report of this study, entitled 'Women and Social Security − Study of the Situation in Five Countries', may be found in *International Social Security Review*, 26, nos. 1−2 (1973), pp. 73−133.
4. ISSA, *Women and Social Security*, Studies and Research, No. 5. Report of Research Conference on Women and Social Security, Vienna, November 2−4, 1972 (Geneva, 1973).
5. Weise Jr, Robert W., 'Housewives and Pensions: Foreign Experience', *Social Security Bulletin* (September 1976), pp. 37−45.
6. Cockburn, Christine and Haskins, Dalmer, 'Social Security and Divorced Persons', *International Social Security Review*, year xxix, no. 2 (1976), pp. 111−43.
7. Kirkpatrick, Elizabeth, 'Alimony and Public Income Support in Fifteen Countries', *Social Security Bulletin* (January 1977), pp. 1−4.
8. ISSA, General Secretariat, 'Income Maintenance for One-Parent Families', Report of a Research Project Undertaken by the General Secretariat of the ISSA for the British Committee on One-Parent Families, *International Social Security Review*, year 28, no. 1 (1975), pp. 3−61.
9. Schnitzer, Martin, *Guaranteed Minimum Income Programs Used by Governments of Selected Countries* (Joint Economic Committee, US Congress, Paper no. 11, Washington, DC, 1968).
10. Burns, Eveline M. (ed.) *Children's Allowances and the Economic Welfare of Children. The Report of a Conference* (New York, Citizens' Committee for Children of New York, 1968).
11. Haanes-Olsen, L., 'Children's Allowances: Their Size and Structure in Five Countries', *Social Security Bulletin*, 35, no. 5 (1972), pp. 17−28.
12. Kafka, Doris and Underhill, Evi, 'Comparative Study of Certain Aspects of Family Law in 16 European and Mediterranean Countries', *International Child Welfare Review*, no. 21 (May 1974), pp. 23−38; and same authors, 'Comparative Study of Certain Aspects of Family Law in 16 European and Mediterranean Countries', *ibid.*, no. 22/23 (October 1974), pp. 27−42.
13. Horlick, Max, 'Social Security Provisions for Young Adults in Industrialized Countries', *Social Security Bulletin*, 34, no. 11 (November 1971), pp. 29−36.
14. Blaustein, Saul J. and Craig, Isabel, *An International Review of Unemployment Insurance Schemes* (Kalamazoo, Michigan, The W. E. Upjohn Institute for Employment Research, January 1977).

15. Fisher, Paul, 'Minimum Old-Age Pensions. I: Their Adequacy in Terms of Consumer Expenditures, Assistance Benefits and Poverty Standards', *International Labour Review*, 102, no. 1 (July 1970), pp. 51–78; 'Minimum Old-Age Pensions, II: Their Adequacy in Terms of Average Earnings, Minimum Wages and National Income and Some Problems of Adjustment', *ibid.*, no. 3 (September 1970), pp. 277–317.

16. Horlick, Max, 'The Earnings Replacement Rate of Old-Age Benefits: An International Comparison', *Social Security Bulletin*, 33, no. 3 (March 1970), pp. 3–16; Haanes-Olsen, Leif, 'Earnings-Replacement Rate of Old-Age Benefits, 1965–75, Selected Countries', *ibid.*, 41, no. 1 (January 1978), pp. 3–14.

17. Horlick, Max and Lewis, Doris E., 'Adjustment of Old-Age Pensions in Foreign Programs', *ibid.*, 33, no. 5 (May 1970), pp. 12–15; Horlick, Max and Tracy, Martin B., 'Adjustments of Old-Age Pensions in Foreign Programs', *ibid.*, 37, no. 7 (July 1974), pp. 33–6; Tracy, Martin, 'Maintaining Value of Social Security Benefits During Inflation: Foreign Experience', *ibid.*, 39, no. 11 (November 1976), pp. 33–49.

18. Horlick, Max and Lucas, Robert, 'Role of the Contribution Ceiling in Social Security Programs: Comparison of Five Countries', *ibid.*, 34, no. 2 (February 1971), pp. 19–31; and Tracy, Martin B., 'Contributions Under Social Security Programmes: Survey in Some Selected Countries', *International Social Security Review*, xxix, no. 1 (1976), pp. 66–85.

19. Horlick, Max and Skolnick, Alfred M., *Private Pension Plans in West Germany and France*, Research Report no. 36, HEW, Social Security Administration, Office of Research and Statistics (Washington, DC, GPO, 1971).

20. Kirkpatrick, E. K., 'The retirement test: an international study', *Social Security Bulletin*, 37, no. 7 (1974), pp. 3–16.

21. Kreps, Juanita M., *Lifetime Allocation of Work and Income. Essays in the Economics of Aging* (Durham, North Carolina, Duke University Press, 1971).

22. Schulz, James, Carrin, Guy, Krupp, Hans, Peschke, Manfred, Sclar, Elliot, and Van Steenberge, J., *Providing Adequate Retirement Income: Pension Reform in the United States and Abroad* (Hanover, New Hampshire, University Press of New England, 1975).

23. Wilson, Thomas (ed.) *Pensions, Inflation and Growth. A Comparative Study of the Elderly in the Welfare State* (London, Heinemann Educational Books, 1974).

24. Kirkpatrick, Elizabeth Kreitler, *Protecting Social Security Beneficiary Earnings Against Inflation: The Foreign Experience*, HEW, Social Security Administration, Office of Research and Statistics. Staff Paper no. 25, HEW Publication No. (SSA) 77-11850 (Washington, DC, GPO, September 1976).

25. Marmor, Theodore, Rein, Martin, and Van Til, Sally, 'Post-War European Experience with Cash Transfers: Pensions, Child Allowances, and Public Assistance', in *Technical Studies*, The President's Commission on Income Maintenance, 1969 (Washington, DC, GPO, 1969), pp. 259–93.

26. Rein, Martin, 'Income Policy in Sweden, Britain and France', *Current History*, 65, no. 384 (August 1973), pp. 80–5.

27. Shlakman, 'The Safety-Net Function'.

28. Rein, Martin, 'Work Incentives and Welfare Reform in Britain and the United States', pp. 151–95 in Stein, Bruno and Miller, S. M.,(eds.) *Incentives and Planning in Social Policy* (Chicago, Aldine Publishing Co., 1973).

29. Rein, Martin and Heclo, Hugh, 'What welfare crisis? – A Comparison among the United States, Britain, and Sweden', *The Public Interest*, no. 33 (Fall 1973), pp. 61–83.

30. Horlick, Max, *Supplemental Security Income for the Aged . . . A Comparison of Five Countries* (Washington, DC, HEW, Social Security

192 Social Socurity and the Individual

Administration, Office of Research and Statistics, DHEW Publication No. (SSA) 74-11850. Staff Paper no. 15, July 1973).

31. Fishbein, Bette K., *Social Welfare Abroad*, Comparative Data on the Social Insurance and Public Assistance Programs of Selected Industrialized Democracies (New King Street, White Plains, New York, 10604, The Institute for Socioeconomic Studies, 1975).

32. Stein, Bruno, *Work and Welfare in Britain and the USA* (London, The Macmillan Press, 1976).

33. Husby, Ralph and Wetzel, Eva, 'Public Assistance in Sweden and the United States', *Social Policy*, 7, no. 5 (March–April 1977), pp. 28–31.

34. UN, Division of Social Affairs, *Minimum Levels of Living*.

35. Rys, 'Problems of Social Security Planning'.

36. UN, Division of Social Affairs, *Minimum Levels of Living*.

37. Mouton, 'Social Security in Africa'.

38. Borelli, Kenneth, 'Social Security in Central America', *International Social Work*, 14, no. 1 (1971), pp. 4–15.

39. ISSA, *The Role of Social Services in Social Security: Trends and Perspectives*, Report of Round Table Meeting, Moscow, May 22–25, 1973. Studies and Research, no. 6 (Geneva, ISSA, 1974).

PART THREE:
PERSONAL SOCIAL SERVICES

Over the years, scholars and experts have devoted considerable attention to delimiting and clarifying the scope and functions of social services in an international perspective. A UN report in 1959 designated the main social service fields as those concerned with problems of family life; special problems affecting individuals and groups (children, juvenile delinquents); difficulties due to lack of material resources; and environmental problems (urbanization) (1:11–13). A comprehensive social service program was conceptualized as addressing all these problems and in addition, providing services 'undertaken within the framework of related services or outside the social field'. This additional group was described as social services in medical, mental health or psychiatric settings; in family planning, rehabilitation of the handicapped, vocational guidance and placement, housing projects, social security agencies, community development programs, schools, armed forces, courts, agencies offering treatment to offenders, and in industry (1:19–20).[1] It was recommended that priority be given to methods 'designed to promote the general welfare of the community rather than to those which are more concerned with the adjustment of the individual to his environment', and that emphasis be placed on prevention, with priority 'to those social services which can be made available to the whole population or the largest segment of it ...' (1:21–2). The responsibility of governments to provide social services and the need in development of a balanced socio-economic approach were stressed.

In 1968, the ministers responsible for social welfare took the position that

> social welfare activities are deeply rooted in each country's unique heritage of cultural and historical values; conditioned by the country's peculiar socio-economic circumstances at any given time, and that it would be neither feasible nor desirable to try to achieve uniformity in national approaches to social welfare and patterns of social welfare organization and operation. It is through the necessary diversity of national experience that some common elements should be looked for, as a basis for a fruitful exchange of ideas and the

development of effective cooperation at the international level (7:34—5).

They argued that social services can contribute significantly to altering the distribution of goods and services so that the poor can share in economic progress more fully; that social welfare's preventive activities can be integrated in national plans as safeguards against the disruptive effects of modernization; and that its intervention can be effective in motivating individuals and groups to change attitudes, values and ways of life, and thus help to commit all members of the society to the objectives of development. They identified the major fields of social welfare activity broadly as (a) providing assistance for those with problems (remedial social welfare); (b) predicting the emergence of social problems and taking measures against their occurrence (preventive social welfare); and (c) helping to create conditions conducive to development (developmental social welfare) (7:76). The crucial role of social welfare personnel in dealing with the human aspects of development and in facilitating attitudinal changes and community participation was underscored.[2]

Basing themselves on a study of social services delivery systems in 22 countries, Thursz and Vigilante in 1975 identified 'basic social service needs for human communities' as including family social services, services for youth and young adults, for the aged, for violators of the law, services in housing and in the health and mental health fields, and in community organization (14:14—21).

Kahn and Kamerman derive their functional definition from findings in eight countries, all highly or moderately developed — Federal Republic of Germany (FRG), France, Israel, Poland, United Kingdom (UK), Yugoslavia, Canada, and the United States (US). In all of them, according to these authors, personal social services perform one or more of eight functions, namely (1) contribute to socialization and development; (2) disseminate information about, and facilitate access to, the entire gamut of social services and entitlements available in a particular country; (3) assure social care and aid for the frail aged, the handicapped, the retarded, and the incapacitated, whether they live in the community or in substitute living arrangements; (4) arrange 'substitute home or residential care or [create] new, permanent family relationships for children whose parents are not able to fulfill their roles'; (5) provide help, counseling, and guidance to individuals and families experiencing problems; (6) support 'mutual aid, self-help, and activities aimed at prevention', deal with problems in community living,

Personal Social Services 195

contribute to planning services and to proposals for changes in policies and programs; (7) assure integration of programs and services for maximum effect; (8) work with deviant individuals to prevent their doing harm to themselves and others, while offering care and guidance to help them change their behavior. They note that countries differ importantly in conceptualizing and assigning priorities to these functions, the outcomes depending on the degrees of a particular country's development and on its dominant views. As to the nature of personal social services, Kahn and Kamerman distinguish between public social utilities, that is, universal programs which enhance development and socialization or provide information and access, to which entitlement is based on status; and case services which are for people with maladjustments, problems, illnesses and difficulties, to which entitlement is via a diagnostic assessment and some sort of certification, formal or informal, which attests to need or eligibility. Case services, they believe, can be universal but, in fact, are not (15:4–8).

That governments may see social service functions quite differently from the way they are seen by operating agencies is vividly illustrated by India's Sixth Plan, 1978–83. Unlike its predecessors, it is a 'radical design' which proclaims that development must begin with the poorest; that economic growth is not enough; and that first priority must be given to redistribution — with a built-in bias in favor of the poor to ensure that redistribution of wealth and income actually takes place. Most important, the poor themselves must assert their rights and mobilize against bureaucratic inertia and vested interests. The strategy to achieve this mobilization is to use 'voluntary agencies engaged in social and developmental work which are close to the people and have the capacity to motivate the rural population for community participation in developmental programs'. Suitable voluntary agencies which do not at present have locally based structures are to be enabled to develop them. But, asks V. K. R. V. Rao, how can the voluntary social service agencies undertake this task — given that they are not now working at the rural and grass-roots level on a national or even a state or a smaller area level. Found in a few local pockets here and there, how can they solve the gigantic problem of motivating and organizing the rural poor? Furthermore, how can they 'counter political pressures and overcome the obstacles created by the existing power, class, and caste structure in rural India that has thwarted all attempts so far to bring about social justice and a more egalitarian growth in the rural areas?' Can government itself, assisted by voluntary social agencies, achieve a socio-economic revolution without a mass movement behind it? (16:22–3).

It is obvious from the above that the 'definitions' produced so far endow personal social services with a tremendous range of activities in a variety of environments while utilizing the skills of many different professionals. It is not surprising, therefore, that although these services have a respectably ancient origin and are recognized as essential components of social provision in modern societies, their boundaries, functions, forms, content, and location in the total network of social undertakings are much less clearly defined than is true of social security. Among the consequences of this difference, as well as of the very nature of personal social services, are greater complexity and specificity of issues they pose, and wider differences in regard to the unique major policy questions they raise.

8 COMPARATIVE NATIONAL EXPERIENCE

As in the case of social security, the selected studies progress from a micro- to a macroscopic view, studies that deal with single countries preceding those that deal with two or more countries, in order to facilitate assessment of what is important for policy when several countries are compared. Some single-country studies are concerned exclusively with personal social services; others discuss these services in a broader context, relating their content, functions, and organizational structures to social security and in some instances, to a variety of other human services. Such a context often reveals the effects of social security and personal social services on each other, the differences and/or similarities in the value base from which each program operates, the gaps in benefits and services, and the weaknesses in administration that diminish potential for effective harmonization and a steadier progress toward desired goals.

Relatively few of the included studies range over the entire spectrum of personal social service programs in a particular country. Most focus on services to children and to the aged — the two groups recognized universally as needing individualized care and protection. Few are explicitly concerned with defining the parameters of services or making manifest their underlying values. Yet, their findings about what is provided and how the task is carried out suggest what a country considers appropriate for inclusion in service activities and indicate these activities' major characteristics.

Personal Social Services within the Network of Social Provision.
Schorr's 1965 study examined French social services from the point of view of their relationship to the country's social security system. He found that this relationship is characterized by three important aspects. The first is that 'through its programs of *health and social action*, social security initiates and maintains a wide variety of social services (17:21). This it accomplishes by paying for services received by social security beneficiaries (in convalescent homes, retraining centers, etc.), as well as by paying for selected social services received by non-beneficiaries. The rationale for this involvement is that the needs of some people go beyond defined benefits and that it is efficient to engage in prevention and in stimulating community services. In addition to providing social

services via grants to agencies outside its jurisdiction, social security provides them through its own administrative apparatus, Applying certain tests of effectiveness — effects on voluntary agencies, flexibility, avoidance of overlapping and confusion — Schorr finds that the French pattern is accomplishing what it intended, namely, that there has taken place 'a rapid buildup of services and a program somewhat more flexible or human that would otherwise have been possible' (17:40). This does not mean, however, that there are no difficulties: among them, fragmentation of services and a hodgepodge of public and voluntary service responsibilities are especially conspicuous and costly.

The system's positive results, Schorr maintains, have been made possible by the second aspect of the French pattern which is that social security employs one-quarter of all French social workers on its own staffs. Their functions are of three kinds: to furnish information for people with special problems and for those who find normal administrative channels inadequate; to complete the case records required for applying for benefits and services; and to provide direct services in collaboration with workers from other public or voluntary agencies. It is in carrying out these functions that programs become more human and flexible, acquire new meaning, lead to greater equity and to more social justice.

The third aspect — the use of a variety of devices to coordinate the social services at national, departmental, and local levels — focuses on avoiding overlapping and confusion. It is at the local level, where services are actually offered and received, that social workers play a crucial role. In this they are guided by three principles: no more than one family social worker may work with a family; each family social worker is responsible for all families in a compact geographic area (unless there are special reasons that make this undesirable); no work is done twice (17:38).

Oram's 1969 study likewise examines New Zealand's social services in relation to the country's social security system — as well as in relation to provisions in health, education and housing. He introduces his discussion by agreeing with Titmuss that the term 'social services' has acquired an elastic quality, that its expanding frontiers now embrace a multitude of heterogeneous activities, and that a consistent definition of the term does not exist. Among these diverse activities he selects those that to him appear especially important, describing and evaluating the protective and supportive roles they play in terms of their overall effect on the economic and social welfare of the country. By including information about expenditures and the financing arrangements they involve, Oram is able to arrive at the relative importance of social service programs within New Zealand's many-faceted network of social provision (18).

Flamm's book on social welfare services and social work in West Germany (1974) is a tightly organized, concise and clearly presented description of his subject in a wide-ranging perspective. It proceeds from an exposition of the constitutional foundations of the social services and the administrative structure within which they are operationalized to a description of their major components, both public and voluntary — social security, social assistance, youth welfare, and public health. Especially illuminating is the discussion of social planning, both 'environmental and functional', as it is shaped by the objectives of social policy. He explains that

> Social planning covers the social requirements of the community in general, the special requirements of the various age-groups and the specific urgent needs of individual human beings . . . planning for demand refers to the planning of social services and institutions and to the planning of the welfare personnel working in them. At the same time, planning must aim to create a sound social structure in the community in order to exercise a positive influence on the extent and type of social requirements (19:135—6).

Environmental structures must be designed 'to promote healthy living and working conditions', an objective that calls for different undertakings in rural and urban areas. Functional planning 'comprises planning of development tasks in the various specific fields'. Flamm emphasizes that 'social planning can be understood only in the context of the entire socio-economic and cultural development process' (19:137). Given this comprehensive approach, it is not surprising that when he looks at social administration and social work, Flamm defines that latter 'in the wider sense' as including 'all those specific activities in organized services and institutions which are designed to implement social tasks'. It follows, therefore, that 'the entire social administration is a part of social work . . . it permeates the education, training and health services systems and is gaining increasing influence on the public authorities in economic life' (19:143).

Madison's analysis of personal social services in the Soviet Union addresses their content and organization, their relationship to the social security system and the manner in which they are shaped by Soviet psycho-social theories and implemented in practice by treatment methods deemed appropriate in socialist society. A major feature of the psycho-social conceptualization is that the inherited factor, seen only as a predisposition, can be made more or less manifest by favorable or unfavorable external factors. Human nature is malleable and psychic influences to which it is subject can be reduced or eliminated by external factors. Because the conscious rather than the 'unconscious' dominates the development of the psyche, the major techniques for molding and changing personality must be rational — persuading, sharpening awareness, strengthening reasoning powers — the ultimate aim being the subjection of all behavior to the control of reason. Therapeutic programs are centered on involving the individual in purposeful activities, with the helping person adopting a rational commonsense attitude concerned primarily with rationally learned behavior rather than with the underlying emotional factors. Psychotherapy is practiced by medical personnel, not by welfare workers (20:25–35).

Three treatment methods are dominant: collective–individual, community participation, and work therapy. Seen as the most powerful element in molding the personality, the collective is defined by Soviet theoreticians as 'a joining of people who are linked together by common work, general interest, and goals'. Each collective — whether the family, the school, co-workers, political or social organizations — should be integrated with the others, guided by the same principles, seeking the same objectives, exhibiting the same basic characteristics, to the end of developing an individual who will feel, think, and act in conformity with the collective system of values. Yet, it is insisted, collective philosophy does not suppress the genuine individuality of each person because it is only through, by, and for the collective that an individual can achieve his particular maximum potential. But collectives are nurturing rather than oppressive for the individual only when correctly organized and do not exceed their proper functions — features which it is not easy to build into them. Community participation is an extension of the collective principle from the small to the large group, a group less intimately involved in the daily life of the individual and more formal in structure. It can exert a quasi-official pressure because of its links to the state and can secure compliance through force if necessary.

Idealization of work has permeated the Soviet welfare scene since the Revolution, itensified by the drive to industrialize, raise productivity and create a powerful military establishment in the face of a growing shortage of labor. Work, it is claimed, is the basic means for developing physical and intellectual abilities, for inculcating desired moral qualities, strengthening the will and discipline. It is the basic force, in growth and regeneration. Both social security and services consistently reward industriousness and punish laziness; they rely on work as the therapeutic tool par excellence to prevent psychic disturbances and a variety of maladjustments — and to cure them if they occur. But to do all this work therapy must also be correctly structured — apparently a requirement beset by many difficulties if one is to judge by the failure of many to internalize the official idealization (20:106—46).

In regard to their location in the total network of provision, services for those who come within the purview of social security are administered by social security agencies; for others, the responsibility for such services is distributed among a variety of organs and delivered by different types of personnel — educators, physicians, nurses, 'up-bringers', trade union activists, correctional workers (both paid and volunteers), etc. The profession of social work, an important participant in the delivery of personal social services in many countries, does not exist in the Soviet Union.

Day Care. Day-care programs provide care for young children during the day, for the most part because their mothers work, but also because their parents want them to have such care, or because the children need it.

A highly laudatory assessment of Cuba's system of day care is presented by Leiner and Ubell who believe that it 'offers research workers, educators, psychologists, and communities everywhere experimental evidence of what is possible in the education of the very young' (21:4). The system's success resides in 'essential and far-reaching features': it is free for families with working mothers; it is accessible to all who apply on a first-come, first-served basis, provided space is available; it admits infants at the age of six weeks and cares for them through age five; it is administered by a single agency (Federation of Cuban Women); in addition to custodial care, it provides medical treatment, preventive health care, and proper nutrition. To cope with the shortage of trained personnel, it relies on young people who are relatively inexperienced and untrained; it builds parent education and participation into the system and gets help from other agencies and from neighboring factories and farms. The constructive potential of the combination of these features, the authors claim, is enhanced by dedication and commitment on the part of all who are involved, including the young paraprofessionals who carry out their duties with enthusiasm and verve (21).

An American group of early childhood development experts visited the People's Republic of China in 1973. Its report — in which the discussion of nurseries and kindergartens is preceded by a description of the salient characteristics of Chinese families and followed by information about primary and middle schools, language development and services to improve nutrition among young children — was published in 1975 (22). The group found that day care is age-related and children are placed in homogeneous age groups. The nursery-age child is typically between two months and three years of age. At age three, he is usually transferred to a kindergarten. As parts of the educational network, both nurseries and kindergartens

> may be operated by factories, by street revolutionary committees, by rural communes, by regions of a city, by cities, or by the state. They may offer daytime care only or, more rarely, may board children from Monday morning until Saturday afternoon; there are some combined day and boarding schools. Some clearly serve children of bureaucrats and Army officers, while others serve children of workers or of peasants (22:74).

Personnel, all female in both, is better trained in kindergartens: a few teachers have college training, many are graduates of middle schools and some complete three years of special training in art, piano, dance, physical culture, language, mathematics, science or 'common knowledge', and teaching methods. In contrast, in nurseries teachers and caretakers are mostly women with some middle-school education or less, 'perhaps selected on the basis of temperament, experience with children and fondness for infants' (22:57—8). The goals for both types of facilities are said to be to free mothers for work, to ease child-rearing burdens for working parents, to promote the moral, intellectual, and physical development of the children, and to educate them to become skilfull and disciplined, so that later they can take their place in a socialist society.

On the qualitative side, the physical environment in both is 'austere', with few toys and primitive amenities. It was observed that nursery caretakers do not worry about interaction with or stimulation of the infant in the first months of life, do not encourage the children to be freely mobile or to play alone for long periods of time, and restrain them from excessive spontaneity and moving about. They prefer groups over individual activity, song and dance over cognitive activities. The kindergarten curriculum, tightly scheduled and structured, deals with six subject areas: Chinese language and politics, arithmetic, singing and dancing, drawing and painting, physical training, and productive labor. In regard to the latter, it was explained that love for manual labor is considered a virtue in Chinese society. Each kindergarten is expected to organize its own 'factory', and all children take part in some form of manual labor each week in order to make useful products.

What impressed the Americans about nursery-age children were their calm, orderliness, and apparent uniformity. Kindergarten children seemed expressive, docile, controlled, of concentrated attention, remarkably skillful in dancing and the arts, nonaggressive, compliant, unfearful, and without obvious symptoms of anxiety or tension. The procedures used by teachers that seemed relevant to developing these attributes were a high ratio of approval to disapproval, reliance on teaching by repetition and by formula, repeated use of models from the past and present, use of persuasion and moralistic reasoning (even with the very young), close connection between words about teaching and teaching practice, and, most important, a serene certainty that the children would do as they were taught. In turn, the children developed confidence that they can acquire the skills and the personality traits that the teachers expect them to acquire.

When the American experts attempted to draw out generalizations from the information they obtained, they were unable to arrive at a unified position 'because the members of the delegation varied radically from one another in their interpretation of what they saw' (22:215). The editor painstakingly outlines the limitations of the information made available to his group, and in concluding, explains what he calls 'a paradox, a proposition and two puzzles': stability in the lives of Chinese children, the pragmatic attitude among adults in regard to high expectations for children, and the acquisition of skills and the management of conflict among Chinese children. His responses to all this are in the form of hypotheses that indicate the need for further knowledge.

In the Soviet Union, day care has made impressive and steady gains: in 1940, permanent nurseries and kindergartens accommodated 2 million children; in 1978, the number stood at 12.7 million (23:99). Yet, these gains mean that in 1978 only 41 percent of all children of pre-school age — three months to seven years — were being cared for in these centers, this percentage being considerably lower than the 65 percent of all eligible children projected for the end of the 1970s. In large cities most three-to-seven-year-olds are accommodated: not so in smaller towns. Shortages for those under three are serious everywhere, resulting in part from the policy initiated in 1959 to decrease the contingent of those younger than three in order to make room for the three-to-seven-year-olds. It was in 1959 that the two types of facilities were unified and the Ministry of Education took over the administration of nurseries from Health. In January 1972 one million children were on the list of 'pending applications' because no republic had fulfilled its plan for the construction of preschools (24:831–2). That shortages are especially severe for rural families is suggested by the fact that of the children in permanent preschools in 1973, 8.2 million lived in urban communities, and only 2.3 million in rural areas. As a matter of fact, 8 million of these children lived in only two republics, the RSFSR and the Ukraine, meaning that only 2.5 million attended preschools in the other 13 republics (25:322).

Because of poor quality of care in some preschools, mothers hesitate to use some facilities, especially for very young children. One problem is the 'thoughtless and inconvenient location' of nursery-kindergartens which causes 'transportation sufferings for parents and children'; another is overcrowding and overloaded personnel; and the most serious, inadequate qualifications and high turnover of personnel. Parents are especially dissatisfied with what they see as a stress on custodial rather than developmental and educational functions and with lack of attention to individual differences among children. In terms of poorly prepared personnel, rural families are the most disadvantaged.

Working mothers likewise have access to facilities for the care of children in primary grades in the form of extended day schools. Established in 1956, these schools are designed to supervise children in off-school hours when no family supervision is available and to assist those who are not making normal progress in school. By 1973, 6 million children were enrolled in these schools, an impressive development but far short of what their advocates predicted in the 1960s when these schools were promoted as the 'prevalent mass-type school' of the future. One important deterrent to their growth has been their relatively high cost: a per capita annual expenditure of 150 rubles, compared with 80–90 rubles for regular primary and secondary schools. To some extent this reflects the expense of the two daily meals provided in these schools, which is shouldered in whole or in part by the state in many cases. But beyond this, the generally low public esteem in which these schools are held has helped to impede their development. It is said that quite often they are a blind alley for the child and for this reason parents are not always willing to avail themselves of their services (20:75, 154—5; 24:832:3; 25:322—3).

In terms of quantitative adequacy, the situation on day care in the Soviet Union must be seen in relation to two major aspects of its society: the changing patterns of family life which mean that working mothers' reliance on their mothers or mothers-in-law to care for their children has diminished because more and more the older and younger generations are living apart; and the fact that by now 68 percent of the nearly 100 million Soviet women over age 16 are employed, accounting for 54.5 percent of all workers (23:98).

Child Welfare. Most single-country studies of child welfare describe either the specific programs contained in this multi-faceted field, ranging from programs for children living in their own homes to those for children living in a variety of settings outside their own homes; or the problems that children experience — the latter generated by a growing number of recognized factors that induce them, such as abuse, neglect, dependency, emotional disturbance, mental retardation, deprived social status, and handicapping conditions; or the methods of professional practice that are likely to be most effective in helping children deal with problems. The few studies selected for inclusion seemed especially pertinent because they either relate child welfare concerns to the social milieu from which they surface and in which their systems of service delivery are organized, or have significant implications for policy.

In a monograph on child abuse published in 1972 (26), Van Stolk presents the available factual information concerning this phenomenon in Canada, the variety of opinions held about its nature and causation, and programs developed to deal with it. She discusses, as well, the legal and administrative complications encountered in implementation. Van Stolk differentiates between 'soft-core abuse', which she views as 'a cultural way of life' caused by the manner in which rights and responsibilities of adults and children are defined and shape relationships between them; and 'hard-core battering' which she considers as rooted in parental or family psychopathology. While both are functions of culture, societal values, social and economic factors, patterns of child rearing, and attitudes toward authority, they call for different intervention methods. 'Hard-core battering', she explains, requires highly specialized diagnostic and treatment approaches.

A book edited by Wolins and published in 1971 (27) contains 26 papers which examine the history, philosophy, achievements and problems of Youth Aliyah in Israel, a program initiated in the 1930s to rescue Jewish children from Germany and other Nazi-menaced countries. Passage of time transformed the program into an experimental undertaking with the aim of resocializing and rehabilitating children from immigrant and economically deprived families living in Israel. To begin with, reliance was placed on group care that maximized the value of work, group experience, and communal responsibility; but with the country's economic and social progress, personal goals emerged as of primary importance. The country required skilled individuals whose need for education burgeoned into a variety of services regulated by government. As focus moved from the influence of the group to the individual and the family, professionalization of the helping personnel increased, replacing the group leader (ideological guide, friend and companion) with a skilled technician ('psychologically distant manipulator'). The discussion of the group formation process, the manner in which a person becomes a group member, and the way in which the group reflects and influences the larger society explain why the group can become a major force for changing personality and values.

Although the subject matter of Rollins's study (1972) is a medical service — child psychiatry in the Soviet Union — she conceptualizes it in such a way as to produce insights useful for clarifying child welfare issues. For example, in discussing the Soviet family she points up features that may have special significance for mental health and illness. She notes that in the home child-rearing practices 'are characterized by warmth, protectiveness, insistence on controlled behavior, and diffusion of parental roles into the wider society'. While the transition from such a milieu to the demands of early schooling may form a vulnerable point, diffusion of parental roles may promote mental health — if it increases the child's feelings of security by offering 'collective alternatives early in life' and thereby influencing profoundly 'the formation of object relations, identification patterns, and capacity for sublimation' (28:44). In order to place treatment practices in a socio-cultural context, Rollins relates aspects of Soviet child psychiatry and of its anti-Freudian orientation to the cultural values of Soviet society she considers especially prominent and important. Drawing on this juxtaposition, she concludes that 'treatment in the USSR acts to desensitize or perhaps to insulate the patient from a frustrating environment, occasionally to give some temporary respite by removing the patient to more tranquil surroundings, but there is little or no attempt to change the environment' (28:240).[3]

In his study of juvenile delinquency in the Soviet Union (1972),

Connor arrives at a similar position on environment, but from a different perspective. His objectives are to portray deviance itself, to give the Soviet explanation for it, and to describe the preventive, rehabilitative, curative and corrective measures used. In regard to causation, he finds that Soviet thought exhibits two trends: the first is to deny that there are delinquency generating factors inherent in Soviet society and to assign responsibility to the malfunctioning of various concrete institutions of socialization and control (family, school, factory, youth organization, etc.); the second is to strive for a deeper understanding of the dynamics and characteristics of the adolescent male personality — such as spirit of adventure, self-assertiveness, desire for independence from parental authority — which may make him particularly susceptible to undesirable influences. Malfunctions are viewed as deviations from the ideal in *some* institutions of socialization and control — not as features of the society as a whole; hence, delinquency is not explained by endemic conditions. Nor do the majority of Soviet criminologists link delinquency to stresses induced by rapid industrialization in their society; some, however, are beginning to realize that such a link exists.

As for the concept of personality, it has established its place in Soviet thinking in the sense that the country's criminologists agree on the need for studying it further. Connor found that despite theoretical differences, the forms of disposition of delinquents in the USSR show little in the way of notable innovations. Writes Connor:

> The range of possibilities, from institutionalization to probation, is no broader than in many other societies, and the tendency to reserve the harsher measures for older delinquents is a familiar one . . . deprivation of freedom, or its threat through a suspended sentence, is a basic . . . means of punishment (29:129).

Services for juvenile delinquents in the Soviet Union, as they evolved since the Revolution, are discussed by Madison in two publications, with special attention focused on the responsible agencies: their structure, functions, personnel and performance (20:172–4; 24:845–50). That juvenile delinquency is on the increase, she finds, is strongly suggested by information from a variety of Soviet sources. It is also clear that the parents of pre-delinquents and delinquents are unable to provide proper supervision or adequate care for their children because of serious social problems they themselves experience — illnesses, difficult work schedules, disorganized family life, and family breakups. These parents especially need services when their youngsters are placed on probation or released on parole so that they either continue to live at home or not far away, in their home communities. Yet preventive work is either absent or ineffective in many jurisdictions, and recidivism among probationers and parolees is high. The reasons for this are said to include the failure of Commissions of Juvenile Affairs — the major responsible official body — to reach all of the youngsters involved or to serve them when they are reached; the insufficient number of paid probation officers; and the lack of training among these officers as well as among unpaid 'social upbringers' who volunteer their services. Similarly, in many localities the militia — another responsible organ — fails to register all juvenile offenders, as it is supposed to do, and confines its preventive and reforming efforts to infrequent and ineffective talks at the militia station.

Personal social services for Soviet children living in their own homes — other than day care — are, strictly speaking, non-existent. Some counseling may be provided by classroom teachers and children's inspectors concerned with learning difficulties and non-attendance; by teachers in special schools for educable 'defective' children; and by medical personnel in a variety of settings, concerned with physical and mental health problems. To what extent these professionals try to help with other problems, such as abrasive personal relationships, is not clear. Not only has the Soviet family undergone changes induced by rapid urbanization and industrialization, but it has also been subject to several violent changes in the official position regarding it. These have ranged all the way from efforts to hasten the 'withering away' of the 'burgeois' family (until the mid-1930s), to a conditional reliance on parents for socialization depending on how well they conformed to standards and expectations set by the Party and the school, to restoring the family to its position as the basic social unit (20:35—49; 147—77; 24:836—9). Nor have measures to strengthen family stability been successful: official statistics show that divorce has sky-rocketed from 3.2 per 100 marriages in 1950 to 27 per 100 marriages in 1973, creating many problems including those involved in child support. This is of great concern to the government, but so far the only agency available for counseling husbands and wives is the divorce court, and only if children are involved. In such cases, the court must 'establish the motives for notice of dissolution of marriage and take measures to reconcile husband and wife' by pointing out to them the importance of the conjugal bond. There exist no specialized services for the unwed mother or for her illegitimate child, despite estimates suggesting that the number of illegitimate children throughout the Soviet period has been sizable and that at least 400,000 illegitimate babies are now being born every year (25:319—20).

Services for children who do not live at home are of two kinds: substitute family care and institutional care. The former refers to adoption and placement with guardians (for those under age 15) and trustees (for those between 15 and 18) who care for them on a long-term or permanent basis. Temporary foster-family care, never extensive, no longer exists. Adoption, although officially highly regarded, in fact remains a rudimentary service: prospective parents must themselves find a child to adopt, usually in an institution; the study of suitability for parenting is superficial; how many children are adopted and how they fare is never reported. Nor is anything written about children in the homes of guardians and trustees. All this suggests that despite the restoration of the family to a pivotal position in the upbringing of children, the major resource for children who do not have one or whose families are unable to offer needed care is the institution, even for those among them who can benefit by family life. Indeed, the heavy reliance on institutions is demonstrated by homes and boarding schools for normal children who are for the most part dependent, neglected and disadvantaged (children of unmarried mothers who do not wish to keep them, of war and labor invalids, orphans, members of large, poor or 'problem' families); and homes for 'defective' children divided into educable and non-educable.

Institutional staffs consist of teachers, upbringers and 'defectologists' —upbringers being teachers with extra training in psychology, while defectologists are teachers with special knowledge about handicapping conditions. With the exception of institutions for non-educable defectives which are administered by welfare organs, all the others are under the aegis of educational authorities who are in charge of substitute family care as well. No authoritatively supported movement to deinstitutionalize can be discerned, although some Soviet upbringers complain about the destruction of the 'most valuable, the most cherished thing' — the feeling of a big friendly family — in 'giant' institutions — for pre-schoolers, homes of 100—160 capacity, for children of school age, boarding schools of 300—600 capacity (20:147—76; 24:839—45).

Aged. Given the well-known fact that the number of aged persons in many countries is increasing — both in absolute terms and as a proportion of the population — it is not surprising that concern about services for them is increasing as well. Among services that are assuming greater importance is 'opencare' — a system that supports community living in order to forestall premature or unnecessary institutionalization. According to Little (1975), in the UK the crucial issue in home help for the elderly is whether the country 'is in fact ready to provide the quantity, quality and range of services required to maintain the elderly and other populations at risk in community living' (30:22). In regard to quantity, while everyone agrees that what is now available in terms of the ratio of home helps per 100,000 population is inadequate, there is some disagreement as to what the target for the future ought to be. In the meantime, advances are being made, but unevenly: there are considerable variations in the planning and provision of services by different localities. As to quality, again there are differences of opinion among researchers about whether consumers are satisfied with the service they get and with the frequency, length and timing of visits by home helps. Studies of consumer satisfaction/dissatisfaction are inconclusive because they omit non-recipients — those who do not apply, are turned down, or drop out. Little is convinced that the British home help service 'is skewed in the direction of providing a little service to many cases at the expense of a more intensive and more meaningful service to some' (30:25). Opinions among personnel also vary on the desirability of retaining fees (generally low and not charged at all to many people). How problems are resolved depends on the answers to such questions as: does a recipient have the right to complain about deficiencies in the service? Do old people have the right to adequate care and attention?

Scholten (1975) discusses issues involved in home help services in the Netherlands in relation to their development since before 1940 (31). One such issue was the need to beef up efficiency. This was achieved by combining small agencies — those working in the same town or region but established by different denominational groups — into one service. This 'denominational enlargement' was adopted in order to maintain the home help service's identity among the other social agencies. Administratively, efficiency was improved by the central government's promulgation of rules on subsidies to the enlarged agencies which spelled out minimum requirements for staff — its number, functions and qualifications. Future improvements in services for the aged, recognized as a multi-faceted problem, were detailed in a five-year plan, initiated in 1970, which called for an increase in part-time home helps, auxiliaries in district nursing services, and service centers. The plan also contained suggestions for developing social services in general. Scholten

Comparative National Experience 211

believes that questions regarding recruitment of staff, quality of work, supervision, and administrative structure must be dealt with on an ongoing basis, to say nothing of the need to constantly update the machinery for cooperating with a variety of other services. All this underscores the need for continuing evaluation and research, to assess results and indicate direction.

Little discusses 'opencare' for the aged in Sweden against a background of the country's social service policies and goals (1978). She described the multiple points of entry into the system and the services provided, noting that 'because a solid base of welfare supports such as income maintenance, rent subsidies, and health care facilities exist, the system is called on primarily to fulfill personal social services functions and is not expected to fill gaps in social and medical areas' (32:285). Among unanswered questions Little includes the lack of information on unmet needs, failure to spell out specific program objectives, scarcity of meaningful outcome measures, absence of clarity about the degree of coordination between medical and health services, on the one hand, and social and environmental services, on the other, and insufficiency of data on cost-effectiveness. She concludes that

> If cross-national comparisons are to be made and the program of one country used as a model for others, a data base that is more substantial than the presently available rough indicators of effort or inputs in needed (32:287).

In the Soviet Union services to support community living for the aged (and disabled) are as yet rudimentary. The only identifiable services seem to be of two kinds: 'material-household assistance' and certain ancillary services. The former provide friendly visiting, supplemented at times by such help as doing the laundry, shopping, light housework, and making sure the pensioner gets the prescribed special diet. The latter assist with job placement, assembling documents required to establish eligibility for pension, checking on working conditions and on sanitation in the home and the work environment, and helping to gain admittance to sanatoria, health, recreational, and educational facilities. The actual provision of these services is entrusted to activists, that is, volunteers. Those in 'material-household assistance' are supervised by local offices of the Ministry of Social Security, those in ancillary services, by local trade unions. In some localities there are relatively more activists than in others, but even in the most advanced centers, such as Leningrad, their potential caseload is well beyond

1,500 clients each. Uneven distribution is characteristic of activists assigned by trade unions as well. All activist groups are quite fluid: they grow or disappear and it is not clear how the need for them is determined. But there is little doubt that many old people who need services but are too timid or depressed to make this known may be ignored; others, who complain or insist, may get some assistance, but its duration and quality usually depend on the character and the commitment of the particular activist.

While there is awareness that aged persons could remain in their own homes longer, thus delaying institutionalization, if adequate outreach and supportive services were developed, the trend continues toward institutionalization. Yet, despite steady growth, in 1975 the country's institutions, unevenly distributed among the 15 Republics, accommodated only 315,000 aged and disabled -- when there were 41.4 million pensioners in these categories (excluding veterans). Institutions are supposed to accept the destitute and those who either have no families or whose families cannot care for them. But waiting lists for the destitute, as well as for others, continue long in most Republics. In most institutions personnel other than medical have no special training (20:177–94; 33:55).

A major policy issue in regard to the aged (as well as retarded children) is raised by Moroney in a study, published in 1976, in which he is concerned with the function of the family as a provider of social care for its members, 'and conversely, the role of the organized welfare system as it affects the family' in the UK – a subject whose 'long-term implications for social policy requirements have been neglected' (34:1). In regard to the elderly he found that 'since 1963 almost one-half of key social welfare expenditures [for social security, health and welfare] have been allocated to this group, representing only 16 percent of the population' (34:35). At the same time, he detected no clear evidence that the family has relinquished the primary responsibility for the care of the elderly or that the State is assuming it. He poses two questions: what would happen if even a small proportion of the families who now care for their handicapped members were to ask the State to take over this function, at a time when 'the issue is not determining priorities for expansion in the social welfare services, but one of controlled retrenchment'; what motivates families to seek relief from this function: are they influenced by unintended consequences of existing policies, are they changing as a social institution, or are they acting in response to interactions between the two? Do existing policies substitute for or complement the family?

Moroney found that the family's traditional functions of socialization and caring are continuing, that the extended family in a modified form exists, but that operating policies seem to neglect the services provided by families to their handicapped members: as a matter of fact, the welfare system makes fewer services available to these families than to other groups. The state is still emphasizing its role as a substitute for the family. To reverse this, social welfare has to offer 'choice from a number of options, flexibility of approach, and an operational commitment to supportive services that share the caring responsibility instead of substituting for the family' (34:112).

In some respects, the situation in Japan is somewhat similar to that described by Moroney in Great Britain — as far as family care for the aged is concerned. Maeda (1975) explains that Japanese culture expects the family to be independent and self-sufficient through mutual assistance of blood relatives. The Japanese find it embarrassing to ask for help from other families, and when such help is given, it is generally on a reciprocal basis: once a family has been helped by others, it is expected to repay that obligation some time later, on equal terms, using either spiritual or material means. Consequently, intervention in other families' affairs is avoided, organized charity and voluntary action have not been well developed, and 'Japanese people tend to expect the state to take action only when the family cannot fulfill its traditional roles' (35:254). Family-based programs of services for the aged have been developed only in the last 10—15 years. Nor is it surprising that three-quarters of the people over 65 live with their children, even in this time of advanced industrialization. These children's families are eligible for income-tax reductions and loans for home improvement and expansion; financial assistance is only available in 'some' localities and apparently, only when the elderly person is bedfast. Services are confined to home helps, community welfare centers, clubhouses for the aged, and organizations of the elderly themselves. Other community services, such as visiting nurses, meals-on-wheels, etc. are 'non-existent'. Among government programs, those that provide institutional care far outnumber those that offer family-based care. The former include nursing homes and homes for ambulatory elderly, with varying fee structures. Both types of facilities with moderate charges are in acute shortage; but priority is being given to expanding nursing homes because of the serious social problems resulting from the fact that the number of bedfast old people whose families cannot look after them is increasing (36:53).

Policy Issues. Underlying the definitional confusion which continues to surround personal social services is the fundamental question about goals to be achieved. Are services to prevent 'social anomalies' and to 'return to productive life everyone who has strayed' from it, as in the Soviet Union? Or are they to prevent social problems generated by the society and to assist each individual to attain his/her highest potential and to enhance his/her quality of life, as in developed democracies? Or are they to organize the poor and the disadvantaged to assert their right to a better life, as in many developing countries? Or are they to do all these things? If so, is this a realistic and feasible goal for a presumably unique professional type of service, and one that, from the standpoint of resources, political clout, and general public understanding, usually finds itself close to the bottom of the human services hierarchy? If they are not to do all these things, how should priorities be fixed?

The 'elastic', hazily defined, fragmented and uneven nature of personal social services underscores the primordial importance of an on-going effort to strive for intra- and inter-service harmonization and for improving coordination with associated and/or contributing services. Important as well is the development of an up-to-date expertise for interpreting both to professionals in other human services and to the lay public the constructive potential of personal social services for advancing the general welfare. What kind of organizational and administrative structure, responsive to changing needs but clear-cut in jurisdictional responsibilities, is likely to achieve this best — given the diversity in governmental systems and arrangements, cultural traditions, economic resources, and political objectives? How well this question is answered is bound up to a considerable extent with the response demanded by yet another issue: how to evaluate what is being achieved (or not achieved) by services, at what cost and why — in short, how to make services accountable. Because the problems of accountability are closely related not only to program effectiveness and professional responsibility, but also to policy-making, politics and ideology, the ability to be accountable, so difficult to attain in services because they are but rarely quantified, profoundly influences policy and planning.

Another vital issue, perhaps even more tenacious in services than in social security, revolves around the kind of personnel that will most effectively implement the policy blueprint and assure a quality of service demanded by a particular society at a given point in time. The teaching and training of personnel raises a host of substantive and technical questions about the location of curricula in the educational establishment, their level, the status they confer, etc. It is here that the professional value base exerts an especially strong influence on the entire educational program. There is no getting away from such questions, for example, as: how do scholars and practitioners explain the presence of social problems in a given society and the responses to them by groups and individuals? Is theory utilized to explain pertinent phenomena or are explanations confined largely to 'facts' — whether statistical, legal or administrative? If theory is brought in, are its bases derived from ideology or is theory tested in the context of empirical data? How are failures to identify and resolve problems explained and to what extent are explanations used to indicate the direction of change in policy? How is the issue of responsibility for initiating and administering services dealt with? Answers to these and other questions which contribute to making personnel 'qualified' in a broader sense than becoming competent technicians is certainly one of the most decisive influences on quality of services and on the degree to which they are truly 'welfare' in nature.

Of crucial concern for all personal social services is 'family policy' an area that is still immersed in much vagueness and many uncertainties. Although the 'family' is universally recognized as the basic social unit, it evokes many and confusing meanings and images. At the same time, it seems obvious that family forms are becoming increasingly diversified, especially in highly developed industrial societies (where singles, childless and homosexual couples are by some considered to be 'families') and less so in tradition-bound societies. It also appears that everywhere the expressed desire is to have the 'family' remain a basic social unit, to provide love, economic support, socialization, health and social care. In most societies, whether this is stated explicitly or implied, the family is expected to raise children who will adhere to certain ideologies, ideals, attitudes. How to help the family perform all these tasks and not weaken or supplant it in the process remains a difficult question, one that leads to policy decisions — whether 'explicit or implicit', 'comprehensive or episodic', 'harmonized to a degree or uncoordinated' (37:476).[4] Even in the economic domain, with general agreement that for family well-being an adequate minimum income is essential, there is concern that providing it collectively should not discourage individual initiative and the striving to meet family needs by its own efforts.

At the same time, it is universally recognized that there are many situations in which the family cannot and/or should not perform the expected tasks. This means that society has to create and maintain a diversified network of services, including institutional care, appropriately used for specific needs. Not only is it difficult and costly to create the network, but there is much debate on what is 'appropriate' use. Involved is the concept of deinstitutionalization — release from institutions of those who can benefit from care in the community — a concept that is intimately related to the issue of community-based services. A policy to institute release must be accompanied by assuring adequate and sufficient facilities in the community to receive all who come. At a deeper level are involved a society's prevailing views concerning the meaning and significance of attributes associated with 'defectives', both physical and mental. These views play an important role in determining whether the separation from the 'normal' will be inflexible or whether a certain amount of integration in specified community settings will be tolerated. Who can benefit by life in the community and who is better served by remaining in the institution raises many emotionally laden issues.

Summary. The findings contained in single-country studies make plain that income provided by cash benefits is not enough: it must be buttressed by a broad, responsive and carefully integrated system of personal social services. These services, in turn, cannot fulfill their functions significantly without a solid base of welfare supports in the shape of employment, health care, housing, education, and income maintenance. What is encompassed by services differs strikingly between countries, much more so than in social security. Countries present different scenarios in the kinds and scope of services they offer, to whom they make them available, for what reasons and on what conditions, in their location in the overall network of social provision, and in the organizational and administrative structures entrusted with their implementation. They also differ in regard to the goals that services are expected to achieve and, of great importance, in relation to a particular society's view of the psycho-social nature of man (including the relationship between genetic and environmental factors) and of the kind of society that is most likely to provide a benign milieu for his ideal all round development.

As in social security, services are influenced by a particular country's level of economic and technological development, by its cultural values, and by its political system. But almost everywhere, in distributing scarce resources, higher priority is assigned to social security than to personal social services. In several types of provision, social security is called upon to respond to values whose evolution has been relatively more rapid and is more readily perceived and understood by the general population — those, for example, that result from demographic and employment

Comparative National Experience

changes. In contrast, personal social services often must take into account values that are still deeply embedded in traditional cultural patterns and are more resistant to change — those, for example, that concern the family, the nurture of children (as in notions of what constitutes neglect and abuse and the reasons for them), and those that reflect religious orientations, especially as they stipulate attitudes between the more and the less privileged.

As a result, what is done in the services domain may range all the way from designing them to permeate the totality of social provision to not providing them at all for large segments of the population whose need for them is patent. The magnitude of the gulf symbolized by these differences between countries appears less wide and deep in social security, while the movement to bridge it is more rapid and more widely accepted and desired.

Notes

1. In regard to social services in industry, policy-oriented information is in short supply. In India, where industrial social work has been important as a professional specialization for decades, it is felt by many that the need for it is 'obvious': industrial social services are concerned with 'the psychological and human relations factors in industry in order to improve individual and group morale, to promote harmonious industrial relations, to increase efficiency and at the same time, in tackling problems of poor productivity, frequent accidents, chronic absenteeism and difficult behavior' (2:410). But it turns out that in fact 'labour welfare officers' for the most part are involved in implementing social legislation that affects the physical work environment (sanitation, lighting, ventilation, etc.). To do this, an officer often has to

> reconcile irreconcilable viewpoints. His job is not easy and often he has been described as being between the devil and the deep blue sea, between the devil of an employer and the sea of workers . . . The workers have often complained that since the Labour Welfare Officers are paid by the management, they will invariably side with their paymasters. The managements often held the opposite view that these officers are too lenient to the workers (3:967).

Some Indian schools of social work have discontinued this specialization as inconsistent with social work values.

In 1971 the UN published a report on industrial social welfare aimed at establishing guidelines for developing countries in the early stages of industrialization. Major sources of information were six country monographs — from Brazil, India, Poland, United Arab Republic, UK, and Zambia. Adoption of a 'wider functional definition' of industrial social welfare facilitated comparisons of its use by industry, government and other organizations (4).

A study published by Carter in 1975 examined industrial social work from the point of view of 'historical parallels' in five industrial nations — UK, France, FRG, US and the Soviet Union. His findings led him to pose the hypothesis that 'the evolution of industrial social work occurs in a pattern which is generally applicable to all industrialized nations; and that the outcome in advanced industrial nations will be the employment of professional social workers in industry' (5).

Quite a different view is presented by Kahn and Kamerman in their review of industrial social services in the eight countries they studied. They found that personal social services are not important in industrial-trade union activities in the UK and Israel, and that their role is limited in FRG, US, and Canada. Only France has seen a comprehensive development; and Yugoslavia provides extensive industrial and union-based social services. 'However', they note, 'to the extent that data are available, it would appear that the industrial or trade union emphasis in all kinds of countries is on utilities: eating arrangements, camps for children, family vacations, or, at the least, child care arrangements' (6:394).

2. Writings on policy concerning social work personnel in an international context are also scarce. Most are focused on whether it is desirable to transfer Western-type social work to developing countries. In his study of social work in the Afro-Asian world, de Jongh found that Western style social work practice has limited use there because of differences in the level of education and division of labor patterns and in the objectives which social welfare programs seek to achieve. Futhermore, Western social work is rational, scientific and adheres strongly to social individualism, whereas in developing countries opportunities for individual responsibility and tolerance of nonconforming behavior are limited. He believes that effective service would be more likely if training of personnel took place in indigenous schools of social work, patterned after indigenous needs and cultural peculiarities (8).

Writing in 1970, Austin came to the same conclusions. 'It may be', he writes, that training for social workers 'must be developed by and among the developing nations on their own terms. Resource persons from the US and other Western nations who have diverse backgrounds may have a role, but only as partners in a common effort to find answers for complex social problems that we in the US do not yet understand or know how to control' (9:106).

The same theme is echoed by Khinduka in 1971. Noting that pervasive poverty is the distinguishing feature of the third world, he points out that the type of social work current in industrialized societies is of limited relevance to poor nations. Since it is the developmental rather than the remedial aspect of social welfare that must have priority, social workers should concentrate on institutional reconstruction rather than on individual rehabilitation. 'It is only when the professional social workers in the third world redefine their targets of intervention that they will acquire a relevance in the context of their societies' needs' (10:71–2).

The doubtful usefulness of transferability in training is also brought out in a comparative study of professional values espoused by American and Turkish social workers, published by Feldman in 1971. He became convinced that the acceptance of certain key values — individual worth and personal liberty — varied cross-culturally, and that these values cannot be viewed as universal attributes of social workers (11).

That the American influence on social work education and through it on social work practice in India, especially in evidence since 1947–8, 'has not been an unmixed blessing' is clearly brought out in a 1975 paper. Efforts to mold the curriculum on the American pattern led 'to the curtailment of the social science content, inadequate emphasis on social action, alienation of the group of trained social workers from the Sarvodaya social workers (largely untrained community workers concerned with the well-being of all), and neglect of social reform' (12:178).

A recent cross-national review of social work education by Kendall, encompassing 79 schools of social work in 65 countries, found that there is enough in common in the curriculum structure and content of these schools for the field to claim legitimacy as an international discipline. Among common educational objectives are certain value commitments: worth and dignity of the individual, social responsibility, solidarity, and authenticity — the latter referring to freedom from imported ideas and the desirability of developing practice that responds to local and national needs. But, 'different levels of education are now very much in evidence' and as for faculty, the patterns were also sharply diversified: of the 79 schools, there were 8 with no full-time faculty while another 8 had 25 or more full-time faculty; in 24 schools the number of part-time faculty varied from 6 to 191 (13:79, 81–2). While training that would prepare for social policy, planning and administration has been accepted in principle, the social workers who emerge are at best equipped with knowledge in these areas that will be useful in the first stages of their careers. Nor is there serious training in research — likewise declared to be important in the preparation of all social workers.

3. In the concluding chapter of her study Rollins attempts to show the ways in which Freudianism is incompatible with values important in Russian culture and compatible with values important in American culture. In the former she includes stress on collectivism, submissiveness to authority, control of external behavior, conscious planning, humanitarianism, warmth, materialism, and cultural isolation; in the latter, individualism, rebelliousness with respect to authority, permissiveness in regard to external behavior, pluralism, permeability, diffusion, and escalation of expectations. She concludes by emphasizing the need to be more aware of the cultural determinants in the two countries' respective ideologies and by advocating a 'healthy skepticism' with regard to all theory (28:230–40).

4. In this book Kamerman and Kahn bring together articles on family policy by experts in 14 countries: Sweden, Norway, Hungary, Czechoslovakia, France, Austria, FRG, Poland, Finland, Denmark, UK, Canada, Israel, the US. They conclude that as yet there are no answers to such questions as: 'What is family policy? What are the costs and benefits of a family policy perspective?' (37:476). Discussion in the 14 articles deals with labor market and population policy; with socialization, protection and control; equality of the sexes; promotion of cultural and ethnic identity; defence; social services; family patterns — these factors, separately or in various combinations, offering clues as to why a particular country does or does not institute particular measures in 'family policy'. As to instruments of family policy, the authors identify income-transfer programs, income-tax systems, family law, child-care services, personal social services, housing, education, and health care. They recognize that family policy can be affected importantly by the type of government structures given operational responsibility in this field. In regard to whether a given family policy 'works', it is necessary to differentiate family types and roles within families, to state standards, to clarify values, to observe and study over long time spans — a formidable task. Kamerman and Kahn take the position that 'family policy as perspective . . . becomes a subset of a *quality-of-life dimension*. It is here that we believe it attains its maximum validity and offers its greatest challenge' (37:497).

References

1. UN, Department of Economic and Social Affairs *The Development of National Social Service Programmes* (New York, UN Department of Economic and Social Affairs, 1959, 60.IV.I).

2. Marfatia, J. C., 'Contributions of Psychiatry to the Profession of Social Work in Twenty-Five Years', pp. 405–11 in Gokhale, S. D. (ed.) *Social Welfare, Legend and Legacy*, Silver Jubilee Commemoration Volume of the Indian Council of Social Welfare (Bombay, Popular Prakashan, 1975).

3. Jacob, K. K., *Methods and Fields of Social Work in India*, revised edition (New York, Asia Publishing-House, 1965).

4. UN, Department of Economic and Social Affairs, *Industrial Social Welfare* (New York, UN, 1971, ST/SOA/112. Sales No., E.71.IV.12).

5. Carter, Irl, *Industrial Social Work: Historical Parallels in Five Western Nations*, PhD Dissertation, University of Iowa, College of Education, May 1975.

6. Kahn and Kamerman, *Social Services in International Perspective*.

7. UN, Department of Economic and Social Affairs, *Proceedings of the International Conference of Ministers Responsible for Social Welfare, 3 to 12 September 1968* (New York, UN, 1969. Sales No., E.69.IV.4).

8. De Jongh, J. F., 'Western Social Work and the Afro-Asian World', *Social Service Review*, 43, no. 1 (March 1969), pp. 50–8.

9. Austin, David M., 'Social Work's Relation to National Development in Developing Nations', *Social Work*, 15, no. 1 (January 1970), pp. 97–106.

10. Khinduka, S. K., 'Social Work and the Third World', *Social Service Review*, 45, no. 1 (March 1971), pp. 62–73.

11. Feldman, R. A., 'Professionalization and Professional Values: a Cross-cultural Comparison', *International Review of Sociology*, 1, no. 2 (1971), pp. 85–97.

12. Pathak, S. H., 'A Quarter Century of Professional Social Work In India', pp. 170–92 in Gokhale.

13. Kendall, K. A., 'Cross-national Review of Social Work Education', *Journal of Education for Social Work*, 13 (2), Spring 1977, pp. 76–83.

14. Thursz, Daniel and Vigilante, Joseph L. (eds.) *Meeting Human Needs*, vol. 1: Social Service Delivery Systems. An International Annual. *An Overview of Nine Countries* (Beverly Hills and London, Sage Publications, 1975); vol. 2: *ibid., Additional Perspectives from Thirteen Countries* (Beverly Hills and London: Sage Publications, 1976). The quotation in the text is from vol. 1. The nine countries included in vol. 1 are: Egypt, Great Britain, Iran, Israel, Italy, Poland, Sweden, US, and USSR. The 13 countries included in vol. 2 are: Canada, Scotland, African Rhodesia, South Africa, Australia, Denmark, Finland, Yugoslavia, People's Republic of China, Japan, Colombia, Brazil, Panama.

15. Kahn and Kamerman, *Social Services in International Perspective*.

16. Rao, V. K. R. V., 'The Seeds of Radical Change', *Development*, vol. xx, nos. 3/4 (1978). pp. 21–3. For a discussion of the highlights of the Sixth Plan see same publication, pp. 17–42.

17. Schorr, *Social Security and Social Services in France*.

18. Oram, *Social Policy and Administration in New Zealand*.

19. Flamm, Franz, *Social Welfare Services and Social Work in the Federal Republic of Germany* (Frankfurt/Main, Eigenverlag des Deutschen Vereins für Offentliche und Private Fürsorge, 1974).

20. Madison, *Social Welfare in the Soviet Union*.

21. Leiner, Marvin, with Ubell, Robert, *Children are the Revolution. Day Care in Cuba* (New York, Viking Press, 1974).

22. Kessen, William, (ed.) *Childhood in China* (New Haven and London, Yale University Press, 1975).

23. Madison, Bernice, 'The 'Problemy' that Won't Go Away', *The Wilson Quarterly* (Autumn 1978), pp. 96–103.

24. Madison, Bernice, 'Social Services for Families and Children in the Soviet Union since 1967', *Slavic Review*, 31, no. 4 (December 1972), pp. 831–52.

25. Madison. Bernice, 'Social Services for Women: Problems and Priorities', pp. 307–33 in Atkinson, Dorothy, Dallin, Alexander, and Warshofsky Lapidus, Gail (eds.) *Women in Russia* (Stanford, California, Stanford University Press, 1977).

26. Van Stolk, Mary, *The Battered Child in Canada* (Toronto, McClelland and Stewart, 1972).

27. Wolins, Martin (ed.) *Group Care: An Israeli Approach: The Educational Path of Youth Aliyah* (New York, Gordon & Breach, 1971).
28. Rollins, Nancy, *Child Psychiatry in the Soviet Union. Preliminary Observations* (Cambridge, Mass., Harvard University Press, 1972).
29. Connor, *Deviance in Soviet Society*.
30. Little, Virginia A., 'Home Help Services for the Elderly: the British Experience', in *Home-Help Services for the Aging Around the World* (Washington, DC, The International Federation on Ageing, 1975), pp. 22—5.
31. Scholten, Dr J. M. P., 'The Development of Home Help Services in the Netherlands', *ibid.*, pp. 28—31.
32. Little, Virginia C., 'Open Care for the Aged: Swedish Model', *Social Work*, 23, no. 4 (July 1978), pp. 282—8.
33. Madison, 'Soviet Income Maintenance Programs'.
34. Moroney, *The Family and the State*.
35. Maeda, Daisaku, 'Growth of Old People's Clubs in Japan', *The Gerontologist*, vol. 15, no. 3 (June 1975), pp. 254—6.
36. Maeda, Daisaku, Chief, Social Welfare Section, Tokyo Metropolitan Institute of Gerontology, untitled letter in *The Rotarian* (December 1974), pp. 52—3.
37. Kamerman, Sheila B. and Kahn, Alfred J. (eds.) *Family Policy. Government and Families in Fourteen Countries* (Columbia University Press, New York, 1978).

9 THE ORGANIZATION OF SOCIAL WELFARE

As in single-country studies, cross-national studies that focus on personal social services range over a broad spectrum. Among them relatively numerous are the studies that investigate special problems affecting certain individuals and groups; by comparison, studies concerned with organization and administration of services are few and some of them are largely descriptive rather than analytical. Yet, the manner in which social service programs are organized and administered — the clarity of administrative goals, the efficiency of operations, and the extent to which procedures are rationalized — has a direct effect on those who seek or receive services. Especially determining in maximizing the welfare aspects of programs and minimizing actual or potential diswelfares is the ability of staff to correctly understand and carry out administrative goals. Consequently, recruitment, retention and proper deployment of staff assume cardinal importance. Equally crucial is a sound financial structure, that is, the raising, distribution, and expenditure of funds, this being no less essential in social services than in any other activity of modern societies. All this being the case, it is necessary to examine continuously the methods and procedures that have been built into organizational and administrative patterns — to the end of making sure that they have not become obsolescent.

Social Welfare in National Development. Pratt's study (1969) analyzes the growth and the organization of social welfare institutions in Ghana, Sierra Leone, Kenya, and Tanzania from the British Colonial era through independence (1). Her findings indicate that there is a significant relationship between the goals of government and the functions assigned to social welfare: primarily remedial in the colonial era, social welfare became developmental during independence. It contributes most effectively to nation-building when it emphasizes national unity, responsible citizenship, maximum use of human and natural resources, an orientation to the future, hard work as a value, sacrifice of immediate material gratification, and mutual aid.

Gueye's study of the health, social and family services offered by social security funds (1973) is based on monographs received from 15 of the French-speaking countries of Africa who were asked to respond to a questionnaire (2). In the majority of these nations, these services are provided directly by the funds; in a few, the funds grant subsidies to public and voluntary agencies that provide them, control being carried out primarily through annual reports required by the funds. While in principle only those insured with the funds are eligible for services, in fact the funds 'appear to an increasing extent' to be unable to limit services to insured persons alone (2:252). Services are generally provided free of charge and include the following: subsidies or loans; financial assistance or cash supplementary benefits; benefits in kind such as medical care, drugs, goods; social centers; social work services, holiday colonies; and low-cost housing. Emphasis is on services that benefit mothers and children. Although it is recognized that services have an advantage over cash benefits in 'that they can be adapted to needs and guided in a particular direction, and it is possible to obtain a concrete appraisal of the results obtained' (2:254), the funds are not using their financial possibilities to meet the need for services to the full. Nor is there enough of an effort made to determine the kind of services that are needed, the manner of achieving balance between cash and in kind benefits, the best way to assure coordination, and to secure greater financial resources for services.

Kramer's study of community development in Israel and the Netherlands (1970), analyzes it as a form of professional practice 'or as a change technology utilized by agents who are employed by a sponsoring organization to engage certain client systems within a distinctive civic culture and socio-political context for community decision making' (3:123). Consequently, the study centers on comparing the socio-political context, sponsors of community work, professional staff, characteristics of community work practice, and the constraints and obstacles it has to deal with. Kramer found that the character and the functions of community work in the two countries differ chiefly because of differences in their socio-political contexts and organizational sponsors. Apparently, the latter are more determining than similarities in philosophy, in goals and methods, and in the encouragement of democratic processes, self-help, and local initiative. As hoped by its author, the study not only yields insights into the practice of community development in advanced countries, but is useful as well for examining critically theories of organization, professionalization, and planned change. Especially thought-provoking is Kramer's discussion of the pivotal influence of sponsorship in community work.

Social Welfare Administration. In 1962, Kammerer published her massive examination of child welfare administration in Great Britain and the United States, its overall aim being to make it possible to 'infer certain generalizations about the organization, leadership, staffing and coordination of treatment services in general as they are presently carried on in certain advanced western nations' (4:6). She studied services to children both in and outside their own homes, linking their administration to the ideological foundations for public child welfare in the two countries as well as to its legal bases, organizational patterns and personnel. The instrument used for evaluative comparisons is a model of child welfare services created by her. Measuring her data against this model, she comes to the following conclusions about organization: (a) within all levels of government, child welfare programs are more effective when integrated within a single agency; (b) 'independence from the administrative direction of public assistance is essential to move child welfare services forward in program development'; (c) administrators and workers should be free of housekeeping functions in order to concentrate on providing services granted by the basic programs, and this can be facilitated by institutionalizing the auxiliary and housekeeping services; (d) coordination is essential, both within and between public and private agencies; the latter requires delegation of authority to the operating level; (e) for management, the board or committee form of overhead structure is not effective; the opposite is true in relation to policy (4:410).

Donnison's and Chapman's study (1965) of Great Britain and Canada derives its findings from a meticulous and penetrating examination of eight case studies of social services at the local level. For their purposes, 'administration' is defined 'not as a distinctive activity or technique, but as consisting of all the processes that play a part in determining the volume, character and distribution of the service being studied' (5:231−2). The people participating in these processes are incorporated into a three-part model as 'providers' of the service, 'controllers of resources' and 'determiners of demand', with the proviso that in certain situations these groups may include the same people — rather than into the more commonly used two-part model of 'bureaucrats and the public', or 'supply and demand', or the 'state and the citizen' (5:232−3).

The three-part model has the advantages of doing away with the misleading dichotomies in two-part models, and of conceptualizing providers of service as taking the initiative in creating and continually modifying the service. Consequently, the providers' perceptions of the nature and extent of needs to be met and of the standards they regard

The Organization of Social Welfare

as appropriate are crucial. Donnison and Chapman place their discussion of the development of social administration within a clearly delineated conceptual framework within which tasks, process and organization are differentiated and defined. While the initiatives for changes in social policies may come from those who control the resources a service requires, or from the consumers of this service, or from those who refer them to the service and act as their advocates, the most important group in this context are again the providers of service. The conflict involved in the evolution of policy is likely to elicit different responses from the groups that make up the three-part model because of differences in perceptions about what the implications of this conflict signify for their particular roles and statuses.

Rodgers' book (1968) compares social welfare administration in France, Norway, Canada and Great Britain. The main purpose is 'to help the student to understand *why* the response to broadly similar problems is different in the particular country under study' (6:14). She notes that while the boundaries of social administration are 'ill-defined', its core is well understood — 'the development of collective action for social welfare', this action involving government, employers, philanthropic bodies and the consumers of services (6:11). She agrees with Donnison and quotes him to the effect that 'policy-making and administration are not separate activities. The "policies" of a social service are its functions — what it does — which may or may not coincide with its official aims. Its "administration" consists of the processes — going on at all levels, inside and outside the organization concerned — which determine those functions. Neither can be studied or understood in isolation from each other' (6:12).

Rodgers develops a case study for each of the four countries she discusses, relating social needs, resources, and forms of social administration to social, demographic, economic and political factors. Her analysis of historical aspects is sufficiently detailed to show how social policies developed in the past and what their future directions are likely to be. The second part of her book is devoted to a systematic comparative analysis of particular problems and of the different forms of social administration designed to meet them. It centers on four areas: social security, coordination at both policy-making and field-work levels, aged and family. Illustrative material is drawn not only from the four countries being compared, but from other western countries with well-developed social service systems.

Preceding Part II, a short chapter deals briefly with a broader theme: the extent and the manner in which the four countries attempt overall planning of resources to meet social needs. This is done in order to stress the interdependence of social policies in the four areas of service, as well as the interdependence of social and economic policies. In relation to the latter Rodgers takes the position that increased opportunities for benefiting from better social provisions 'must be regarded and presented as are wages and interest rates, as an incentive and reward for the savings and the hard work of the whole population on which increased productivity ultimately depends'; and at the same time it must not be forgotten that 'most increases in social investment ... inevitably lead to new or increased social expenditure on current account. Improved development resulting from new investment is immediately reflected in higher working costs' (6:230).

Glennester's book (1976) compares the roles of planning, program budgeting and evaluation in social welfare in Great Britain and the United States (7). He is critical of the application of 'managerial' and 'incrementalist' methods of resource allocation in social welfare. Instead of rationalizing the allocation process, he argues, these methods have tended to overcentralize decisions and to exaggerate the importance of budgets. What is more desirable, he believes, is a 'pluralist social planning' approach — one that combines rationalization with recognition of the importance of the political process which makes possible maximum participation by diverse groups. This approach is supported by Glennester's findings that it is the historical, economic and political characteristics of the two countries that determine program objectives and their desired 'outputs', the factors integrated into budgets. He then discusses efforts to evaluate welfare programs in the two countries, pointing out that in this area the US has made greater strides than Great Britain. The final chapter, which summarizes the two countries' differing experiences, sheds light on the ways in which politics, socioeconomic conditions, and bureaucracies generate different planning, budgeting and administrative patterns.

Ferguson's study of UNICEF (1972), utilizing reports and information obtained through visits to projects in Asia and South America, compares the administrative structure and policies of this international agency with those of HEW (8). While he recognizes that the two agencies differ in regard to certain major responsibilities, he finds that in several important respects they are alike. His comparisons address the use of authority, funds and information in administration, coordination of services, delegation of responsibility, evaluation of services and policies, and the quality of leadership. Ferguson makes suggestions which he believes would help the US to move toward a unified social development system of services.

Kramer's important study reports

... selected findings from an international comparative study of the structure and function of 80 voluntary agencies serving the physically, sensorially, and mentally handicapped in four countries: England, Holland, Israel and the US. The purpose of the study was to identify and analyze the principal external and internal factors influencing the performance of the four major roles usually attributed to voluntary agencies: pioneering, advocacy, promotion of voluntarism, and service provision (9:2).

Kramer describes national fiscal policies and their consequences for the selected agencies. He presents several important findings: (a) the most frequent type of transfer was payment or reimbursement for service provided by a voluntary agency to an individual for whom there was a public responsibility; (b) indications were that organizational autonomy is a function of multiple, diverse sources of financing: the less the dependence on any single source, whether voluntary or governmental, the greater the possibility that the agency will determine its own policies; (c) militating against governmental control of the voluntary agency was the distribution of power between government and agency and the presence of countervailing resources at the agencies' disposal in the shape of virtual monopoly of services required by government, as well as their capacity for political pressure; and (d) the strongest factor militating against any challenge to the freedom of the voluntary agency was the low level of accountability demanded by the government. Overall, reliance on governmental funding did not seem to constrain voluntary agency autonomy. Kramer discusses some of the dysfunctional aspects of what he calls bureaucratic symbiosis.

Social Service Delivery Systems. Perhaps the most ambitious effort to date to explore 'the architecture of various national social service delivery systems' is personified by *An International Annual*, its first volume appearing in 1975 (10), and its second, in 1976 (11). In all, the diverse countries studied total 22: nine — Egypt, Great Britain, Iran, Israel, Italy, Poland, Sweden, United States, and the Soviet Union — are included in volume 1; 13 — Canada, Scotland, African Rhodesia, South Africa, Australia, Denmark, Finland, Yugoslavia, People's Republic of China, Japan, Colombia, Brazil, and Panama — are found in volume 2. Reports for the included countries were prepared by 'well known social welfare experts' who were provided with an outline which asked for certain content from all of them. At the same time, it is

228 The Organization of Social Welfare

stressed, the experts were not expected to confine themselves to this outline, since the editors 'felt that it was important *not* to attempt to limit writers to our own preconceived notions as to the relevant content of social service systems' (11:7). Consequently, the experts varied considerably in how they described particular systems.

As was to be expected, the editors found that the variables which affect or shape social service structures in different countries 'are endless', for

> Each country presents a special set of circumstances, and the structure of its delivery system is inevitably affected by its history, economic ability, political iedology, cultural heritage, religious traditions, degree of ethnic heterogeneity, military needs, whether imaginary or real, and so on (11:273).

But in addition to differences, the editors were able to identify similarities. Among these they include first of all, the importance of human values in the organization and development of social services, whether these values emphasize the dignity and worth of the individual, or solidarity and mutuality, or both. In response to values, there appears to be taking place some movement toward melding individualized services with social responsibility. All countries show that there exist relatively wide gaps between needs and services; and that there is a desire to build into services 'a caring scale' which seems almost unattainable when services are delivered by large public bureaucracies. As a result, there is observable a common trend toward decentralization and toward exploring communal, as contrasted with institutional methods, of meeting needs. Another common problem is that social service systems are not consciously designed; that is, they are not created to carry out long-range policy, but rather, to respond to crises and urgent needs. A haphazard scenario results in a situation in which crisis-oriented programs often remain and resist change. In all countries, regardless of ideology, policy-makers disagree about the role of government in providing social services and about the desirability of making them available on a universal basis. Everywhere, the areas of major concern are intrafamily problems which bring on tensions in family relationships; the care of the aged; deviance among youth, ranging from truancy, vagrancy, and delinquency to drug and alcohol abuse; and the particular needs of minority or so-called native populations which are generating growing challenges to social service capabilities (11:274—7).

The Organization of Social Welfare

Differences in the way social services are delivered frequently spring from several major difficulties faced almost universally by administrative structures and staffing patterns in social service sub-cultures. Thus, the desire to move toward decentralized service systems creates serious problems when decentralization in services is not simultaneous with decentralization in decision-making. The desirability of orienting social services toward planned goals raises the question as to whether it is better to place administration in a single central government department rather than to disperse administration among separate state or federal agencies or ministries such as housing, labor, etc. A continuing controversial issue is whether social security should be fused with social services. At present, the more common, and continuing, arrangement is for social security to be either centrally administered or to be administered under specific national regulations. As to personnel, in line with ideological positions as well as pragmatic considerations, the concept of a professionally trained social worker is so far rejected in the Soviet Union and in the People's Republic of China. In other countries, the level of special education for social work remains low (none exists in universities), and on-the-job training is the only source of professional education. In still others, like the United States, professional social work training is available in university-based schools, but its relevance to the provision of concrete assistance, especially to low-income groups in the population, is being questioned (11:278-9). The social work profession in the United States, as mentioned earlier in this book, is still struggling to define itself and to achieve consensus on what its unique functions are, assuming that uniqueness can be drawn out of the multitude of social work activities in diversified settings.

Overall, write the editors,

these similarities and differences have significant implications not only for the organization, administration, and manpower development for the social services but also for the possible transferability of services from one country to another (11:274).

The editors project the publication of volumes 3 and 4, the former to be devoted to 'the use of the neighborhood as a locus of organization of social welfare services'; the latter, to the 'special aspects of delivering services to the aging' (11:7).

Social Services in International Perspective. A book by Kahn and Kamerman (1975) describes certain social services in five European countries — England, Sweden, France, Denmark and the Netherlands (12). The included services are health visiting and school meals in England; daytime care of young children, helping people at home, and housing for the elderly in Sweden; housing for the young, and family vacations in France; housing for the young in Denmark; and helping people at home in the Netherlands. Since the same set of programs is not investigated in all of the five countries, cross-national comparisons cannot be made. As for findings with policy implications, the ones that are suggestive are that social services cannot amount to much unless they are built on 'foundation blocks' which provide a decent income, basic health services and adequate housing; and that social services should be available for all people, not just for the poor.

Perhaps the most ambitious undertaking aimed at producing cross-national comparisons that has appeared so far is represented by a three-year study of social services in eight countries — United States, Canada, Great Britain, France, Israel, Poland, West Germany, and Yugoslavia. The final report, written by Kahn and Kamerman (who are also the authors of the United States study), was published in 1976 (13). As described by Kahn,

> the study focused in each country on the governmental and societal context for services and on six specific topics. The country reports are thus organized to cover the societal context for social welfare — child care; child abuse and neglect; children's institutions and alternative programs; community care of the aged; family planning; and the local social service delivery system . . . this provided a useful 'purposive sample' . . . To avoid ambiguities deriving from language problems and to assure data comparability, stress was placed upon operational definitions and descriptive reporting, in accord with a standard (if general) data collection instrument . . . The study was interested in several major policy and program issues but dealt with them inductively, and thus not definitively, by assembling significant data rather than by studying them directly . . . (14:172—3).

Kahn and Kamerman conceptualize services as 'personal' in the sense that they are 'individualized, whether in delivery, assuring access to rights or benefits, or offering counseling and guidance' (13:3).
As already noted, these authors divide services into public social utilities and case services. The former are supposed to serve average people facing ordinary circumstances, are institutionally permanent,

The Organization of Social Welfare

and offer entitlement on the basis of status. They are universal and access to them is not limited to low income groups. In contrast, case services are for people with maladjustments, problems, illnesses, difficulties in the social domain. They are not universal in most countries.

According to these authors, the very character of personal social services calls for a localized and decentralized delivery system — one that will make possible local control and decision-making, and locally accessible service outlets. In regard to such a system, the detailed findings about differences of delivery arrangements in the nine countries lead Kahn and Kamerman to present the following list of eight groups of issues: (a) Does the country have one personal social service system or are there two or more categorical systems related to particular client groups? If one system, what is its scope? If categorical systems, are they interconnected? (b) Are personal social services a separate entity, or are they adjuncts to other service systems? If the former, what linkages are provided? If the latter, what arrangements are used to achieve coherence and identity? (c) What is the nature of the local service outlet? (d) Are the practitioners generalists or specialists? How are their roles conceptualized and integrated? What is required of them in terms of education and training? Do they work alone or in teams? (e) What is the content of services? (f) What arrangements are used to assure quality, sufficient quantity, access, integration, coordination, evaluation, feedback and accountability? (g) Who are the sponsors of services, and if several sponsors are involved, how are their roles differentiated, who has the leading role, and what are the arrangements to assure interelationships and accountability? (h) Does the delivery system provide services on a universal or selective basis, and what are the conditions governing access in either case? (13:314—15).

Policy Issues. Many organizational and administrative issues in personal social services appear to be generic to administration in almost all human undertakings. As an example, there is the need to determine how funds are being spent and to account for unit costs of service. The generic aspect also means that social service structures, like other bureaucracies, are faced with issues that stem from and revolve around bureaucratic strains — such as ritualism, overconformity, unwillingness to expose themselves to community scrutiny, etc. — and consequently, with the need to prevent, mitigate or compensate for these strains. At the same time, there are certain distinctive aspects of administration in personal social services that create a somewhat different set of administrative problems. For example, there is the emphasis on individualized service and on altruism as a motive for offering service. The former may clash with the administrative urge to rationalize and streamline the methods by which services are organized; the latter may spell a less efficient operation than can be achieved by a business motivated by profit-seeking and therefore utilizing a strictly rational approach.

Several basic questions in organization and administration flow out of the resource problems: how to ascertain the magnitude and the nature (cash or kind) of resources available or that can be made available for services within a given period of time; how to determine the extent and nature of the need for personal social services, current and potential; what should be the criteria for resource allocation and the priorities for program development? Assuming a scarcity of resources, how to create an organizational structure that will meet at least the essential service needs and at the same time be flexible enough to detect new needs and to mount a timely response to changing goals and priorities?

Directly or indirectly these questions call for responses to the entire galaxy of issues that must be resolved by administration: centralization, decentralization, or both in a variety of combinations; relationship to other programs; separation versus integration of programs. A continuing problem is how to show what personal social services are achieving and how to make clear their contribution to a society's well-being – an issue that becomes especially serious when competition for scarce resources is severe. And because to be effective and accessible, services have to be delivered at the neighborhood level, they are particularly subject to the inevitable introduction of new tiers of bureaucracy that devolution entails – another sensitive issue.

Throughout, a pivotal question is how to imbue administration with humanistic values without sacrificing reasonable efficiency. Since administrative mechanisms per se do not determine quality nor the underlying philosophy in which values reside, standards and guidelines for achieving program goals combine into a crucial issue. This, in turn, leads to questions about qualified personnel, a complex area because in personal social service programs (with few exceptions) there is no single professional discipline that predominates. Services are delivered by several disciplines, some more important in certain programs than in others. Consequently, not only is it necessary to decide what should

The Organization of Social Welfare

be the level and the content of education and training essential for staff in social services, but also to deal with conflicts that are likely to develop around leadership roles and methods for assuring a coordinated and harmonious working together.

Underlying all this are the central questions about what should be the role of government in providing services and what should be their objectives. Associated with these is the question whether services should be universal or selective, and whether they should be fused with cash benefit programs. If universality is the desired outcome, the role of government becomes paramount since voluntary agencies are not likely to be able or to want to reach everyone. Universality in combination with fusion of the two types of social protection (social security and personal social services), if it leads to large, impersonal bureaucracies in which downgrading of the 'caring' function relegates it to a subservient position, may become a particularly sharp issue.

Summary. There is a growing consensus that in policy implementation means are as powerful as ends; that how conflicts in principles and objectives are analyzed and resolved depends not only on policy decisions but on the capacity of the organizational structure to transform these decisions into services; that the manner in which this transformation is carried out shapes policy. As a matter of fact, the two are indivisible: policy is decision on administrative objectives. Such decisions are made both outside and within the organization, via legislation, for example, and through agency rules. Administration, however, includes participating in making far-reaching policy decisions on the outside, as well as internal, implementing decisions. In a broader perspective, an increasing number of investigators are making the point that while the society determines administrative structures and service delivery processes, these structures and processes, in turn, influence the nature of the society.

As the number of countries that are studied increases, it is found that differences outnumber similarities in the ways they deal with broadly similar problems. Social service structures, administrative patterns, budgeting and planning processes differ because of differences in the character of the countries' bureaucracies as well as in their socio-political and economic contexts. The number of variables is further increased by the interdependence of social and economic policies everywhere. Since there exists a meaningful relationship between the goals of government and the functions assigned to services, differences in goals also add to organizational differences. In countries with similar philosophies and goals, organizational sponsors inject still another diversifying element.

Among important similarities is the recognition that social services cannot accomplish much unless there exists an infrastructure of services and provisions on which they can draw for basic support and in relation to which they can construct their own organizations. As to the similarities specific to the services themselves, these include the primordial importance of values, the gaps between needs and available services, and the tendency of services to respond to emergencies rather than to develop in line with consciously designed plans.

In regard to methods that seem particularly promising for comparative studies of social service organizations, a few investigators are emphasizing the importance of models that encompass as many as possible of the major determining features and influences, inside and outside the organization. These conceptual constructs are useful not only for meaningful descriptions of similarities and differences between organizations, but for providing standards against which performances can be evaluated.

References

1. Pratt, Mildred, *Social Welfare in National Development*, Doctoral Dissertation in Social Work, Pittsburgh (April 1969).
2. Gueye, Amadou, 'Health, Social and Family Services of Social Security Funds in Africa', *International Social Security Review*, xxvi, no. 3 (1973), pp. 250–87.
3. Kramer, Ralph M., *Community Development in Israel and the Netherlands, A Comparative Analysis* (Institute of International Studies, University of California, Berkeley, 1970).
4. Kammerer, *British and American Child Welfare Services*.
5. Donnison and Chapman, *Social Policy and Administration*.
6. Rodgers, *Comparative Social Administration*.
7. Glennester, H., *Social Service Budgets and Social Policy: British and American Experience* (New York, Barnes & Noble, 1976).
8. Ferguson, Dwight H., 'The Twenty-fifth Anniversary of UNICEF, with Implications for the United States', *Social Service Review*, 46, no. 2 (June 1972), pp. 170–92.
9. Kramer, Ralph M., 'Public Fiscal Policy and Voluntary Agencies in Welfare States', *Social Service Review*, vol. 53, no. 1 (March 1979), pp. 1–15.
10. Thursz and Vigilante, *Meeting Human Needs*, vol. 1.
11. Thursz and Vigilante, *Meeting Human Needs*, vol. 2.
12. Kahn, Alfred J. and Kamerman, Sheila B., *Not for the Poor Alone, European Social Services* (Philadelphia, Temple University Press, 1975).
13. Kahn and Kamerman, *Social Services in International Perspective*.
14. Kahn, Alfred J., pp. 166–78 in International Council of Social Welfare, *The Struggle for Equal Opportunity. Strategies for Social Welfare Action*. Proceedings of the XVIIIth International Conference on Social Welfare, San Juan, Puerto Rico, July 18–24, 1976 (New York, Columbia University Press, 1977).

10 SERVICES FOR SPECIAL GROUPS

As noted earlier, cross-national studies that investigate personal social services for certain groups are quite numerous. Not surprisingly, most of them are concerned with children and the aged, everywhere the two most vulnerable groups in the population. Only a few compare services for delinquents and criminals, although criminal and delinquent behavior is becoming more widespread and is on the increase and societal concern in regard to it is escalating. Although none of the included studies compare the circumstances and needs of families as such, in a general way some insight into the familial environment may be gained from the findings concerning children and the aged. This is clearly illustrated, for example, in the case of the children of migrants – a group whose membership is increasing and whose problems and needs require international cooperation both in the legal domain and in the provision of cash and noncash benefits and services.

Social Services for Children. Studies of services for children range from global overviews to intensive investigations of specific programs in two countries. In order to facilitate comparability and to assist the reader in getting a sense of the persistence or change in concerns, they are divided into studies carried out under UN auspices with their primary focus on the problems of children in developing nations; studies of child care; and studies in the broad field of child welfare.[1]

UN Studies. A report published for UNICEF in 1963 deals with the needs of children in developing countries (9). Its preparation involved most of the organizations and agencies active in the international child welfare field and brought together most of the relevant information available at that time on the health, nutritional and educational requirements of children, and on their needs in the field of social welfare, labor and vocational preparation. Twenty-four UNICEF beneficiary countries – in Africa, Asia, Europe, and the Americas – submitted reports on the needs of their children and on the measures that might be taken with UNICEF assistance to meet them. The report examines the environments in which children live from the point of view of their demographic, social and economic characteristics, as well as the social values they embody. Within this broad context, the

specific needs of children are identified, priorities analyzed and implications for UNICEF policy pinpointed.
In relation to the field of social welfare,

> the fundamental importance of assisting in the improvement, extension, and establishment of comprehensive national systems of social services and related programs to strengthen the family, improve levels of living, and provide children with needed care and protection (9:134)

is stressed. The manner in which children's social welfare needs are generated by broader societal forces such as the suffering and upheavals brought on by poverty, population growth, urbanization, and lack of adequate housing is explained. In order to respond effectively to these needs, social services must achieve several basic objectives: in regard to the family and child welfare, emphasis should be placed on preventing the breakdown or disintegration of families; harmful and/or inadequate environmental conditions should be eradicated in both urban and rural areas; the rights and responsibilities of both parents and the status of children, legitimate and illegitimate, ought to be defined and the rights of children to care and protection, recognized. Community development programs can make a tremendous contribution toward realizing these objectives, provided they establish multi-purpose social services, their priorities determined with due regard for economic, social, and cultural factors, and offer experience to people for assuming responsibility for improving their own ways of life. To prevent delinquency, strengthening the family and improving the environment are essential; but because not all delinquency is likely to be prevented, treatment and rehabilitation services must be available. 'To alleviate or minimize some of the negative effects of urbanization on family life, it is necessary to provide a variety of community services to help the family adjust to a new pattern of living' (9:136); these services should be especially sensitive to the desire of women to learn better methods of homemaking, including family nutrition and better child care and training. Slum clearance must be undertaken; new housing, to be of maximum benefit, must offer the necessary community services for both adults and children — a concept that must be incorporated into long-range plans.

These objectives are not likely to be realized to a significant degree, however, unless 'gaps and weaknesses' that characterize national efforts are removed. Among these, the most urgent is the failure to build greater integration of all skills within the child welfare field, do away with fragmentation of services, and establish guidelines via viable long-range plans. Further, creating necessary legal framework to protect the integrity of the family and the equal rights of its members is of primordial importance. The neglect of rural areas and over-concentration of scarce resources on services for children who are deprived temporarily or permanently of normal home life should give way to providing adequate services in rural as well as urban areas and to helping families to discharge their functions more adequately — although services outside the home must continue to receive attention. And 'the lack or inadequacy of reliable information regarding social welfare needs of families and children and about methods by which such needs are met is a continuing problem requiring urgent attention in many countries' (9:137).

The first international conference, under UN auspices, devoted to planning for the needs of children was held in 1964 (10). Policy positions developed by the participants included a national policy for children that should not be confined to dealing with the underprivileged and handicapped but should cover *all* children; such a policy should address *all* needs — health, nutrition, education, vocational training and social welfare; the meeting of needs should be integrated into the general objectives of development. Welfare services, available to all and not only to vulnerable children and youth, should include the adaptation of the family to changing social conditions and social demands; hence, measures for strengthening family life should be emphasized with attention directed to preventing emotional as well as physical deprivation. As resources increase, special provision should be made for the vulnerable — the abandoned, neglected, illegitimate, delinquent and handicapped children.[2]

The UN's 1971 *Report on Children* attempts to 'highlight problems of children, both with regard to the national and international situation' (14:2–3). It is explained that

> Although a brief world view has been attempted, stress has been placed on the conditions of children in the developing countries. The underlying emphasis of this report is on the right of the child to adequate protection and effective preparation for a useful life. Attention has been directed to sectoral and intersectoral problems, programmes and prospects. The report considers the following main headings: demographic trends and social changes in relation to the needs of the child; the child's protection — including his health and nutrition and the necessary physical, social, psychological and

238 Services for Special Groups

economic prerequisites; preparation for life — including education and the process of socialization and modernization; and appraisal of action aimed at the child — including plans and programmes related to children's needs and national planning and policy for children (14:3).

An examination of development plans of 46 countries revealed that most of them present children's programs in three sectors — education, health, and social welfare. 'The social welfare content ranges from reformatories for juvenile delinquents to youth-vacation resorts and children's clubs' (14:7); but the total amounts allocated to this 'content' are not indicated and it is impossible to estimate them by aggregating project allocations, since financial data on many projects are not available.

The *Report* does not have a separate section on social welfare. It appears that social services are thought of as especially necessary in efforts to assist 'children needing special attention'. Among these are handicapped children for whom early medical and educational assessment 'requires a close working relationship between doctors, teachers, psychologists, social workers and parents' (14:5); children who are victims of war for whom the report recommends a special study of their physical and social plight; children born out of wedlock for whom the most urgent undertaking is considered to be the enactment of legislation embodying the principle of equality; abused children for whom the most effective approach is seen as the alleviation of 'social ills affecting those who abuse, as well as those who are abused, with imagination and sympathy' (14:5); exploited children who need protective legislation effectively enforced, but 'it may be advantageous in certain situations to allow the child to do certain types of work' provided working conditions are proper and the child can still continue his education; and children whose mothers are working who require properly staffed day-care centers or equivalent institutions.

The designation of 1979 by the UN as the 'Year of the Child' suggests that further stocktaking and hopefully, significant and worldwide action to improve the lives of children will take place.

Child Care. Meers' and Marans' study of group care of infants (1968) wished 'to highlight philosophic or ideologic views of other countries relevant to and reflected in the methods of selection, training, and practices of the child care-takers in group day-care and residential centers' (15:238). They studied centers in the Soviet Union, East

Services for Special Groups 239

Germany, Czechoslovakia, Hungary, Israel, Greece, and France. They found it difficult to make direct comparisons between the United States and countries of 'collectivistic' orientations because of 'differing assessments of infant vulnerability and individual differences, differing social and philosophic goals for the children and differences in willingness to provide the staff needed for large-scale child care programs' (15:275). Hence, they confine themselves to rather limited conclusions.

In 1971, Jensen published the results of his survey and comparison of day-care practices for infants and small children in Belgium, Czechoslovakia and England, with emphasis on the mental health aspects of such care (16). He found that differences emerge when practices are ranged on a continuum of rigidity, control and richness of environmental stimuli, but that in all three countries, care of normal children is effectively integrated into the day-care system. Because administrative patterns have important implications for mental health, he takes them into account in presenting models and options which, he believes, should be considered as America begins to develop policies and programs (16:432).

Thomas's dissertation (1972) describes day care for young children in selected centers provided by government and adjacent to industries in the Soviet Union and day care in selected centers in inner-city areas in Atlanta, Georgia (17). Her comparison of the two systems focuses on the qualifications of personnel, the interaction between teachers and children, and the use of paraprofessionals. She also tries to evaluate the emotional climate in the centers, the noise level and the kind of noise that exists, and the relationship of children to children. Some attention is likewise given to describing similarities and differences in curricula.

Drawing upon findings from the project on social services in international perspective (reference 13 in Chapter 9), Kamerman discusses child care programs in nine countries — France, Israel, Canada, Sweden, UK, Poland, West Germany, United States and Yugoslavia (18). She reports that most child-care programs are universal and nonmeans tested, although income may be taken into account as a basis for requiring payment on a sliding-fee scale. The social changes that have stimulated demand for day care are similar in the studied countries; namely, the increased numbers of women with children under age six in the labor force; the increased number of female-headed families; the decreased number of families who can count on relatives for child care; the larger gap in levels of achievement in the primary grades between different groups of children; and the movement to provide equality for women and more options from which to choose their life styles. Kamerman maintains that the United States differs in one respect: during the 1960s efforts to expand day-care facilities were oriented toward freeing welfare mothers for work and training — a feature she did not find in the other eight countries. Policy issues which, according to Kamerman, each country faces center on day care's unclear objectives, problems around priorities and allocations of resources, lack of data on need or demand for child care, the relationship between child care and other child welfare programs, the structure and nature of child care programs, and what should be the guide lines for future development and what considerations support the directions they project. Commenting on the study, Meier (the director of the Office of Child Development in HEW at the time of its publication) voiced 'one possible conclusion'; namely, 'that there are clear grounds for diversity, and that the standards which are enforced and the guidelines which are encouraged may be the crucial issue' (18:Foreword).

In her dissertation (1976), Calkins investigated government-sponsored child care centers in the Soviet Union and California (19). She examined the historical, philosophic and political influences in each country as they are reflected in the two systems of child care. Also reviewed are patterns of financing, state control of the program, curriculum content, parent involvement, and teacher training. Of special interest are Calkins' efforts to assess the moral values exemplified in pre-school education in the two societies.

In their book on group care for pre-school children (1978), Glickman and Springer examine the programs in Israel, Russia, China and Sweden (20). They briefly sketch in the social background which influenced the creation of group care in the first three of these countries and contrast it with goals and life styles in the United States. This leads them to say that 'rather than a community of consensus, we [the United States] have an agreement to disagree, a national commitment to diversity' (20:132). They then note that even in these three countries, the number of children utilizing group care represents a relatively small proportion of all children of pre-school age and that very little research has been done on children brought up in groups, especially from the point of view of long-term effects. Their belief is that parents 'should want more for their children and more for themselves than infant group rearing allows'; that is, children capable of independent thought and action, creative and unique; parents who would receive love, warmth, and 'caring of one human being toward another' (20:141—2). Glickman and Springer point to Sweden as a society that, while improving provisions for group care, is placing greater emphasis on measures that make it possible for parents to either stay home with their children or to spend a great deal of time with them. Especially important, they think, is Sweden's 'firm governmental policy to support families and children and an understanding that children's welfare cannot be separated from the welfare of the family' (20:229).

Bronfenbrenner's comparative study of childhood in the US and the Soviet Union (1970) focuses major attention on similarities and differences in the process of socialization in two principal contexts, the family and the children's group. The study 'began with descriptive facts, considered their implications in the light of data and theory from the social sciences, and ultimately ended with a blueprint for change within our own society' (21:165), specifically for the classroom, the family, the neighborhood, and the larger community. Among the most important findings about Soviet children are the following: (a) 'in the process of growing up, Soviet children are confronted with fewer divergent views both within and outside the family and, in consequence, conform more completely to a more homogeneous set of standards' (21:81). To a significant extent, this explains their obedience; (b) at the same time, Bronfenbrenner detected signs of flexibility in Soviet upbringing which he also saw in other spheres of Soviet life. In the family this took the shape of a shift away from dependency and conformity to greater individuality and independence. He thinks that this may reduce 'the primacy of the collective and its powerful sanctions against deviance in word and action' (21:89); (c) he found the emotional ties between Soviet parents and children 'exceptionally strong', notwithstanding collective upbringing. Even though these parents have less time at home than American parents because of longer working hours and time lost in shopping and commuting, more of the time they do have is 'spent in conversation, play, and companionship with children than in American families' (21:99). Consequently, segregation by age is not as great.

In the US society 'gives decreasing prominence to the family as a socializing agent' and has tended to 'decrease opportunity for contact between children and parents. . .' (21:99). He warns that if this continues and 'if the resulting vacuum is filled by the age-segregated peer group, *we can anticipate increased alienation, indifference, antagonism, and violence on the part of the younger generation in all segments of our society* — middle-class children as well as the disadvantaged' (21:117). He calls for a 'greater involvement of parents, and other adults, in the lives of children, and — conversely — greater involvement of children in responsibility on behalf of their own family, community, and society at large' (21:165).

242 Services for Special Groups

A book edited by Roby (1973) examines child care from the perspective of social policy and programming as contrasted with the pedagogical perspective (22). One part of the book is devoted to presentations by early childhood experts from Sweden, Finland, Hungary, Norway, England and Wales, Japan and Israel who describe their nations' child-development policies, including prenatal and postnatal health care, children's allowances, maternity leaves, nutrition programs, and child care; the presentation on the Soviet Union is written by an American. The reason for discussing child care in this broader framework is that policies governing it 'should be considered only in the context of a *comprehensive* social policy for the promotion of children's well-being and development and the well-being of their parents' (22:300).

Perhaps the most authoritative undertaking in research on early child care is the work initiated by a group of concerned professionals, each a voluntary participant and none an official representative, which founded the International Study Group for Early Child Care in 1969 (23). Among them were specialists in education, medicine, psychology, sociology, and social welfare from twelve countries. By 1978, seven countries' monographs — from Hungary, Sweden, United States, Switzerland, Great Britain, France and Israel — were published. The remaining five — from Cuba, Poland, India, Yugoslavia, and the Soviet Union — are said to be in active preparation.

Each of the monographs follows a common outline. This will make possible the final volume in which the twelve completed monographs will be integrated to the end of comparing the systems, cultural values, conditions, ideas and practices that affect early child care across the world — in countries at different stages of development, and governed by different political, economic and social goals.

Each monograph includes material on the particular country's demographic and economic characteristics, major historical developments, and religious factors. Within this socio-economic context, the uniqueness of each country's child-care system becomes visible and the reasons for it become discernible. Authors then address a number of topics specifically concerned with child care; that is, child-rearing practices and attitudes; planning of services for families as they relate to changing family patterns; specific programs especially important in bringing up young children (family allowances and other income support programs; maternal and child health services; social services; child-care facilities for working mothers; educational programs for pre-schoolers); training of child care professionals and paraprofessionals (if the latter receive

Services for Special Groups 243

training); information for and/or involvement of parents; and research on child care and child development. Based on an analysis of these materials, a brief discussion focuses on future desirable directions and makes recommendations for improving practices and programs — to the end of improving the quality of life for small children and their families.

Child Welfare. In 1963 Wolins compared group care for children in Israel, Russia, Yugoslavia and Poland (24). He took the position that in comparative work, the researcher should seek 'some understanding of how the problem of families, children, and society are seen from *within* a society...' (24:369). This approach will provide an understanding of the different goals that different societies have for children, and a basis for evaluating the extent to which each is achieving its goals. Wolins related his findings to these different goals, as well as to certain practical factors that play a role in group care programs.

Continuing his work in this area of services for children, in 1974 Wolins edited an impressive volume on successful group care in Austria, England, Israel, Poland, the Soviet Union, the United States, and Yugoslavia presenting it as one of the options in providing care for culturally disadvantaged, economically and emotionally impoverished, disturbed and delinquent children. The editor includes group care for young children and adolescents and shows what can be accomplished by focusing on those 'explorations in the powerful environment' that are sound, either from the point of view of research findings or because they conceptualize practice at a well-grounded level of generalization. He relates accomplishments to relevant historical, ideological, and political factors which illumine the reasons behind them (25).

As noted earlier, the Kafka and Underhill comparative study of family law in 16 European and Mediterranean Countries (1974) is part of a larger investigation concerned with children of migrants, initiated by the IUCW. 'Migrant' is defined as anyone working in a foreign country (26). In addition to family allowances and maintenance provisions for children, the two authors studied the divorce laws of these countries, their aim being to answer the following questions: who can apply for divorce? On what grounds can a divorce be granted? If a divorce is granted, who is awarded custody of the children — family or others? Focusing on divorce was motivated by the authors' view that

> Perhaps the most serious problem connected with migration is the breakdown of the family. The nature of migration today is such that the family of the migrant worker is left behind in the country of

origin. The obstacles to the migration of the entire family fall into two categories — financial and legal. Either the migrant worker chooses to leave his family behind . . . or [is] *forced* to leave his wife and children behind . . . In either case, the family is separated and the preservation of family ties is often difficult (26:27).

This is one aspect of the problem; the other is the breakdown of marriages between migrant workers and the spouses which they may take in the receiving countries. Divorce in either case is likely to be a complicated matter. The material in the table constructed by Kafka and Underhill vividly illustrates both the character and the range of these complications, as they revolve around two key problems: the determination of the applicable law and the recognition of the divorce abroad.

Since 'migration is partly responsible for another serious social and legal problem — the number of children born out of wedlock every year' (26:38), Kafka and Underhill seek to answer the question: what are the rights of the illegitimate children of emigration; that is, under what conditions is the father obliged to maintain the child? They compare the different laws governing the establishment of filiation and the rights and obligations that ensue, with special attention to the maintenance obligation. Again, complications are many. Filiation must be determined separately for the mother and the father; consequences of the establishment of paternity vary according to the laws of each country. While in general, maintenance obligations are legally binding once filiation has been established, there are exceptions. The overall impression is that the answer to the IUCW's original question in initiating this study — are progenies of international economics, are migrants' children the orphans of nations? — is 'yes'.

Veillard-Cybulska's impressive study concerning the legal welfare of children in a disturbed family situation (1975) is divided into three parts: part I examines the existing provisions for children living in a complete family (parental rights and duties, the competent authority when coercive measures must be instituted and the legal coercive measures available) and for children living in an incomplete family (legitimate and illegitimate, children of divorced or separated parents or those whose parents are in prison); part II examines the main legal provisions which implement parental authority, both its rights and obligations (custody of minors, guardianship, curatorship, placement in foster care, residential care, adoption); part III discusses the difficulties in applying legal provisions and proposes some improvements.

Services for Special Groups

The data for this study were obtained from questionnaires received from 21 countries of Europe, North America, Asia, Africa, and the Middle East (27).

Part I opens with the explanation that the 'family', although generally conceived 'as a spiritual entity which is not simply based on blood ties or legal constitution', nevertheless has very different meanings from country to country (27:35). From a legal standpoint the situation of children in complete families is governed in 'very different ways', but generally, priority is given to bringing up the child in his own family because his parents are viewed as the natural upbringers. Coercive measures are instituted as a last resort, involve a progression from lesser to greater severity, and may be rescinded when no longer necessary. As to children in incomplete families, while the principle of equal rights for all children is proclaimed, in fact 'there are still many countries where the law does not treat children born in or out of wedlock equally' (27:42). The situation of unmarried mothers is also determined by differing provisions. In many countries, divorce is preceded by conciliation attempts but often, these are looked upon as merely a formality. When marriages are dissolved, the law everywhere tries to safeguard the welfare of the child. It appears that in many countries the welfare of prisoners' children is a forgotten problem; in those that remember it, it is the responsibility of social security services, or of guardianship authorities.

Part II opens with the explanation that legal protection is brought to bear when the family is unable to properly exercise its parental authority, but that in practice, it is often difficult to determine what parental rights and duties are. Veillard-Cybulska then clarifies the various ways (see above) that are used in relation to such families in order to safeguard the child's physical, moral, intellectual and social welfare. In regard to foster care, Veillard-Cybulska finds that everywhere it comes up against difficulties. ' "Some consider foster care to be like marriage, often seeing it as a lottery" ' (27:55). Residential care is often regarded as a necessary evil. In contrast, not only is adoption universally known (except in tribal and customary law in Africa), but is highly regarded. Nevertheless, 'it often happens that initially well-intentioned adoptive families become quickly discouraged when faced with problems or lack of experience, with the result that the effects of adoption are somewhat less beneficial than expected' (27:58). It is noted that the range of available measures for children who must live outside their own homes is increasing, spurred on by experiments carried out in several countries.

In part III Veillard-Cybulska states that 'unfortunately, the kind of difficulties encountered in applying the law have not always been fully revealed to us'; consequently, the question as to whether all the 'eloquent legal texts' (Declaration of Human Rights, Rights of the Child, as well as laws of particular countries) are 'so significant in practice' remains unanswered (27:33). Within these limitations she highlights the problems 'revealed' by some of the questionnaire respondents, ranging from Spain where the difficulties are 'innumerable' to Bulgaria where none exist. As to proposed improvements, some require adherence to elementary principles of modern justice; others call for State intervention in order to insure payment of maintenance allowances to children in incomplete families and involvement of competent authorities in all placements who would adhere to the 'golden rule' of cooperating with a whole range of psycho-social services; still others stress better training of personnel and the primordial importance of being guided by scientific research. At the same time, it is believed that too much intervention is not advisable, that individual and familial responsibility must not be reduced, and that 'the legal welfare of young people and the family should focus on the personal commitment of the interested parties' (27:34). Veillard-Cybulska thinks that

> the most effective means of determining the socio-cultural factors that foster juvenile and familial maladjustment, whilst at the same time providing support for assistance to young people and families, would seem to lie in diversifying available kinds of legal and social welfare, perfecting intervention methods and techniques, providing a greater number of specialised facilities, and improving and coordinating efforts guided by scientific research and supported by community action in cooperation with the persons concerned (27:35).

She draws up a 'balance sheet' between the positive and the negative aspects of the legal welfare of children in disturbed families which leads her to say that 'these contradictions between the eloquent principles and the sad reality could be at least partially resolved by developing international law in this field' (27:38).

Again drawing on findings from the project on social services in international perspective (reference 13 in Chapter 9) Kamerman discusses child abuse/neglect in seven western-type democracies and in Poland and Yugoslavia (28). She reports that perceptions of this baffling problem differ in these nine countries: some recognize child

Services for Special Groups

abuse/neglect as a separate, identifiable problem but assume 'that to the extent the problem exists, adequate response is being provided within the existing child protective . . . service' (28:34); others see it as a minor phenomenon that requires no special provision; still others are becoming increasingly aware of it, as well as of the 'battered child syndrome', and are trying to deal with it, finding it especially difficult to arrive at a definition that would be meaningful and acceptable. In no country are there reliable data on the incidence of child abuse/neglect, not even in countries that recognize its existence as a separate phenomenon.

From a review of the legislation pertaining to child abuse/neglect, the machinery for identifying the children who are victims of it, and the programs that are currently available — all quite different in the nine countries — Kamerman considers the major issue to be whether child abuse/neglect signifies 'a phenomenon distinct from maltreatment of children generally and whether it warrants special policies and programs' (28:37). Apparently, the consensus is that abuse/neglect is one form, in some cases an extreme one, of maltreatment in general and that the policy should be to improve services for all children and families rather than to develop separate programs for the abused/neglected contingent. This calls for doing away with the inadequacies of traditional programs such as insufficient resources (financial and human), fragmentation, absence of accountability and conflicts between the different professions and organizations involved — to say nothing of the fact that valid and reliable knowledge is still limited in scope.

A report about youth advisory services — youth information centers, drop-in centers, hotlines, drug information and counseling centers — in Denmark, Sweden, the United Kingdom, the Netherlands, Poland, and Czechoslovakia was published by Shore in 1976 (29). He studied only those that employed mental health professionals (some, only on a consultant basis) and 'aimed at finding solutions to mental health problems on a community level' (29:24). Shore found important similarities in services in the six countries. Mental health problems among young people were on the increase in all of them. Government played an important role in youth development in all by providing sex education in the schools and free medical care; abortion is legal in each; and several had well developed and well attended recreational programs. While not all citizens agreed with national policy, youth advisory services were accepted everywhere as legitimate mental health services — they were not identified with the counter-culture. In treatment, the medical model was rejected; rather, emphasis was placed on the young people's economic, social, educational, legal, and medical needs — as well as on their emotional difficulties. Consequently, personnel represented a variety of disciplines with psychiatry playing a minor role. Everywhere staff devoted much effort to making services accessible. Shore concludes that despite differences in social philosophy, these similar features have several counterparts in the United States. One of the major differences between what he found in Europe and the United States, however,

> can be seen in the issues of legitimation and sanction. In the United States there still remains a deeply-held belief that [youth advisory services] are of low quality, coddle the young and foster inappropriate behavior. The services are constantly in search of funds, often depending upon the ability of dedicated professionals to donate some of their precious time. In general, they are seen as inadequate ways of receiving help, approaches that might be necessary for certain 'way out' young people, but not acceptable to the general populus or to professionals operating out of traditional settings. Such an attitude seemed much less prevalent in these European countries, permitting a greater degree of confidence in exploration, initiative and creativity (29:35).

Social Services for the Aged. A pioneering study on aging in Western societies — France, Italy, the Netherlands, Sweden, the United Kingdom, and West Germany, with quite extensive references to Belgium, Denmark, and Switzerland as well — was published under the editorship of Burgess in 1960 (30). It surveys the problems experienced by elderly people and the programs developed to deal with them, and relates both to the social and economic changes that generated them to begin with.

The authors found that problems facing older people are similar in all countries of Western culture. For the most part, the differences that exist are in degree, in practices designed to meet the special needs of the elderly, and in the extent to which they are or are not met. Major problems arise because of inequality of opportunity for employment, inadequate income, unsuitable housing, lack or insufficiency of social services and of provisions for sustaining physical and mental health, stresses and strains produced by changing family patterns and family relations, lack of meaningful activities in retirement, and paucity of research on the social and psychological aspects of aging.

The significance of these findings is made vividly meaningful by 14 case studies and by selected statistical data. In the concluding section, an attempt is made to answer questions pertaining to what European experience suggests in regard to ways of dealing with older people and their problems; to issues that emerge when action is taken to cope with these problems; to implications for the United States; to contributions of cross-national research to social gerontology; and to the effect of social action in behalf of old people on their independence, initiative, and autonomy.

A massive landmark study was published by Shanas and her associates in 1968 (31). It surveys living conditions and behavior of elderly people in Denmark, Britain, and the United States, in a systematic comparative framework. Considered are the capacity of older persons for self-care, their role in the family network and their ability and opportunity to provide for themselves in old age. The authors believe that the most important theoretical question in social gerontology today is: 'Are old people integrated into society or are they separated from it?' (31). How this question is answered affects all social policies concerning the aged. Hypotheses in regard to five major aspects of aging in industrial societies — health, medical and social services, the family, work and retirement and financial resources — are posed. Analysis separates phenomena that are nation-related from those that are common for the aged in industrial societies. The authors' rigorous control, coordination and consistency both of the theoretical framework and of definitions makes this study a valuable contribution to research in gerontology and one that offers important insights into comparative social welfare, as well as into policy in regard to the aged.

Subsequently, national sample surveys on the elderly were initiated in Israel, Poland, and Yugoslavia. Questionnaires and research techniques were similar to those used by Shanas in order that the findings from the six countries would be comparable. Under UN sponsorship, a discussion of the findings concerning all six took place in 1969 (32). The overall conclusion arrived at by the participants was that the similarities among the aged in terms of life situations and problems faced appear to be greater than cultural differences.

Havighurst *et al.* in 1969 published the results of a pilot study for a cross-national investigation of adjustment to retirement (33). The study groups included teachers and steelworkers in five European countries and the United States. An important purpose was to learn the extent to which available methodology can produce reliable cross-national comparisons around such factors as role activity and degree of satisfaction with such activity. Two hypotheses tested by the authors were that occupational differences have more effect than national differences in the total role activity of the retirees, and that people in expressive occupations, like teachers, remain more widely engaged than those in more technical or instrumental ones, like steelworkers. The first hypothesis was not sustained — a finding that suggests that culture outweighs class in determining role activity — while the second was confirmed.

A study of modernization and status of the aged by Palmore and Manton (1974) is especially important because it raises questions about the usual assumption that

> the social status of the aged, relative to the non-aged, declines with modernization. The decreased importance of land as a source of status, decreased importance of the extended family, increased geographical mobility, the rapidly changing technology, social structure, and cultural values have been postulated as the major aspects of modernization contributing to this decline in status (34:205).

They base their analysis on an examination of 31 countries with available data. By 'status of the aged' they mean the relative socio-economic position of the aged, which they measure in relation to the non-aged (aged are persons of 65 or over; non-aged are those age 25 through 64) by means of an 'equality index'. This index is used with three measures of socio-economic status: employment, occupation of those economically active, and education. They stress that their equality indexes 'are measures of the status of the aged *relative to the non-aged in the same country*. They cannot be used to compare the economic well-being of the aged in one country with that of the aged in other countries' (34:207).

Their findings are several. The general hypothesis that modernization leads to a decline of the status of the aged is supported by the finding that this status is almost equal that of younger adults in some underdeveloped countries, but is equal to about half that of younger adults in some of the developed countries. At the same time, however, it is learned that different aspects of the status 'may change at different rates and that different aspects of modernization may affect one kind of status more than others' (34:207). It is the shift from agriculture and increased education, rather than productivity, that are the determining aspects of modernization in this context. As to why most aged stop working in industrialized countries, Palmore and Manton think that this is due to growth of retirement benefits, compulsory retirement policies, shift from self-employment to work for employers, and obsolescence of skills.

They consider their most significant findings those that

imply that the occupation and education status of the aged decrease in the advanced stages of modernization; but that after a country has gone through a rapid period of modernization, these aspects of status stabilize and may begin to rise. . . Longitudinal analysis of changes in status of the aged within modernizing countries are needed to test the applicability of these theories to specific countries. If these . . . patterns are found to apply longitudinally, they will indicate that the aged need not fear the advanced stages of modernization, because their average occupation and education status should no longer fall as in the early stages, and it may even begin to rise (34:210).

Contributors to a book on geriatric care in advanced societies edited by Brocklehurst (1975) are experts from six countries: Great Britain, the Netherlands, the United States, Sweden, the Soviet Union, and Australia (35). Advanced societies are defined as those in which at least 10 percent of the population is 65 or older (by this definition, Australia should not have been included). These rather than other advanced societies were chosen because, according to the editor, they 'tend to have a more developed system of medical care for the elderly than a number of other advanced societies and they do encompass a number of very different approaches to national administration and are, therefore, useful to compare' (35:3). To some extent, the contributors do cover the same issues — as they are viewed in their respective countries and as they affect geriatric care in them. All give some attention to health care, chronic long-term care, home care, coordination of services, and educational manpower issues. But despite the coherence this provides, it is not clear why they differ in philosophy and practice: development of geriatric care is not related to the socio-economic and political development of each country.

It does become clear that in all countries the elderly face multiple problems. Consequently, no one service or provision can alone meet their needs. The contributors agree that a diversified network of services ought to be available. This raises the usual problem of coordination. Brocklehurst proposes the creation of a geriatric specialist, closely identified with the medical model of care. To what extent such a specialist would know how to respond appropriately to other than medical needs of the elderly remains a question.

In her 1975 review of selected in-home services in Western European countries (Sweden, Denmark, Norway, Belgium, Great Britain, Netherlands, France, West Germany, Switzerland, and Finland), Trager ranges over many topics (36). She introduces them by explaining that these services differ from country to country, but 'they are alike in one respect: the keen interest which is expressed by government in the development, maintenance and expansion of the services' (36:3). This, she thinks, is because these services have a longer history in Europe than in the United States (since 1892) and because they have demonstrated their potential value. Furthermore, in Europe preservation of family life is deeply embedded in cultural attitudes while social changes have made the extended family less available in periods of crisis. European governments have been involved in providing home help services, both administratively and financially, because they consider such services essential. As a result, everywhere the volume of home help services has been expanding.

The topics explored include European attitudes toward home help, characteristics of home-help workers, the quality of training for them, the scope and duration of services, who the recipients are, funding, auspices, and program direction. Some of the findings appear to have significance for policy. A positive attitude toward home help among the citizenry is essential. Well developed and clearly formulated notions about the desirable traits for home-help workers are likewise of primordial importance, as are training requirements. Especially interesting in this connection is the focus in all training programs on social and psychological factors in the helping process, including responsibility to support the family 'vis-à-vis an external world which is largely indifferent, a society which is neutral' (36:10), and knowledge of community resources, both those that provide monetary benefits and those that offer personal social services. Trager concludes that home care has become a social institution in European countries because of the belief in the right of an individual 'to protection of his "personal" self in his "own family" environment in times of stress, crisis or failing vigor' (36:14).

Little's discussion of homemaker–home-help services in developed countries (1975) focuses on the sources of information about them, national and international, and on the highlights of what is being done to improve them, quantitatively and qualitatively (37). She notes that the question of standards of service remains a 'thorny one', although considerable work has been done on it by the UN. In attempting to suggest an answer to what should be a world-wide policy on aging, she

Services for Special Groups

develops the concept of a minimum-indicative-maximum standards approach.

> A minimal-standards policy is one which would respond to the needs of older persons by providing a mix of institution-based services . . . An indicative-standards policy is one which would recognize the increase in the numbers and proportion of the aged in all countries by providing a level of services designed to meet the defined needs of this population at risk. A maximum-standards policy is one which would recognize not only the increase in numbers but also the deficits in existing services, and would therefore plan to increase both institution-based and community-based services at a faster rate than the rate of population increase, with a greater investment in community-based services (37:21).

In a companion article Little discusses homemaker—home-help services in developing countries (1975), applying a conceptual model which distributes them along a 'residual-institutional' continuum because such a model

> reflects the degree of public responsibility assumed as well as offering a possible fit with the minimum-indicative-maximum standards approach . . . (38:33).

Movement from residual to institutional provision is marked by greater public responsibility for basic social services. She summarizes her observations about home-help services in a number of developing countries and arrives at the overall conclusion that 'while lip-service is given to the value of community living for the elderly, home-delivered services to supplement family care are seriously deficient and in most countries available only on a minimal basis' (38:35).

In an unpublished paper (1976), Little analyzes issues and problems in providing home-care services for the aging by using data from studies in 20 countries in several regions of the world (39). She found that these issues and problems are similar even though different societies are at disparate stages of economic and social development. But these societies do differ in the way home care is managed and in the level of effort allocated to it. She suggests that an index of incapacity may be a better and more usable base for planning and evaluation than other types of data, and stresses the need to develop coordinating mechanisms to accompany service expansion.

A *Handbook of Aging and the Social Sciences* (1976), edited by Binstock and Shanas, marks an important step toward bringing together comprehensive information and major reference sources on aging, including knowledge and points of view from abroad, and toward illumining contemporary research issues on the 'phenomenon' of aging (40). The *Handbook* is one of three, the first two addressing the biology of aging and the psychology of aging.

In order to achieve its purposes, contributors were selected from among the best experts in the various social science disciplines and the social aspects of aging were broadly conceived. The topics dealt with in the 25 chapters are divided into five parts: the social aspects of aging, aging and social structure, aging and social systems, aging and interpersonal behavior, and aging and social intervention. The editors claim that in addition to providing historical perspectives on their topics, contributors constructed their presentations so as to ensure that the usefulness of the *Handbook* would not be limited by specific time referents.

A monograph by Kane and Kane, a physician and social worker team (1976), presents the results of a study of long-term care in six developed countries — Norway, Sweden, Netherlands, England, Scotland and Israel (41). The focus is on the elderly although the authors acknowledge and disavow the tendency to view chronic illness as for the most part affecting the aged. Information was obtained from official reports, visits to observe selected programs, and discussions with professional personnel. Kane and Kane strove for comparability by using a common guide for obtaining information, but found it difficult to achieve because of unique features — as well as common ones — exhibited by programs in different countries.

Among the latter they include the finding that 'in all countries the elderly experienced losses — in power, functional ability, memory and mental faculties, friendships, and social roles' (41:169). Everywhere, the family is seen as the most constant support for the elderly person; hence, provision of considerable official assistance for families of elderly individuals. Everywhere there is unequal distribution of services between the urban and the rural areas. In all countries it is recognized 'that community services do not replace the need for institutional services — they may only postpone and reduce their use' (41:171). Yet, nowhere were the authors able to find adequate research data that would throw light on the benefits of community-service programs or on their costs. While everywhere care for the elderly is conceptualized as both a social and a health problem so that theoretically, division of responsibilities between the social service and the health departments is clear-cut, in practice much confusion exists 'and the elderly resident is often caught in the middle' (41:171).

In regard to the fragmentation between social welfare homes and long-term hospitals, one of the solutions that is being proposed 'is the multi-level institution that may combine housekeeping flats, old-age-home beds, and long-term-care beds within the same facility' (41:172), even though it is recognized that this would not obviate the need for establishing clear guidelines for coordination and for handling financial and monitoring responsibilities. Another proposal, less popular, is to join reimbursement for care to prognosis and outcome of care, even though it is well known that deterioration is a gradual process and that distinctions between competence and incompetence are difficult to make. In this connection, in regard to the 'most insurmountable problem'— the disoriented — disagreement is widespread: most professionals felt that this group should be separated from the merely physically ill, while others argued that each old-age facility could easily accept and assimilate a small number of the disoriented. 'This would make it easier for competent staff who would not have to deal *only* with mentally confused or mentally retarded individuals' (41:175).

Guided by their findings, Kane and Kane draw up a list of major differences between what they found in the six countries they studied and the United States, couched in terms that raise policy issues and outline implications for the United States. They produce a proposal for the future development of long-term care in this country (41:175—90). This assumes the continuation of the profit motive as pivotal in providing such care in the United States — although in none of the six studied countries 'does the profit motive figure as importantly as in the United States. Public social services are much more involved in the direct administration of both community and institutional services ...' (41:175) and this makes possible the projection of desired goals and long-term planning.

A UN report on the aging in slums and uncontrolled settlements (1977) is based on four country studies carried out in Colombia, Jamaica, Hong Kong and Lebanon by consultants (42). It deals with the urban populations in these countries. Detailed are the demographic characteristics of aged persons who live in slums and uncontrolled areas, their social status, their living conditions and their needs. Policies that govern what is provided for them in the way of programs and services are also discussed.

A study edited by Shanas and Sussman (1977), another landmark contribution, has as its major theme

the linkage of aged persons with bureaucratic organizations in
complex societies and the role of family networks in such linkages.
The problematics of this linkage are how these organizations
constrain or support the aged person in developing and using
available human services; how family networks operate to assist or
hinder the aged family member in developing competence to 'handle'
bureaucracies; and how bureaucracies may affect the character and
quality of relationships between aged members and their families
(43:xii),

a theme that has not been investigated up to now because in the social
sciences, studies of bureaucracy, family, and the elderly developed
separate research traditions — a dysfunctional approach.

Contributors to the study were selected from among international
scholars from eight countries — Great Britain, the United States,
Netherlands, France, Poland, Austria, Yugoslavia and Israel — all of
them competent and knowledgeable about social systems, family
structure, and aging. Each contributor

was asked to prepare a paper describing how a selected social
system operates vis-à-vis the elderly and extended kin network; how
this system influences the quality of family relationships; what criteria
are being used to measure quality; and, finally, what current research
findings are available and what research is needed to understand the
relationships between bureaucratic structure and the quality of
family life (43:xv).

Overall, the contributions by the selected experts focused on theoretical
perspectives, historical/demographic analyses, empirical studies, and
interpretive analysis.

Gordon F. Streib (one of the contributors) introduced his discussion
of common themes and directions for further research by noting that
'one of the major advantages of cross-national studies is the opportunity
to note some of the common patterns which mark the conditions of the
aged in societies with different cultures, religious, and political
traditions' (43:204). What are these common patterns in the investigated
countries? Problems experienced by the aged are similar from the point
of view of social forces that generate them: the nature and size of the
aging population, the degree to which a high proportion of the
employed population is in agriculture, and the amount of social and
health services which the society pays for or can afford. This combines

Services for Special Groups

into the premise that as societies move toward modernization, the problems they face in relation to family and bureaucracy become similar. 'Indeed one can note a continuum related to the issue involved' (43:214). A largely agricultural society may mitigate the problems of the aging temporarily. The new norms and values that appear as the society moves toward modernity – brought about by the longer life span, changes in family relations, and the change-over from dealing with problems via traditional roles of families and religious groupings to formal agencies – do not rapidly coalesce into coherent systems. In answer to the question 'which is easier to change in modern societies: the bureaucratic structures or the family?' the consensus of opinion among contributors is that it is the former. They indicate what research and demonstration projects need to be undertaken to throw more light on 'how bureaucratic structures in modern societies can be developed, adapted, and improved to meet the emerging problems of older persons and their families' (43:214).

In the final chapter, Shanas and Sussman discuss bureaucracies and their activities in general and within them, the human service bureaucracies. In their view, there are major developments in progress which may inhibit 'the continuous encroachment of human service bureaucracies upon the affective territory of primary groups such as the family' (43:217); namely, limits being reached in providing financing for expanded service systems, and the poor track record of these systems in performing the non-uniform tasks of daily life and of socialization – activities which afford affection and individualized help needed by all human beings, especially the elderly. In line with these prognostications, they write:

> Viewing the family and its elderly member or members as an ecosystem with the provision of general services in centralized institutions when required is an appropriate option. It need not be a universal pattern in a society, but we insist that it be considered as an option. It would yield reciprocal benefits to both service practitioners and family members. The professional could best use his skills as an expert and consultant. He would not be required or tempted to assume complete control over the life of the elderly person and the family. Nor would the professional be 'pushed' into tasks, such as providing affection for his clients, which may not be in consonance with idealized professional roles (43:217).

As to social systems, Shanas and Sussman note that the demographic changes affecting older people in all of the included countries have not substantially changed the basic pattern of interaction between adult children and older parents. In regard to economic support and increased social services which have been developed in these countries, it is the conditions, under which the right to subsistence for the elderly is implemented, that differ from country to country. In this connection, relative responsibility laws tend to destroy good child—parent relations by injecting threat into a situation previously personal and private. While in some countries there exist 'advice bureaus', to discuss problems and/or to refer old people to proper community agencies, most of the social service systems are concerned with health and housing.

Shanas and Sussman devote special attention to what they call 'the emergence of the social worker as a family surrogate'. They believe that this role is not appropriate for

> One does not need professionals to provide everyday types of interactions, including everyday socialization. One does not need professionals whose training has created specialized cognitive styles, techniques of problem analysis, methods of communication, and perception well suited to handle those cases which may be 'two standard deviations from the norm' to handle idiosyncratic daily events (43:222).

Instead, they believe, social workers ought to utilize their skills in organizing the elderly and their families for lobbying and political action aimed at enlarging and improving the services available to them; in serving as managers and administrators of their interests; and in being advocates or ombudsmen for them.

In regard to future developments, Shanas and Sussman see no reasons why bureaucratic organizations cannot perform more effectively 'the uniform tasks for which they have been specifically organized', and families cannot perform more effectively 'the nonuniform tasks to which their structures are most suited' (43:225). What is called for, it would appear, is to assist both to develop their potentials to the full.[3]

The aged were included in the eight-country study of social services published by Kahn and Kamerman in 1976 (45). They found that the most important aspects pertinent to the social provisions made for them are pensionable age (rather than age per se) since it influences the size and composition of the aged cohort; the changing composition of the aged cohort in the direction of an increasing number who are older than 75 which augments the group of the 'frail elderly'; the fact that

Services for Special Groups 259

most of the aged live in urban areas; the fact that 'those who usually suffer most in old age in all countries are women'; and the impossibility of judging, for comparative purposes, the quantitative adequacy of a country's provision for the elderly outside of its overall system of provision — even after account has been taken of differences in terminology. Although everywhere needs are identified as income on retirement, medical care, 'shelter and care for the incapacitated with no families', all countries are stymied in developing objective criteria of need for varying levels, types and frequencies of care and services. The major policy issues revolve around failure to implement the decisions made for meeting needs and/or lack of harmonization between implementation strategies in different systems such as income support, health services and housing. In administration, the two questions singled out as the most important are: who is responsible for policy and for operating programs — which governmental organ, at what level in the governmental hierarchy, for what type of responsibility — and what should be the relationship between the public and private sectors? (45:245–68).

On the basis of a detailed listing of the major models and programs in community services for the aged used and operated in the eight countries they studied, Kahn and Kamerman conclude that despite extensive similarities, 'there are substantial differences among the countries'. These spring from differences in program emphasis, administrative auspices, the extent to which services are adequate quantitatively, eligibility conditions and financial arrangements, and the degree to which delivery of services is integrated or fragmented. Among major issues in services for the aged are familiar problems: how to determine the need for services and how to establish priorities for resource allocation; how to balance cash and in-kind benefits; what should be the objectives of personal social services for the aged; how to design the most effective delivery system to achieve these objectives; and how to integrate what is done for the aged into a broader family policy (45:269–312).

Social Services for Delinquents and Criminals. Conrad's international survey of attitudes and practices in regard to crime and its correction, published in 1965, is based on visits to facilities and agencies in the United States, Canada, Israel, and 14 countries in Europe, including the Soviet Union (46). His major discovery was that corrections constitute 'an instrument of social control which, in spite of local differences, is wielded in much the same way throughout the world', that it requires 'a complex apparatus for its operation', and that it conveys the same message — 'punishment' (46:301).

Two years later, Conrad produced a study on trends in European corrections. He outlines 'certain regularities which hold generally true of all continental countries west of the Communist bloc' (47:1) and compares them to the situation in the United States. Forces which are challenging the present correctional patterns in Europe and 'new departures' in continental correctional systems are discussed. Out of this analysis, Conrad draws implications for American practice and policy: for example, it is feasible to plan comprehensively for delinquent youth; correctional methods which are compatible with or make use of allied services such as schools, child welfare services and recreational programs have much more potential for success than correctional programs in isolation.

The impressive study published in 1973 by Clinard and Abbott is a pioneering investigation of crime in *developing* countries (48). In these countries, they note, development is bringing about a general increase in crime. 'In fact, one measure of the effective development of a country probably is its rising crime rate' (48:v). Yet, they explain, despite this increase and its generating forces, references to developing countries are omitted from criminological literature and from writings dealing with the development process or with the effects of urbanization in developing countries. The two authors describe their methodology and aims as follows:

Within the framework of a number of theoretical constructs derived from criminological research in the United States and Europe we have brought together most of the existing findings on crime in Africa, Asia, and Latin America, and the results of our own extensive research in Uganda. Throughout this book we have tried to show the similarities and differences between the developed and the less developed countries. In a cross-cultural setting we have discussed the relation to criminal behavior of urbanization, migration, the social organization of slum areas, differential association and peer-group structures, and differential opportunity (48).

The theoretical value of their work, they believe, lies in expanding criminological research into the 'third stage', namely, to developing societies 'that may be considered to be dissimilar to the developed countries of the world ... but, at the same time, are undergoing many similar processes' (48:2). The first stage (according to Durkheim) is the

Services for Special Groups

study of a single culture at one point in time, and the second stage, the study of societies characterized by similar cultural, economic and technological features.

Clinard and Abbott found that the increase in crime is especially pronounced in thefts; in contrast, homicide rates and prostitution (the latter closely related to sexual imbalance in cities, limited employment opportunities for women and their low social status) are likely to decrease with development. Sharp increases in thefts, for the most part, occur in 'primate cities' which attract the young, unskilled, migrant males who are drawn more easily into criminal activities. They migrate from distant villages not by stages but by sharp leaps. Their initial adjustment to the city plays a crucial role in their involvement in criminal activities especially because 'maintenance of rural ties does not appear to reduce the likelihood of [such] involvement' (48:127).

The two authors discovered that as in developed countries, developing countries' concentrations of crime are in slum areas. In these, older inhabitants, especially if their tribal background is identical with that of the younger newcomers, do play a vital role in determining the character of slum communities. Furthermore, among various factors, it is the internal relations and the patterns of behavior within these communities that are the more important in controlling property crime; they exert an influence quite independent of linkages outside the slums. It was found that ability of community members to control behavior within its boundaries is not necessarily increased by attainment of a higher average socio-economic status (48:165). In this connection, the authors' reminder that in developed countries

> With discouraging regularity the higher general standards of living, better distribution of wealth, and new urban housing programs ultimately appear to have little or no effect on crime rates (48:187)

is revealing.

As to characteristics of offenders, the study showed that while similar proportions of offenders and non-offenders were unemployed or had no education, educational aspirations were much lower among offenders. In contrast, their perceptions of blocked access to better jobs and their level of cynicism toward the nepotism and corruption in business and government were sharper and higher than among non-offenders. In regard to the theory of differential opportunity which emphasizes the importance of access to illegitimate means, Clinard and Abbott write:

it is this aspect that may represent the key, rather than the blocking of economic and educational opportunities, to an understanding of criminality in less developed countries. . . A major principle . . . is that criminal behavior is learned by processes of differential association. As in developed countries, there is ample evidence that the major social groups that transmit and perpetuate criminal norms are youth and adult gangs (48:188, 210).

A recent international survey (1976) on juvenile justice is the result of a joint effort by the UN Social Defense Research Institute and the World Health Organization (49). The decision to carry out this cross-cultural undertaking by combining the expertise and resources of these two bodies was motivated by the realization that their specialized perspectives are not broad enough separately to deal with juvenile problems: the Institute is a policy research body focusing on deviance and its criminal justice connotations, while the Organization is particularly concerned with mental health aspects of deviance. In addition to the survey, the Institute and the Italian Ministry of Justice commissioned an in-depth study of the operation of the juvenile justice system in Naples.

The survey is a descriptive one by design: it was felt that as a beginning stage in a larger study of juvenile delinquency, it could serve as a back-drop 'against which specific trends, problems, innovations and their significance could be identified and assessed' (49). The countries in which it was conducted were considered as 'representative' — India, Japan, Scotland, Afghanistan, France, Indonesia, Mexico, and South Australia. The Soviet Union contributed a description of its treatment processes, with special attention to the degree of their effectiveness. Effort was concentrated on eliciting information on the nature and magnitude of juvenile problems, on the administration of juvenile justice, the role and contribution of mental health and related organs, and on discovering whether or not data for more specific research and analysis were available.

It became evident to the researchers 'that additional efforts are needed not only to describe and assess systemic performance over time, but to elicit trend data and especially to identify and evaluate the effectiveness, viability and potential transferability of particular innovations or improvements for coping with juvenile maladjustment and deviance' (49:12). They pinpointed three innovative approaches that seemed to them especially worthy of investigation: developing community resources for juveniles without referring them to specialized agencies or institutions; developing community youth services for coping with particular problems; and assisting developing countries in creating juvenile justice systems.

In an exceptionally competent study (1977), Gurr analyses official records of offenses against persons and property in London, Stockholm, and Sydney over a period of 150 years, from 1820s to 1970s (50). In the process, he deals with two recurring research problems: the accuracy of crime statistics and how public order changes over time. He found that from about 1840 to 1930, indicators of common crime fell by an average ratio of 8:1; but that since then, and especially since 1950, these indicators have increased by a similar ratio.

Gurr maintains that the dramatic increases since 1950 cannot be attributed to institutional factors — changes in criminal law, police systems, and judicial policies. Rather, these increases represent a real increase in threatening social behavior in the aftermath of World War II, far more rapid than the earlier decrease. Whether this finding is generalizable to other Western societies is a problem which Gurr investigates in a forthcoming study in which he analyzes trends in public order since 1945 on the basis of official data on known offenses and convictions, in 16 Western democracies. All of them, he found, have experienced accelerating rates of crime against persons and property. 'Interestingly enough', he notes, 'the English-speaking and Scandinavian countries have experienced the sharpest and most consistent increases' (50:135).

In regard to causality, Gurr notes that his study does not support the position of those who claim that the increase in crime since the 1950s can be attributed to changes in the operations of the police and criminal justice systems. On the contrary, the workings of the police, courts, and penal institutions do not have consistent effects on the magnitude of crime. The valid explanation must be sought, he suggests, in the workings and effects of more fundamental social forces — not on 'repressive' or 'inefficient' officials.

Policy issues. Many policy issues in personal social services for children and the aged are basically the same. Among these, an issue that is assuming greater importance is the relationship between the welfare establishment responsible for services and the family — still the major social institution for providing affection, socialization and care to children and the elderly alike. Specifically, the question is how to avoid reducing familial responsibility and encroaching on its functions, and at the same time assuring a diversified network of services and specialized facilities that the family cannot and/or should not provide. Related questions are how to determine the extent and nature of the need for such services and facilities and how to balance resources between urban and rural areas so that the latter do not remain shortchanged.

Similarities permeate the usual major administrative and organizational issues, namely, how to design the most effective and responsive delivery system, how to establish priorities for resource allocation, how to design feasible and flexible long-range plans, how to achieve coordination and harmonization, how to assure quality services and related to this, how to resolve the many problems concerning personnel. In regard to the latter, the main questions are what should be the training for professionals and paraprofessionals (if the latter receive training), and how can a commitment to strengthening the family rather than becoming family surrogates be built into the professional value base; how to integrate diverse professional skills and clarify the division of responsibilities between the different professions involved.

An important issue in care for the aged and in child care concerns the auspices and financial arrangements. Because in many countries both government and voluntary agencies offer services and operate facilities for children and the aged, the question of the place and/or desirability of the profit motive and the role of official organs in enforcing standards can become acute – especially when voluntary agencies have a monopoly on services needed by government agencies to implement their legal responsibilities toward eligible individuals. A perennial problem is how to involve service users and the community in developing and improving services. While the necessity for integrating services for children and the aged into the general objectives of development in line with a particular country's economic, social and cultural characteristics is recognized everywhere, the issues that it poses are especially pronounced in developing countries – given the tendency in the past to transplant western designs and methods without adapting or modifying them, a tendency that is still influencing service delivery.

An issue important for the aged is how to balance cash and in-kind benefits. Among the crucial issues specific to child welfare is whether policy should be comprehensive, that is, should extend to all children and parents rather than only to certain groups among them, usually the underprivileged and the handicapped. Equally important is how to define and recognize the status of children and the rights and responsibilities of parents and children in a way that will protect equality of all family members (especially of women and of children other than legitimate). An issue that affects all services for all groups,

Services for Special Groups

but is especially sharp in relation to young persons whose behavior defies societal mores or breaks laws, is how to secure public legitimation and sanction of new and/or innovative service programs. Tied into this is the necessity of overcoming difficulties in evaluating the effectiveness, viability and potential transferability of innovations or improvements. This goes to the question of securing sufficient knowledge and consensus among the professionals and experts about the implications and consequences of changes in programs and beyond this, to the mounting of effective public relations and educational campaigns that would interpret what is being done to the general public.

Summary. Throughout the literature on cross-national studies reviewed in this chapter there are frequent references to the paucity of adequate and reliable information and to the meagerness of scientific research — whether in relation to the service needs of children, or long-term effects of day care, or trend data in delinquency, or benefits of community-service programs and their costs, or ways to refine intervention methods and techniques. Complaints are also voiced about the lack of clarity concerning objectives. For example: should the emphasis in day care be on freeing mothers for work or on socializing children or on preparing them for elementary school? The answer to this question is likely to determine what children do and learn in day care and how the program is organized and operated and by whom.

But scientific data are not altogether lacking. In regard to children, they illumine differences in child-rearing practices and attitudes in the family and in the school as they are influenced by different societal contexts and by the degree of importance attached to assessing individual differences in children. Knowledge about the salient characteristics of effective group care for young children and adolescents is considerable. Reliable analyses of the legal position of migrant children and of youngsters in 'disturbed' family situations, as well as of the problems that the legal framework often engenders for them and their families, is at hand. The social changes that stimulate the demand for day care are becoming more clearly visible. There is some indication that administrative patterns have important implications for the mental health of users of service. Sound information about how to organize and administer services so that they will implement the goals of policy more fully and effectively is accumulating.

In regard to the aged, the volume of scientific research is impressive. It has shed light on the biological, social and psychological aspects of aging; on the similarity of problems faced by aged people in industrial nations and of the social forces that generate them; on the dissimilarity in the practices of different societies in meeting needs as well as in the extent to which needs are met as they reflect ideological and sociopolitical differences; and on the influence of different cultures and religious and political traditions on the role activities of the aged in various societies. We are beginning to understand better the impact of modernization on the status of the aged and on the problems they face vis-à-vis the family and the bureaucratic structures, as both are affected by the pace at which changes induced by modernization coalesce into discernible systems that embrace values, life styles and ways of dealing with social problems.

Much less is known about delinquency. What has been learned so far seems to point to the notion that higher average socio-economic status has little effect on crime rates, in both developing and developed nations; rather, it is access to illegitimate means that is the more potent. In a time-related perspective, reasons for increases in crime cannot be pinned on repressive or inefficient officials; rather, they must be sought in more fundamental social forces. From the point of view of treatment, there is some indication that better results, especially with young delinquents, can be achieved when correctional services are integrated with allied services in the community.

Information that is not scientific but does represent consensus among experts suggests that in developing countries, as elsewhere, children's needs are better met when their families are strengthened by improvement in their levels of living. Strengthening families likewise calls for improving the situation of women in general (in employment, social status, educational and health areas) and for helping mothers to enhance their skills in homemaking, child care and nutrition.

Notes

1. Understanding of problems experienced by children likely to require social service intervention calls for knowledge concerning their family situations. Among works that provide such knowledge in an international perspective may be included Goode's pioneering *World Revolution and Family Patterns* published in 1963 (1) and his shorter discussion on 'Industrialization and Family Change' which appeared in 1968 (2); Pearlin's cross-national study (1971) which focused on class context and family relations (3); the volume of papers which discussed 'the changing family: East and West' (1973), edited by White (4); and a 1972 book edited by Gordon on 'the nuclear family in crisis' (5). A recent book (1976) by Rosenblatt, Walsh and Jackson seeks to enhance our understanding of the manner in which families and individuals are affected by grief and mourning and how to help them deal with these experiences, in a cultural perspective involving

various countries. This is an area of concern that is acquiring increasing importance (6).

Anthropologically oriented investigations of child rearing patterns are also useful, especially for insights on how to offer services to children. Among such investigations may be included *Childhood in Contemporary Cultures*, a 1955 work edited by Mead and Wolfenstein (7); and the well-known work on cross-cultural socialization, initiated in 1953 and directed by Beatrice and John Whiting, which culminated in the publication of two volumes (1963, 1975), both concerned with children in six cultures — Kenya, India, Okinawa, Mexico, Philippines, and the United States (8). The 1975 volume attempts to answer the following questions: are children brought up in societies with different customs, beliefs, and values radically different from each other? Do differences attributable to sex, age, and birth order override these cultural differences? Does the situation and setting influence a child's behavior or are his actions similar across environments?

2. Among UN international surveys that have policy implications for children's services are those, for example, that studied discrimination against persons born out of wedlock (11), compared services for juvenile delinquents (12), or examined national youth service programs (13).

3. Several of the studies included in this section have considered the cultural environment as an important variable in the experience of aging in particular societies. A recent book under the editorship of Barbara G. Myerhoff and Andrei Simic (1978) reports on the research of five anthropologists, each of whom considers old age and aging in relation to a particular cultural environment. Sponsored by the National Science Foundation, the research sought to discover common elements in the lives of the informants (44).

References

1. Goode, William J., *World Revolution and Family Patterns* (New York, The Free Press, 1963).

2. Goode, William J., 'Industrialization and Family Change', pp. 47–61 in Eisenstadt, S. N. (ed.) *Comparative Perspectives on Social Change* (Boston, Little, Brown and Company, 1968).

3. Pearlin, Leonard I., *Class Context and Family Relations: A Cross-National Study* (Boston, Little, Brown and Company, 1971).

4. White, Henry E. (ed.) *An Anthology of Seminar Papers: The Changing Family, East and West* (Hong Kong, Hong Kong Baptist College, no date, but seminar held on May 14–16, 1973, sponsored by the Department of Sociology-Social Work of the Baptist College).

5. Gordon, Michael (ed.) *The Nuclear Family in Crisis: In Search for an Alternative* (New York, Harper & Row, 1972).

6. Rosenblatt, Paul C., Walsh, Patricia R., and Jackson, Douglas A., *Grief and Mourning in Cross-Cultural Perspective* (New Haven, Conn., HRAF Press, 1976).

7. Mead, Margaret and Wolfenstein, Martha (eds.) *Childhood in Contemporary Cultures* (Chicago, University of Chicago Press, 1955).

8. Whiting, Beatrice B. (ed.) *Six Cultures. Studies of Child Rearing*, Laboratory of Human Development, Harvard University (New York, John Wiley and Sons, 1963); and Whiting, Beatrice B. and Whiting, John W. in collaboration with Longabaugh, Richard, *Children of Six Cultures; A Psycho-Cultural Analysis* (Cambridge, Mass., Harvard University Press, 1975).

9. Sicault, Georges (general ed.) *The Needs of Children. A Survey of the*

268 Services for Special Groups

Needs of Children in the Developing Countries, Report prepared by UNICEF, WHO, The Food and Agriculture Organization, UNESCO, the UN Bureau of Social Affairs, and the ILO for the guidance of the UNICEF Executive Board (New York, The Free Press of Glencoe, 1963).

10. Stein, Herman (ed.) *Planning for the Needs of Children in Developing Countries*, Report of a Round-Table Conference, April 1–7, 1964, Bellagio, Italy (New York, UNICEF, 1964).

11. UN, Department of Economic and Social Affairs, *Study of Discrimination against Persons Born out of Wedlock* (New York, UN, 1968, Sales No., 68, XIV. 3).

12. UN, Department of Economic and Social Affairs, *Comparative Survey of Juvenile Delinquency*, Part 5: Middle East (New York, UN, 1965).

13. UN, Department of Economic and Social Affairs, *Report of the Interregional Seminar on National Youth Service Programmes*. Organized jointly by the UN, the ILO and the Government of Denmark; Holte, November 17–30, 1968 (New York, UN, 1968).

14. UN, Department of Economic and Social Affairs, *Report on Children* (New York, UN, 1971).

15. Meers and Marans, 'Group Care of Infants'.

16. Jensen, Gordon D., 'Day Care Centers in Europe: A Focus on Consequences for Mental Health', *Mental Hygiene*, 55, no. 4 (October 1971), pp. 425–32.

17. Thomas, Jean McKamy, *A Study of Day Care in the USSR and USA*, PhD dissertation, University of Georgia, 1972.

18. Kamerman, Sheila B., *Child Care Programs in Nine Countries* (Office of Child Development, Office of the Secretary, PO Box 1182, Washington, DC 20013).

19. Calkins, Joan Sweitzer, *Two Worlds of Early Childhood: Government-Sponsored Child Care Centers in the Soviet Union and California*, PhD dissertation, Claremont, 1976.

20. Glickman, Beatrice Marden and Springer, Nesha Bass, *Who Cares for the Baby? Choices in Child Care* (New York, Schocken Books, 1978).

21. Bronfenbrenner, Urie, *Two Worlds of Childhood* (New York, Russell Sage Foundation, 1970).

22. Roby, Pamela (ed.) *Child Care – Who Cares? Foreign and Domestic Infant and Early Childhood Development Policies* (New York, Basic Books, 1973).

23. Robinson, Halbert B., and Robinson, Nancy M. (eds.) *International Monograph Series on Early Child Care* (London, Gordon and Breach). Vol. 1: *Early Child Care in Hungary* by Alice Hermann and Sandor Komlosi; vol. 2: *Early Child Care in Sweden* by Ragnar Berfenstam and Inger William-Olsson; vol. 3: *Early Child Care in the United States of America* by Halbert B. Robinson, Nancy M. Robinson, Martin Wolins, Urie Bronfenbrenner and Julius B. Richmond; vol. 4: *Early Child Care in Switzerland* by Kurt K. Luscher, Verena Ritter and Peter Gross; vol. 5: *Early Child Care in Britain* by Mia Kellmer Pringle and Sandhua Naidoo; vol. 6: *Early Child Care in France* by Myriam David and Irene Lezine; and vol. 7: *Early Child Care in Israel* by Chanan Rapaport, Joseph Marcus, Miriam Glikson, Witold Jedlicki and Sheldon Lache.

24. Wolins, 'Some Theory and Practice in Child Care'.

25. Wolins, Martin (ed.) *Successful Group Care. Explorations in the Powerful Environment* (Chicago, Aldine Publishing Company, 1974).

26. Kafka, Doris and Underhill, Evi, 'Comparative Study of Certain Aspects of Family Law in 16 European and Mediterranean Countries', *International Child Welfare Review*, no. 22/23 (October 1974), pp. 27–42.

27. Veillard-Cybulska, Henryka, 'The Legal Welfare of Children in a Disturbed Family Situation', *International Child Welfare Review*, Part I, no. 25 (May 1975), pp. 34–48; Part II, no. 26 (September 1975), pp. 45–59; Part III, no. 27 (December 1975), pp. 29–39.

28. Kamerman, Sheila B., 'Eight Countries: Cross-National Perspective on Child Abuse and Neglect', *Children Today* (May–June 1975), pp. 34–7.
29. Shore, Milton F., 'Youth Advisory Services in Six European Countries', *Children Today*, 5, no. 1 (January/February 1976), pp. 23–7, 35.
30. Burgess, E. W. (ed.) *Aging in Western Societies* (Chicago, Chicago University Press, 1960).
31. Shanas et. al., *Old People in Three Industrial Societies*.
32. UN European Social Development Programme, *Symposium on Research and Welfare Policies for the Elderly*, Herzlya, Israel, June 1–9, 1969 (New York, UN, 1970).
33. Havighurst, Robert J., Joep, M. A., Munnichs, Bernice Neugarten, and Thomae, Hans (eds.) *Adjustments to Retirement: A Cross-National Study* (New York, Humanities Press, 1969).
34. Palmore, E. B. and Manton, K., 'Modernization and Status of the Aged: International Correlations', *Journal of Gerontology*, 29, no. 2 (1974), pp. 205–10.
35. Brocklehurst, J. C. (ed.) *Geriatric Care in Advanced Societies* (Baltimore, University Park Press, 1975).
36. Trager, Brahna, 'Home Help Abroad, A Review of Selected In-Home Services in Western European Countries', in *Home-Help Services for the Aging Around the World* (Washington, DC, International Federation on Ageing, 1975), pp. 3–16.
37. Little, Virginia A., 'Present Status of Homemaker-Home Help Services in Developed Countries', in *ibid.*, pp. 16–22.
38. Little, Virginia A., 'Homemaker-Home Help Service in Developing Countries', in *ibid*, pp. 32–43.
39. Little, Virginia A., 'Issues and Problems in Providing Home Care Services for the Aging: A Cross-Cultural Perspective'. Mimeographed. (The University of Connecticut School of Social Work, West Hartford, Connecticut, September 15, 1976).
40. Binstock, Robert H. and Shanas, Ethel (eds.) *Handbook of Aging and the Social Sciences* (New York, Van Nostrand Reinhold Co., 1976).
41. Kane, Robert L. and Kane, Rosalie A., *Long-Term Care in Six Countries: Implications for the United States*, Fogarty International Center Proceedings no. 331 (Washington, DC, HEW, 1976).
42. UN, Department of Social and Economic Affairs, *The Aging in Slums and Uncontrolled Settlements* (New York, UN, 1977).
43. Shanas, Ethel and Sussman, Marvin B. (eds.) *Family, Bureaucracy, and the Elderly* (Durham, NC, Duke University Press, 1977).
44. Myerhoff, Barbara G. and Simic, Andrei (eds.) *Life's Career – Aging: Cultural Variations on Growing Old*, Sage Series in Cross-Cultural Research and Methodology, vol. 4 (Beverly Hills, California, Sage Publications, 1978).
45. Kahn and Kamerman, *Social Services in International Perspective*.
46. Conrad, John P., *Crime and Its Correction. An International Survey of Attitudes and Practices* (Berkeley, California, University of California Press, 1965).
47. Conrad, John P., *Trends in European Corrections*, Report submitted to the President's Commission on Law Enforcement and Administration of Justice, 1967. Mimeographed.
48. Clinard, Marshall Barron and Abbott, Daniel J., *Crime in Developing Countries. A Comparative Perspective* (New York, John Wiley and Sons, 1973).
49. UN, Social Defense Research Institute, *Juvenile Justice: An International Survey. Country Reports, Related Materials and Suggestions for Future Research* (Rome, Publication no. 12, February 1976).
50. Gurr, Ted Robert, 'Contemporary Crime in Historical Perspective: A Comparative Study of London, Stockholm, and Sydney', *The Annals of the American Academy of Political and Social Sciences*, 434 (November 1977), pp. 114–36.

PART FOUR: PLANNING

Many social scientists take the position that in one form or another and in varying degrees, planning is an essential part of social and economic policies of different countries. Writes Aiyar:

Planning is the outward expression of the technological impact on modern societies and is, therefore, inevitable at all levels of development. The modern problem is not, to plan or not to plan, but the nature and degree of state intervention in the different sectors of society. Modern democratic states, of which the welfare state is but one variant, rest on the view that while overall planning is required at the national level under the supervision of the state, at the micro-economic level, the market mechanism has still a useful function to perform in diversifying the economy and for competitive efficiency. While collectivist economic planning supplants the market process, democratic planning seeks in many ways to supplement it . . . The nature and degree of planning is, of course, tied up with the structure of economic and political power in the modern state (1:xxi).

It is the nature and degree of state intervention that underlie the essential, structural differences between the Soviet planning process, which effectively melds economic and social planning with the political power structure, the French 'indicative' planning process, where the government sets certain priorities and targets which the conjunction of governmental and non-governmental actions tends to approximate, the 'free enterprise' planning whereby private and non-national government bodies as well as agencies of the national government make and execute plans. Since different degrees of state intervention reflect different power structures and different scales of social and individual values, they have a profound impact on the quality of life. The goals of social welfare may be expressed in similar words, yet reflect radically different views of the nature of man and project quite different means to achieve superficially similar ends. Common basic ideas about social planning emerge from declarations and conventions of international organizations. Nevertheless, 'in the international sphere', writes Flamm, 'there is no uniform concept of social planning' (2:135). The planning that is undertaken depends on a country's or a region's socio-political order and on its 'real-life' situation.

Furthermore, doubts about the feasibility of planning persist. As recently as 1972, for example, Donnison raised the question:

> Is planning, in any synoptic or far-reaching sense, a feasible operation at all? If it is not, social ideologies of a comprehensive kind will not greatly interest practical men because there is not much they can do with them. I . . . conclude that, although planning should be a more modest proceeding than some of its practitioners have been prepared to concede, reports of its death are greatly exaggerated (3:97).

That social and economic planning must become inseparable is almost universally acknowledged. The need for an integrative approach inspired all documents pertaining to the second UN Development Decade and has been enthusiastically endorsed by writers on social welfare (for example, see (4)). It springs from the conviction that the lack of integration characteristic of development planning ignores the social determinants and the social consequences of development and befuddles efforts to understand the relationship between social and economic factors that is essential for genuine progress. But to achieve a synthesis between economic and social variables is, as will be seen later, a difficult task.

In a technical sense, planning in any society is an institutionalized process to achieve a more rational use of resources with distinctions usually made between policy and program planning: the former concerned with attaining overall societal goals, the latter, with attainment of goals for specific functional activities or sectors (5:196). But there are differences between different societies in the extent to which planning is confined to theoretical, somewhat rigid and largely unimplemented designs on the one hand, and planning that is intimately connected with the authoritative allocation of values (that is, practical politics and governmental machinery of a given society) on the other.

Pertinent in this context is Friedmann's distinction between allocative and innovative planning. While closely related, the former guides the process of change in a political system by maintaining overall balances in the attainment of given objectives while the latter seeks to accomplish the guiding function by 'fostering imbalances in the existing order so as to legitimize new values or to render vaguely formulated

Planning 273

purposes specific through new institutional arrangements' (6:203). Planning and implementation are not distinct and separable activities, and making planning decisions more rational is no more important to Friedmann than improving the quality of action. He proposes an action-planning model which 'fuses action and planning into a single operation so that the conceptual distinctions of planning—decision—implementation—recycling are washed out' (7:312). In this approach, the planner moves to the action line as a person whose success will depend partly on how skillful he is in interpersonal relationships. To implement his action-planning model, Friedmann proposes a type of planning more suitable for linking technical know-how to organized action and for bringing about new mechanisms of control and conflict resolution (8:315—27).

11 SOCIAL WELFARE PLANNING

This chapter opens with a discussion of the efforts that have been made to clarify the meaning of the term 'planning', of its potential importance in advancing the cause of social welfare, and of the reasons why difficulties continue to surround welfare planning wherever it has been undertaken. This is followed by an analysis of studies in social welfare planning which, although not comparative in a strict sense, do examine the planning process in an international perspective and provide a good deal of information about the basic common principles that should guide them.

Planning and development. There is a tendency among some writers to treat planning as almost synonymous with development. To some extent, this may be due to the fact that planning is considered by many as especially important for developing nations so that much of the literature that deals with planning from an international point of view is concerned with the efforts of such nations to improve the quality of life for their people (9:20, 10, 11:3). The interchangeable use of the two concepts may also stem from the position held by some experts that planning and development are complementary in the sense that development is seen as a goal while planning is thought of as method (12:15).

At the Symposium on Social Policy and Planning held under UN auspices in 1970, *development* was more precisely described as 'a process of improving the capacity of national institutions and value systems to meet increasing demands, whether of a social, economic or political character' (13:17). This is similar to Myrdal's definition: development is the movement of the whole social system upwards (14:29). It also reflects the use of the term as defined in the Pearson Commission report as:

> a composite concept describing the interdependent development of cultural, social and economic resources of a country whose condition of life has previously been largely static, at a low socio-economic level, for long periods of history. The objective of development in this sense is to enable the country concerned to live and move as a viable partner in the modern world of nations (15:63).

276 *Social Welfare Planning*

In contrast, *planning* was defined by the Symposium:

> as signifying essentially the process of choosing or selecting among alternative courses of action, with a view to allocating scarce resources, in order to reach specified objectives, on the basis of a preliminary diagnosis covering all the relevant factors that could be identified. Such relevant factors were considered to include the social and political, as well as the economic, structures of countries seeking to plan, and the choices to be made to include the selection of instruments and approaches that would be workable within these structures (13:17).

Participants saw planning as contributing to a more comprehensive formulation of the objectives of development. Kuusi also views planning as a long-term pattern of action adopted to promote the indispensable social aims of a country — to rationalize its social policies by degrees. It is a method, he explains, for developing the decision-making machinery of the community gradually so that choices made by its citizens enter into attaining its social aims more effectively (16:8).

That development and planning are neither synonymous nor complementary is aptly explained by McGranahan. He writes that under a system model

> development is an evolving system of factors that influence and are influenced by each other, directly or indirectly. This means, conversely, that social or economic elements that are not . . . interdependent with other factors, are excluded from the definition of development, although they may have a one-way relationship as causes or consequences . . . Under this approach, some other expression, such as 'social progress', would have to be used for desirable changes not part of development, such as reductions in crime . . . and progress towards other ideals of human society which do not appear to be part of development as an interdependent system. These values . . . should be involved in *planning which would not then be coterminous with development planning* (17:98, emphasis added).

There is general agreement that to think of social welfare planning as concerned primarily with welfare activities of public and private social agencies is to distort reality and needs (18). Social 'programming' by these agencies is only one part of implementing the social goals of a particular community which, in turn, are a reflection of social goals for the nation. Planning should be tied into both of these levels of action. The need for such comprehensiveness also emerges when planning is looked at as a process (5) or when prognostications have to be made about future directions (19, 20).

Importance of Social Welfare Planning. The need for social welfare planning has been recognized by the UN and by international social welfare organizations for some time.

As early as 1957, a group of experts convened by the UN stressed the need for centralized planning, for planning to be based on precise data supplied by methodical organization of research and evaluation processes, and for flexibility so that plans may be kept abreast of development (21). In 1959, another group was asked to recommend guiding principles for the planning and implementation of social service programs (22), and in 1967 a third group was brought together to examine the problems of social welfare organization and administration (23). In 1968, the ministers responsible for social welfare assigned top priority to devising effective social welfare planning (10). But in 1970, on the basis of a review of 50 national plans in Asia, Middle East and Africa, 14 in Latin America and four in the Caribbean, the UN staff wrote the following:

> The methodology of sectoral planning is already well advanced in the fields of education, health, manpower and the like. In the field of social welfare, however, methodological progress has been generally slower, a fact which has contributed to the tendency among national planners to treat this sector as a 'poor relation' (24:1).

And in 1971, Wolfe noted that social welfare planning 'is more talked about than practised' (25:37).

The theme of the XIIth International Conference of Social Work in 1964 was 'social progress through social planning — the role of social work'. Its working party analyzed a large number of national reports and found that approaches to national planning varied considerably; that interpretation and treatment of the subject likewise varied, differing importantly according to economic, socio-political, cultural and social structure of different countries and regions. It was clear, however, that although there was awareness of the need for more active and effective participation in planning by social welfare bureaucracies, very little of it in fact took place.

That diversity, as well as the slow pace of planning in the welfare field, are likely to continue is suggested by more recent discussions. At the 1974 International Conference on Social Welfare, for example, it was proposed that development, in addition to facilitating greater production, must help attain equitable distribution, satisfaction, self-sufficiency, and self-fulfillment. It should, therefore, concentrate on benefiting the poor, on eliminating class distinctions and exploitation, and on community welfare — and it should always derive its goals from the aspirations of the people. This broad policy statement, accepted by most of the Conference participants, produced very different scenarios when translated into strategy and planning. These ranged from giving priority to therapeutically oriented personal social services, to focusing on community development, land reform, institution building, adult education, social action, and industrial development with self-management. Social action was to create the 'inevitable society', agrarian in form and based on communal institutions; industrial development with self-management was to introduce 'a profound change wherein man, the worker, with his primordial, inalienable, and sovereign rights occupies the place of honor' (26:55, 258).

Difficulties in Planning. After a careful and wide-ranging examination, Hodge concludes that there is still 'considerable confusion about the definition of social planning and its conceptual base'; that how social planning is defined depends 'upon the background, education and profession or occupation of the person' who is doing the defining; and that movement toward greater clarity will be assisted 'if social planners will make clear what they mean by social development, and how they propose to measure progress made along the road of such development' (27:8, 23). Because planners must take into account the organizational and political circumstances in which they find themselves — and then devise strategies and techniques that seem most appropriate to these circumstances — they often come up against unresolved issues in political philosphies of different countries. Many of these issues have a bearing on planning and befuddle the meaning of social development.

The report of the working party at the XIIth International Conference of Social Work in 1964 saw planning as conveying two aspects of development: social policy with regard to developmental planning as a whole, and sectoral (functional) planning of what are called social services, such as social security and personal social services (9:20). But a continuing problem has been a lack of clarity in defining

Social Welfare Planning

the functions of welfare, and particularly the failure to demonstrate the concrete contributions it can make to overall development. This has complicated the governmental task of deciding where to locate the responsibility for specifying the goals to be achieved; who will be responsible for devising and harmonizing the optimum use of resources for reaching these goals; who will assess the feasibility of proposed programs within the context of national development; and who will evaluate the results as compared to stated objectives. That these complications may diminish the role of government in the social welfare field was recognized, for example, by the European ministers responsible for social welfare at their conference in 1972. They were especially concerned with securing appropriate governmental direction in inter-sectoral relationships, in determining the degree and kind of decentralization of welfare, and in creating social welfare strategies that would be constructively attuned to social change (28:26–32).

Additional difficulties center on the fact that planners abhor generalities; they want and need quantification but the social welfare establishment does not produce it. The orientation of economic and social planners is different: the former are interested in increasing output; the latter are concerned with meeting human needs. Consequently, means to achieve economic and social objectives may be in conflict (29:126). Furthermore, as noted earlier, the traditional function of social welfare in most countries has been residual and remedial; the preventive and planning functions are not yet accepted by all countries or by all social welfare agencies (9:28). As a result, planners get little help from social welfare personnel with quantifying welfare proposals and relating them to an agreed-upon conceptual base – a situation reflecting absence of formal social welfare planning methodology, an unscientific approach to decision-making, and failure to state problems and criteria of choice systematically, precisely and objectively.[1]

Still other difficulties stem from broader conceptual and methodological problems involved in efforts to achieve integration between social and economic planning. Such integration, explained Tinbergen in 1964, requires dealing with 'social' policy as a component of general development policy and making choices 'based on the maximization of human well-being'. But how to define 'well-being'? We can accept the definitions of 'wise men', he said; that is, of parliaments in democracies and rulers in non-democratic nations. Or we may attempt to create more sophisticated yardsticks to measure it. Essentially, what the 'wise men' must decide is 'whether the marginal satisfaction of each family is about equal' (32:63); if it is, 'general well-being' is presumed to characterize the population's living situation. More sophisticated yardsticks require 'splitting up well-being into such elements as nutritive sufficiency, psychical balance, etc, to which a certain meaning has already been attached by the scientists dealing with the subject' (32:68). From this should emerge more objective socio-economic planning in the shape of projects that would yield a correct knowledge of their consequences and as objective a valuation as possible of the effect these consequences have on general well-being.

Central planning for national economic development has been instituted, in one form or another, in at least 100 countries, from preindustrial Tanganyika to post-industrial France and England. But integration or even coordination of social and economic planning is spotty, ineffective and, in many countries, non-existent. In 1970, the UN reported that in most developing countries, what is referred to as 'social planning' is still nebulous in conception, in substance and application — despite formal commitments to a comprehensive approach (33). In practice, such planning is confined to a few sectors which are traditionally regarded as important in improving living standards, so that in fact little activity is undertaken toward integrative welfare strategies. In 1972, Fisher found that:

> In practice, integration between 'social' and 'economic' planning — except in the sense of combining the two in one document — has not been achieved anywhere even when differences in the meaning of the term 'planning' in various market economies are disregarded (34:19).[2]

Studies in Social Welfare Planning. The subjects covered by the included studies are overall development planning, planning for social security, for children and youth, and for the disabled.

Planning for Balanced Social and Economic Development. The UN has been actively concerned with planning, especially in the past 20 years. A report issued in 1957 centered on the mechanics of planning for the development of social policy, stressed the need for centralized planning, for basing it on precise data through the methodical organization of research and evaluation processes, and for flexibility so that plans might be kept in line with development (37).

A European seminar on the problems and methods of social planning, held in 1964, was attended by participants from 15 countries

(38). Introductory papers by experts ranged over a wide spectrum of concerns: the diverse approaches to social planning; the institutional and economic framework for decision-making in social planning; concepts of social policy and social planning and the relations of social to economic planning. Discussion focused on three aspects: basic data essential for social planning (to make possible the assessment of needs, determination of available means, and the evaluation of effects); the establishment of standards and priorities; and the primordial importance for planning that it take place within the country's actual institutional and political framework. It was noted by one of the experts that the approaches to planning of the socialist countries of Eastern Europe differ in several respects from those typical of Western European countries, but that in practice, approaches showed a marked tendency to converge (38:10). Another expert pointed out that the difference between the quick- and slow-growing economies could not be explained solely in terms of varying rates of input of capital and of labor. Consequently, economists 'were being driven' to pay more and more attention to the economic growth-producing effects of expenditures on the social sector, that is, to the sphere of *social* policy (38:12−13). Balanced social and economic development was defined as development which 'implies both the growth that may be measured quantitatively and the changes of a social and cultural nature which are qualitative and do not lend themselves to quantitative measurement' (38:14).

A meeting of experts convened by the UN in 1969 addressed the subject of 'social policy and planning in national development' (39). The experts were averse to continuing the artificial dichotomy between 'economic' and 'social' phenomena in development, and strongly affirmed the need for more attention to factors often neglected by economists and inappropriately labelled 'social' (39:1). In an international context, they thought that the UN should give priority to central unification of data collection; to the design of uniform definitions for use in collecting data; and to more critical and constructive evaluation of the quality of data and of indicators. The group felt that in work defining an international development strategy, the following elements should be stressed: (a) elaboration of the minimal level of adequacy in services; (b) designing an illustrative planning scheme of development goals, their indicators and units for planning − a scheme that could be adapted by each country; (c) devising regional plans of development which could reduce disparities by taking into account regional interactions; and (d) taking specific account in sectoral planning of the impact of particular policies, projects and programs on various groups in the population. In this connection, the experts noted that 'technological, regional and social dualism result from the whole nexus of forces operating in a society and only integration of planning for all sectors with reduction of dualism as a specific goal was likely to be effective' (39:5).

Between 1957 and 1964 six country case studies – of India, Poland, Puerto Rico, Netherlands, Senegal and Yugoslavia – were completed under UN auspices (40). Their planning needs were presented in relation to their respective historical, social, and economic evolutions. Based on the findings of these studies, subsequently augmented by case studies in seven other nations and by surveys of 68 developing countries of Africa, the Middle East, Asia and Latin America, in 1970 the UN produced an important report concerned specifically with social welfare planning in the context of national development plans (41).

In this document, the case study material provided data for an analysis of social welfare planning in countries at different stages of industrialization – Iran, Lebanon, Netherlands, Poland, Tunisia, and Uganda; the survey material yielded descriptions of programs which the 68 developing countries include under 'social welfare'. The spectrum that emerges from this survey is broad but does exhibit some common characteristics. Because focus is on developing countries, the emphasis in these programs 'is usually . . . on community action of a preventive and developmental nature, rather than on personal services of the remedial type' (41:3). For purposes of the survey, a social welfare program was defined as 'any means of intervention, requiring special skills in human relations, social diagnosis or informal education, which is basically meant to enable individuals, groups or communities to improve their own conditions and participate in developmental programs' (41:49). This definition meant that the survey included among social welfare activities not only those listed in various plans in separate social welfare sections, but also others which 'may legitimately be considered a social welfare activity' such as health, housing, rural development, etc.

The report notes that a majority of national plans do devote a separate section to social welfare, except Latin America. This may be partly due, it is explained, to the fact that in this part of the world, social welfare is considered the responsibility of voluntary agencies, while government involvement is seen as a secondary responsibility of the ministries of health and/or labor. Furthermore, because social welfare has been identified with remedial functions, it is not considered

Social Welfare Planning

significant for development.

The report explains that many of the methods used for social welfare planning are similar to those of any other field; some, however, are specific to the welfare field and it is on these that the report concentrates. Specific methods emanate from the three sets of objectives to be achieved by planning: provide support for the achievement of planning objectives of related sectors; 'enable local citizens to participate in self-help projects and help . . . create the social climate' essential for development; and directly help vulnerable groups in the population to achieve minimum social standards (41:65). It is only in implementing the third objective that planning is the primary responsibility of the welfare institution; for the first two objectives, responsibility is with the concerned sectors. 'Minimum social standards' refer to what each country wishes to happen to its people within a given period of time as a result of development and, states the report, 'despite the variety of ideologies and forms of government, there exists across the world a striking degree of consensus about what each country wants to happen to its people' (41:69).[3]

The objective of a UN Symposium held in 1970 was to encourage a better dialogue between planners, researchers and decision-makers. Planning was defined as the process of selecting a course of action, among possible alternatives, that would allocate resources in a way most likely to reach specified objectives. This requires that the plan be based on a diagnosis of all relevant factors that can be identified; that is, economic, social and political structures, as well as the instruments and approaches that would be effective within these structures. One of the main functions of social planning was seen as a more comprehensive formulation of overall development objectives, a formulation which would also ensure consistency and compatibility between sectoral and overall objectives (45).

A 1972 UN report, although not centered on social welfare, is of importance because it is concerned with a unified approach to development analysis and planning (46). It was produced in response to:

> a judgment that the many previous attempts did not penetrate deeply enough into the reasons why the processes of economic growth and societal change . . . are having such ambiguous consequences for human well-being, and why the disciplines of development analysis and planning from which so much was expected a few years ago are demonstrating so limited a capacity

to explain or direct these processes of growth and change (46:2).

The objective was to develop 'a more adequate conceptual frame of reference for thinking about development — a frame of reference leading to strategic orientations governing choices among policies and planning techniques under defined conditions' (46:3). In this frame, 'the identification of development with economic growth' is seen as totally discredited — 'however much influence the conception may still exert in national planning and in political discourse' — and its identification with 'industrialization' or 'modernization' is also severely criticized. Instead, a 'unified approach' must see development in two complementary ways; 'as a perceived advance toward specified ends based on societal values, and as the system of interrelated societal changes that underlies and conditions the feasibility of the advance' (46:9). This means that the essential prerequisite for planning is the identification and understanding of interrelationships called for by this 'unified approach'.

To be effective, planning must be continuous, diffused, and diversified but simultaneously, coherent and part of the real decision-making process. It must address successfully four major methodological problems: relations between ends and means, relations between different time horizons, control of uncertainty, and methods for cross-sectoral integration. All this is discussed cogently in the report (46:38—53). Effective planning exhibits three characteristics: it is the 'diffusion of an attitude or approach of rationality and efficiency at all levels of decision-making'; it is 'a *strategic approach* in which, on the basis of diagnosis, key issues are selected for special attention and intensified planning effort, and all relevant sectors, instruments and types of planning are oriented toward the solution' of these issues; and it 'implies an *innovative* approach' toward resources, ends and means, implementation and evaluation (46:53—6). Considerable attention is also given to 'diagnosis, information and indicators'. In regard to the latter it is stressed that 'indicators cannot or should not be derived purely theoretically: they must also be empirically validated' (46:69); and that

> What is needed at the national level is not a single indicator but a pattern or profile of indicators for each country. Through this means, it can be seen in what respects and in what amounts a country has been changing over a given period of time. But these changes cannot be added together (aggregated) meaningfully into

a single synthetic indicator . . . (46:67).

Social Security Planning. In response to the growing importance of the role of sociology in social policy planning, ISSA arranged a meeting on the sociology of social security (at the VIIth World Congress of Sociology) in 1970 (47). The ten papers presented by experts from both market economy and socialist countries addressed a wide range of topics: conceptual problems such as political choices by decision-makers in regard to social security objectives and technical choices by planners in procedures to reach these objectives; differences in planning situations related to the planners' frame of reference, that is, whether the focus is on one best solution within a given socio-economic system, or on alternative solutions within this system, or on solutions implementing changes in the system; the need to guarantee strict scientific principles in planning procedures, especially because social policy planning has political significance.

In the major paper read at this meeting, Rys compares basic theoretical planning principles with the actual situation in 17 countries whose planning practices were surveyed by ISSA. Questioning the wisdom of solely economic planning, Rys first examines certain conceptual issues related to social planning in general: separation of planning from decision-making, recognition of the political nature of decisions about social goals and priorities, clearer determination of ends and means, recognition of limitations of planning. He notes that in applying current planning techniques to the social sector

> The essential problem is how to achieve some degree of commensurability as between costs and gains; in order to do so gains must be expressed in terms of some single or multiple effectiveness indicators. This makes the whole question of social planning dependent on the development of social indicators . . . It would appear that work in this area is the key to any major advance in social planning (47:20).

Among prerequisites for successful planning in social security specifically, Rys includes the need for conceptual and structural unification, integration of social security and economic planning, and the development and creation of effective planning methods. Analysis of information from the 17 surveyed countries indicates that a number of the principles and postulates posed by Rys are applied in practice.

The survey revealed a wide range of attitudes and policies with regard to social security planning. In order to describe this range cogently, Rys divided the 17 countries into market economy countries without any national economic plans, market economy countries practising some form of national economic planning, and countries with centrally planned economies. He found that

> If planning is understood to mean 'an attempt at rationally calculated action to achieve a goal', its presence will be noted in all countries covered by the survey. It is the time-span of the planning cycle and the degree of a systematic effort to arrive at a planning methodology which will differ . . . Two general features [that] emerge [are] . . . the importance of the planning issue in the vast majority of countries surveyed [and the] universal presence of research efforts . . . in conjunction with . . . planning (47:58).

Following up on this 1970 meeting, in 1973 ISSA brought together a group of experts (30 participants from 13 countries) to examine current experience in social security planning in countries of Western Europe and North America and to analyze issues related to the basic concepts and techniques used in the planning process (48).

In line with this charge, in the first part of the meeting, approaches to social security planning in four countries (West Germany, Belgium, France, and Bulgaria) were described and discussed. In three of these countries social security planning has become a required part of overall planning, with its own administrative bureaucracy and covering both the economic and social aspects. But despite this integrated socio-economic approach, it is still difficult to avoid giving priority to economic criteria in evaluating program progress. In the second part of the meeting, with discussion centering on basic concepts, the question: 'what relations exist or should be established between economic and social planning?' elicited different responses. Some stressed the difficulties involved in global planning when choices are dominated by value judgments and political attitudes and urged caution in extrapolating unquantifiable values proper to the social sector. Others thought that only one type of study is likely to throw more light on the available political choices; namely, an in-depth examination of interconnections between social security and other sectors of social policy and of the relationship between social policy and economic policy. Still others expressed the position that coordination of sectoral plans is preferable to fully integrated planning of the whole social field. But this position was attacked by those who noted that since

Social Welfare Planning

everybody agreed that there should be a separation between planning and political decision-making, social planning in the sense of assessing the consequences of alternative types of actions and based on cost-benefit analysis techniques can measurably assist decision-makers by providing necessary information related to their objectives. Some participants were concerned that planning be conducive to innovation rather than to rigidity; that it be democratic rather than coercive. Nor was there any unanimity among the experts when they attempted to answer the question: 'Are there fundamental principles of social security planning different from those governing planning generally'? The summarizer of the discussion concluded that a wide consensus could probably be obtained on only one basic idea; namely,

> Whatever definition you give to social planning, whatever technical content it may have, whatever degree of precision it may achieve, social planning will always mean, above all, the affirmation of a will to act, of a will to achieve something, of a will to determine the direction we wish to follow (48:55).

In the third part of the meeting, speakers discussed social security planning techniques such as the setting of standards, the use of models, and the creation of social indicators and their application to social security. Rys introduced his presentation on the latter subject by a succinct and competent analysis of available studies on social indicators — both at the national and the international levels.[4] He then examined the ongoing research on social indicators, discovering that it is sparked by the desire to control the development of society and that the quantification of life's social aspects is its central theme. International studies, in developing their own concepts and approaches, reflect the main interests of the organizations that sponsor them, as well as trends emerging at the national level. Work under UN auspices is in line with the concept of planning for unified socio-economic development. While none of the studies surveyed by Rys address social security as a subject of analysis, many contain references to it — 'pointers' which he discusses briefly. Lastly, Rys constructs his own conceptual framework of social security indicators which requires, first, that the function of each measure in the social security system be defined within the general function and objectives of the system; second, the results obtained be examined for their economic and social effects; and third, that the effect of social security measures on members of society, individuals and groups, be evaluated. Rys warns, however, that the tools needed to implement this optimum design 'will be long to fashion, while planning is urgent. Consequently, it is necessary to start by regrouping the data at hand and improving data collection — to better serve the needs of planning' (48:56–116).

In an article based on two lectures which he delivered at a symposium organized by the ILO in 1973, Rys brings together his thoughts concerning social security planning in industrialized and developing countries, and he does this in a lucid and perceptive manner (49). As a backdrop, he cautions that planning is not a cure for all social ills, but rather, a tentative device to be applied with a good measure of common sense. His historical survey of planning exposes the error of identifying societal with economic planning and of assuming that economic planning is of necessity linked to a particular ideology, and shows how unrealistic was the expectation that general well-being would automatically follow growth of the national product. Departure from an exclusive emphasis on economic considerations in development planning resulted from deeper insight which illumined its complex nature — an insight gained especially from experience in low-income countries which showed that development was concerned with important societal functions which must be studied via a multi-disciplinary approach — and revealed the essentially political nature of decision-making. From efforts to improve levels of living on a sectoral basis in poor nations, focus shifted to a unified socio-economic approach. Research projects incorporating this focus were launched at a 1969 UN Meeting of Experts on Social Policy and Planning, in Stockholm.

Rys then summarizes the ideas which he discussed on previous occasions. Among the major issues in planning, he stresses the need to define planning and to adopt a holistic approach which shows that in reality, economic, social, and political forces are interdependent; the need to advance the evaluation of social needs by providing more and better information to political decision-makers; in relation to setting priorities and limiting planning to a 'rational' undertaking, the need to provide the political decision-maker with estimates of the likely consequences of different choices. As for techniques, Rys maintains that all of them — cost-benefit analysis, cost-effectiveness analysis, and the planning, programming, budgeting system (PPBS) — suffer from the unsolved problem of the quantification of social objectives. Behind the social indicators movement was the desire to develop social statistics which would measure social progress and define social objectives. The systems analysis approach propounded the idea that this can be done

Social Welfare Planning

only if society is seen as a system with social values arrived at through general consensus which can be used to guide development.

Specifically in the social security field, planning requires adherence to its basic function: 'to guarantee to all citizens a certain level of living based on a certain concept of social justice' (49:326) which entails the carrying out of three tasks: 'prevention of social risks, income compensation for losses caused by social accidents, and social reintegration of victims' (49:327). Evaluation of the results obtained by existing social security measures should be concerned with their *social* effectiveness in reaching these objectives. The preparation of a plan and its implementation should be guided by these findings and the plan must be harmonized with other important components of social development, both quantifiable — such as demographic and economic factors — and non-quantifiable — such as social, structural and political aspects.

Planning for Children and Youth. UNICEF's 1963 study of the needs of children surveyed 18 countries in Africa, Asia, Europe and the Americas (50). In addition, the study incorporated information from the Inter-American Children's Institute and from the International Union for Child Welfare. This study helps countries assess the needs and possibilities of the prevailing situation of their children and youth, in the process drawing attention to neglected problems, to the need to look ahead, and to interrelate children's needs administratively and in relation to successive age groups.

At the 1964 international conference on planning for children, there was general agreement that planning procedures should include an assessment of the situation of children and youth as the starting point; then should follow the setting of goals for the development of children and youth; and finally, the fitting of goals into appropriate sectors of the overall development plan (51). The latter may be dealt with by relating goals to separate sectors in the total plan, on the one hand, and to those units of the total plan that can best handle cross-sectoral problems, on the other. Non-social sectors should not be excluded from this process because some at least have the potential for generating negative repercussions which would cause problems for children and youth. The position was taken that there need be no separate body concerned solely with planning for children; rather it is more important to achieve coordination of effort to ensure that the interests of children are safeguarded. In regard to welfare services — one among many planning aspects — it was insisted that there do exist quantitative data that can be used (such as costs, numbers and classification of consumers of service, etc.) to show benefits that can accrue in quantified form. The social welfare expert must strive to make them as clear and explicit as possible for the planner, by statistical and other means. It was stated that:

> One cannot assume beforehand that the economist-planner would be unsympathetic to these objectives . . . or insensitive to their importance; but he has to know what to be sympathetic and sensitive about (51:64).

The conference stressed the principle of complementarity among services and urged that initially, plans should not be for too long periods (better information will require revisions); long-range plans should be developed when a certain minimum level of resources, personnel and income has been reached.

Periodic conferences under UNICEF auspices in various regions of the world (see for example, (52) and (53)) likewise provide information that has implications for planning. At the conference in Asia (in 1966), it was noted, for example, that children's 'vital residual needs' — those that are not met by provisions for health, education and employment — were widely neglected. Accurate assessments of needs were lacking. It was pointed out that

> the prime obstacle to promoting a better understanding of the crucial role of social welfare services has been a lack of clarity in explaining and defining the functions of such services, and particularly the failure to demonstrate the concrete contributions which they can make to over-all development (53:32—3).

Reports by UNICEF's executive directors are likewise suggestive. Thus, in 1967 (54) 'strategy for children' left no doubt that planning for maximum efficiency required assessing needs and possibilities; looking ahead in the light of development forecasts covering a considerable period of years; taking into account the interrelationship of children's needs (among the different ministries and among the successive age groups of infancy, pre-school, school and adolescence); and relating specific services for children to those for the family and the community.

Reubens' 1967 publication marked another important step in planning for children and youth within national development plans

Social Welfare Planning

(55). His study is centered on Asia, Latin America and Africa, although it includes some references to more developed countries, with due allowance for differences in prevailing conditions. The study addresses requirements of planning; the specific problems involved within the basic constraints of development planning as a whole; the main steps in framing a policy on children and youth and in converting that policy into programs; and practical devices and rule-of-thumb procedures, elicited from theory and experience, for coping with the dilemmas and constraints.

A UN report concerned with long-term policies and programs for youth, published in 1970, again stresses the importance of integrated planning. This requires that:

> the planner . . . should have the over-all view of young people, their needs and capacities, their problems and potentialities seen in the context of the social and economic situation of the countries. It is his responsibility to draw the strands of youth interests together from all the sectors, from all the agencies and organizations concerned, whether official or unofficial. Where the task is beyond him he has the responsibility for devising the planning machinery to promote intersectoral coordination and public and private coordination in preparing the plan which will translate the national policy into real terms making use of a social planner to coordinate social sectors whenever possible . . . the plan should not merely be integrated by continuous coordination from an early stage, it should be purposive and should provide the motive power for the various programs in its allocation of resources (56:23).

A seminar on child welfare in East and Central Africa in 1971 elicited individual reports from Kenya, Ethiopia, Malawi, Mauritius, Somalia, Sudan, Tanzania, Uganda, Zambia and Lebanon (57). Prepared in line with guidelines applicable to all, they formed a basis for recommendations on planning. Among them, the most important emphasized the primordial importance of creating effective machinery for planning and coordination in social welfare — largely non-existent at that time in these countries; the desirability of basing programs, as far as possible, on a society's traditional systems — on beginning where the people are and linking up new knowledge and techniques with old teachings; on channeling aid to children through their families, and on ensuring firm links with the home for children placed in institutions. All this requires properly trained personnel. Training should be offered

292 *Social Welfare Planning*

in centers whose geographic locations and teaching programs should also be carefully planned, coordinated, and evaluated.

Summarizing the major features of planning for children as it saw them in 1970, the UN concluded that

> neither the developed, the centrally planned, the free market economy countries, nor the developing countries have yet formulated an integral plan for the young . . . nevertheless, a number of countries . . . have established inter-ministerial machinery to deal with the affairs of children and youth. These attempts are being directed towards the development of policies which stress the interrelationship and co-ordination between sectoral services (58:7).

Convinced that planning has 'clear advantages' over isolated approaches, the UN document outlines the steps that empirical planning methods should involve.[5] But it notes that each country will have to choose among them in line with its children's needs and will have to set priorities according to its resources and development requirements.

Rehabilitation Planning. Principles which should govern planning of rehabilitation services for the disabled are discussed in a 1972 UN report which resulted from a meeting of experts (59).[6] Disability covers many types of conditions, in terms of severity, number of disease categories, and social and economic factors. How it is perceived is affected by cultural and religious traditions. All this means that a comprehensive plan is perforce complex and requires the cooperation of a variety of services.

A number of government departments must be involved, with health, welfare, education and labor playing the most important roles, assisted, when necessary, by recreation, community development, and architecture. This brings in professionals from a variety of disciplines, and on occasion involves interested lay individuals. A carefully designed rehabilitation plan becomes essential if these agencies and personnel are to be utilized to the full.

Insofar as it is feasible to do so, the disabled should not be segregated from their families and the community. At the same time, special facilities to meet their specific needs should be established via a coordinated plan. Such a plan must be responsive to existing cultural, economic and political factors, and must be realistic in terms of the resources of the country. In initial stages, emphasis should be placed on pilot projects and the adequate training of personnel. The plan must incorporate mechanisms for periodic reviews of progress and for evaluation of effectiveness in relation to both short-term and long-term targets. This means that the plan must be flexible so that it can be modified when and where necessary. While aware that responsibility for rehabilitation planning differs from country to country, the experts felt that the most effective way of achieving a coordinated and comprehensive plan was through a national rehabilitation board or council.

Policy Issues. There is no dearth of issues that beset social welfare planning. They spring from confusion about how to define planning, whether in a strictly technical sense or extended to include policy initiated at the political level; how to make more precise and usable the meaning of 'well-being' toward which planning objectives are directed; how to cast these objectives — anticipation of social problems, dealing with factors that impede development, and creating the social prerequisites for development — into coherent operational terms; how to construct effective planning machinery, one capable of evaluating the social effectiveness of provisions and of averting undesirable unforeseen consequences; how to imbue the planning process with values conducive to innovation and democracy rather than to rigidity and coercion. Underlying these questions and determining for the very concept of planning is the need to decide the nature and the degree of state intervention in different sectors of the society, basically a political decision. In relation to it, social planners need to decide how they can assist political decision-makers with the information, expertise and experience at their disposal.

Perhaps the most persistent issue at this point in time, however, is how to integrate social and economic planning. It continues to pose difficult and frustrating dilemmas, partly because social planners still think of themselves as different from economists, especially in regard to causation of social problems and the goals they wish to achieve through social programs. Yet the economists themselves have rejected the notion that they are theoretical scientists who rely on mathematical and quantitative methods of analysis. At the Stockholm meeting of experts on social policy and planning, for example, it was stressed

> that economic phenomena are, in fact, social phenomena: they are social in nature, are socially conditioned and have social consequences, and any development planning, if limited to economic interrelationships and neglecting social conditions and social

implications, is bound to be misleading ... It is most necessary to view the development process as a complex whole, comprising economic elements, *censu stricto*, but also other social as well as political and administrative elements. Any design for development strategy, national or international, has to cover all the above-mentioned fields if it is to be meaningful, internally consistent and capable of effective implementation'(39:5).

As noted by writers with important experience in planning and well disposed toward social planners (61), the problem is not that economists and social planners disagree about objectives; rather, the disagreement revolves around which measurements and which methodologies to use to assess the achievement of objectives. Social planners wish to use as measurements 'levels of living' rather than '*per capita* national income'. They wish to attain these levels by concentrating on 'quality'; on increases in conventional budgetary resources; on stressing that social variables that enter into 'quality' are not amenable to quantification; and on participation by the citizenry in decisions about objectives. But they have few proposals about how to deal with the ambiguities that arise. So far, attempts to develop a unitary index of the levels of living have not been quite successful. Quantity and quality are not antithetical, the former entering into the latter at many points. Conventional budgetary resources, even if ample, are not per se the kind to generate changes in values, institutions and organizations so ardently desired by social planners. Stress on the unquantifiable nature of social variables will not produce the scientific base so eagerly sought by social planners. And participation by the citizenry often complicates the attainment of needed consensus on objectives since the preferences of the public and the planners do not always coincide.

Basically, key issues in planning seem to point to the similarities between them and issues in policy, underscoring the indivisible nature of the policy and planning processes.

Summary. Among planners, as among policy-makers and administrators, there is much concern about the insufficiency and inadequacy of data essential for a constructive conduct of their activities. This is, predictably, more pronounced among developing nations and influences what they can do in planning compared to what can be done in developed countries. While data must originate in individual countries, the UN is seen as an organization that should play a leading role in unifying data collection, designing uniform definitions, and evaluating the quality of data. This would help toward evolving a uniform concept of social planning, now absent, and doing away with current confusions — to say nothing of producing more realistic and sound plans.

Despite data problems, much has been learned about the characteristics of the planning process, the elements to be considered in devising plans, and about methods and mechanics that seem most fruitful for reaching planned objectives — as well as about the limitations of planning. There is universal appreciation of the need in planning for a continuing dialogue between planners, researchers and decision-makers. And it has become clear that social-welfare planning is complicated by fuzzy definitions and by the vagueness about what welfare can contribute to development. Disagreement still exists as to whether planning for social security is different from planning generally; but discernible is a tendency to view the methods used for social welfare planning as similar to those used in other human services fields. On the other hand, consensus is considerable that overall, the objective of planning is to move the society toward specified ends based on societal values; hence, the importance of philosophies and ideologies, and the recognition that similarly expressed welfare ends may be accompanied by radically different means. When means are in their essence diswelfares, they may seriously impair the welfare elements of the ends.

Notes

1. That the negative impact of these failings has not gone unrecognized is indicated by the urging of some participants at the XIVth International Conference of Social Work in 1968 that claims for social welfare expenditure be made in terms of human rights and values, but that at the same time methods be found for estimating the advantages to be derived in monetary terms (30:307). Rodgers suggests that the benefits of social welfare 'must be regarded and presented as are wages and interest rates, as an incentive and reward for the savings and the hard work of the whole population on which increased productivity ultimately depends' and at the same time it must be shown that these benefits 'inevitably lead to new or increased social expenditure on current account' (31:230).

2. This is clearly illustrated by the situation in the Soviet Union, for example. The concept of 'social planning' is not found in the *Bol'shaia Sovetskaia Entsiklopediia* (The Large Soviet Encyclopedia), where the word 'planning' is followed in parentheses by the word 'economic'. This adherence to economic planning dominated the discussion of the then current five-year plan in welfare (35), concerned almost entirely with material values. It appears, however, that a lack of labor reserves is compelling economic executives to consider 'social planning' whose principal task would be to satisfy workers' daily needs, both

material and psychological, and to improve their working conditions (36).

3. For planning strategies in developing countries, see also (42); and for planning in post-industrial societies see (43,44).

4. Among those at the international level, especially important are studies by the UN Research Institute of Social Development aimed at constructing a level-of-living index that would provide a single measure of the levels of living in a number of specified social fields, and those aimed at defining empirically the contents of development by identifying measurable characteristics that distinguish countries at different levels of development. Important as well is the work under the auspices of UN's Division of Social Affairs on quantification and standards in social planning (standards often being indistinguishable from indicators). Pertinent likewise is the work of the UN Statistical Commission. Rys viewed as the most relevant the work carried out by the UN Economic Commission for Europe in three meetings: the first, in Geneva in 1970 to examine methodology of long-term studies in the social area; the second, in Geneva in 1971, to review what had been accomplished by participating institutes and research centers; and the third and most important, in France in May 1972, to evaluate the results of the joint research and seek methodological conclusions. Rys considers this third meeting as 'one of the most important international exchanges on questions of social planning' at which discussion of problems involved in the construction of social indicators was a recurring theme. Rys noted that the systematic study of social indicators begun by OECD in 1971 (see earlier discussion under *Assessing social reality and progress: 'Where are We and Where Are We Going?'*) is the only research project devoted exclusively to social indicators. Among other international organizations in the 'UN family' that are involved in the study of social indicators, Rys included the ILO, the International Institute for Labour Studies, and UNESCO.

5. These steps are detailed as follows: the recognition of the problem as an interrelationship of economic as well as social factors requiring economic and social measures; the gathering and analysis of information on the existing situation of children in order to select the most important programmes and aspects for concentration; the preparation within a national development plan of comprehensive measures reflected in a strategy for children from the point of view of the problems and the instruments which can be provided by various functional ministries, including activities that are not the direct responsibility of a particular ministry; the search for a rational development of services within each sector; the coordination of the plans of the different sectors concerning children rather than the organization of a special sector for them; and the need to consider the problems of children as related to different geographical, cultural and economic areas and conditions, including national regional differences as well as urban and rural factors (58:7).

6. A 1964 report dealt with the legislative and administrative aspects of rehabilitation (60).

References

1. Aiyar, *Perspectives on the Welfare State*.
2. Flamm, *Social Welfare Services*.
3. Donnison, 'Ideologies and Policy'.
4. Rohrlich, George F. (ed.) *Social Economics for the 1970s* (New York, Dunellen Co., 1970).
5. Friedmann, John, 'Response to Altshuler: Comprehensive Planning as a

Social Welfare Planning

Process', *Journal of the American Institute of Planners*, xxxi, no. 3 (August 1965), pp. 195–7.

6. Friedmann, John, *Regional Development Policy: A Case Study of Venezuela* (Cambridge, MIT Press, 1966).
7. Friedmann, John, 'Planning as Innovation: The Chilean Case', *Journal of the American Institute of Planners*, xxxii, no. 4 (July 1966), pp. 194–204.
8. Friedmann, John, 'Notes on Societal Action', *Journal of the American Institute of Planners*, xxxv, no. 5 (September 1969), pp. 311–18.
9. Leaper, 'Report of the Pre-Conference Working Party'.
10. UN, *Proceedings of the International Conference of Ministers Responsible for Social Welfare, 3 to 12 September 1968*.
11. Fox, 'Report of the Pre-Conference Working Party'.
12. Aptekar, 'The Values, Functions, and Methods of Social Work'.
13. UN, Department of Economic and Social Affairs, 'Highlights of the Symposium on Social Policy and Planning', Copenhagen, Denmark, June 22–July 2, 1970, *International Social Development Review*, no. 3. Unified Socio-Economic Development and Planning: Some New Horizons (New York, UN, 1971), pp. 16–22.
14. Thorsson, Inga, 'The Social Aspects of Development', *Assignment Children*, no. 13 (January–March 1971), pp. 23–32.
15. Wedell, E. G., 'Development for What?', *ibid.*, pp. 63–74.
16. UN, Bureau of Social Affairs, *European Seminar on the Problems and Methods of Social Planning*, Kallvik, Finland, August 2–12, 1964 (Geneva, UN, 1965. SOA/ESWP/1965/3).
17. McGranahan, 'Development Indicators'.
18. Dyckman, John W., 'Social Planning, Social Planners, and Planned Societies', *Journal of the American Institute of Planners*, xxxii, no. 2 (March 1966), pp. 66–76.
19. Perloff, 'New Directions in Social Planning'.
20. Frieden, 'The Changing Prospects for Social Planning'.
21. UN, Department of Economic and Social Affairs, *Report on a Coordinated Policy Regarding Family Levels of Living* (New York, UN, 1957; IV.7).
22. UN, Department of Economic and Social Affairs, *The Development of National Social Service Programmes* (New York, UN, 1959. 60.IV.1).
23. UN, Department of Economic and Social Affairs, *Report of the Interregional Expert Meeting on Social Welfare Organization and Administration*, Geneva, August 7–18, 1967 (New York, UN, 1968. SF/SOA/83. Sales No.: E68.IV.8).
24. UN, Department of Economic and Social Affairs, *Social Welfare Planning in the Context of National Development Plans* (New York, UN, 1970. ST/SOA/99).
25. Wolfe, Marshall, 'Between the Idea and the Reality: Notes on Plan Implementation', *International Social Development Review*, no. 3 (New York, UN, 1971).
26. International Council of Social Welfare, *Development and Participation: Operational Implications for Social Welfare*, Proceedings of the XVIIth International Conference on Social Welfare, Nairobi, Kenya, 1974 (New York, Columbia University Press, 1975).
27. Hodge, Peter, 'Social Planning for Growing Cities', *Social Planning for Growing Cities: Role of Social Welfare*, Proceedings of the ICSW Regional Conference for Asia and Western Pacific, September 1–5, 1975, Hong Kong.
28. UN, *Conference of European Ministers Responsible for Social Welfare.*
29. Schottland, Charles I., 'Issues in Social Planning for the Future –

Implications of the Conference', *Social Progress Through Social Planning* — *The Role of Social Work*, XIIth International Conference of Social Work, 1964 (New York, Columbia University Press, 1965), pp. 117—36.

30. Turner, John B., 'Report of the Pre-Conference Working Party', *Social Welfare and Human Rights*, Proceedings of the XIVth International Conference on Social Welfare, Helsinki, Finland, August 18—24, 1968 (New York, Columbia University Press, 1969), pp. 305—8.

31. Rodgers, *Comparative Social Administration*.

32. Tinbergen, 'Social Aspects of Economic Planning', pp. 61—9.

33. UN, Department of Economic and Social Affairs, *1970 Report on the World Social Situation* (New York, UN, 1971).

34. Fisher, 'Social Reports of the German Federal Republic'.

35. Buzlyakov, N., *Welfare — The Basic Task. Five-Year Plan 1971—1975* (Moscow, Progress Publishers, 1973).

36. Wekesser, Irina, 'What is Social Planning?', *Radio Liberty Dispatch*, October 29, 1973.

37. UN, *Report on a Coordinated Policy regarding Family Levels of Living* (UN, Sales No., 1957.IV.7).

38. UN, Bureau of Social Affairs, *European Seminar on the Problems and Methods of Social Planning*, Kallvik, Finland, August 2—12, 1964 (Geneva, UN, 1965. SOA/ESWP/1965/3).

39. UN, Economic and Social Council, *Social Policy and Planning in National Development*, Report of the Meeting of Experts on Social Policy and Planning held at Stockholm from 1—10 September, 1969 (New York, UN, E/CN.5/445. December 11, 1969).

40. UN, Department of Economic and Social Affairs, *Planning for Balanced Social and Economic Development: Six Country Studies* (New York, UN, 1964.ST/SOA/56.E/CN.5/346/Rev.1. Sales No., 64.IV.8).

41. UN, Department of Economic and Social Affairs, *Social Welfare Planning in the Context of National Development Plans* (New York, UN, 1970. ST/SOA/99).

42. *Journal of The American Institute of Planners*, 'Planning Strategies in Developing Countries', xxxiv, no. 6 (November 1968).

43. Mertins Jr, Herman, and Gross, Bertram M. (co-eds.) 'Special Symposium. Changing Styles of Planning in Post-Industrial America', *Public Administration Review*, xxxi, no. 3 (May/June 1971), pp. 254—403.

44. Flamm, *Social Welfare Services*.

45. UN, 'Highlights of the Symposium on Social Policy and Planning'.

46. UN, Economic and Social Council, *Report of a Unified Approach to Development Analysis and Planning* (New York, UN, October 25, 1972. E/CN.5/477). Mimeographed.

47. ISSA, *The Planning of Social Security*, Studies and Research no. 2. Papers presented at the meeting on the Sociology of Social Security at the VIIth World Congress of Sociology: Varna, Bulgaria, September 16—17, 1970 (Geneva, 1971).

48. ISSA, *Current Issues in Social Security Planning: Concepts and Techniques*, Studies and Research no. 4. Reports and Summary of Discussion of the Group of Experts on Social Security Planning, Brussels, October 19—21, 1972 (Geneva, 1973).

49. Rys, 'Problems of Social Security Planning'.

50. Sicault, *The Needs of Children*.

51. Stein, Herman (ed.) *Planning for the Needs of Children in Developing Countries*, Report of a Round-Table Conference, April 1—7, 1964, Bellagio, Italy (New York, UNICEF, 1964).

52. UN Children's Fund, *Children and Youth in National Development in*

Latin America, Report of a conference held in Santiago, Chile, November 28– December 11, 1965 (New York, UN, 1966).

53. UN Children's Fund, *Children and Youth in National Planning and Development in Asia*, Report of a conference held in Bangkok, Thailand, March 8–15, 1966 (New York, UN, 1966).

54. UNICEF, *Strategy for Children*, and subsequent reports of UNICEF's Executive Director.

55. Reubens, *Planning for Children and Youth*.

56. UN, Department of Economic and Social Affairs, *Long-Term Policies and Programmes for Youth in National Development* (New York, UN, 1970.ST/SOA/103. Sales no., 70.IV.12).

57. Nduba, G. Kaburu, seminar rapporteur. KNCSS. Report of the Seminar on *Planning and Coordination in the Field of Child Welfare in East and Central Africa*, Nairobi, August 16–21, 1971. Sponsored by the International Union for Child Welfare and held under the auspices of the Kenya National Council of Social Service.

58. UN, Department of Economic and Social Affairs, *Report on Children* (New York, UN, 1971).

59. UN, Department of Economic and Social Affairs, *Planning, Organization and Administration of National Rehabilitation Programmes for the Disabled in Developing Countries: Report of a Meeting of Experts*, Geneva, September 27– October 6, 1971 (New York, UN, 1972. ST/SOA/115. Sales No., E.72.IV.1).

60. UN, Department of Economic and Social Affairs, *Study of the Legislative and Administrative Aspects of Rehabilitation of the Disabled in Selected Countries* (New York, UN, 1964. ST/SOA/51. Sales no., 65.IV.2).

61. Sovani, 'Whither Social Planners?'.

12 CONCLUSION

There is little doubt that cross-national studies useful for social welfare policy and planning will continue to proliferate, perhaps at an increasingly faster pace. Even the initial effort that this book represents shows that their potential for enlarging our understanding of social continuity and change and of the needs and relationships they generate in an interdependent world is indeed considerable. And this amplified discernment, in turn, makes for a more relevant and a more profound understanding of the meaning of social policy and is suggestive for ways most likely to transform policy into 'real life'. Cross-national studies have certainly expanded the array of alternatives from which those concerned with social welfare policy-making in different nations can choose; and they can assist policy-makers in selecting policies and policy instruments most appropriate for their particular countries and in realizing their possibilities more fully.

These important contributions to the welfare field have come about because, despite disagreements among their creators concerning the significance of certain findings (and perhaps because of them), the included studies have yielded a great deal of practically and theoretically important knowledge. They have uncovered world-wide trends in social security and personal social services, and in relation to this vast panorama, have shed light on the direction and the speed (or the slowness) of change in individual countries. They have analyzed substantive provisions, organizational and administrative structures and processes, effects on those who seek or receive cash benefits and noncash services, and why nations create different policies to cope with roughly similar problems. Ample evidence has been furnished in support of the essential need for welfare provisions and related activities to support and reinforce each other, substantively and administratively. It has been made abundantly clear that descriptions of administration must be interpreted in light of the relationship between the social welfare institution and its social environment – if one is to form a correct judgment about the ramifications of the administrative role in the welfare field and how this role can be played most effectively.

More wide-ranging and better substantiated information about the reasons that determine the nature of issues in welfare, as they reflect and alter societal aspirations and systems of beliefs, has highlighted the promising methods for achieving desired policy objectives. That planning is inseparable from policy has been convincingly demonstrated: simultaneously, planning designs instruments to carry out policy decisions and provides influential inputs into policy content. Mechanisms to assure continuing coordination must be firmly implanted into plans, not only to avoid fragmentation, duplications and gaps, but to inject purpose and motive power into programs for which the plan allocates resources, and to make certain that these programs reinforce and support each other. Like policy, the plan must be comprehensive and unified; that is, it must take into account as many of the relevant factors as possible — economic, social, cultural and political — and must integrate them into a realistic, purposive and flexible blueprint for action.

Findings from cross-national studies reaffirm that implementation, the manner in which benefits and services are delivered, not only determines whether policy decisions will be carried out, but has a powerful influence on the very content of decisions — on what is provided, for whom, and under what conditions. These findings also make evident that legal blueprints are rarely carried out fully in 'real life', leading to disparity between protection intended by law and protection that results from the process of implementing legal norms. Sometimes there is a sizable gap between operating programs and the commitment of a nation. In fact, the difference between ideologically approved goals and practical policies can be quite pronounced. Comparative knowledge discloses that, like other types of human service bureaucracies, welfare administrations are constrained by technical difficulties, by the need to get the most out of usually scarce resources — human, financial and technological — and by the requirement to take into account the most inclusive possible range of probable outcomes of their operations.

Studies concerned with decision-making in the political arena as it affects welfare have shown who the most powerful movers and shakers are and how they initiate new and modify old policies through expertise, interest group pressure, and mobilization of public opinion. Accumulating knowledge is making it possible to better assess the outcomes of policy choices and to better forecast future developments. Continuing work on social indicators has clarified their potentials and limitations, thereby contributing to more penetrating descriptions of welfare's components, more astute evaluations of its programs, and keener appreciation of its normative requirements — all part and parcel of the policy development process. The knowledge gained so far has also pointed up the elements that enter into a functionally refined selection of transferable ideas and administrative patterns from one country to another and into the process of adapting them for use in the receiving country.

At the same time, the included studies reveal a number of unresolved problems, unexplored areas and unanswered questions that limit the understanding of what is involved in arriving at sound policy in social welfare and in realizing its objectives at a given point in time, in a given society.

There is no denying that the paucity of valid, reliable and sufficient data about various aspects of social security and personal social services in most countries is a serious limiting factor and sometimes, a deterrent to undertaking needed investigations. One cannot help but agree with Rys that to find ways and means of obtaining data is one of the tasks of social scientists engaged in cross-national studies. At best, however, this can fill only part of the need. Essential for a genuine breakthrough is a more active participation by the UN and its specialized agencies, encouraged and vigorously supplemented by international and national organizations of welfare professionals.

To a significant extent, the situation on data influences the selection of countries included in cross-national studies. *Social Security Programs Throughout the World* for 1977 lists 129 countries with such programs, spread over all continents and touching the lives of all races, be it unevenly and unequally. Yet available studies repeatedly compare social security in a relatively small number of countries, while the systems of many nations are left out or described in narrowly circumscribed frameworks with few comparative connotations — those in Latin America, the Middle East, Asia, Africa and the Pacific region. Another element that has a bearing on selection is the assumption by some investigators that to study countries dissimilar from their own in historical, cultural, economic and political respects would not be useful for their own policy concerns. That this is open to question is demonstrated by studies that include 'dissimilar' countries. In addition to the substantial and important insights already gained from them, it seems reasonable to speculate that such studies could be useful in welfare policy deliberations in countries with heterogeneous populations whose different ethnic groups aspire to retain their own identities: studies with dissimilar participants could reveal the distinctive features of different value systems which are equally decisive for forming identities and for designing responsive welfare

Conclusion

programs. Absence of comparative analyses of social welfare policy in large and densely populated areas of the world cannot but constrict our perception of the global forces of continuity and change and of their meaning for huge segments of mankind. This may contribute to a dysfunctional, stereotyped view of peoples beyond our borders thus depriving us of cross-cultural awareness so essential for understanding other people with other values and interests.

That most cross-national studies, both in social security and personal social services, center on the aged, children and women is understandable: the first two represent the most vulnerable and dependent groups in all countries; women are among social security's proletariat and intimately involved in the lives of children and the aged. But the relative scarcity of comparative knowledge about the welfare needs and problems of other population groups leaves wide gaps and makes difficult an inclusive, integrated approach to social policy. Especially insufficient is policy-oriented knowledge concerning the unemployed, young workers, and the physically disabled.

Given that unemployment is a destructive and growing problem in large areas of the world, comparative analyses of unemployment compensation provisions and of their effects on the unemployed, both personal and societal, appear to be highly in order. A beneficial side-effect might be the production of more and better data and a steadier and more rapid movement toward uniform terminology and a common understanding of concepts. In regard to young adults, even the limited knowledge now available indicates that their preparation for employment, their safety on the job, protection during unemployment, and benefits in retirement can be affected by what social security provides prior to and at the beginning of their work careers. Comparative knowledge now at hand has demonstrated that it can reveal this many-sided connection in sharper perspective and can offer a broader range of policy alternatives than is likely to be found in any one country. The same can be said in regard to the physically disabled — a dependent and often helpless group whose needs, possibilities and aspirations are given low priority in too many places. That such knowledge could measurably enrich policy choices in personal social services for these groups has been established as well.

All this is not to suggest that we have 'enough' comparative knowledge about children, the aged, and women. Far from it. For example: how can social security move toward adequacy in providing for these categories, usually the ones that make up the bulk of public assistance recipients and thus among the poorest of the poor in most nations? How does adequacy of provision affect the living standards and living arrangements of beneficiaries in different countries? 'Adequacy' is a fundamental concept upon which depends not only what is done in benefits as of right and in benefits based on need, but what decisions are taken about equity — a companion concept that affects an unending series of specific actions. Yet so far comparative studies have not produced a common understanding of what adequacy means and involves or laid down guidelines for achieving it in an equitable manner and with proper regard to differences in levels of development and cultural traditions. In regard to women, it should be added that their situation is so complex and volatile — reflecting changes in women's roles both in the home and in the larger society — that it must be reassessed on a continuing basis to be of genuine usefulness for policy formulation in both social security and personal social services.

Of central importance in the lives of all who come within the purview of social welfare is 'the family', however it is defined and whatever meanings it projects. In most nations the family's position as a basic social unit has not been seriously challenged; in some nations this attribute is being 'rediscovered'. Yet hardly any comparative studies shed light on what happens to families under alternative forms of social welfare protection; that is, to what extent (if any) and why do some cash benefits and some personal social services strengthen family stability and cohesion while the influence of others is negligible or even destructive. In short, what is their significance in family life? Admittedly, investigations that would yield such knowledge are difficult to mount, not only because of the technical problems they would pose, but also in terms of securing access to families in certain countries in order to obtain essential original data. Yet the development of 'a sound family policy', to which all nations say they are deeply committed, is not likely to make headway without comparative knowledge that would illumine the consequences of alternative welfare policies.

Closely related to what happens to families in different welfare subcultures is the problem of juvenile delinquency — a spreading phenomenon in many countries, developed and developing, with market and nonmarket economies, with democratic and oppressive governments. Again, comparative studies are few, especially those that would reveal the results (if any) of different kinds of cash and noncash interventions. Rare likewise are investigations that show how different legal prescriptions, administrative arrangements, philosophies and

Conclusion

qualifications of personnel, types of settings, and service objectives enter into bringing about the results that are revealed. To do this is also difficult and touchy because delinquency is often seen as an unspoken judgment about whether a given organization of society is 'successful'. Do not the poor often vote by means of delinquency and crime? And is not a decent provision for the poor the true test of a civilized society? But without the kind of comparative knowledge suggested here the billions now spent on correctional services are not likely to be reduced or even held in check — to say nothing of preventing delinquency or at least diminishing the cruel inroads it makes into the lives of all, delinquent and straight.

In studies focused on planning and administration, so determining for social welfare policy, gaps and inadequacies likewise are not rare. Comparative studies of welfare planning are extremely scarce. Comparative studies of administration frequently fail to describe the actual functioning of policies and therefore shed but a dim light on certain fundamental administrative issues. For example: when administrators and personnel 'interpret the law' in social security, as they do almost constantly, in what direction do they go? Toward making the lot of the least productive and of the nonworkers more tolerable by applying the most generous interpretation possible, or toward making it more meager by applying the entire galaxy of legal stipulations to each case as strictly and narrowly as possible? When trade unions are involved in administration, does this mean that the more generous interpretation will hold sway or is there evidence that, on the contrary, the possibilities of 'going around the law' will not be exploited because the least productive do not 'overfulfill plans' and the nonworkers are not active in unions? Does trade union involvement assure that what welfare provisions do for or to people in daily life becomes feedback, to be considered fearlessly and honestly in policy deliberations? To answer these and similar questions — and thus begin to illumine the configurations of power in policy determination — it is necessary to find out how programs work in actual practice. In short, there is a crying need for empirical research. Massive, global statistical data have their uses; but they are not a substitute for painstaking work in disaggregated contexts. And when empirical evidence is available, to deduce what it signifies is no simple matter, demanding as it does a solid understanding of the cultural, economic and political histories and traditions of the nations being studied and the ability to relate this understanding to social welfare.

Empirical studies in a cross-national perspective are also essential for deciding whether social insurance and public assistance or social security and social services ought to be integrated into unified systems as compared to organizing them in separate systems. In addition to revealing the impact on beneficiaries within separate systems, on the one hand, and in united administrative structures, on the other, such studies would clarify what the components of unification should be and what they require in cooperative arrangements. This seems to be true as well in regard to transforming personal social services into 'freestanding' systems, separate and distinct from other human services systems such as health and education. The basic question is: how would consumers of service fare in a 'freestanding' system as compared to how they fare under contrasting settings? The consequences of policy are meaningful not only in relation to expectations of policy-makers, administrators and practitioners but, more importantly, in the light of their actual effect on service consumers compared to what these consumers had anticipated would be the effect.

Because social security and personal social services are integral parts of society, they are not only influenced by but also influence the society in which they are found. Is not the history of social welfare 'a record of successive redefinings of the unacceptable' as is true of public health (Geoffrey Vickers)? Yet cross-national studies that explore the impact of social welfare on the larger society leave many unanswered questions that have both economic and social implications.

For example: do social security and personal social services help to translate economic growth into human betterment and if so, in what ways and to what extent? Do they discourage or promote individual initiative, the desire to work and to acquire and improve skills, and the striving to meet one's needs by one's own efforts? Do they affect spending and saving patterns? Does social security discourage needed investment in capital formation? Do contributory social security programs affect wage levels? Does welfare help to reconcile economic efficiency with ethical considerations — judged by some to be one of the most difficult tasks in the administration of wage policy? Does welfare integrate people into the society by facilitating social adaptation and cohesion, or does it accentuate class distinctions? Do welfare's eligibility conditions tend to strengthen conformity and weaken diversity and pluralism? Does welfare advance social justice by equalizing individual resources so that the less-advantaged can meet their basic needs in a dignified manner and without jeopardizing their individual liberty, or are its effects in this direction negligible and restrictive? Does it discourage or stimulate eligible individuals to utilize

Conclusion

constructively the benefits and services provided collectively? Does it motivate its consumers to be participants, so essential in democratic societies, or does it alienate them? Does more adequate fulfillment of welfare requirements tend to decentralize government direction and planning, strengthen working-class organizations, unify the middle classes, and lessen the influence of the military establishment?

The included studies offer useful suggestions for dealing with certain problems in cross-national research. They present substantial evidence that theoretical constructs — conceptual frames of reference, models — help to cull from masses of data those that are essential, relevant and clearly significant and to arrange them in a meaningful order. This reveals where data are lacking or deficient so that researchers can avoid using irrelevant data to fill information voids. There is then less chance of basing comparisons on evidence whose comparability is questionable, or generalizations on information that is insufficient or narrowly specific or, in contrast, marshaling data highly general in nature to support specific policies for particular nations. By establishing a rationale for judging the quality and quantity of data, models may stimulate the production of better and more information as well as contribute to delimiting social welfare's parameters and clarifying its objectives.

Social scientists agree that when the properties of a model correspond to the important properties of some part of the real world, the model is theoretically useful because the behavior of the model can help to explain the behavior of that part of the real world. It would seem, therefore, that by their very nature models are capable of explaining not just what is being done (or not done) but also why: why certain policy enactments over time, why they interact with the societal environment as they do, why the consequences of specific policies, good and bad. It is such explanations that endow with meaning the similarities and differences between what nations do in social welfare. Without such meaning, derivation of general concepts and assessment of transferability across nations will at best be equivocal and at worst, misleading. Models also provide standards against which what is being achieved (or not achieved) and at what cost can be evaluated. In short, theoretical frames of reference are constructs within which 'facts', data, information can be organized, integrated, explained, and evaluated — thereby making more certain that research outcomes can assist authoritatively in designing policies that should govern action and can actually do so.

When working as investigators in a social science discipline, social welfare's scholars and researchers are concerned with developing concepts for all aspects of practice, including policy-making; when working as professionals in an applied field, welfare's policy practitioners are concerned with relatively short-term applications of broader social science concepts to specific issues. If social welfare is conceived as largely a technology, it becomes possible to use a variety of models relevant to particular concerns, rather than a single model. Some models are more appropriate to one time or place than another, and it is not likely that any one model is fully adequate to the analysis of as complex a field as social welfare. Action-planning models built on system relationships, rather than on one-way associations, isolated programs or events, may be useful. They derive from the concept of interdependence in social change, of a dynamic intermeshing of processes and consequences. In them some ends act as means to attain other ends, and some effects as causes to produce other effects. Action-planning models may have much to recommend them to social welfare when they utilize welfare's ability to create interpersonal relationships between the planner and the community that reinforce each other and produce the desired movement.

Since social welfare operates in organic and dynamic relationships with its surrounding environment, models must take into account as inclusive a range of pertinent factors as possible, and thus provide a frame of reference as comprehensive as possible. Nevertheless, the advice given by Rys seems especially suggestive: to include without fail those factors known to be relevant to the subject of investigation, leaving for subsequent examination factors which may be 'interesting' but are not known in advance to be relevant; to give priority to those factors in the socio-economic environment which are closely related to the subject of study, that have a direct bearing on its formation and development rather than to factors of general economic or cultural environment which are connected with the subject of study only inasmuch as all phenomena are interconnected in a social whole. Equally, researchers ought to draw freely on what appear to be the best and most relevant social science conceptualizations, but ought not to hesitate to discard those which turn out to be of little use. This kind of selective approach is probably more promising for producing insights that are genuinely significant for policy and planning – given the state of empirical studies in social welfare at this time. By restraining social welfare's tendency toward expansions – and the multitude of interconnections they generate – that are but vaguely defined and legitimated, a selective approach may also facilitate the derivation of

Conclusion

welfare's unique features and in this way make easier the establishment of productive linkages between welfare and society.

It is apparent that most of the problems involved in cross-national research in welfare policy and planning are not different in kind from those that confront social scientists in other disciplines — although in certain areas they may differ in degree. Social welfare provisions are not automatic responses to economic forces, but rather to deeper and more varied strains affecting the society, its organization and its distinctive features. Hence, welfare policy must embody a unified socio-economic approach. The emergence of social economics — the application by economists of their analytical skills to problems outside the sphere of traditional economics — is a development that underscores the need to deal with questions about the 'quality of life' from a perspective broader than mainly economic and reinforces the wisdom of a more comprehensive approach. Non-economic aspects of economic activities turn out to be just as influential as the activities themselves. Such commonalities indicate that what is called for is 'interdisciplinary creativity', to be activated via a more conscious and purposeful alignment among social scientists working in the comparative field, in settings and organizations most capable of supporting it. And this, in turn, means that those associated in interdisciplinary endeavors must be less rigid in their adherence to separate research traditions which deter the formation of linkages between the various disciplines involved. Flexibility would develop the ability to think in interdisciplinary and generalist, as well as specialist, terms.

Now, what can we say about the meaning of social policy as it has been depicted by comparative studies in social welfare? To begin with, welfare policy can never be final. And this holds when the issues policy addresses are old (but probably dressed in modern garb) or new. Nor can any policy command universal or permanent approval. In modern times, conditions of life change rapidly so that it becomes ever more difficult to trace the continuity between the past, the present and the future, between what is done now and emerging needs, between traditional values and those called for by an interplanetary age. In short, welfare policy and planning, no matter how competent their makers, are subject to substantive and temporal limitations. And it should not be forgotten that not everything that happens in welfare is determined by policy.

Welfare policy is a plan of action based on choices and priorities. Indicated are what policy-makers perceive as essential objectives and the implementing structures and practices they intend to attain them.

The questions welfare policy needs to answer in the process of formation are quite similar to those that have to be answered by any organization that undertakes to deliver a good or a service; namely, what resources are needed and are projected costs commensurate with what the intended beneficiaries will receive; how is the policy to be implemented so that there is no doubt on the part of all concerned about what its makers have in mind, that is, what they wish to accomplish and by what means; what elements and forces in the society are likely to generate changes that will affect policy significantly in the foreseeable future; what are the relevant criteria for ascertaining 'success' and 'failure' and what mechanisms are most likely to ensure meaningful feedback for this evaluation; what are likely to be the components of controversies that may ensue, how can differences be reconciled sufficiently to permit movement toward policy goals, and who will be the supporters and opponents of the proposed policy in the reconciliation process. These are the generic questions.

However, the considerations that enter in when answering these questions for social welfare policy differ in several important respects from those that enter in when the delivery of goods and services is a function of the market. Social provision is basically an expression of collective, public responsibility. Consequently, the role of government in financing, managing and monitoring the social welfare institution assumes special power, all the more because welfare is expanding and becoming more necessary to an ever increasing number of people. Decisions in regard to the universality—selectivity options and to the relative advantages of an individualized as contrasted to a standardized, mass approach must be sensitive to the possible stigmatizing effects of selective and individualized policies.

Being socially determined, welfare policy projects a particular view about how a human being grows and matures, what his salient characteristics are, what he requires in the way of nurture and support from the society, and what should be the relationship between him and the state. This view has a strong influence on the way policy can analyze and tackle, or not tackle, social problems, on the kind of status it assigns to the individual who comes within its purview, the kind of rights it confers on him, and on how it legitimates what it does. Access becomes not only a matter of cost and physical location, but how people perceive accessibility as an expression of the eligibility conditions it imposes.

Creative integration of pertinent social and economic aspects in welfare policy as equal partners means that social value, the fulfillment

Conclusion

of the needs and aspirations of people as human rather than merely as actual or potential productive or consuming units, must have high priority. Principles by which policies in the welfare field can be judged demand a reconciliation of many-faceted, subtle and often clashing expectations. In short, the making of social welfare policy is an extremely complicated business which demands appropriate use of an enormous amount of diversified data broad in scope, of intricate patterns of relationships, of facts based on knowledge and of preferences based on attitudes — to say nothing of impressive technical know-how and the ability to forecast consequences for beneficiaries, the welfare establishment, the politicians and the general public. Vivekananda was wise when he said: 'There is no good work that has not a touch of evil in it . . . We should engage in such works which bring the largest amount of good and the smallest measure of evil.'

And underlying the entire policy-making process is the primordial importance of infusing it with humanitarian values. As global aspirations, values exist in all societies — aspirations toward social and economic equality, social justice, freedom, democracy, 'a standard of living adequate for the health and well-being of himself and of his family'. But to become operative values must be integrated into policies in specific forms that harmonize with the particular cultural and political characteristics of the given country. It is in creating these specific forms that differences between countries arise: countries hold different views about and promulgate different prescriptions to deal with social 'needs' and 'problems'; they put forth different levels of effort and employ different practices to meet these needs and problems; hence, different consequences emanate from programs that are oriented toward similar goals. In short, roughly similar policy issues elicit dissimilar policy decisions, their humanitarian value components ranging from minimal to respectable.

Progress toward achieving global aspirations is a process that itself creates new and more complicated problems, difficult to solve because 'consciousness' — thoughts, values, feelings — changes more slowly than social and economic conditions. This slower pace issues from several characteristics of values as determiners of attitudes that coalesce into systems of beliefs. Adherence to these beliefs is a condition of an individual's membership in the social group. When he accepts them he becomes committed to a way of life, to behaving in the way preferred by the social group, to choosing the means, ends and conditions of life that the group prefers — all this almost invariably accompanied by strong feelings. In the process the individual develops his sense of self and the manner in which he uses it to interact with his environment. This includes the manner in which he works through the interaction between egoism and altruism within his inner self and thereby determines the degree to which he can achieve disciplined social consciousness. It is the values related to one's sense of self that are the hardest to change involving as they do deeply felt constellations of beliefs. If they are changed, the individual may be faced with having to make wrenching adjustments in his self-concept. This he may resist doing because it may threaten his own, long-established identity and integrity. 'If I should be someone else, who would be me?' (Yiddish proverb).

Yet societies do arrive at meaningful agreements on preferences and social welfare policies must express them and at the same time contribute to making attitudes and man's inner nature more genuinely humanitarian. Perhaps then nobody will say: 'Look at people on welfare. They are deprived of volition, they lose their existence in the name of virtuous government' (Kobo Abé).

SELECT BIBLIOGRAPHY

Aaron, Henry 'Social Security: International Comparisons', pp. 13–48 in Eckstein, Otto (ed.) *Studies in the Economics of Income Maintenance* (Washington, DC, The Brookings Institution, National Committee on Government Finance, 1967)

Binstock, Robert H. and Shanas, Ethel (eds.) *Handbook of Aging and the Social Sciences* (New York, Von Nostrand Reinhold Co., 1976)

Blaustein, Saul J. and Craig, Isabel *An International Review of Unemployment Insurance Schemes* (Kalamazoo, Michigan, W. E. Upjohn Institute for Employment Research, January 1977)

Brocklehurst, J. C. (ed.) *Geriatric Care in Advanced Societies* (Baltimore, University Park Press, 1975)

Bronfenbrenner, Urie *Two Worlds of Childhood* (New York, Russell Sage Foundation, 1970)

Brown, Joan C. *How Much Choice. Retirement Policies in Canada* (Ottawa, The Canadian Council of Social Development, November 1975)

Bubeck, A. E. *International Perspectives on Social Welfare Research: Report of a Symposium*, The Brookings Institution, May 23–June 9, 1971 (Washington, DC, The Brookings Institution, 1971)

Burgess, E. W. (ed.) *Aging in Western Societies* (Chicago, Chicago University Press, 1960)

Burns, Eveline M. (ed.) *Children's Allowances and the Economic Welfare of Children. The Report of a Conference* (New York, Citizens' Committee for Children of New York, Inc., 1968)

Caputo, David A. 'New Perspectives on the Public Policy Implications of Defense and Welfare Expenditures in Four Modern Democracies: 1950–70', *Policy Sciences*, iv (1975), pp. 423–46.

Clinard, Marshall Barron and Abbott, Daniel J. *Crime in Developing Countries. A Comparative Perspective* (New York, John Wiley and Sons, 1973)

Cockburn, Christine and Haskins, Dalmer 'Social Security and Divorced Persons', *International Social Security Review*, no. 2 (1976), pp. 111–51

Connor, Walter D. *Deviance in Soviet Society. Crime, Delinquency and Alcoholism* (New York, Columbia University Press, 1972)

Conrad, John P. *Crime and Its Correction. An International Survey of*

Attitudes and Practices (Berkeley, California, University of California Press, 1965)

Cutright, Phillips 'Political Structure, Economic Development, and National Social Security Programs', *American Journal of Sociology*, lxx, no. 5 (March 1965), pp. 537–50

David, Henry P. (ed.) *Child Mental Health in International Perspective*, Report of The Joint Commission on the Mental Health of Children (New York, Harper & Row, 1972)

Fisher, Paul 'Minimum Old-Age Pensions. I: Their Adequacy in Terms of Consumer Expenditures, Assistance Benefits and Poverty Standards', *International Labour Review*, 102, no. 1 (July 1970), pp. 51–78; 'Minimum Old-Age Pensions. II: Their Adequacy in Terms of Average Earnings, Minimum Wages and National Income and Some Problems of Adjustment', *ibid.*, no. 3 (September 1970), pp. 277–317

Flamm, Franz *Social Welfare Services and Social Work in the Federal Republic of Germany* (Frankfurt/Main, Eigenverlag des Deutschen Vereins für Offentliche und Private Fürsorge, 1974)

Furniss, Norman and Tilton, Timothy *The Case for the Welfare State. From Social Security to Social Equality* (Bloomington, Indiana, Indiana University Press, 1977)

George, Victor *Social Security and Society* (London, Routledge and Kegan Paul, 1973)

Gil, David G. *Unravelling Social Policy. Theory, Analysis, and Political Action Towards Social Equality* (Cambridge, Mass., Schenkman Publishing Co., 1973)

Gilbert, Neil and Specht, Harry *Dimensions of Social Welfare Policy* (Englewood Cliffs, New Jersey, Prentice-Hall, Inc., 1974)

Glennester, H. *Social Service Budgets and Social Policy: British and American Experience* (New York, Barnes & Noble, 1976)

Glickman, Beatrice Marden and Springer, Nesha Bass *Who Cares for the Baby? Choices in Child Care* (New York, Schocken Books, 1978)

Gordon, Margaret S. *The Economics of Welfare Policies* (New York, Columbia University Press, 1963)

Gueye, Amadou 'Health, Social and Family Services of Social Security Funds in Africa', *International Social Security Review*, xxvi, no. 3 (1973), pp. 250–87

Gurr, Ted Robert 'Contemporary Crime in Historical Perspective: A Comparative Study of London, Stockholm, and Sydney', *The Annals of the American Academy of Political and Social Science*, 434 (November 1977), pp. 114–36

Select Bibliography 315

Habib, Jack *Redistribution Through National Insurance in Israel by Income and Demographic Groups*, Discussion Paper 7 (Jerusalem, Israel, The National Insurance Institute, Bureau of Research and Planning, November 1975)
Haskins, Dalmer and Bixby, Lenore E. *Women and Social Security: Law and Policy in Five Countries* (Washington, DC, Research Report No. 42, HEW, Social Security Administration, Office of Research and Statistics, 1973. HEW Publication No. (SSA) 73-11800)
Havighurst, Robert J., Joep, M. A., Munnichs, Bernice Neugarten and Thomae, Hans (eds.) *Adjustments to Retirement: A Cross-National Study* (New York, Humanities Press, 1969)
Heclo, Hugh *Modern Social Politics in Britain and Sweden: From Relief to Income Maintenance* (New Haven, Yale University Press, 1974)
Heidenheimer, Arnold J., Heclo, Hugh, and Adams, Carolyn Teich *Comparative Public Policy: The Politics of Social Choice in Europe and America* (New York, St Martins Press, 1975)
Hodge, Peter 'Social Planning for Growing Cities', in *Social Planning for Growing Cities: Role of Social Welfare*, Proceedings of the ICSW Regional Conference for Asia and Western Pacific, September 1–5, 1975, Hong Kong
Horlick, Max *Supplemental Security Income for the Aged . . . A Comparison of Five Countries* (Washington, DC, HEW, Social Security Administration, Office of Research and Statistics, DHEW Publication No. (SSA) 74-11850. Staff Paper No. 15, July 1973)
Inkeles, Alex and Smith, David H. *Becoming Modern. Individual Change in Six Developing Countries* (Cambridge, Mass., Harvard University Press, 1974)
International Council on Social Welfare *Developing Social Policy in Conditions of Rapid Change. Role of Social Welfare*, Proceedings of the XVIth International Conference on Social Welfare, The Hague, Netherlands, August 13–19, 1972 (New York, Columbia University Press, 1973)
International Social Security Association (ISSA) *The Planning of Social Security*, Papers Presented at Meeting on the Sociology of Social Security at the VIIth World Congress of Sociology, Varna, Bulgaria, September 16–17, 1970 (Geneva, ISSA, 1971)
ISSA *Current Issues in Social Security Planning: Concepts and Techniques*, Reports and Summary of Discussions of the Group of Experts on Social Security Planning, Brussels, October 19–21, 1972. Studies and Research No. 4 (Geneva, ISSA, 1973)
— *Women and Social Security*, Report of Research Conference on

Women and Social Security, Vienna, November 2—4, 1972. Studies and Research No. 5 (Geneva, ISSA, 1973)
— *The Role of Social Services in Social Security. Trends and Perspectives*, Report of Round Table Meeting, Moscow May 22—25, 1973. Studies and Research No. 6 (Geneva, ISSA, 1974)
— General Secretariat 'Income Maintenance for One-Parent Families', *International Social Security Review*, year 28, no. 1 (1975), pp. 3—61
Jenkins, Shirley (ed.) *Social Security in International Perspective* (New York, Columbia University Press, 1969)
Kafka, Doris and Underhill, Evi 'Comparative Study of Certain Aspects of Family Law in 16 European and Mediterranean Countries', *International Child Welfare Review*, no. 21 (May 1974), pp. 23—38; and no. 22/23 (October 1974), pp. 27—42
Kahn, Alfred J. *Social Policy and Social Services* (New York, Random House, 1973)
Kahn, Alfred J. and Kamerman, Sheila B. *Social Services in International Perspective. The Emergence of the Sixth System* (Washington, DC, HEW, Social and Rehabilitation Service, Office of Planning, Research and Evaluation, SRS 76-05704)
Kallgren, Joyce K. 'Social Welfare and China's Industrial Workers', pp. 540—74 in Barnett, A. Doak (ed.) *Chinese Communist Politics in Action* (Seattle, Washington, University of Washington Press, 1968)
Kammerer, Gladys M. *British and American Child Welfare Services. A Comparative Study in Administration* (Detroit, Wayne State University Press, 1962)
Kane, Robert L. and Kane, Rosalie A. *Long-Term Care in Six Countries: Implications for the United States*, Fogarty International Center Proceedings, no. 331 (Washington, DC, HEW, 1976)
Kassalow, Everett M. (ed.) *The Role of Social Security in Economic Development* (Washington, DC, HEW, Social Security Administration, Office of Research and Statistics. Research Report No. 27, 1968)
Kessen, William (ed.) *Childhood in China* (New Haven, Yale University Press, 1975)
Kilby, Peter and Taira, Koji 'Differences in Social Security Development in Selected Countries', *International Social Security Review*, 22, no. 2 (1969), pp. 139—54
Kirkpatrick, Elizabeth Kreitler *Protecting Social Security Beneficiary Earnings Against Inflation: The Foreign Experience*, HEW, Social

Security Administration, Office of Research and Statistics, Staff Paper No. 25, HEW Publication No. (SSA) 77-11850, September 1976 (Washington, DC, Government Printing Office (GPO))

Kramer, Ralph M. *Community Development in Israel and the Netherlands. A Comparative Analysis* (Berkeley, California, Institute of International Studies, University of California, Berkeley, 1970)

Kreps, Juanita M. *Lifetime Allocation of Work and Income. Essays in the Economics of Aging* (Durham, North Carolina, Duke University Press, 1971)

Kuusi, Pekka *Social Policy for the Sixties. A Plan for Finland* (Helsinki, Finnish Policy Association; published in Finnish in 1961; translated into English in 1964)

Lally, Dorothy *National Social Service Systems. A Comparative Study and Analysis of Selected Countries* (Washington, DC, HEW, Social and Rehabilitation Service, September 1970)

Laroque, Pierre 'Social Security and Social Development', *Bulletin of the International Social Security Association*, xix, nos. 3–4 (March–April 1966), pp. 83–90

— 'Women's Rights and Widows' Pensions', *International Labour Review*, 106, no. 1 (July 1972), pp. 1–10

Lawson, Roger and Reed, Bruce *Social Security in the European Community*. Lawson: *Social Security and Medical Care in Britain and the Continent*; Reed: *Social Security and Medical Care in the Context of the European Community* (London, Chatham House, PEP, 1975)

Leiner, Marvin with Ubell, Robert *Children are the Revolution. Day Care in Cuba* (New York, Viking Press, 1974)

Leman, Christopher 'Patterns of Policy Development: Social Security in the United States and Canada', *Public Policy*, 25, no. 2 (Spring 1977), pp. 261–91

Little, Virginia A. 'Present Status of Homemaker-Home Help Services in Developed Countries', *Home-Help Services for the Aging Around the World* (Washington, DC, The International Federation on Ageing, 1975), pp. 16–22

— 'Home Help Services for the Elderly: the British Experience', *ibid.*, pp. 22–5

— 'Homemaker-Home Help Services in Developing Countries', *ibid.*, pp. 32–43

— 'Open Care for the Aged: Swedish Model', *Social Work*, 23, no. 4 (July 1978), pp. 282–8

Littrell, Boyd W. and Sjoberg, Gideon (eds.) *Current Issues in Social*

318 *Select Bibliography*

Policy (Beverly Hills, Sage Publications, 1976)
Livingstone, Arthur *Social Policy in Developing Countries* (London, Routledge and Kegan Paul, 1969)
Lynes, Tony *French Pensions*, Occasional Paper in Social Administration, no. 21 (London, G. Bell and Sons, 1967)
Madison, Bernice 'The Organization of Welfare Services', pp. 515–41 in Black, Cyril E. (ed.) *The Transformation of Russian Society* (Cambridge, Mass., Harvard University Press, 1960)
— *Social Welfare in the Soviet Union* (Stanford, California, Stanford University Press, 1968)
— 'The Welfare State: Some Unanswered Questions for the 1970s', *Social Service Review*, 44, no. 4 (December 1970), pp. 434–51
— 'Social Services for Families and Children in the Soviet Union since 1967', *Slavic Review*, 31, no. 4 (December 1972), pp. 831–52
— 'Soviet Income Maintenance Policy for the 1970s', *Journal of Social Policy*, 2, part 2 (April 1973), pp. 97–116
— 'Social Services for Women: Problems and Priorities', pp. 307–33 in Atkinson, Dorothy, Dallin, Alexander, and Lapidus, Gail Warshofsky (eds.) *Women in Russia* (Stanford, California, Stanford University Press, 1977)
— 'Trade Unions and Social Welfare', in Kahan, Arcadius and Ruble, Blair A. (eds.) *Industrial Labor in the USSR* (Pergamon Press, 1979)
Marmor, Theodore, Rein, Martin, and Van Til, Sally 'Post-War European Experience with Cash Transfers: Pensions, Child Allowances, and Public Assistance', in *Technical Studies*, US, President's Commission on Income Maintenance, 1969 (Washington, DC, GPO, 1969), pp. 259–93
Marshall, T. H. *Social Policy*, 3rd edn (London, Hutchinson University Library, 1970)
Mencher, Samuel *Poor Law to Poverty Program. Economic Security Policy in Britain and the United States* (Pittsburgh, University of Pittsburgh Press, 1967)
Minkoff, Jack and Turgeon, Lynn 'Income Maintenance in the Soviet Union in Eastern and Western Perspective', pp. 176–211 in Horowitz, Irving Louis (ed.) *Equity, Income and Policy. Comparative Studies in Three Worlds of Development* (New York, Praeger Publishers, 1977)
Moroney, Robert *The Family and the State: Considerations for Social Policy* (London and New York, Longman, 1976)
Mouton, Pierre *Social Security in Africa. Trends, Problems, Prospects* (Geneva, International Labour Office (ILO), 1975)

Select Bibliography

Oram, C. A. *Social Policy and Administration in New Zealand* (Wellington, New Zealand University Press, 1969)
OECD, The OECD Social Development Programme, 1. *List of Social Concerns Common to Most OECD Countries* (Paris 1973)
—, The OECD Social Indicator Development Programme, 3. *Measuring Social Well-Being*, A Progress Report on the Development of Social Indicators (Paris, 1976)
—, The OECD Social Indicator Development Program. *1976 Progress Report on Phase II. Plan for Future Activities* (Paris, 1977)
—, The OECD Social Indicator Development Programme: Special Studies, no. 4. *Basic Disaggregations of Main Social Indicators* (Paris, 1977)
— *Public Expenditure on Income Maintenance Programmes*, Studies in Resource Allocation, no. 3 (Paris, July 1976)
— *Old Age Pension Schemes* (Paris, 1977)
Osborn, Robert J. *Soviet Social Policies: Welfare, Equality, and Community* (Homewood, Illinois, The Dorsey Press, 1970)
Palmore, E. B., and Manton, K. 'Modernization and Status of the Aged: International Correlations', *Journal of Gerontology*, 29, no. 2 (1974), pp. 205–10
Perrin, Guy 'The Future of Social Security', *International Social Security Review*, xxii, no. 1 (1969), pp. 3–28
— 'Reflections on Fifty Years of Social Security', *International Labour Review*, 99, no. 3 (March 1969), pp. 249–92
Pratt, Mildred *Social Welfare in National Development*, Doctoral Dissertation in Social Work, Pittsburgh, April 1969
Pryor, Frederic L. *Public Expenditures in Communist and Capitalist Nations* (Homewood, Illinois, Richard D. Irwin, Inc., 1968)
Rein, Martin *Social Policy: Issues of Choice and Change* (New York, Random House, 1970)
— 'Work Incentives and Welfare Reform in Britain and the United States', pp. 151–95 in Stein, Bruno and Miller, S. M. (eds.) *Incentives and Planning in Social Policy* (Chicago, Aldine Publishing Co., 1973)
Rein, Martin and Heclo, Hugh 'What Welfare Crisis? – A Comparison Among the United States, Britain, and Sweden', *The Public Interest*, no. 33 (Fall 1973), pp. 61–83
Rein, Martin 'Equality and Social Policy', *Social Service Review*, 51, no. 4 (December 1977), pp. 565–88
Reubens, Beatrice G. *The Hard-to-Employ: European Programs* (New York, Columbia University Press, 1970)

Rimlinger, Gaston V. *Welfare Policy and Industrialization in Europe, America and Russia* (New York, John Wiley and Sons, 1971)
Robinson, Halbert B. and Robinson, Nancy M. (eds.) *International Monograph Series on Early Child Care* (London, New York, Paris, Gordon & Breach, 1974), vols. 1–7.
Roby, Pamela (ed.) *Child Care – Who Cares? Foreign and Domestic Infant and Early Childhood Development Policies* (New York, Basic Books, 1973)
Rodgers, Barbara N. *Comparative Social Administration* (New York, Atherton Press, 1968)
Rohrlich, George F. *Social Security for the Aged: International Perspectives*, A Working Paper Prepared for a Hearing on 'International Perspectives on the Economics of Aging', August 25, 1969. Special Committee on Aging, US Senate (Washington, DC, GPO, 1969)
Rollins, Nancy *Child Psychiatry in the Soviet Union. Preliminary Observations* (Cambridge, Mass., Harvard University Press, 1972)
Rosenthal, Albert H. *The Social Programs of Sweden: A Search for Security in a Free Society* (Minneapolis, University of Minnesota Press, 1967)
Rys, Vladimir 'Comparative Studies of Social Security: Problems and Perspectives', *Bulletin of International Social Security Association*, 19, nos. 7/8 (July–August 1966), pp. 242–68
– 'Problems of Social Security Planning in Industrialized and Developing Countries', *International Social Security Review*, nos. 2–3 (1974), pp. 314–46
Safran, William *Veto-Group Politics: The Case of Health Insurance Reform in West Germany* (San Francisco, California, Chandler Publishing Co., 1967)
Schorr, Alvin *Explorations in Social Policy* (New York, Basic Books, 1968)
Schultz, James, Garrin, Guy, Krupp, Hans, Peschke, Manfred, Sclar, Elliott, and Van Steenberge, J. *Providing Adequate Retirement Income: Pension Reform in the United States and Abroad* (Hanover, New Hampshire, University Press of New England, 1975)
Shanas, Ethel *et al. Old People in Three Industrial Societies* (New York, Atherton Press, 1968)
Shanas, Ethel and Sussman, Marvin B. (eds.) *Family, Bureaucracy, and the Elderly* (Durham, North Carolina, Duke University Press, 1977)
Shlakman, Vera 'The Safety-Net Function in Public Assistance', *Social Service Review*, 46, no. 2 (June 1972), pp. 193–212

Select Bibliography

Stein, Bruno *Work and Welfare in Britain and the United States* (London, The Macmillan Press, 1976)

Stevens, Cindy *Public Assistance in France*, Occasional Paper on Social Administration, no. 50 (London, G. Bell and Sons, 1973)

Thursz, Daniel and Vigilante, Joseph L. (eds.) *Meeting Human Needs, Social Service Delivery Systems*, An International Annual. Vol. I: An Overview of Nine Countries (Beverly Hills, Sage Publications, 1975); vol. 2: Additional Perspectives from Thirteen Countries (Beverly Hills, Sage Publications, 1976)

Titmuss, Richard M. *Commitment to Welfare* (New York, Pantheon Books, 1968)

— 'Equity, Adequacy, and Innovation in Social Security', *International Social Security Review*, xxiii, no. 2 (1970), pp. 259–69

— Keynote Address, in *Developing Social Policy in Conditions of Rapid Change. Role of Social Welfare*, Proceedings of the XVIth International Conference on Social Welfare, The Hague, Netherlands, August 13–19, 1972 (New York and London, Columbia University Press, 1973)

Tracy, Martin B. 'World Developments and Trends in Social Security', *Social Security Bulletin*, 39, no. 4 (April 1976), pp. 14–22

Trager, Brahna 'Home Help Abroad, A Review of Selected In-Home Services in Western European Countries', *Home-Help Services for the Aging Around the World* (Washington, DC, The International Federation on Ageing, 1975), pp. 3–16

Uhr, Carl G. *Sweden's Social Security System* (Washington, DC, HEW, Social Security Administration, Office of Research and Statistics, Research Report No. 14, 1966)

UN, Department of Economic and Social Affairs *Proceedings of the International Conference of Ministers Responsible for Social Welfare, 3 to 12 September 1968* (New York, UN, 1969)

—, Department of Economic and Social Affairs *Social Policy and the Distribution of Income in the Nation* (New York, UN, 1969)

—, Department of Economic and Social Affairs *Long-Term Policies and Programmes for Youth in National Development* (New York, UN, 1970)

—, Department of Economic and Social Affairs *Social Welfare Planning in the Context of National Development Plans* (New York, UN, 1970)

—, Department of Economic and Social Affairs *Report on Children* (New York, UN, 1971)

—, Department of Economic and Social Affairs 'Highlights of the

322 Select Bibliography

Symposium on Social Policy and Planning', Copenhagen, Denmark, June 22–July 2, 1970, *International Social Development Review*, Unified Socio-Economic Development and Planning: Some New Horizons (New York, UN, 1971), pp. 16–22

—, Department of Economic and Social Affairs *Planning, Organization and Administration of National Rehabilitation Programmes for the Disabled in Developing Countries: Report of a Meeting of Experts*, Geneva, September 27–October 6, 1971 (New York, UN, 1972)

—, Division of Social Affairs *Minimum Levels of Living and Their Role in Social Policy. Comparative Study*, Working paper no. 1, prepared for the Expert Group on Minimum Levels of Living which met in Czechoslovakia on October 4–8, 1976 (Geneva, UN, 1976)

—, Economic and Social Council *Social Policy and Planning in National Development*, Report of the meeting of experts on social policy and planning held at Stockholm, September 1–10, 1969 (New York, UN, March 1970)

—, Economic and Social Council *Conference of European Ministers Responsible for Social Welfare*, The Hague, Netherlands, August 22–26, 1972 (Geneva, UN, 1972)

—, European Social Development Programme *Symposium on Research and Welfare Policies for the Elderly*, Herzlya, Israel, June 1–9, 1969 (New York, UN, 1970)

US, Department of Commerce, Office of Federal Statistical Policy and Standards and Bureau of the Census *Social Indicators, 1976* (for sale by the Superintendent of Documents, Washington, DC, 20402. Stock # 041-001-00156-5)

US, HEW, Social Security Administration *The U.S. Social Security Mission to the Union of Soviet Socialist Republics . . .* report on the 1971 cultural exchange visit by the American delegation (Washington, DC, DHEW Publication no. (SSA) 73-11901, February (1972)

US, HEW, Social Security Administration, Office of Research and Statistics *Social Security Programs Throughout the World, 1977* (Research Report No. 50. HEW Publication No. (SSA) 78-11805)

Van Stolk, Mary *The Battered Child in Canada* (Toronto, McClelland and Stewart, 1972)

Veillard-Cybulska, Henryka 'The Legal Welfare of Children in a Disturbed Family Situation', *International Child Welfare Review*; Part I, no. 25 (May 1975), pp. 34–48; Part II, no. 26 (September 1975), pp. 46–59; Part III, no. 27 (December 1975), pp. 29–39

Vogel, Lynn Harold and Lund, Michael S. *Cross-National Research in*

Select Bibliography

Social Policy, Report of a Seminar, April 14—16, 1972, sponsored by The Center for the Study of Welfare Policy, School of Social Service Administration, University of Chicago

Wilensky, Harold L. *The Welfare State and Equality. Structural and Ideological Roots of Public Expenditures* (Berkeley, University of California Press, 1975)

Wilson, Thomas (ed.) *Pensions, Inflation and Growth. A Comparative Study of the Elderly in the Welfare State* (London, Heinemann Educational Books, 1974)

Wolins, Martin (ed.) *Successful Group Care. Explorations in the Powerful Environment* (Chicago, Aldine Publishing Co., 1974)

Woodsworth, David E. *Social Security and National Policy, Sweden, Yugoslavia, Japan* (Montreal and London, McGill-Queen's University Press, 1977)

NAME INDEX

Aaron, Henry 127, 152n3
Abbott, Daniel J. 260-2
Abel-Smith, Brian 105
Adams, Carolyn Teich 31, 52
Aiyar, Sadashin Prahakar 271
Akabas, Sheila H. 53
Alber, Jens 31
Appelbaum, Diana Karter 60
Arrow, Kenneth Joseph 53

Baier, Kurt 27
Bauer, Raymond A. 13
Berliner, Joseph S. 53
Binstock, Robert H. 254
Bixby, Lenore E. 158-9
Blakeley, T. J. 12
Blaustein, Saul J. 170
Borelli, Kenneth 183-4
Boulding, Kenneth 52
Bouwmeesters, Jan 134-5
Brocklehurst, J. C. 251
Bronfenbrenner, Urie 241
Brown, Joan C. 101-2
Brown, J. Douglas 36-7
Burgess, E. W. 248-9
Burns, Eveline M. 167-8

Calkins, Joan Sweitzer 240
Cantril, Hadley 29, 31
Caputo, David A. 131-2
Chapman, Valerie 50, 54, 224-5
Clinard, Marshall Barron 260-2
Cockburn, Christine 163-4
Coleman, J. S. 40
Connor, Walter D. 32, 206-7
Conrad, John P. 259-60
Craig, Isabel 170
Cutright, Phillips 32, 126-7, 152n2

Dallin, Alexander 32
Danziger, Sheldon H. 75
Donnison, David 28, 50, 53-4, 54, 224-5, 272
Durkheim, Emile 12

Eames, Edwin 60
Elkin, Robert 50
Erikson, Erik H. 36

Fein, Ricca 74-5
Ferguson, D. Frances 60
Ferguson, Dwight H. 226
Field, Mark G. 32
Fishbein, Bette K. 180
Fisher, Paul 75, 97-8, 120-1, 135, 171, 280
Flamm, Franz 199, 271
Freeman, Howard E. 73
Friedlander, Walter 95-6
Friedmann, John 21n3, 272-3
Friis, Hennino 94, 102
Furniss, Norman 30, 75, 143-4

Galenson, Walter 134-5
Gandhi, Mohandas Karamchand 36
Gartner, Alan 34
Gavin, William J. 12
George, Victor 97, 106
Gil, David G. 57
Gilbert, Neil 60
Glazer, Nathan 58
Glennester, H. 226
Glickman, Beatrice Marden 240-1
Goode, Judith Granich 60
Gordon, Margaret S. 126
Grant, James P. 33
Gueye, Amadou 222-3
Gurr, Ted Robert 263

Haanes-Olsen, Leif 168
Habib, Jack 107
Harris, Robert 57
Hasan, Saiyid Zafar 99-100
Haskins, Dalmer 158-9, 163-4
Havighurst, Robert J. 249-50
Heady, Ferrel 49, 85n1
Heclo, Hugh 31, 52, 57, 139-42, 178
Heidenheimer, Arnold J. 31, 52, 138-9
Henriot, Peter J. 73-4
Higgins, Benjamin 136
Hodge, Peter 278
Horlick, Max 169-70, 178-80
Husby, Ralph 181-2

Inkeles, Alex 71-2, 72

324

Name Index

Jensen, Gordon D.   239

Kafka, Doris   168–9, 243–4
Kahn, Alfred J.   57–8, 72–3, 194–5, 218n1, 219n4, 229–30, 230–1, 258–9
Kaim-Caudle, P. R.   144
Kallgren, Joyce K.   108–9
Kamerman, Sheila B.   72–3, 194–5, 218n1, 219n4, 229–30, 230–1, 239–40, 246–7, 258–9
Kammerer, Gladys M.   71, 223–4
Kandel, Denis B.   12
Kane, Robert L.   254–5
Kane, Rosalie A.   254–5
Kassalow, Everett M.   134
Katona, George   29
Kilby, Peter   71, 129–30
Kirkpatrick, Elizabeth   164–5, 174–5
Kolakowski, Leszek   33–4
Kramer, Ralph   223, 227
Kremen, Eleanor   53
Kreps, Juanita M.   171–2
Kuusi, Pekka   94–5, 276

Lampman, Robert J.   75
Land, Kenneth C.   75
Laroque, Pierre   96, 133–4, 157–8
Lawson, Roger   144–6
Leiner, Marvin   201
Leman, Christopher   31, 142–3
Lesser, Gerald S.   12
Little, Virginia L.   210, 211, 252–3, 253
Littrell, W. Boyd   52, 54–5, 69, 70–1
Livingstone, Arthur   47, 56–7
Lynes, Tony   103

MacGranahan, Donald   76, 276
Madison, Bernice Q.   32, 105, 110, 111, 111–12, 117nn2,3,4, 199–201, 205–6n2, 207–8, 208–9
Maeda, Daisaku   213
Manton, K.   250–1
Marans, Allen E.   72, 238–9
Marmor, Theodore   175–6
Marshall, T. H.   27–8, 61, 152n5
Mead, Margaret   12
Meers, Dale R.   72, 238–9
Mencher, Samuel   136–7
Merriam, Ida   162

Miller, Leonard S.   130–1
Miller, S. M.   39, 62
Minkoff, Jack   146–7
Mishra, Ramesh   33
Morgan, John S.   93–4
Moroney, Robert   52, 212–3
Mouton, Pierre   13, 123–5, 152n1, 183
Moynihan, Daniel P.   55–6, 57
Myrdal, Gunnar   27, 28, 85n1, 275

Nizan, A.   100

Oram, C. A.   108, 198–9
Osborn, Robert J.   32–3, 105

Palmore, E. B.   250–1
Parke, Robert   73, 75
Paukert, Felix   135
Perrin, Guy   121–2, 122–3
Petersen, Wallace C.   106
Plessas, Demetrius J.   74–5
Portes, Alejandro   60
Pratt, Mildred   222
Pryor, Frederic L.   11, 32, 72, 127–9
Pusic, Eugen   49, 50

Rao, V. K. R. V.   195–6
Reed, Bruce   144–6
Rein, Martin   12, 30, 53, 56, 175–6, 176–8
Reubens, Beatrice G.   72
Reubens, Edwin P.   53, 290–1
Riessman, Frank   34
Rimlinger, Gaston V.   135, 137–8
Rivlin, Alice M.   74
Roby, Pamela   242
Rodgers, Barbara N.   71, 225–6, 295n1
Rohrlich, George F.   120, 121, 135
Rollins, Nancy   206, 219n3
Rosenfeld, Jona M.   81
Rosenthal, Albert H.   105
Rothenberg, Jerome   53
Rys, Vladimir   70, 81, 82, 120, 136, 152nn2 and 5, 182, 183, 285–6, 287–8, 288–9, 296n4, 302, 308

Safran, William   99
Schnitzer, Martin   166–7, 175, 189n2

326 Name Index

Scholten, J. M. P.   210–11
Schorr, Alvin L.   102–3, 197–8
Schottland, Charles I.   81
Schulz, James   172–3
Seidman, David   72, 75
Shanas, Ethel   11, 71, 249, 254, 255–8
Sheldon, Eleanor Bernert   73
Shlakman, Vera   71, 176
Shore, Milton F.   247–8
Singer, Hans W.   134
Smith, David H.   72
Sommer, John J.   53
Spilerman, Seymour   75
Springer, Nesha Bass   240–1
Stein, Bruno   39, 58, 62, 71, 180–1
Stein, Herman   81
Stevens, Cindy   96–7
Streib, Gordon F.   256–7
Sussman, Marvin B.   255–8

Taira, Koji   71, 129–30
Thomas, Joan McKamy   239
Thursz, Daniel   194
Tilton, Timothy   30, 75, 143–4
Tinbergen, Jan   134–5, 279–80

Titmuss, Richard   13, 30–1, 38–9, 50–1, 57, 58, 64n2, 104, 135–6
Tracy, Martin B.   125–6
Trager, Brahna   252
Turgeon, Lynn   146–7

Ubell, Robert   201
Uhr, Carl C.   107–8
Underhill, Evi   168–9, 243–4

Van Stolk, Mary   205
Van Til, Sally   175–6
Veillard-Cybulska, Henryka   244–6
Vigilante, Joseph L.   194

Weiner, Hyman J.   53
Weise, Robert W.   162
Wetzel, Eva   181–2
Wickenden, Elizabeth   46
Wilensky, Harold L.   130
Wilson, Thomas   61, 173–4
Wolfe, Marshall   277
Wolins, Martin   32, 205–6, 243
Woodsworth, David E.   147–8

Zimbalist, Sidney E.   60–1

SUBJECT INDEX

Bhagavadgītā, freedom of choice   35
Brookings Institution, symposium on social welfare research   81

comparative studies:
author's definition   18; conceptual framework and holistic approach   81–2; practical and theoretical importance   11–14; predictive potential   13; 'transnational' and 'crossnational'   21
Conference of European Ministers Responsible for Social Welfare: changes in social welfare   46; definition of social welfare   48; effects of vagueness re functions and contributions of social welfare   279; minimum levels of living concept   59; selectivity and universality   59

data and information:
ambiguity, inadequacy and lack 69–71, 125, in corrections   262, in social security, child welfare, psychiatry, services for aged, social welfare   70, 81, 178, 211, 240, 247, 254; importance as first step in research   81–2; role of UN in data collection and evaluation   281, 302; useful sources, their limitations   79–82

First International Conference of Ministers Responsible for Social Welfare:
comparative studies   11; roots of social welfare   193; social welfare planning   277

Historical Indicators of the Western European Democracies project   80

ideologies:
definition and functions   28; influence on policy, programs and delivery systems   31–3, 130, 135–6, 137, 138, 140, 228; influence on planning   288
Inter-American Children's Institute, UNICEF study of needs of children   289
International Conference of Social Welfare:
efforts to define social welfare 48; lack of empirical data   70; role of social indicators   74; role of social work in social planning   277–8; strategy in planning   278
International Labour Organization (ILO):
definition of social security 152; functions and publications 80; social security standards 124; symposium on social security planning   288
International Social Security Association (ISSA):
effect of divorce on rights to social security   163–4; income maintenance for one-parent families   165–6; membership, functions, publications   79–80; social security and social services 184–6; security planning in Western Europe and North America   286–8; sociology of social security   285–6; women and social security   159–62
International Study Group for Early Child Care   242
International Symposium on Social Welfare Research   81
International Union on Child Welfare (IUCW):
family allowance for children of migrants   168–9; maintenance provisions for children of migrants 169; planning child welfare in East and Central Africa   291–2; publications   80; UNICEF study of needs of children   289

New Zealand Royal Commission, values underlying income

327

328 Subject Index

maintenance programs   34

Organization for Economic
  Cooperation and Development
  (OECD):
  basic human needs concept   59;
  member countries   64–5; old-
  age pensions   156–7, for
  women   162–3; public
  expenditures on income
  maintenance   132–3; social
  indicators   76–9; standardized
  relative poverty line   61–2

Pearson Commission report on
  development   275

personal social services
  aged experiencing problems:
  adjustment to retirement
  249–50; effect of modernization
  on status   250–1; factors
  generating similar needs   248,
  249, 253, 256–7, 258–9, 259
  aged in national systems:
  countries in several regions of the
  world   253; developed
  countries   252–3; developing
  countries   253, 255; socialist
  countries   111, 211–12, 230–1,
  249, 251, 255–8, 258–9; Western
  type democracies   39, 212, 213,
  230, 230–1, 248–9, 249, 251,
  252, 254–5, 255–8, 258–9
  *aged in relation to problems of
  implementation:*
  coordination and harmonization
  251, 253, 254–5, 259; functions
  of bureaucracies, families and
  professionals   212–13, 213,
  249, 252, 254, 255–8; funding
  210, 252, 255; standards of
  service   210, 211–12, 252–3;
  unequal distribution between
  urban and rural   254; universal
  vs selective   210; welfare
  supports as a base   211
  aged, provisions for them:
  differences in provisions   249,
  252, 253, 259; home help
  services   210–11, 213, 251,
  252; long-term care   212, 213,
  251, 254–5, 257; 'open
  (community) care'   210, 211,
  230–1; research questions   249,
  254–6, 257
  child care:
  goals: diversity of   239, 240,
  242, ease child-rearing burdens for
  working parents   202, free
  mothers to work   202, 238, 239,
  prepare to carry out society's goals
  and values   202, 203, 240, 241,
  promote intellectual and physical
  development   201, 202, provide
  custodial care   201; problems:
  curriculum construction   202–3,
  differing uses of environmental
  stimuli   239, high cost   204,
  involvement of parents   243,
  poor quality of care   204,
  204–5, relationship to
  demographic and socio-economic
  factors   242, relationship to
  other programs   240, 242,
  shortages of facilities   203–4,
  205; shortages of trained
  personnel   201, 204, training
  of personnel   242
  child care in national systems:
  socialist countries   201, 202–3,
  203–5, 230–1, 238–9, 239–40,
  240, 240–1, 241, 242; Western
  type democracies   230–1,
  238–9, 239, 239–40, 240,
  240–1, 241, 242, 242–3
  child welfare programs:
  child abuse and neglect   205,
  230–1, 238, 246–7, children
  borne out of wedlock   208,
  238, 244; children in disturbed
  family situations   243–6;
  children in their own homes
  208–9; children of migrants
  243–4; children outside their
  own homes   209, 230–1;
  exploited children   238; group
  care   205–6, 243; relationship
  to child-rearing practices and
  family situations   205, 206,
  208, 209, 241, 243, 244–6, 247;
  youth advisory services   247–8
  children in developing countries:
  factors generating needs   236–8;
  goals   236; measures to attain
  goals   235–7
  delinquents and criminals:
  attitudes toward 259–60;

Subject Index

concepts of causation 207–8, 241, 261–3; correctional practices 259–60, 262–3; innovative approaches 260, 262–3; need to improve treatment services 236; research problems 262–3; ways to strengthen prevention 236
general problems:
differences in perceptions re role of government 195–6, 228; difficulties in defining 198; diversity 223, 229–30; fragmentation 198, 237, 247; gaps between needs and services 228; influence of assumptions about man 200; integration of values 34, 36–40, 41–2, 180, 200–1; legitimation and sanction 248; programs not consciously designed 228; relationship between programs 198, 240, 247, 259
in societal development:
socialist countries 199–205, 230–1; Western type democracies 197–99, 230–1
problems in implementation:
accountability and evaluation of outcomes 211, 226, 231, 247; assurance of access 78, 231, 248; balance between cash and in kind benefits 223; determining need for services 211, 223–4, 259; interconnectedness of policy and administration 225; resource allocation 226; roles of agencies 210, 227, 231, 259; standards of service 211, 224–5, 231; type and training of personnel 209, 210–11, 224, 229, 231, 248, 251–2, 257–8
problems of organization:
centralization vs dispersion 210, 224, 229, 231; coordination and harmonization 211, 224, 226, 231, 251, 253, 254–5, 259; detailing functions and scope 193–4, 194, 194–5, 199, 222–3, 231; factors leading to differences in structure 228; factors leading to similarities in structure 228; sponsorship 211, 224, 225, 228, 231

structure in national systems:
at local level, Canada and Great Britain 224–5; at local level in 8 developed and moderately developed countries 230–1; by voluntary agencies 223, 227; in child welfare in Great Britain and US 223–4; in Africa 222, 222–3; in 22 diverse countries 227–9; in Soviet Union 109–12, 201; in Western democracies 198, 199, 223, 225–6

planning
basic elements:
availability of data and information 280, 281; balanced, integrated socio-economic approach 272, 279–80, 288, 295–6; clarified and elaborated objectives 281, 283; diagnosis 283; estimates of consequences and impacts 281–2, 288; incorporation of essential characteristics 281, 284; integration into institutional and political framework 281; resolution of major methodological problems 284; standards and priorities 281, 283; use of prior studies 282–3
for children and youth,
effective implementation:
built-in coordination and complementarity 289–90, 292; clarified functions and contributions of services 290; clarified role of planner 291; manpower policy 291–2; relating to each society's traditions 291; viewing children's needs 290
for children and youth,
essential components:
assessment of needs 289, 290, 292; assessment of resources 289, 290, 292; comprehensive, long-term approach 237, 260; elaboration of goals 289; elaboration of steps in methodology 291, 292, 296; integration into overall welfare plan, 237, 289–91; stress on strengthening family 237,

Subject Index

290–1; use of quantified data 289–90
for disabied:
factors influencing perceptions 292; flexibility in goals 293; governing principles 292–3; need for community-based and special facilities 292; need to respond to cultural and socio-economic factors 292; periodic reviews of progress 292–3; securing cooperation of services and professionals 292; trained personnel 292
for social security:
conceptual problems 285, 286–7; effectiveness in reaching goals 286–7, 289; integration of social and economic aspects 285–8; location within administrative structures 286; need to define social security 288; need to guarantee scientific principles 285–8
general considerations:
concepts: action-planning model 273, allocative 272–3, environmental 199, functional 199, index of incapacity for aged 253, innovative 272–3, lack of uniform concept 271, 278, 280, pluralist social 226; definitions and clarifications: differences between planning and development 275–7, differences between development and economic growth 283–4, 288, feasibility 272, importance of 199, 277, nature and degree of state intervention 271
problems:
diversity of 210, 277–8; in maintaining dialogue between planners, researchers and decision-makers 54–5, 288; in relating objectives to planning methods 283; inadequate quantification 279, 295; re functions and contributions of welfare 279–80; slow pace 277–8
public (means-tested) assistance:
aged 178–80; approaches to determining size of benefits 179; ascertaining pertinent program characteristics 178, 180–1; difficulties in conceptualizing 57, 104; interrelationship with other forms of social provision 96, 125–6, 140, 173, 175–6, 178–9, 180, 182; level of assistance 117, 180–2; need for assistance programs 95, 109–11, 175–6, 179; reasons for need 96–7, 176, 179; relation to negative income tax 177–8, 189; single-parent households 166, 181, 189–90; work-incentive strategy 117, 176–8, 180–2

selecting countries to be compared, criteria 71–3, 138, 144, 147, 179, 251
social indicators:
conceptual base for social security indicators 287–8; definitions 73–4; OECD program, 76–9; problems and limitations 74–6; reasons for renewed interest in 73, 77, 288; 'UN family' of agencies 296; use of: in measuring socio-economic development 85; in social security planning 285, 287; in social welfare planning 284–5
social policy development, general considerations:
anti- and pro-incrementalist positions 57–8; difficulties in defining 52–3, 55; elements and questions in formulating 55, 58, 140; factors influencing 225–6; importance of dialogue 54–5, 139–41, 152, 225; importance of harmonization 57, 140, 173; importance of policy 'inheritance' 139–40; integration of specific policies 59–61; interdependence of economic and social policies 56–7, 62, 226, 281; issues in policy research 52; role of values and assumptions about man 53–6
social policy in relation to poverty:
defining 'minimum level of living' or 'poverty line' 59–60, 117, 173–5: absolute and relative

Subject Index

concepts 60–1, 132–3, as part of 'basic human needs' 59, 64, standardized relative concept 61–2; reasons for relative poverty 133; social security provisions and poverty 182; studies in measurement of levels of living and welfare 85
social policy issues, personal social services 214–16; 231–3; 263–5
social policy issues, social security: impact on individuals 186–8; impact on society 148–50; in planning 293–4; national provision in: Canada 112, Denmark 112, France 112–13, Great Britain 113, India 114, Israel 114, Japan 113, New Zealand 113–14, Sweden 114, People's Republic of China 114–15, Soviet Union 115

social security
and income redistribution:
developed and less developed countries 122, 134–5; France 106; Great Britain 106; Israel 107; Sweden 107–8
and social services:
advantages and disadvantages of integration 185–6; complex of factors determining relationship 184; continuing disagreements 229; difficulties of integration in Central America 183–4; integration in Africa 124, 125, 183, 222–3; need for complementarity and integration 122, 182–3
as factor in economic and social development:
effect on productivity 134–6; effect on redistribution of income *see* social security and income redistribution; movement from agrarian to industrial society 135; national solidarity 133–4; social protection 135–6
as influenced by cultural and socio-political factors:
Canada 31, 142–3; developing countries 135–6; France 137–8, 145; Great Britain 30–1, 136–44; Japan 30–1, 147–8; market and planned economies 32; Soviet Union 137–8, 146–7; Sweden 138–44, 147–8; United States 30–1, 136–44; West Germany 137–42, 145; Yugoslavia 147–8
development, problems, principles and values:
Africa 120, 123–5, 152; Asia 120; India 99–100; Japan 97–9; Latin America 120; Mexico 120; socialist countries 37–8, 100–1, 105, 138, 146–7; Western type democracies 36–9, 93–7, 99–105, 138, 143
expenditures:
factors that may influence size: age of program 126–9, 131, age structure of population 130–1, 144, degree of unionization 128, 138–9, 141, geographical location 129–30, level of economic development 126, 128–30, 144, 171, method of financing 127, per capita income 127, type of political and economic organization 127, 129–31, 141; relationship between public and private sectors 126, 128; relationship between welfare and defense expenditures 130–2, 141
for the aged, national systems:
17 countries 171; socialist countries 37–8, 108–12, 117, 146–8; Western type democracies 38, 94–5, 97–9, 101, 147–8, 156–7, 171–5
for the aged, problem areas:
adequacy of pensions 108–9, 111, 171–3; adjustments for inflation and recession 156, 171–5; ancillary benefits and services 101, 156, 173; categories of protection 156; contribution ceilings 171; differences based on sex *see* social security for women; equity 104, 172; extension of coverage 126, 172; financing and taxation 156, 173–4; freedom of choice re retirement age 101, 156–7; functions of private plans 171,

173; graduated vs flat benefits
173; income-loss replacement
ratios 146–7, 171–3; increases
related to productivity 147,
171–4; level of benefits 156,
180; manner of stopping to work
101, 117, 157; retirement test
171; survivors' pensions 146,
156
*for children, principles and
provisions:*
family allowance program:
Belgium 145, 158, Canada
166–8, Denmark 166–7,
effect of divorce in 26 countries
164, five Western type
democracies 168, for children
of migrant workers 168–9,
France 145, 166–8, Great
Britain 166–8, industralized
democracies 180, Soviet Union
111, Sweden 166–8;
maintenance obligations 169,
178
*for women, principles and
provisions:*
alimony and public income
support 164–5; benefits for
divorced women 163; income
maintenance for one-parent
families 141–2; in Latin
America 161–2; maternity
allowances 111, 146–7, 160–1;
old-age pensions 111, 146–7,
158–60, 163; pensions for
housewives 162; position of
women 111, 158, 162–3, 174;
rights of women who stop work
to care for children 158;
survivors' pensions 111, 146–7,
158–9; widows' pensions 157–8,
160
*for young adults, in industrialized
Western democracies* 169–70
forecasts and trends:
current problems: administrative
123, financial 123, 132, 135,
inflation 125, place of social
security in development 123–4,
relationship to demographic
situation 124, relationship to
economy and level of
development 122, 124, 136,
138, relationship to medical care
124; expansion in post-World
War I era 120-5, 132; reasons
for expansion 120–1, 135;
future developments 122–6,
136
*implementation, national
systems:*
Japan 147–8; New Zealand
108; People's Republic of China
108–9; Soviet Union 105,
109–12, 146–7; United States
139; Yugoslavia 147–8
in Nordic Countries 80
social welfare:
disadvantages of vague definitions
49–50; difficulties in defining:
by individual scholars 47, by
UN and International Conferences
on Social Welfare 46–9, 81,
by professionals 49
social workers' education and
functions 198–9, 217–19, 229,
258

unemployment insurance in 36
countries 170
UN activities and reports:
children in 46 developing
countries 237–8; conferences
on social welfare planning 277;
efforts to define 'social welfare'
46–7; 50 national social welfare
plans 277; first international
conference on planning for
children 237; functions and
scope of social services 193–4;
planning for disabled 292–3;
planning long-term policies and
programs for youth 291;
publications 82; report at
International Symposium on
Social Welfare Research 81;
report on aged in slums and
uncontrolled settlements 255;
social policy and planning 275,
280–4, 288; sponsorship of
conference on aging 249;
survey of juvenile justice 262–3
UNICEF:
administration of 226;
conferences on planning for
children and youth 289–90;
reports on needs of children in
24 developing countries 235–7;

Subject Index

reports of executive directors 290
US Department of Health, Education and Welfare (HEW):
administration of 226; publications 80, 109–10; reports on social security in the Soviet Union 109; sponsorship of symposium on social welfare research 249; studies on various aspects of foreign pension systems 171
US, Social Security Act 142

values:
at varied levels of generalization 28–30; 143–4; debate re influence on convergence and divergence in welfare 30–5; difficulties in securing consensus 27–8, 34–6, 40–1; in New Zealand's income maintenance programs 34; in policy-making 36–7, 180, 228; in policies of 'social welfare state', 'positive state', and 'social security state' 30, 137–8, 143; in professional practice 34; normative and instrumental values 30; problems in applying to policy and practice 40–2, 53–4; short- and long-run outcomes 148
voluntary professional organizations, publications 80

welfare models:
'active trends' and 'latent conflicts' 122–3; capital investment 134; human betterment 134; human investment 134; industrial achievement-performance 64; institutional-redistributive 50–1; residual 64; residual-institutional 252–3
World Health Organization (WHO), survey of juvenile justice 262–3